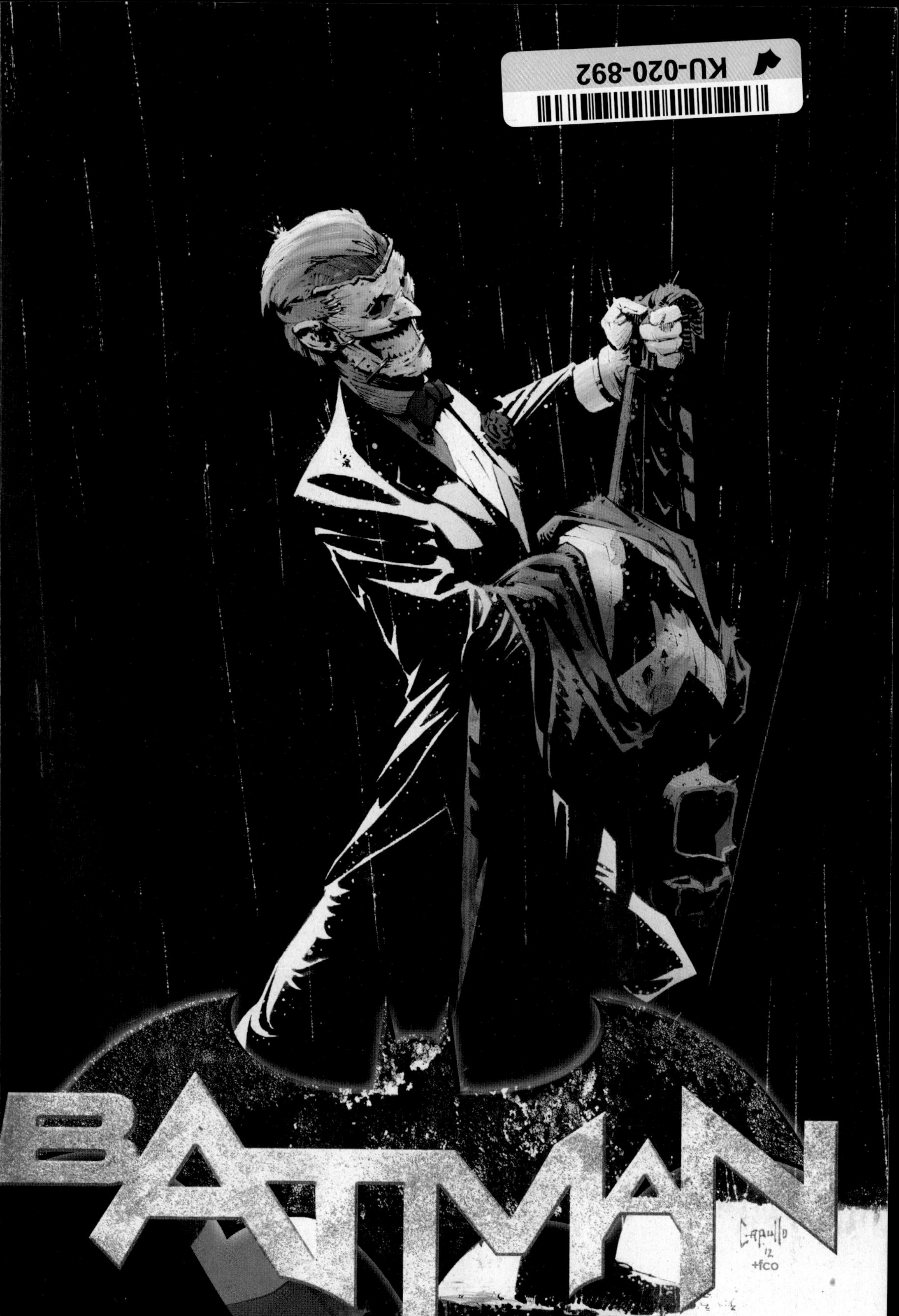
Capullo
'12
+fco

BATMAN

VOLUME 3 **DEATH OF THE FAMILY**

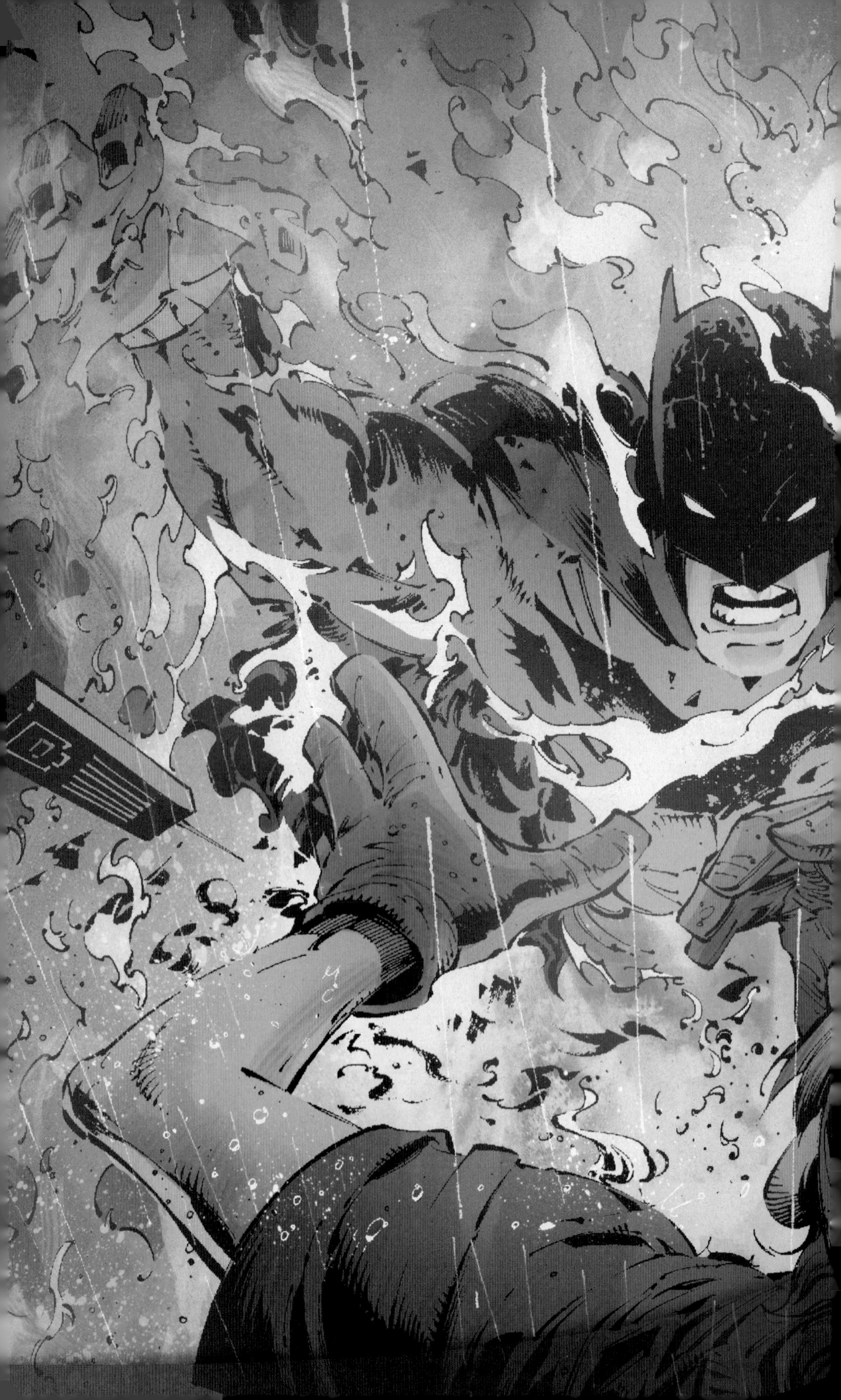

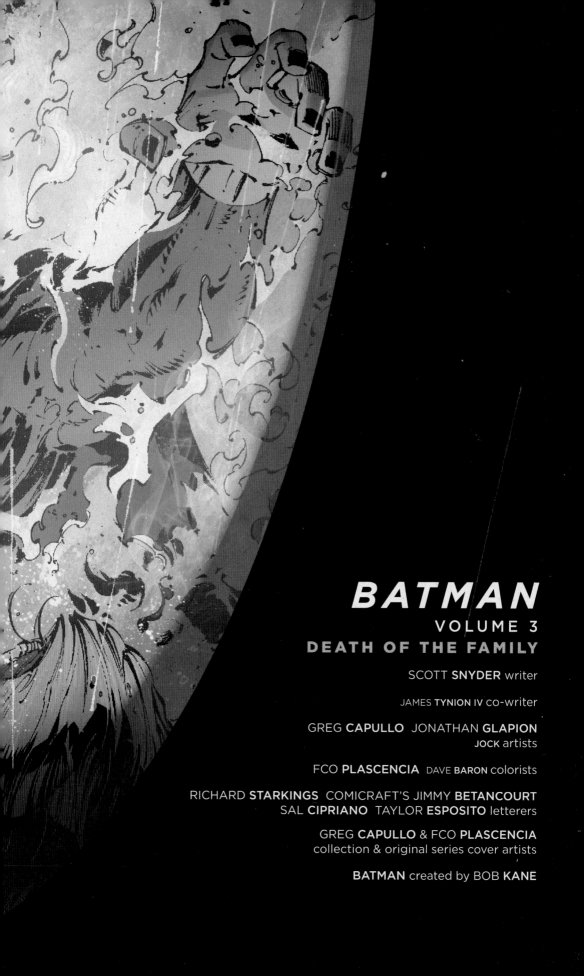

BATMAN

VOLUME 3
DEATH OF THE FAMILY

SCOTT **SNYDER** writer

JAMES **TYNION IV** co-writer

GREG **CAPULLO** JONATHAN **GLAPION**
JOCK artists

FCO **PLASCENCIA** DAVE **BARON** colorists

RICHARD **STARKINGS** COMICRAFT'S JIMMY **BETANCOURT**
SAL **CIPRIANO** TAYLOR **ESPOSITO** letterers

GREG **CAPULLO** & FCO **PLASCENCIA**
collection & original series cover artists

BATMAN created by BOB **KANE**

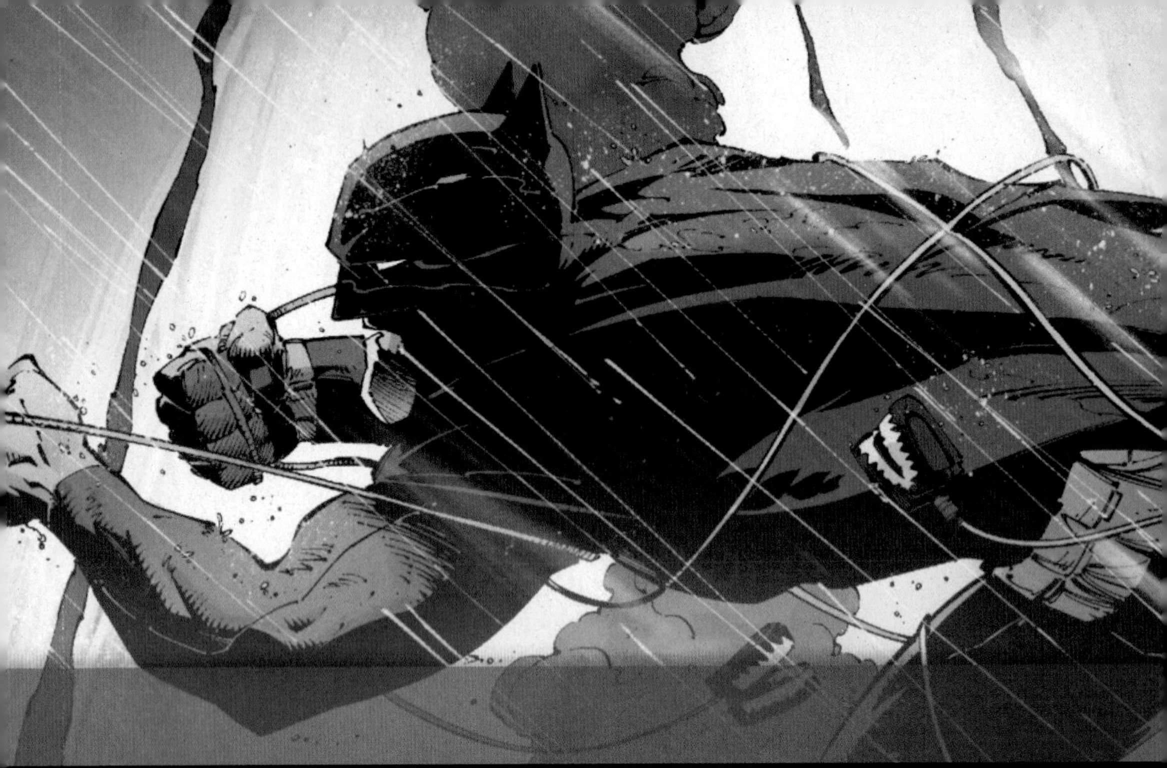

MIKE MARTS Editor - Original Series KATIE KUBERT Associate Editor - Original Series PETER HAMBOUSSI Editor
ROBBIN BROSTERMAN Design Director - Books ROBBIE BIEDERMAN Publication Design

BOB HARRAS Senior VP - Editor-in-Chief, DC Comics

DIANE NELSON President DAN DIDIO and JIM LEE Co-Publishers
GEOFF JOHNS Chief Creative Officer
AMIT DESAI Senior VP - Marketing & Franchise Management
AMY GENKINS Senior VP - Business & Legal Affairs NAIRI GARDINER Senior VP - Finance
JEFF BOISON VP - Publishing Planning MARK CHIARELLO VP - Art Direction & Design
JOHN CUNNINGHAM VP - Marketing TERRI CUNNINGHAM VP - Editorial Administration
LARRY GANEM VP - Talent Relations & Services ALISON GILL Senior VP - Manufacturing & Operations
HANK KANALZ Senior VP - Vertigo & Integrated Publishing JAY KOGAN VP - Business & Legal Affairs, Publishing
JACK MAHAN VP - Business Affairs, Talent NICK NAPOLITANO VP - Manufacturing Administration
SUE POHJA VP - Book Sales FRED RUIZ VP - Manufacturing Operations
COURTNEY SIMMONS Senior VP - Publicity BOB WAYNE Senior VP - Sales

BATMAN VOLUME 3: DEATH OF THE FAMILY

DC Comics, 1700 Broadway, New York, NY 10019
A Warner Bros. Entertainment Company
Printed by Transcontinental Interglobe, Beauceville, Qc, Canada. 07/25/14. Second Printing.

ISBN 978-1-4012-4602-0

Library of Congress Cataloging-in-Publication Data

Snyder, Scott, author.
Batman. Volume 3, Death of the Family / Scott Snyder, Greg Capullo.
pages cm
"Originally published in single magazine form as Batman 13-17."
ISBN 978-1-4012-4602-0
1. Graphic novels. I. Capullo, Greg, illustrator. II. Title. III. Title: Death of the Family.
PN6728.B36S684 2013
741.5'973—dc23
2013020537

SUSTAINABLE FORESTRY INITIATIVE Certified Chain of Custody Promoting Sustainable Forestry www.sfiprogram.org SFI-00507
This Label only applies to the text section

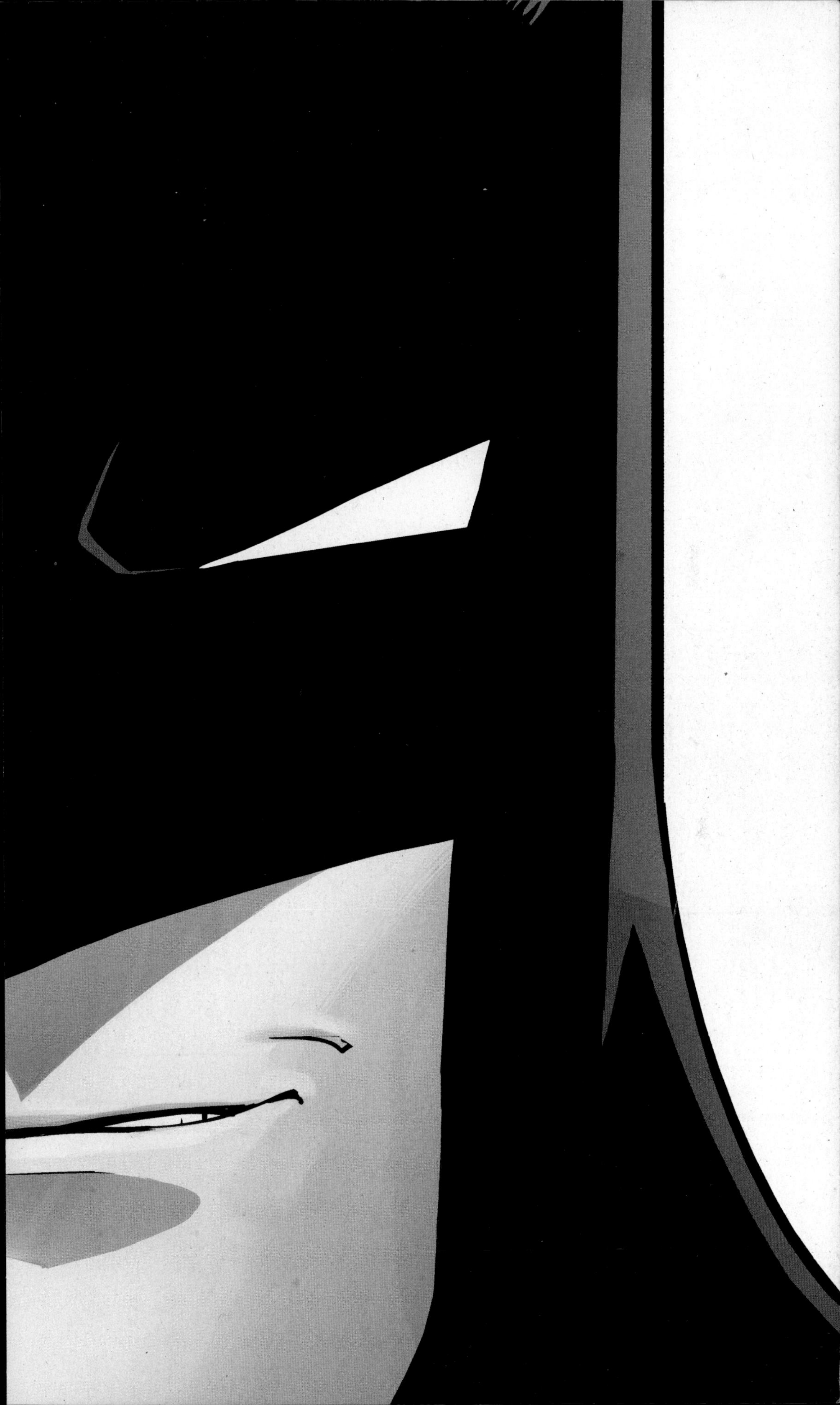

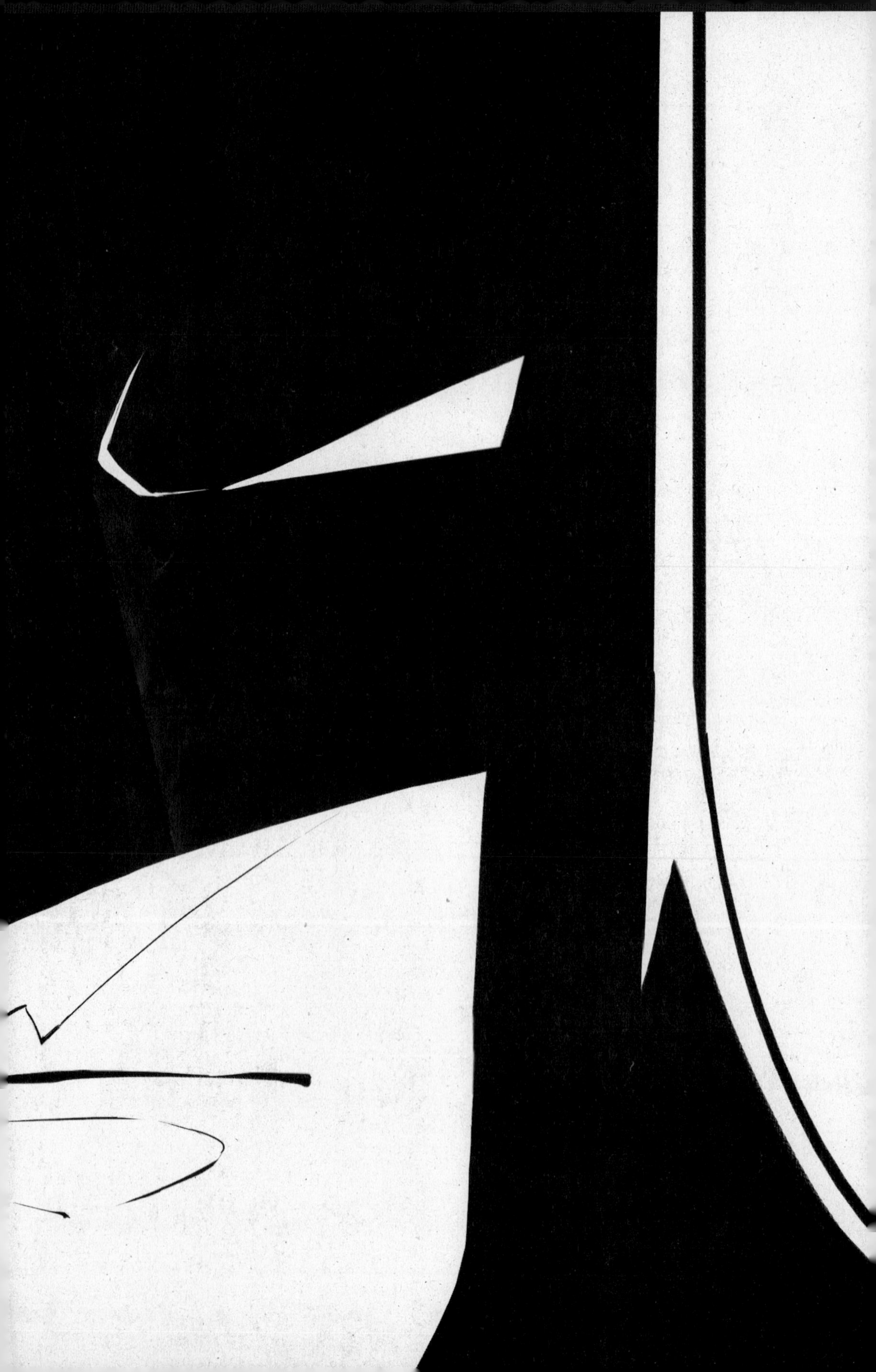

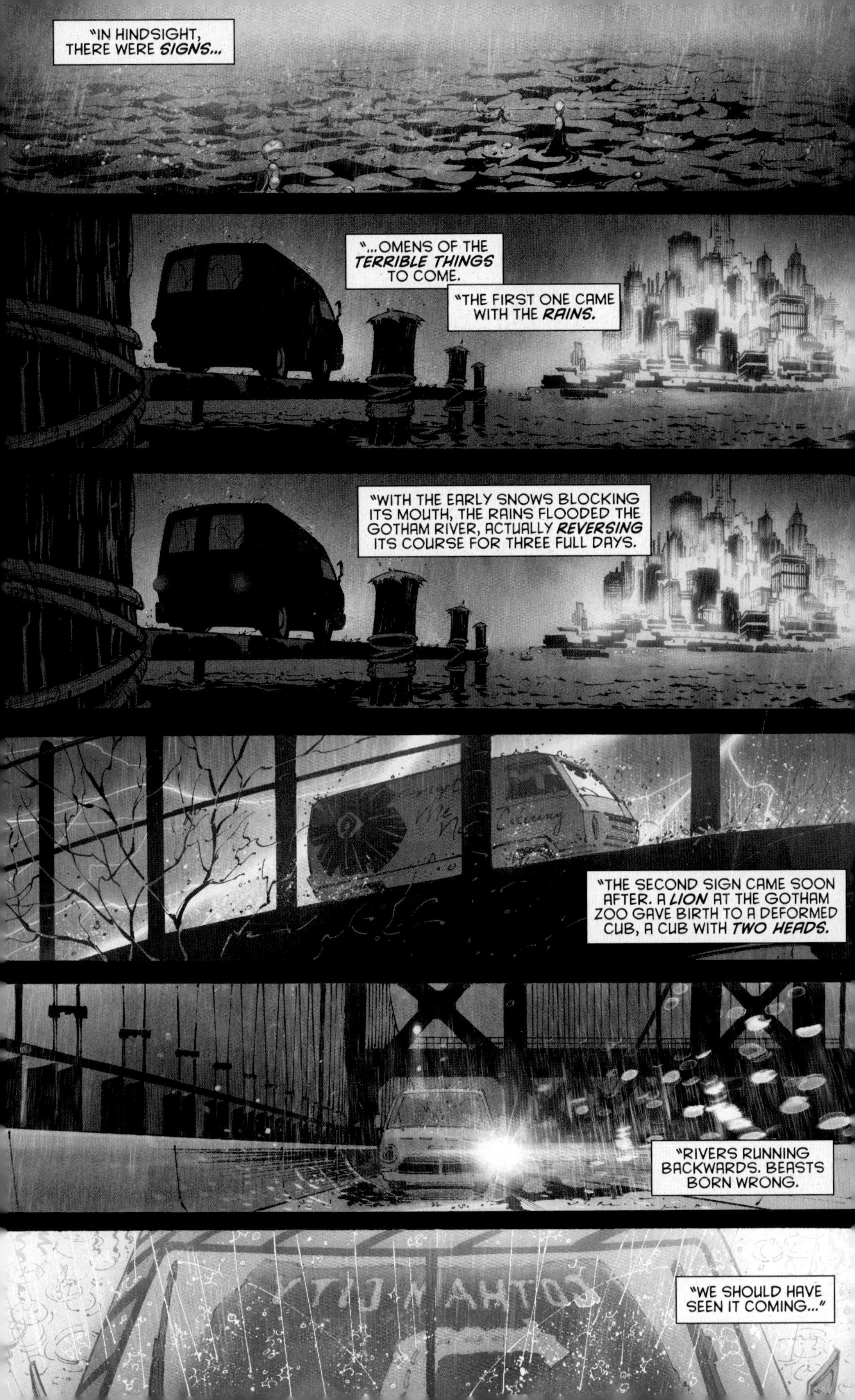
"IN HINDSIGHT, THERE WERE *SIGNS*...
"...OMENS OF THE *TERRIBLE THINGS* TO COME.
"THE FIRST ONE CAME WITH THE *RAINS*.
"WITH THE EARLY SNOWS BLOCKING ITS MOUTH, THE RAINS FLOODED THE GOTHAM RIVER, ACTUALLY *REVERSING* ITS COURSE FOR THREE FULL DAYS.
"THE SECOND SIGN CAME SOON AFTER. A *LION* AT THE GOTHAM ZOO GAVE BIRTH TO A DEFORMED CUB, A CUB WITH *TWO HEADS*.
"RIVERS RUNNING BACKWARDS. BEASTS BORN WRONG.
"WE SHOULD HAVE SEEN IT COMING..."

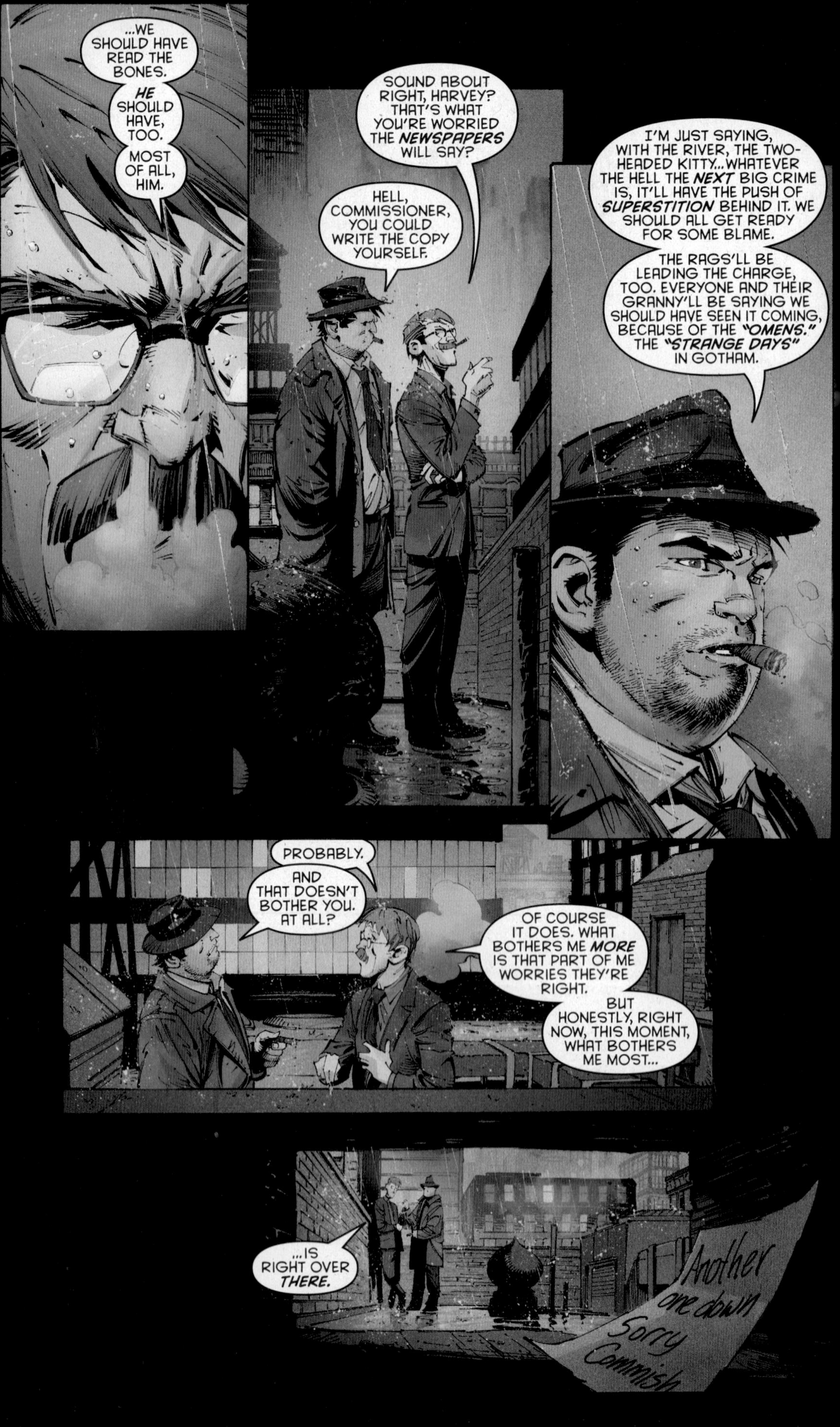
...WE SHOULD HAVE READ THE BONES.
HE SHOULD HAVE, TOO.
MOST OF ALL, HIM.
SOUND ABOUT RIGHT, HARVEY? THAT'S WHAT YOU'RE WORRIED THE *NEWSPAPERS* WILL SAY?
HELL, COMMISSIONER, YOU COULD WRITE THE COPY YOURSELF.
I'M JUST SAYING, WITH THE RIVER, THE TWO-HEADED KITTY...WHATEVER THE HELL THE *NEXT* BIG CRIME IS, IT'LL HAVE THE PUSH OF *SUPERSTITION* BEHIND IT. WE SHOULD ALL GET READY FOR SOME BLAME.
THE RAGS'LL BE LEADING THE CHARGE, TOO. EVERYONE AND THEIR GRANNY'LL BE SAYING WE SHOULD HAVE SEEN IT COMING, BECAUSE OF THE *"OMENS."* THE *"STRANGE DAYS"* IN GOTHAM.
PROBABLY.
AND THAT DOESN'T BOTHER YOU. AT ALL?
OF COURSE IT DOES. WHAT BOTHERS ME *MORE* IS THAT PART OF ME WORRIES THEY'RE RIGHT.
BUT HONESTLY, RIGHT NOW, THIS MOMENT, WHAT BOTHERS ME MOST...
...IS RIGHT OVER *THERE.*
Another one down
Sorry Commish

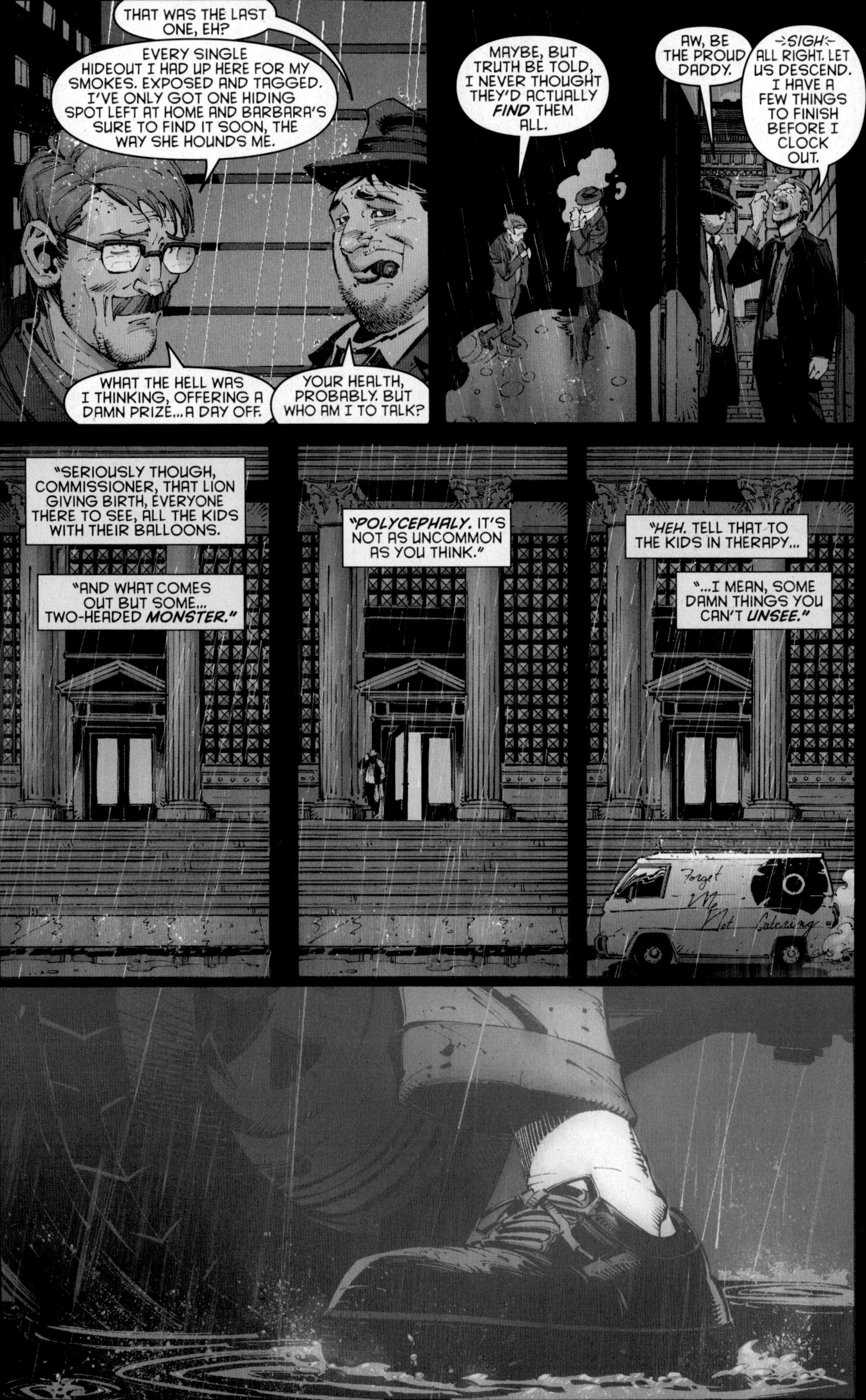
THAT WAS THE LAST ONE, EH?
EVERY SINGLE HIDEOUT I HAD UP HERE FOR MY SMOKES. EXPOSED AND TAGGED. I'VE ONLY GOT ONE HIDING SPOT LEFT AT HOME AND BARBARA'S SURE TO FIND IT SOON, THE WAY SHE HOUNDS ME.
WHAT THE HELL WAS I THINKING, OFFERING A DAMN PRIZE...A DAY OFF.
YOUR HEALTH, PROBABLY. BUT WHO AM I TO TALK?
MAYBE, BUT TRUTH BE TOLD, I NEVER THOUGHT THEY'D ACTUALLY FIND THEM ALL.
AW, BE THE PROUD DADDY.
SIGH ALL RIGHT. LET US DESCEND. I HAVE A FEW THINGS TO FINISH BEFORE I CLOCK OUT.
"SERIOUSLY THOUGH, COMMISSIONER, THAT LION GIVING BIRTH, EVERYONE THERE TO SEE, ALL THE KIDS WITH THEIR BALLOONS.
"AND WHAT COMES OUT BUT SOME... TWO-HEADED MONSTER."
"POLYCEPHALY. IT'S NOT AS UNCOMMON AS YOU THINK."
"HEH. TELL THAT TO THE KIDS IN THERAPY...
"...I MEAN, SOME DAMN THINGS YOU CAN'T UNSEE."
Forget Me Not Catering

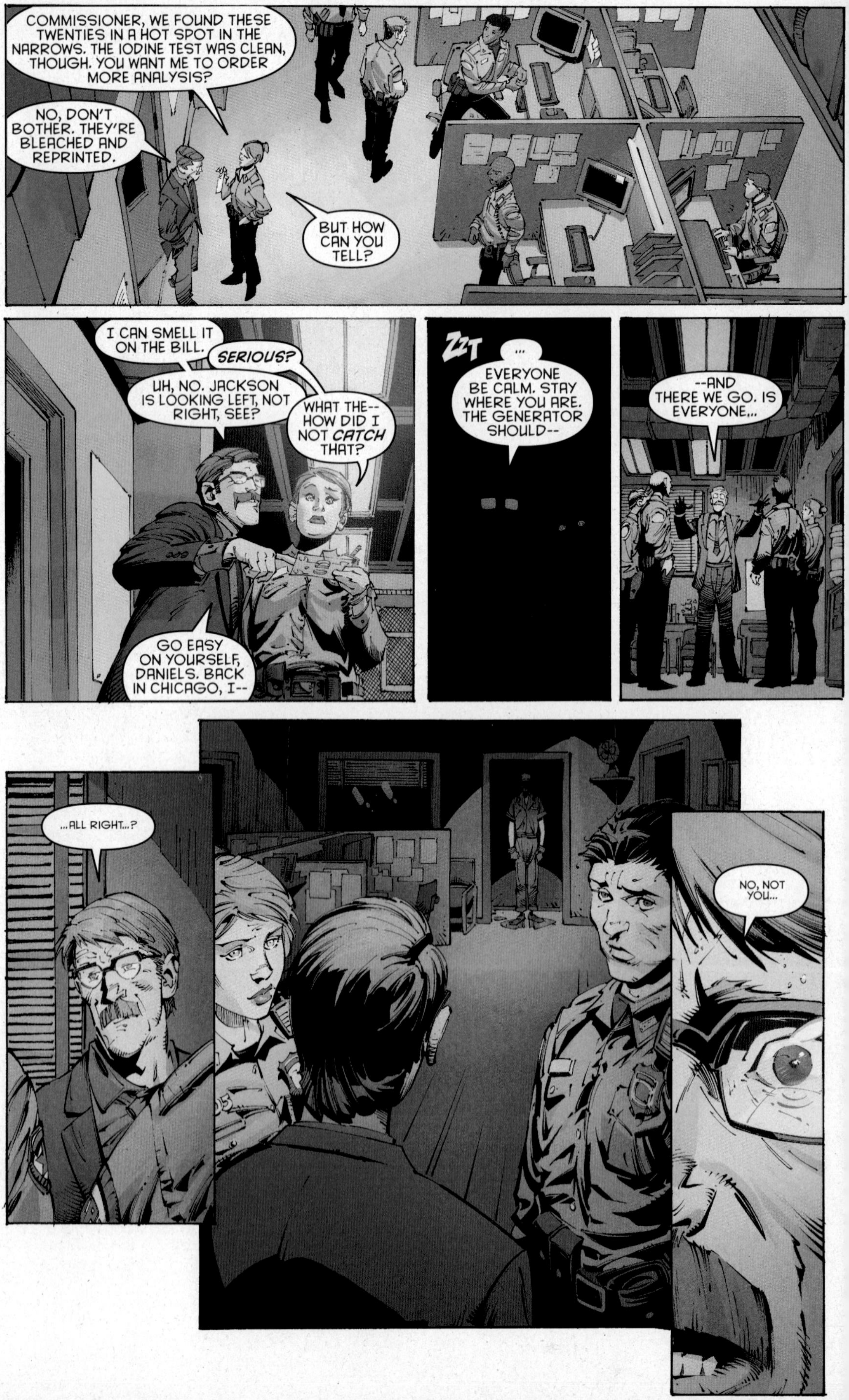
COMMISSIONER, WE FOUND THESE TWENTIES IN A HOT SPOT IN THE NARROWS. THE IODINE TEST WAS CLEAN, THOUGH. YOU WANT ME TO ORDER MORE ANALYSIS?
NO, DON'T BOTHER. THEY'RE BLEACHED AND REPRINTED.
BUT HOW CAN YOU TELL?
I CAN SMELL IT ON THE BILL.
SERIOUS?
UH, NO. JACKSON IS LOOKING LEFT, NOT RIGHT, SEE?
WHAT THE-- HOW DID I NOT CATCH THAT?
GO EASY ON YOURSELF, DANIELS. BACK IN CHICAGO, I--
ZZT
...
EVERYONE BE CALM. STAY WHERE YOU ARE. THE GENERATOR SHOULD--
--AND THERE WE GO. IS EVERYONE...
...ALL RIGHT...?
NO, NOT YOU...

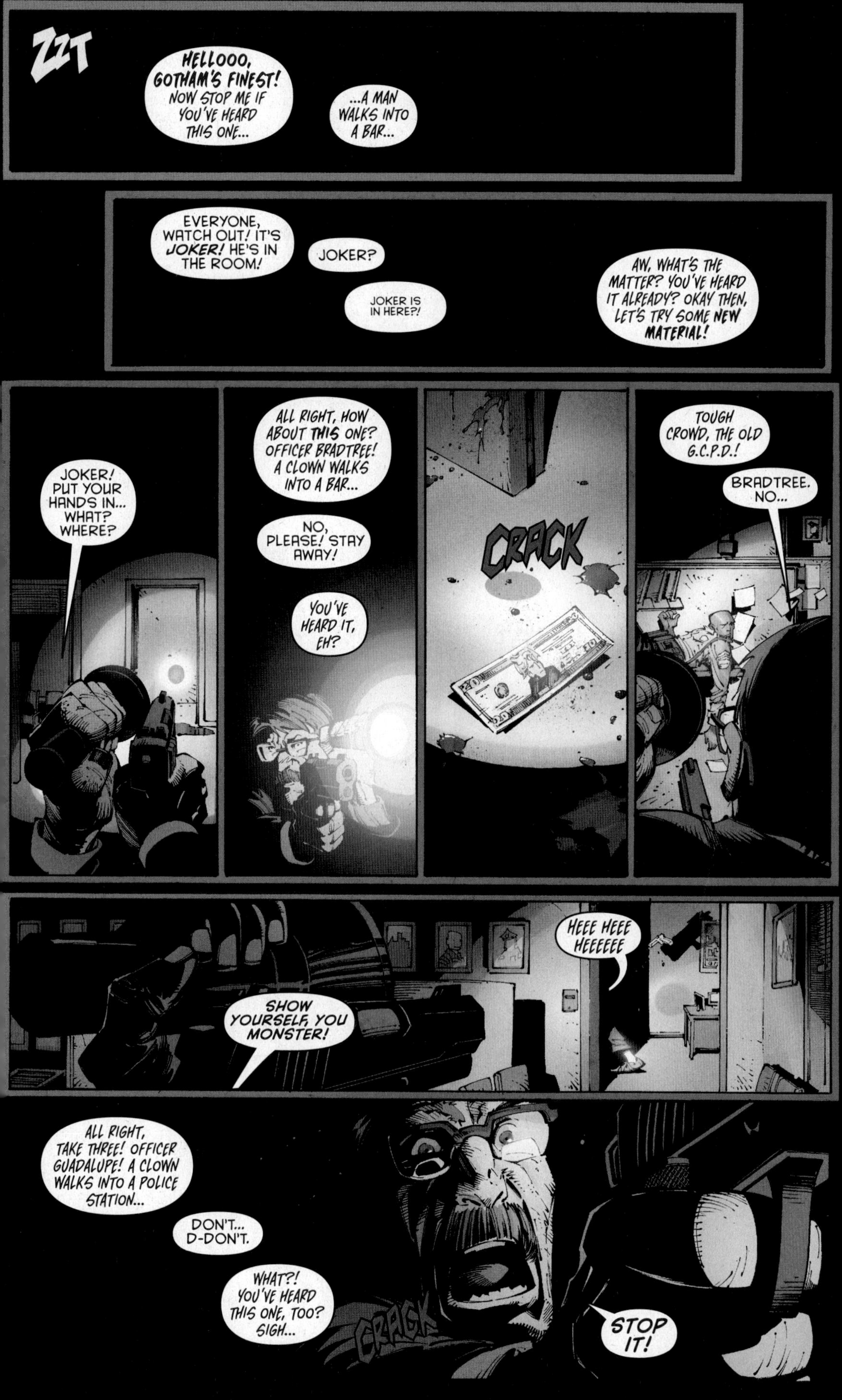
ZZT
HELLOOO, GOTHAM'S FINEST! NOW STOP ME IF YOU'VE HEARD THIS ONE...
...A MAN WALKS INTO A BAR...
EVERYONE, WATCH OUT! IT'S JOKER! HE'S IN THE ROOM!
JOKER?
JOKER IS IN HERE?!
AW, WHAT'S THE MATTER? YOU'VE HEARD IT ALREADY? OKAY THEN, LET'S TRY SOME NEW MATERIAL!
JOKER! PUT YOUR HANDS IN... WHAT? WHERE?
ALL RIGHT, HOW ABOUT THIS ONE? OFFICER BRADTREE! A CLOWN WALKS INTO A BAR...
NO, PLEASE! STAY AWAY!
YOU'VE HEARD IT, EH?
CRACK
TOUGH CROWD, THE OLD G.C.P.D.!
BRADTREE. NO...
HEEE HEEE HEEEEEE
SHOW YOURSELF, YOU MONSTER!
ALL RIGHT, TAKE THREE! OFFICER GUADALUPE! A CLOWN WALKS INTO A POLICE STATION...
DON'T... D-DON'T.
WHAT?! YOU'VE HEARD THIS ONE, TOO? SIGH...
CRACK
STOP IT!

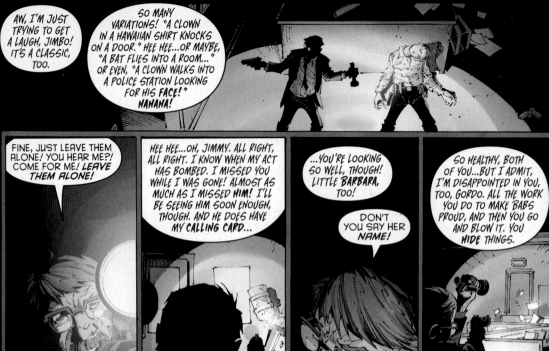

AW, I'M JUST TRYING TO GET A LAUGH, JIMBO! IT'S A CLASSIC, TOO.

SO MANY VARIATIONS! "A CLOWN IN A HAWAIIAN SHIRT KNOCKS ON A DOOR." HEE HEE...OR MAYBE, "A BAT FLIES INTO A ROOM..." OR EVEN, "A CLOWN WALKS INTO A POLICE STATION LOOKING FOR HIS FACE!" HAHAHA!

FINE, JUST LEAVE THEM ALONE! YOU HEAR ME?! COME FOR ME! LEAVE THEM ALONE!

HEE HEE...OH, JIMMY. ALL RIGHT, ALL RIGHT. I KNOW WHEN MY ACT HAS BOMBED. I MISSED YOU WHILE I WAS GONE! ALMOST AS MUCH AS I MISSED HIM! I'LL BE SEEING HIM SOON ENOUGH, THOUGH. AND HE DOES HAVE MY CALLING CARD...

...YOU'RE LOOKING SO WELL, THOUGH! LITTLE BARBARA, TOO!

DON'T YOU SAY HER NAME!

SO HEALTHY, BOTH OF YOU...BUT I ADMIT, I'M DISAPPOINTED IN YOU, TOO, GORDO. ALL THE WORK YOU DO TO MAKE BABS PROUD, AND THEN YOU GO AND BLOW IT. YOU HIDE THINGS.

DOESN'T HE HIDE THINGS, OFFICER MCCABE?

GET ME, YOU--

CRACK

NO!

YESSSS, COMMISH...YES YOU DO HIDE THINGS.

LIKE THAT LAST PACK OF SMOKES!

THE ONE YOU HIDE IN YOUR APARTMENT...

...IN THAT FINAL HIDING SPOT WHERE BARBARA WON'T LOOK... WHERE NO ONE WILL.

UNDER YOUR BED, IN THE WIRE NETTING.

SOMETIMES I LIE UNDER THERE AT NIGHT AND LISTEN TO YOU SLEEP. THE SAD THINGS YOU SAY... HOW I WANT TO JUST REACH MY ARMS UP AND...

HAHAHA HAHA!

CREAK

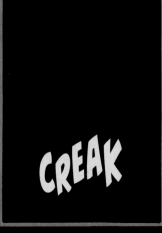

BLAM BLAM

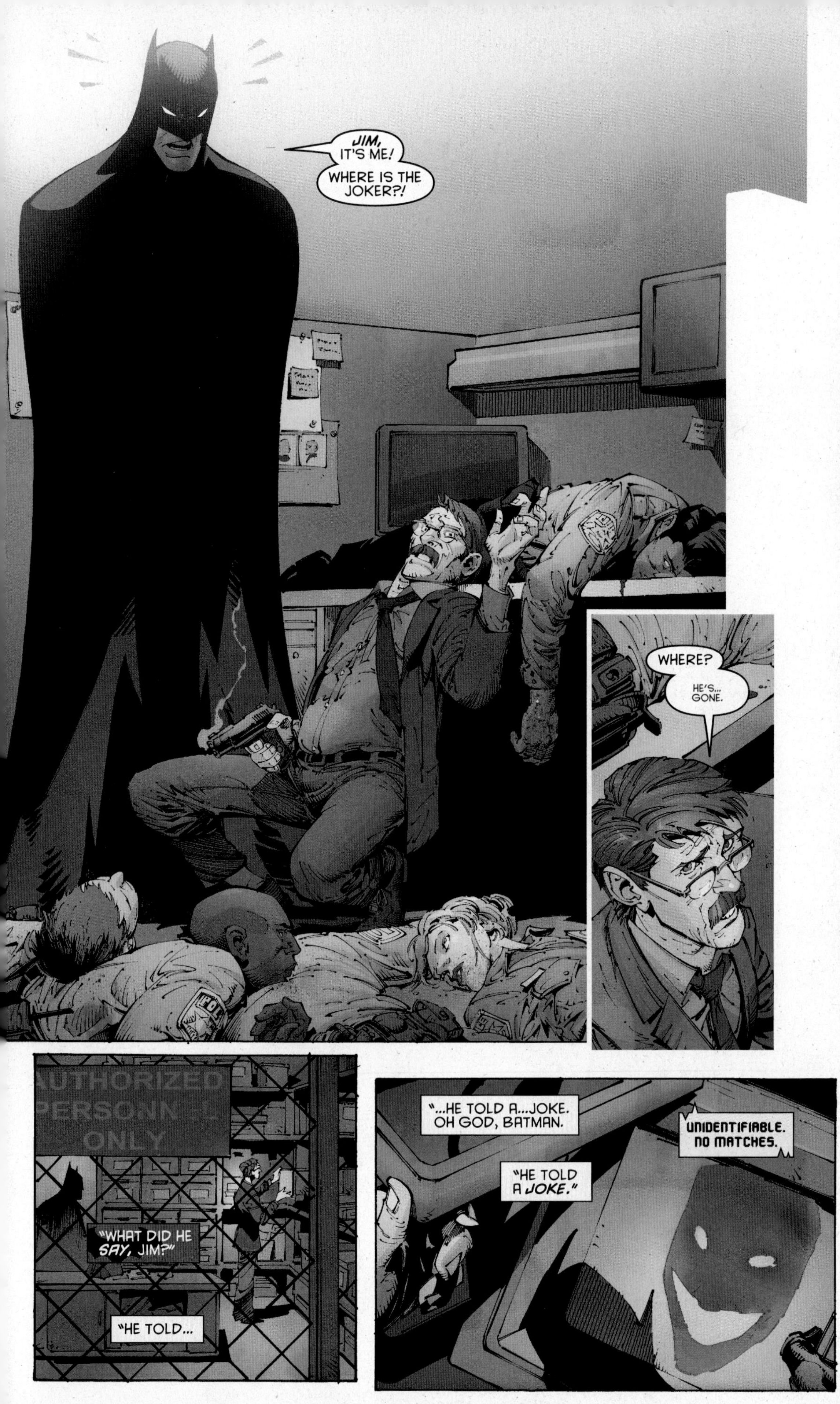
JIM, IT'S ME! WHERE IS THE JOKER?!
WHERE?
HE'S... GONE.
AUTHORIZED PERSONNEL ONLY
"WHAT DID HE SAY, JIM?"
"HE TOLD...
"...HE TOLD A...JOKE. OH GOD, BATMAN.
"HE TOLD A JOKE."
UNIDENTIFIABLE. NO MATCHES.

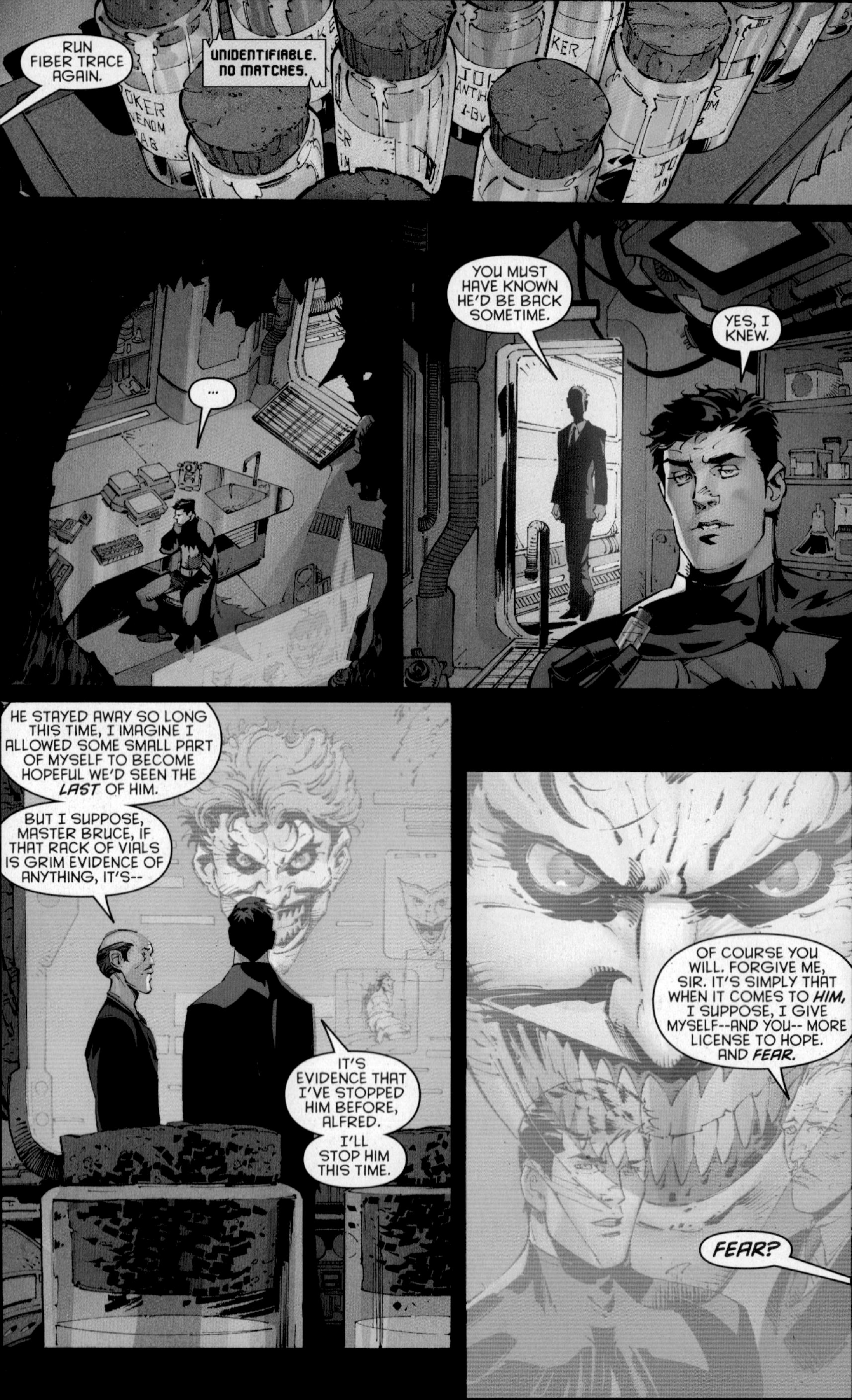
RUN FIBER TRACE AGAIN.
UNIDENTIFIABLE. NO MATCHES.
...
YOU MUST HAVE KNOWN HE'D BE BACK SOMETIME.
YES, I KNEW.
HE STAYED AWAY SO LONG THIS TIME, I IMAGINE I ALLOWED SOME SMALL PART OF MYSELF TO BECOME HOPEFUL WE'D SEEN THE LAST OF HIM.
BUT I SUPPOSE, MASTER BRUCE, IF THAT RACK OF VIALS IS GRIM EVIDENCE OF ANYTHING, IT'S--
IT'S EVIDENCE THAT I'VE STOPPED HIM BEFORE, ALFRED.
I'LL STOP HIM THIS TIME.
OF COURSE YOU WILL. FORGIVE ME, SIR. IT'S SIMPLY THAT WHEN IT COMES TO HIM, I SUPPOSE, I GIVE MYSELF--AND YOU-- MORE LICENSE TO HOPE. AND FEAR.
FEAR?

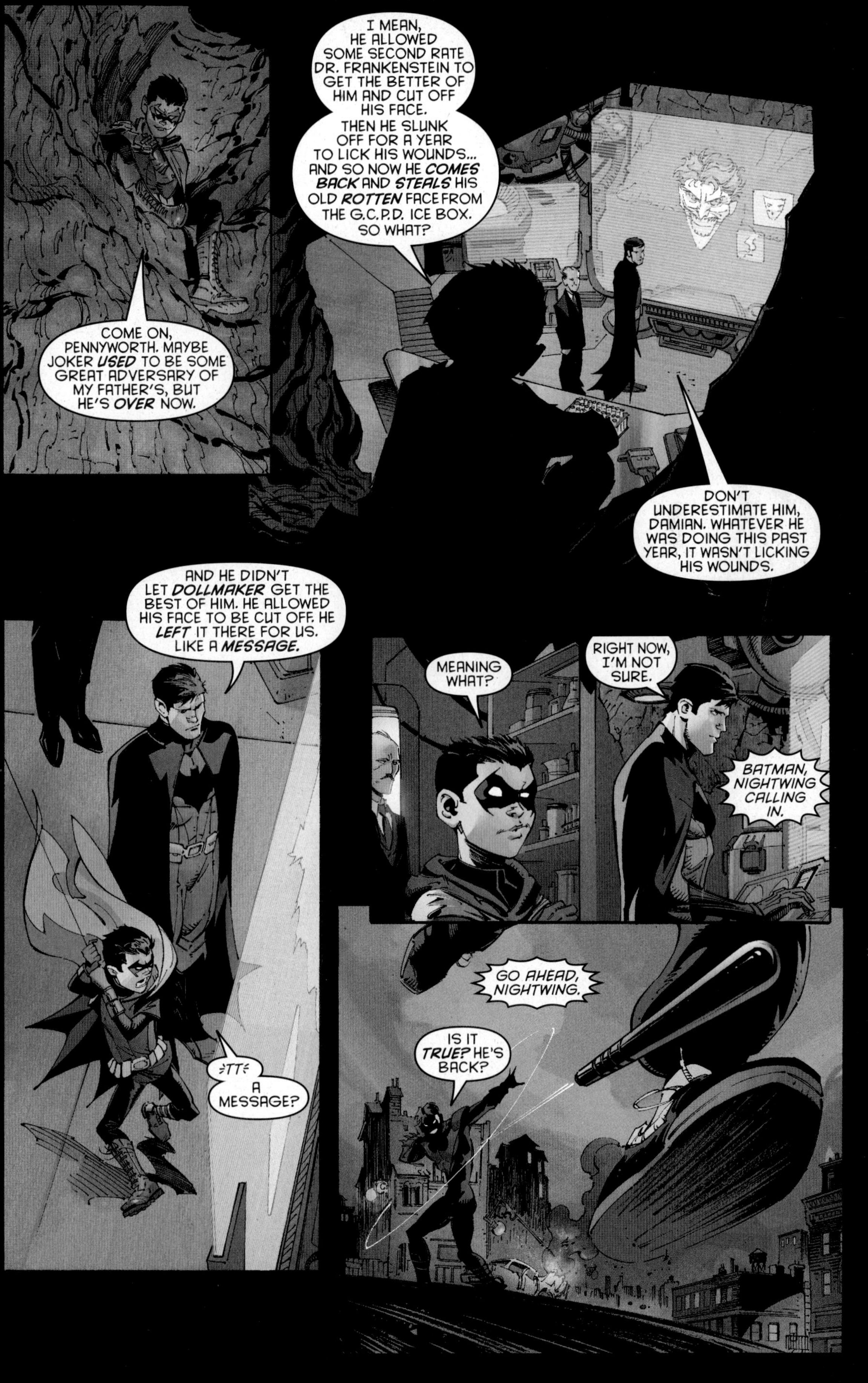

COME ON, PENNYWORTH. MAYBE JOKER *USED* TO BE SOME GREAT ADVERSARY OF MY FATHER'S, BUT HE'S *OVER* NOW.
I MEAN, HE ALLOWED SOME SECOND RATE DR. FRANKENSTEIN TO GET THE BETTER OF HIM AND CUT OFF HIS FACE.
THEN HE SLUNK OFF FOR A YEAR TO LICK HIS WOUNDS... AND SO NOW HE *COMES BACK* AND *STEALS* HIS OLD *ROTTEN* FACE FROM THE G.C.P.D. ICE BOX. SO WHAT?
DON'T UNDERESTIMATE HIM, DAMIAN. WHATEVER HE WAS DOING THIS PAST YEAR, IT WASN'T LICKING HIS WOUNDS.
AND HE DIDN'T LET *DOLLMAKER* GET THE BEST OF HIM. HE ALLOWED HIS FACE TO BE CUT OFF. HE *LEFT* IT THERE FOR US. LIKE A *MESSAGE.*
TT
A MESSAGE?
MEANING WHAT?
RIGHT NOW, I'M NOT SURE.
BATMAN, NIGHTWING CALLING IN.
GO AHEAD, NIGHTWING.
IS IT *TRUE?* HE'S BACK?

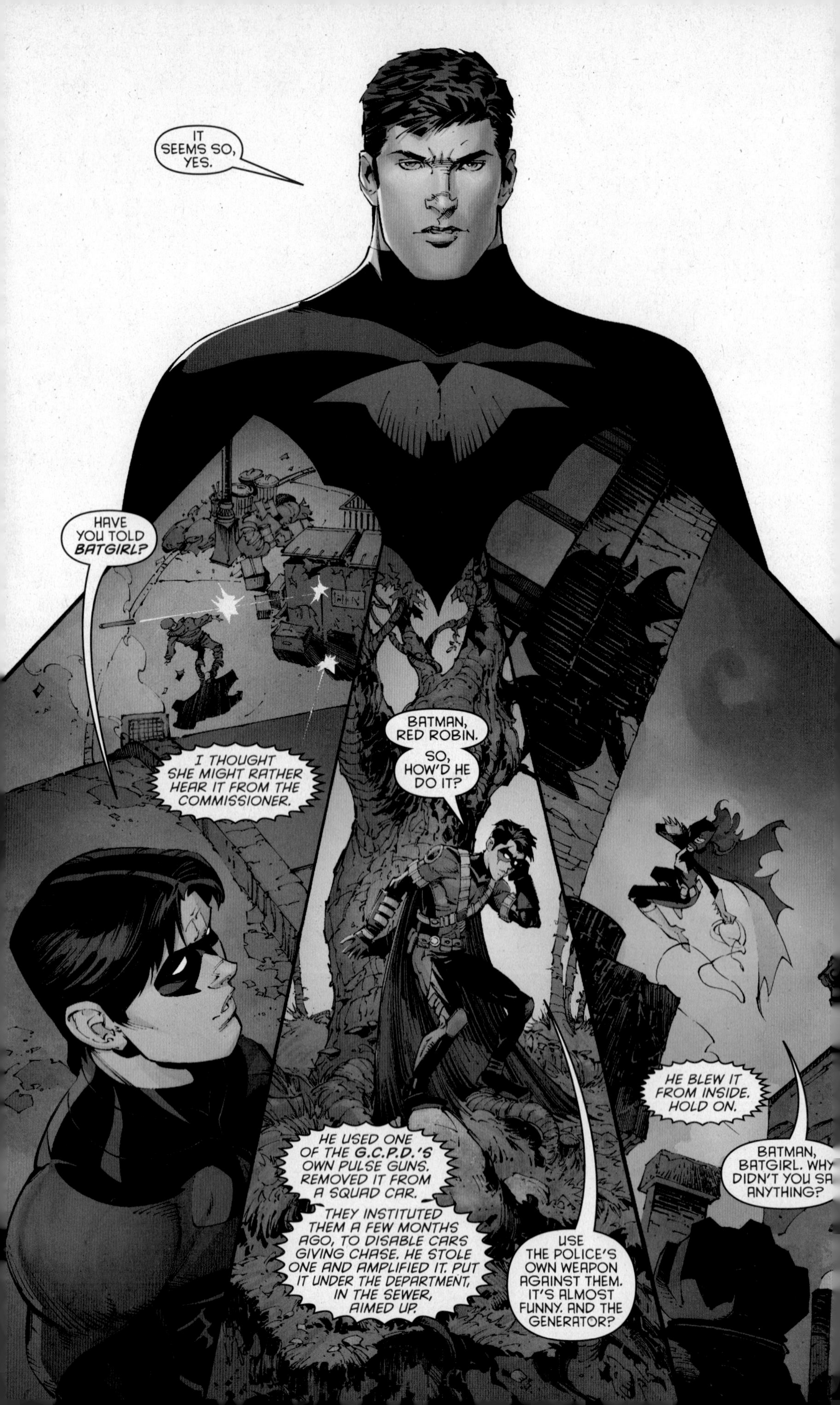
IT SEEMS SO, YES.
HAVE YOU TOLD BATGIRL?
I THOUGHT SHE MIGHT RATHER HEAR IT FROM THE COMMISSIONER.
BATMAN, RED ROBIN.
SO, HOW'D HE DO IT?
HE USED ONE OF THE G.C.P.D.'S OWN PULSE GUNS. REMOVED IT FROM A SQUAD CAR.
THEY INSTITUTED THEM A FEW MONTHS AGO, TO DISABLE CARS GIVING CHASE. HE STOLE ONE AND AMPLIFIED IT. PUT IT UNDER THE DEPARTMENT, IN THE SEWER, AIMED UP.
USE THE POLICE'S OWN WEAPON AGAINST THEM. IT'S ALMOST FUNNY. AND THE GENERATOR?
HE BLEW IT FROM INSIDE. HOLD ON.
BATMAN, BATGIRL. WHY DIDN'T YOU SA ANYTHING?

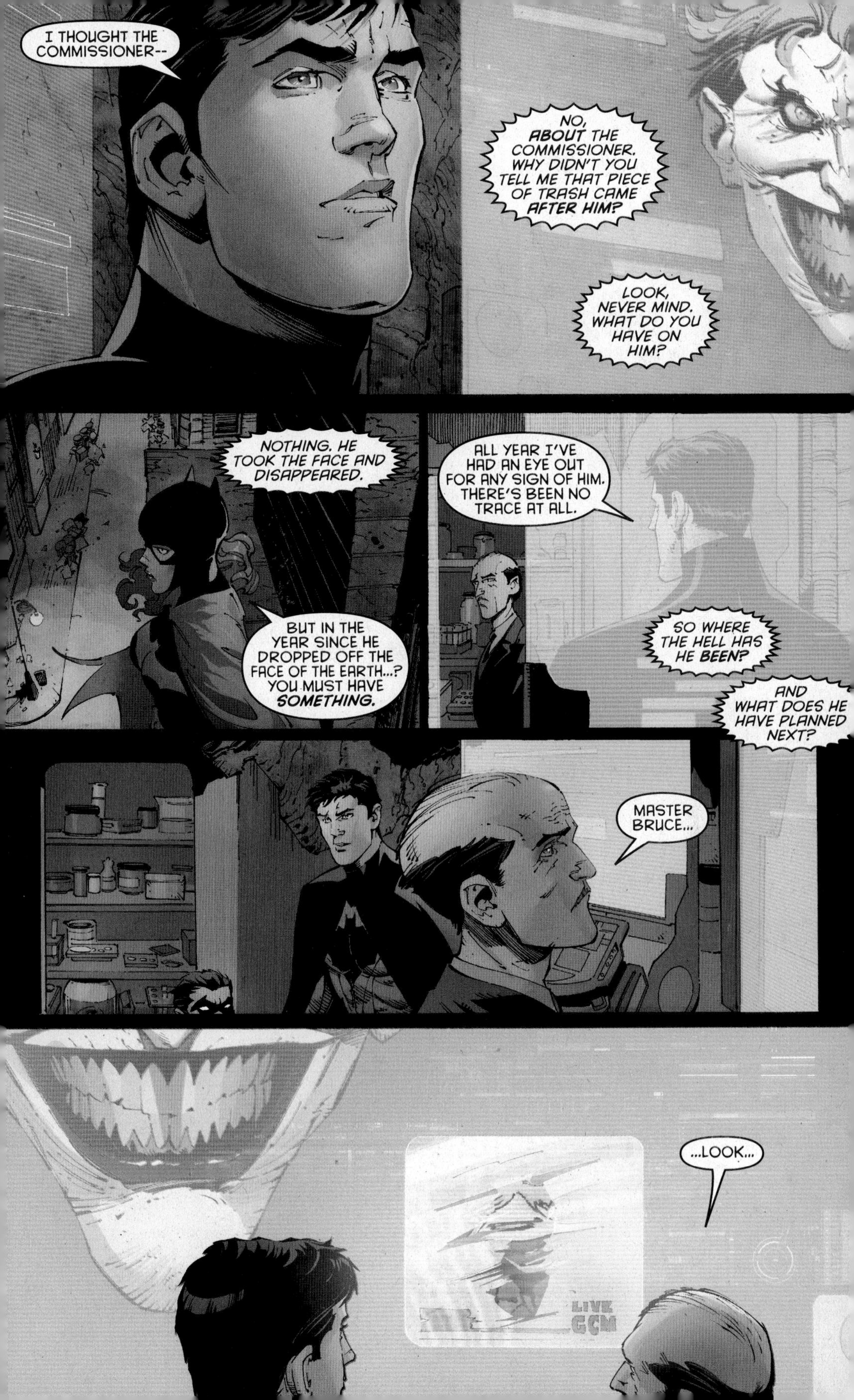
I THOUGHT THE COMMISSIONER--
NO, ABOUT THE COMMISSIONER. WHY DIDN'T YOU TELL ME THAT PIECE OF TRASH CAME AFTER HIM?
LOOK, NEVER MIND. WHAT DO YOU HAVE ON HIM?
NOTHING. HE TOOK THE FACE AND DISAPPEARED.
BUT IN THE YEAR SINCE HE DROPPED OFF THE FACE OF THE EARTH...? YOU MUST HAVE SOMETHING.
ALL YEAR I'VE HAD AN EYE OUT FOR ANY SIGN OF HIM. THERE'S BEEN NO TRACE AT ALL.
SO WHERE THE HELL HAS HE BEEN?
AND WHAT DOES HE HAVE PLANNED NEXT?
MASTER BRUCE...
...LOOK...
LIVE GCN

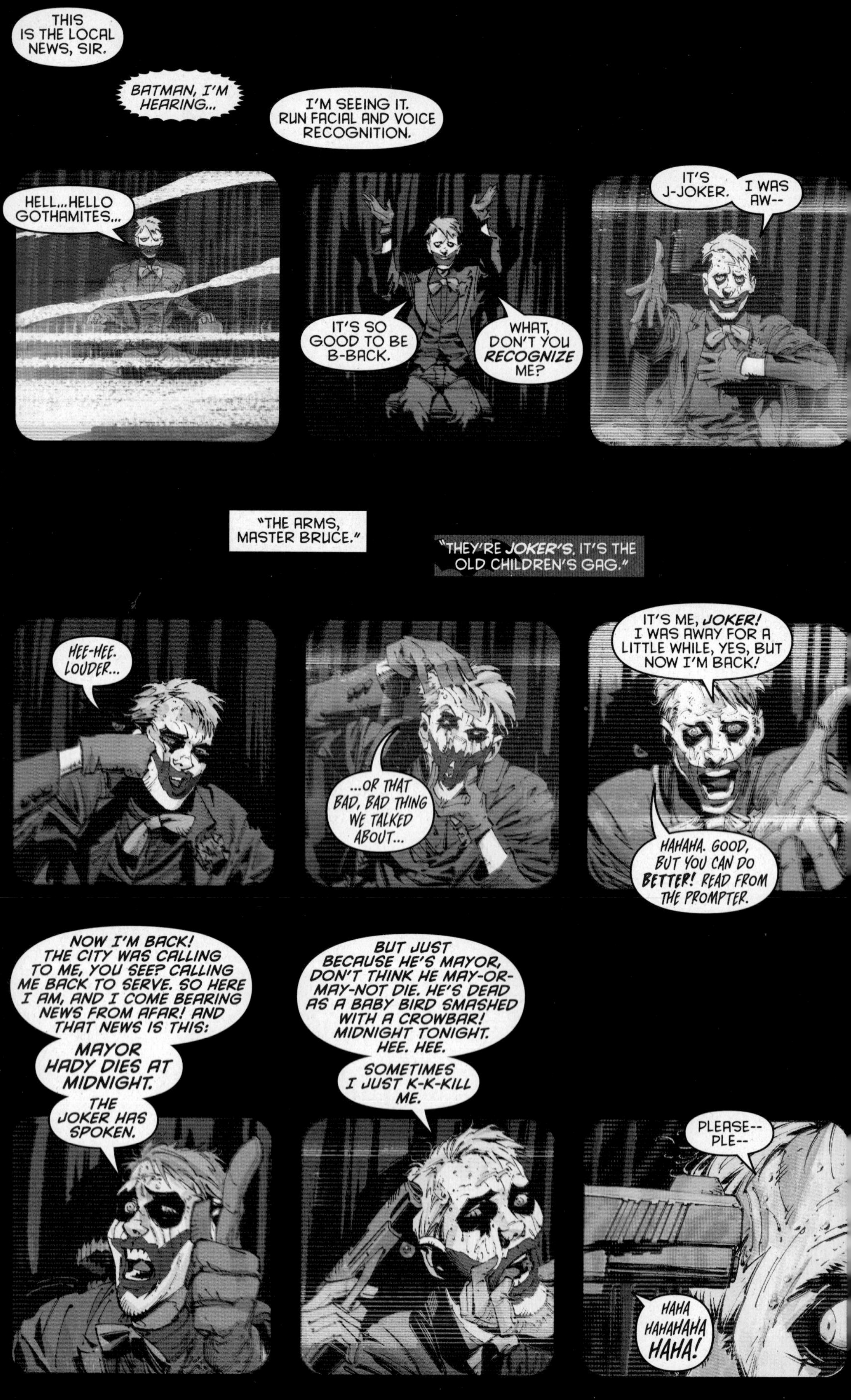

THIS IS THE LOCAL NEWS, SIR.
BATMAN, I'M HEARING...
I'M SEEING IT. RUN FACIAL AND VOICE RECOGNITION.
HELL...HELLO GOTHAMITES...
IT'S SO GOOD TO BE B-BACK.
WHAT, DON'T YOU RECOGNIZE ME?
IT'S J-JOKER.
I WAS AW--
"THE ARMS, MASTER BRUCE."
"THEY'RE JOKER'S. IT'S THE OLD CHILDREN'S GAG."
HEE-HEE. LOUDER...
...OR THAT BAD, BAD THING WE TALKED ABOUT...
IT'S ME, JOKER! I WAS AWAY FOR A LITTLE WHILE, YES, BUT NOW I'M BACK!
HAHAHA. GOOD, BUT YOU CAN DO BETTER! READ FROM THE PROMPTER.
NOW I'M BACK! THE CITY WAS CALLING TO ME, YOU SEE? CALLING ME BACK TO SERVE. SO HERE I AM, AND I COME BEARING NEWS FROM AFAR! AND THAT NEWS IS THIS:
MAYOR HADY DIES AT MIDNIGHT.
THE JOKER HAS SPOKEN.
BUT JUST BECAUSE HE'S MAYOR, DON'T THINK HE MAY-OR-MAY-NOT DIE. HE'S DEAD AS A BABY BIRD SMASHED WITH A CROWBAR! MIDNIGHT TONIGHT. HEE. HEE.
SOMETIMES I JUST K-K-KILL ME.
PLEASE-- PLE--
HAHA HAHAHAHA HAHA!

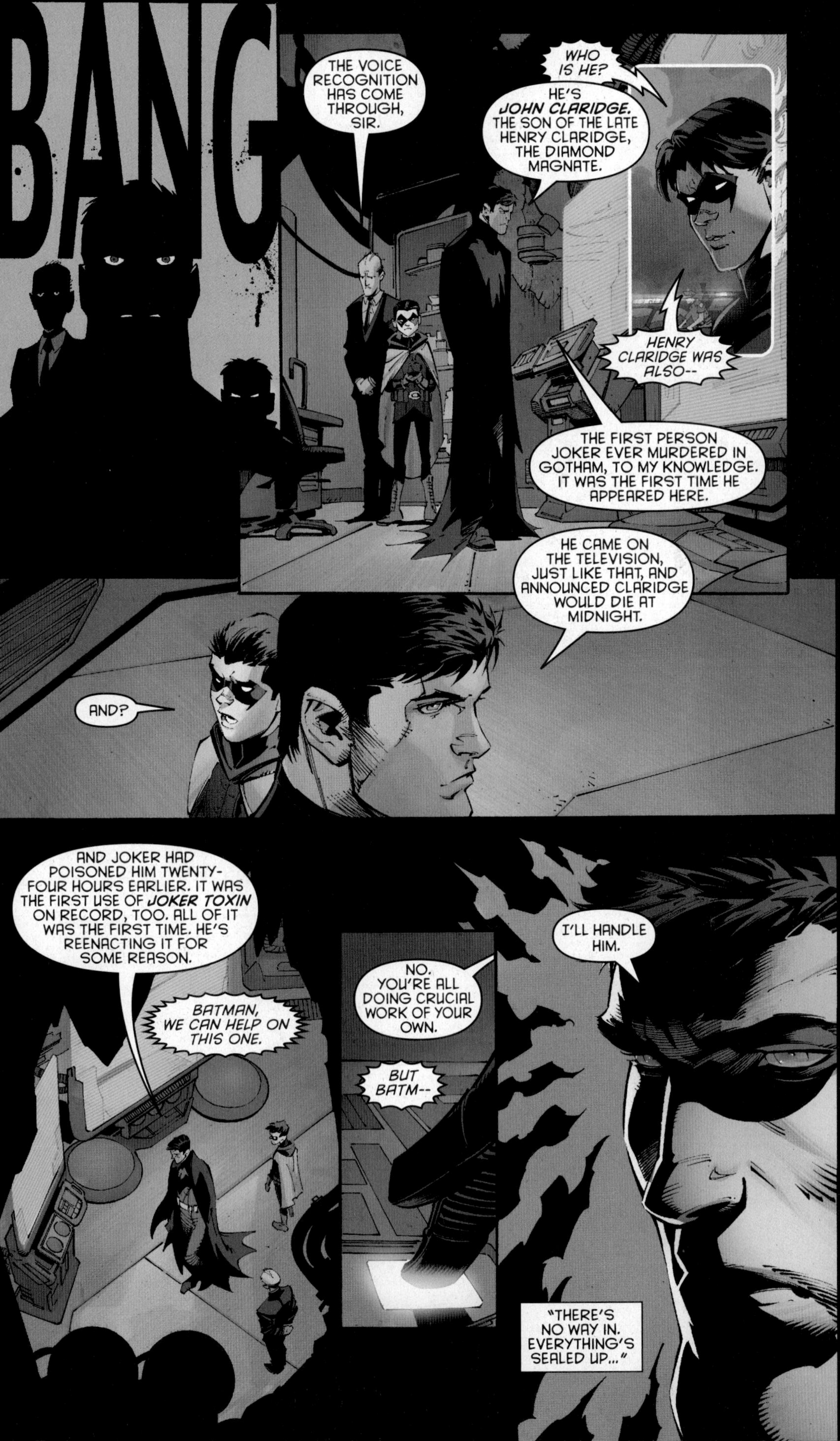
BANG
THE VOICE RECOGNITION HAS COME THROUGH, SIR.
WHO IS HE?
HE'S JOHN CLARIDGE. THE SON OF THE LATE HENRY CLARIDGE, THE DIAMOND MAGNATE.
HENRY CLARIDGE WAS ALSO--
THE FIRST PERSON JOKER EVER MURDERED IN GOTHAM, TO MY KNOWLEDGE. IT WAS THE FIRST TIME HE APPEARED HERE.
HE CAME ON THE TELEVISION, JUST LIKE THAT, AND ANNOUNCED CLARIDGE WOULD DIE AT MIDNIGHT.
AND?
AND JOKER HAD POISONED HIM TWENTY-FOUR HOURS EARLIER. IT WAS THE FIRST USE OF JOKER TOXIN ON RECORD, TOO. ALL OF IT WAS THE FIRST TIME. HE'S REENACTING IT FOR SOME REASON.
BATMAN, WE CAN HELP ON THIS ONE.
NO. YOU'RE ALL DOING CRUCIAL WORK OF YOUR OWN.
BUT BATM--
I'LL HANDLE HIM.
"THERE'S NO WAY IN. EVERYTHING'S SEALED UP..."

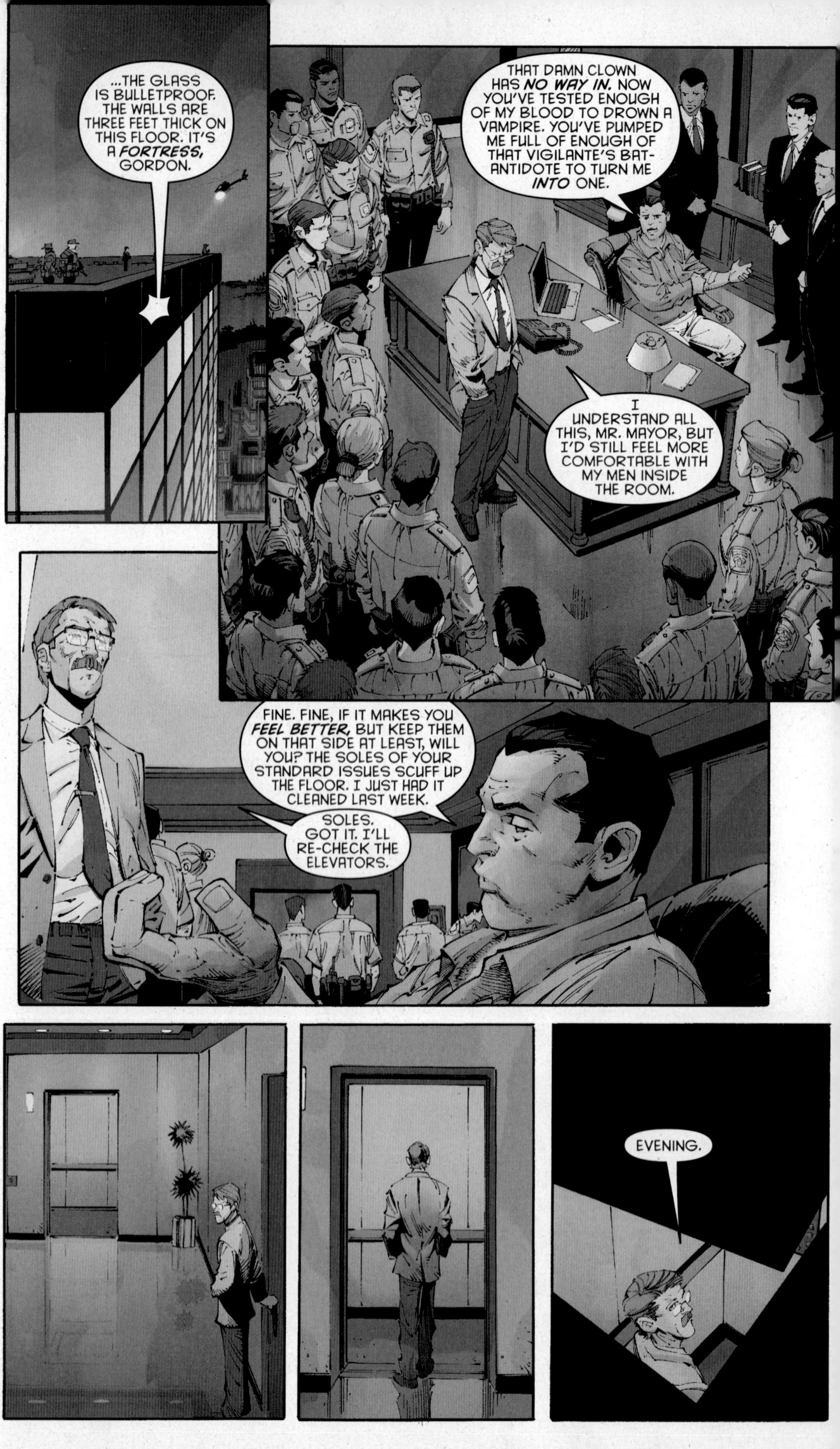
...THE GLASS IS BULLETPROOF. THE WALLS ARE THREE FEET THICK ON THIS FLOOR. IT'S A FORTRESS, GORDON.
THAT DAMN CLOWN HAS NO WAY IN. NOW YOU'VE TESTED ENOUGH OF MY BLOOD TO DROWN A VAMPIRE. YOU'VE PUMPED ME FULL OF ENOUGH OF THAT VIGILANTE'S BAT-ANTIDOTE TO TURN ME INTO ONE.
I UNDERSTAND ALL THIS, MR. MAYOR, BUT I'D STILL FEEL MORE COMFORTABLE WITH MY MEN INSIDE THE ROOM.
FINE. FINE, IF IT MAKES YOU FEEL BETTER, BUT KEEP THEM ON THAT SIDE AT LEAST, WILL YOU? THE SOLES OF YOUR STANDARD ISSUES SCUFF UP THE FLOOR. I JUST HAD IT CLEANED LAST WEEK.
SOLES. GOT IT. I'LL RE-CHECK THE ELEVATORS.
EVENING.

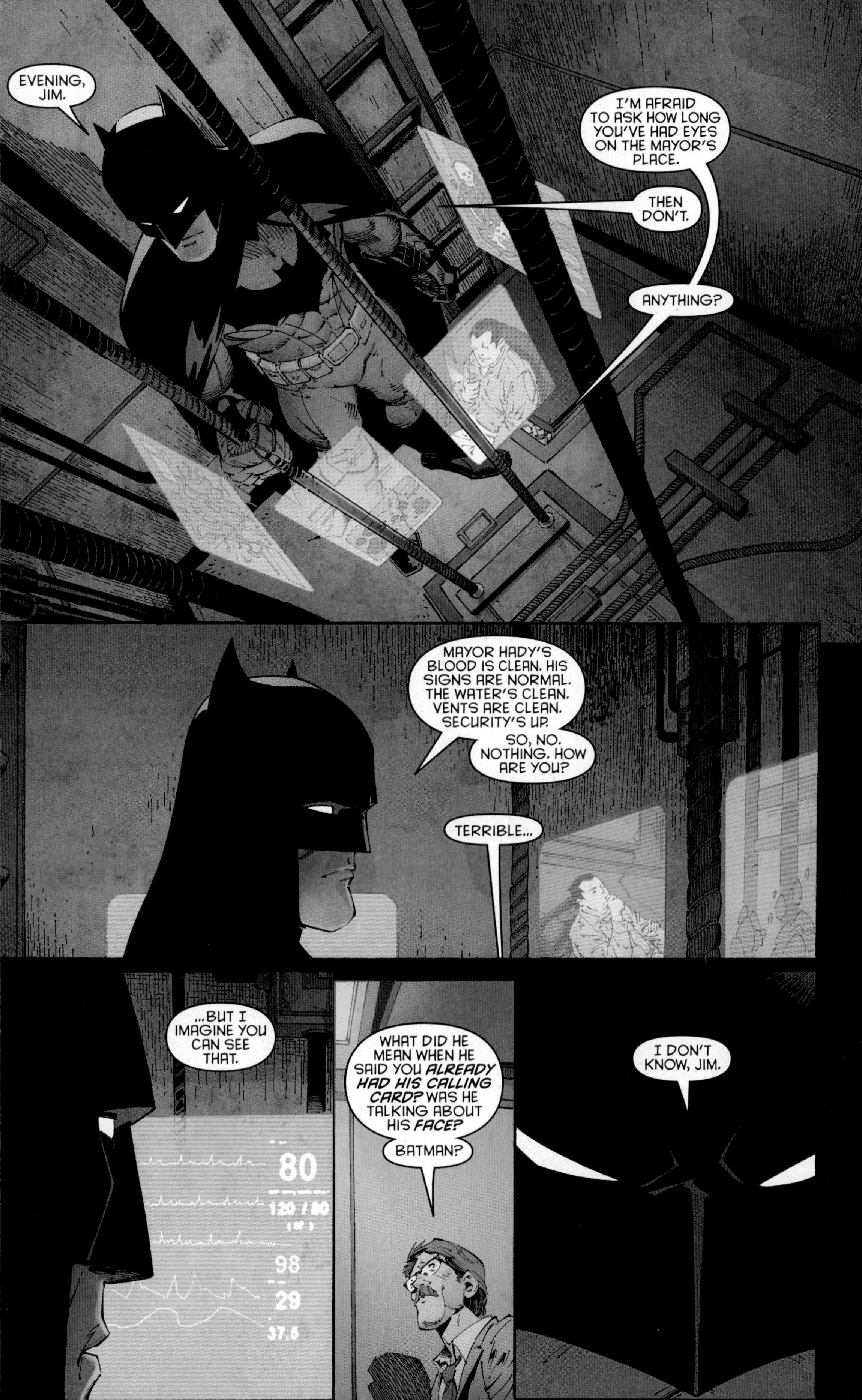

EVENING, JIM.
I'M AFRAID TO ASK HOW LONG YOU'VE HAD EYES ON THE MAYOR'S PLACE.
THEN DON'T.
ANYTHING?
MAYOR HADY'S BLOOD IS CLEAN. HIS SIGNS ARE NORMAL. THE WATER'S CLEAN. VENTS ARE CLEAN. SECURITY'S UP.
SO, NO. NOTHING. HOW ARE YOU?
TERRIBLE...
...BUT I IMAGINE YOU CAN SEE THAT.
80
120 / 80
98
29
WHAT DID HE MEAN WHEN HE SAID YOU *ALREADY HAD HIS CALLING CARD?* WAS HE TALKING ABOUT HIS *FACE?*
BATMAN?
I DON'T KNOW, JIM.

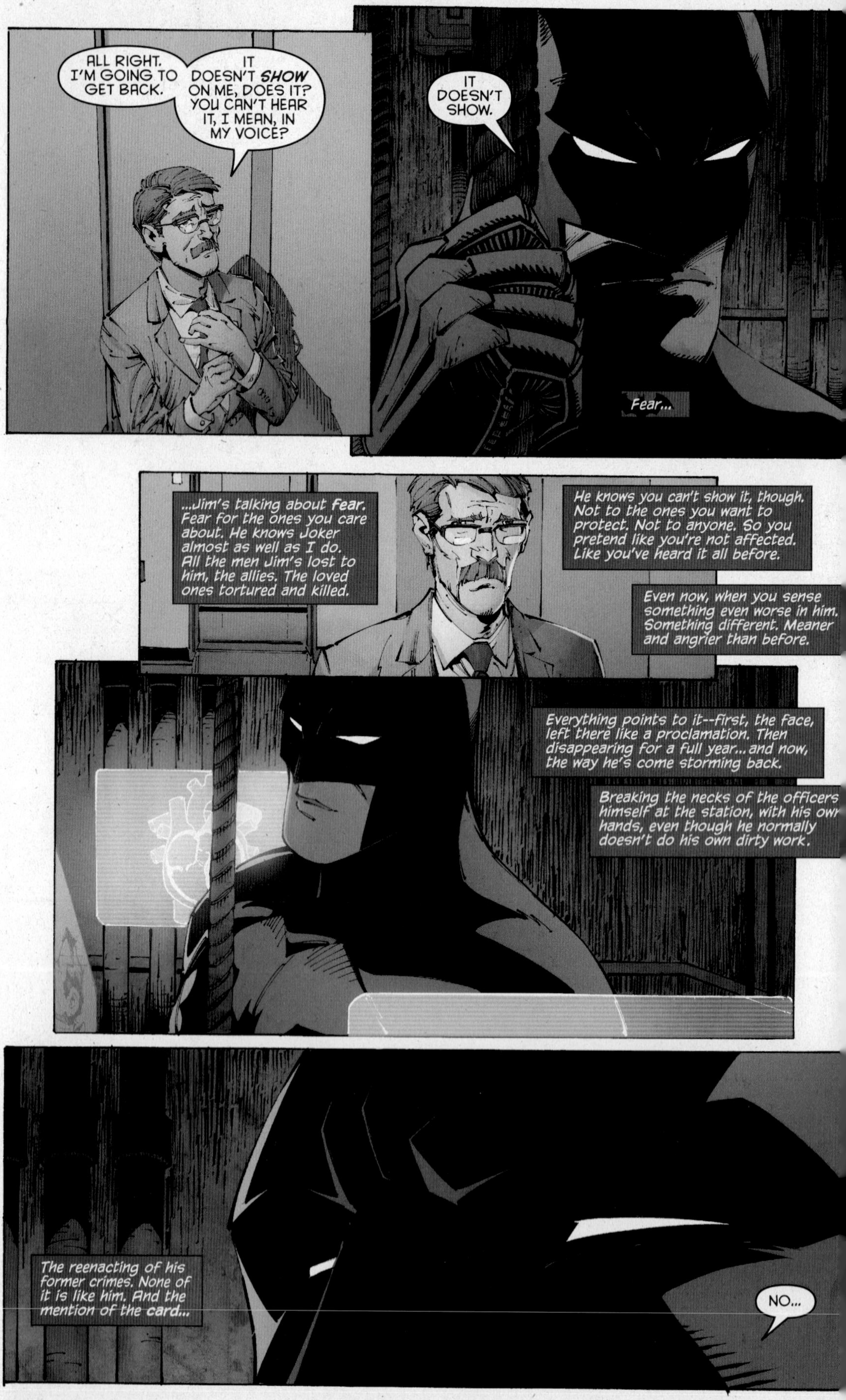
ALL RIGHT. I'M GOING TO GET BACK.
IT DOESN'T **SHOW** ON ME, DOES IT? YOU CAN'T HEAR IT, I MEAN, IN MY VOICE?
IT DOESN'T SHOW.
Fear...
...Jim's talking about **fear**. Fear for the ones you care about. He knows Joker almost as well as I do. All the men Jim's lost to him, the allies. The loved ones tortured and killed.
He knows you can't show it, though. Not to the ones you want to protect. Not to anyone. So you pretend like you're not affected. Like you've heard it all before.
Even now, when you sense something even worse in him. Something different. Meaner and angrier than before.
Everything points to it--first, the face, left there like a proclamation. Then disappearing for a full year... and now, the way he's come storming back.
Breaking the necks of the officers himself at the station, with his own hands, even though he normally doesn't do his own dirty work.
The reenacting of his former crimes. None of it is like him. And the mention of the **card**...
NO...

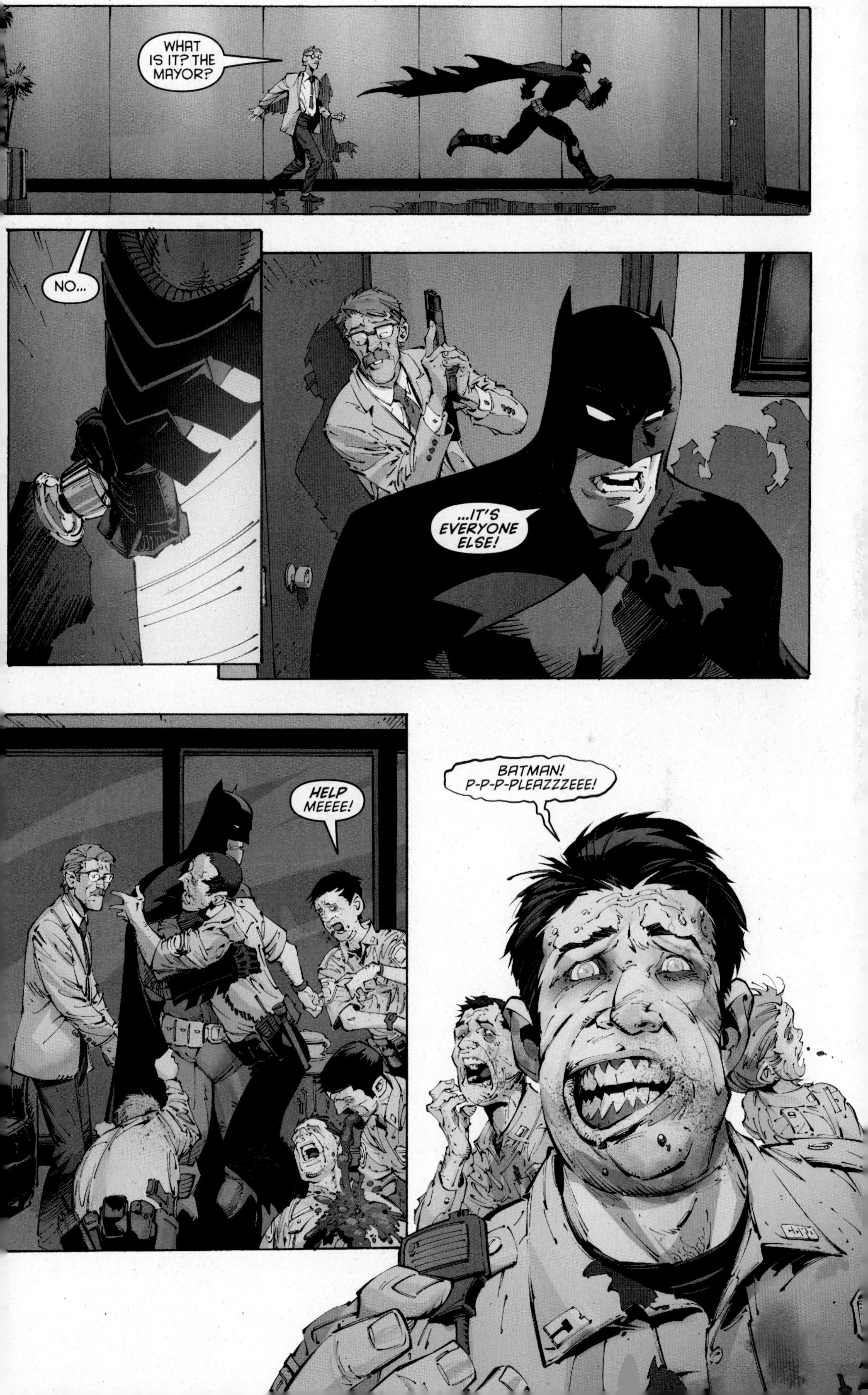
WHAT IS IT? THE MAYOR?
NO...
...IT'S EVERYONE ELSE!
HELP MEEEE!
BATMAN! P-P-P-PLEAZZZEEE!

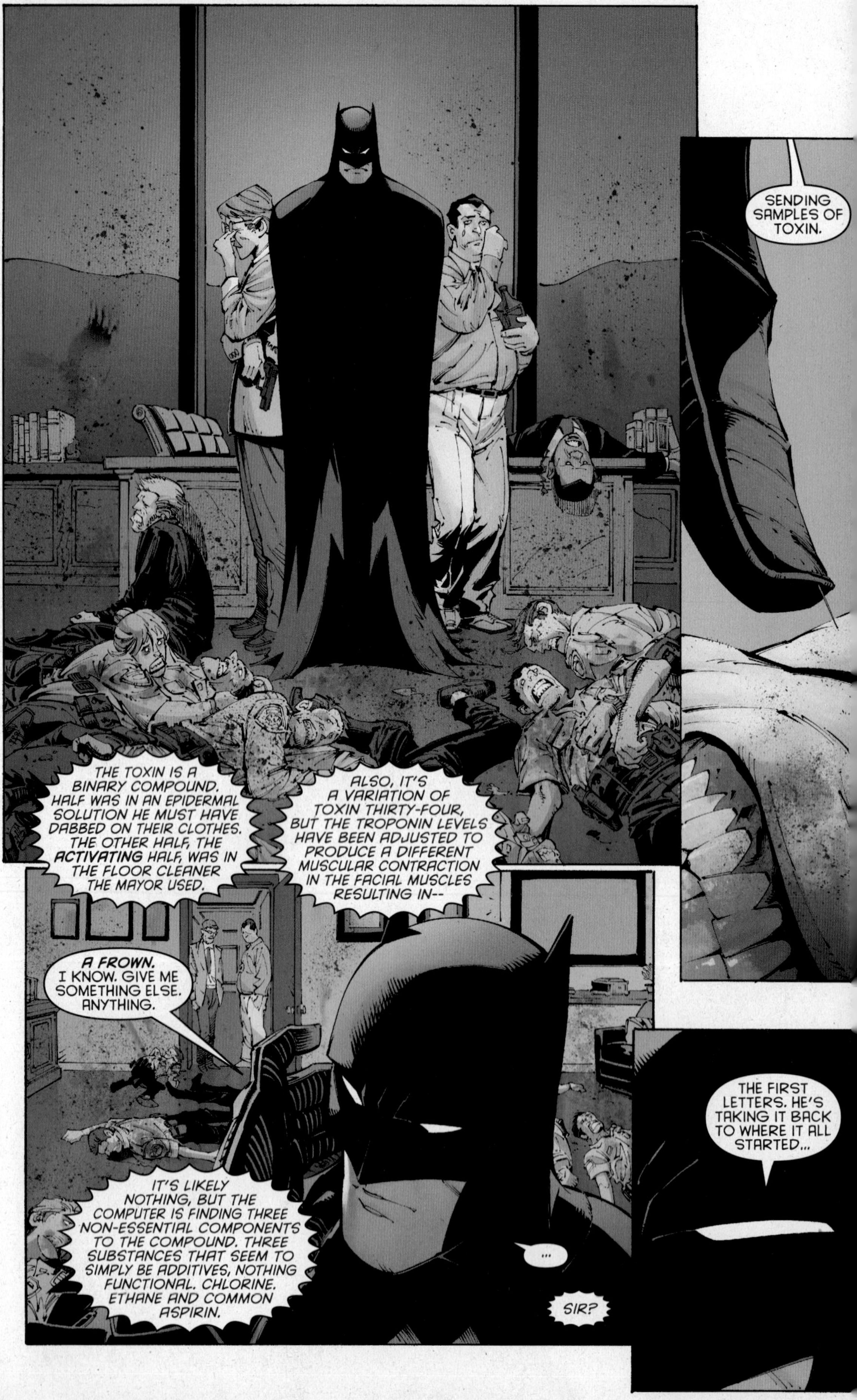
SENDING SAMPLES OF TOXIN.
THE TOXIN IS A BINARY COMPOUND. HALF WAS IN AN EPIDERMAL SOLUTION HE MUST HAVE DABBED ON THEIR CLOTHES. THE OTHER HALF, THE ACTIVATING HALF, WAS IN THE FLOOR CLEANER THE MAYOR USED.
ALSO, IT'S A VARIATION OF TOXIN THIRTY-FOUR, BUT THE TROPONIN LEVELS HAVE BEEN ADJUSTED TO PRODUCE A DIFFERENT MUSCULAR CONTRACTION IN THE FACIAL MUSCLES RESULTING IN--
A FROWN. I KNOW. GIVE ME SOMETHING ELSE. ANYTHING.
IT'S LIKELY NOTHING, BUT THE COMPUTER IS FINDING THREE NON-ESSENTIAL COMPONENTS TO THE COMPOUND. THREE SUBSTANCES THAT SEEM TO SIMPLY BE ADDITIVES, NOTHING FUNCTIONAL. CHLORINE. ETHANE AND COMMON ASPIRIN.
...
SIR?
THE FIRST LETTERS. HE'S TAKING IT BACK TO WHERE IT ALL STARTED...

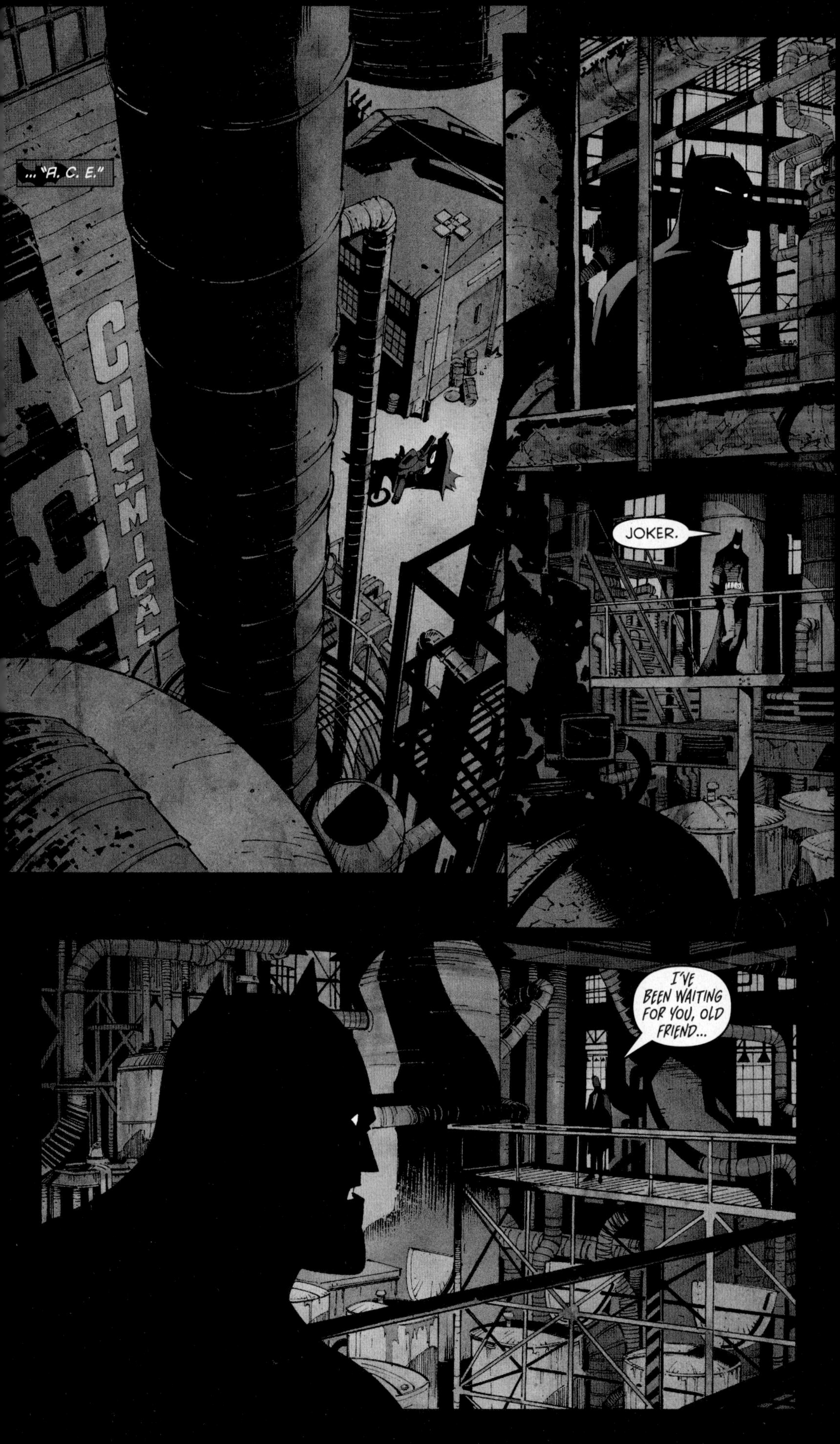
..."A. C. E."
CHEMICAL
JOKER.
I'VE BEEN WAITING FOR YOU, OLD FRIEND...

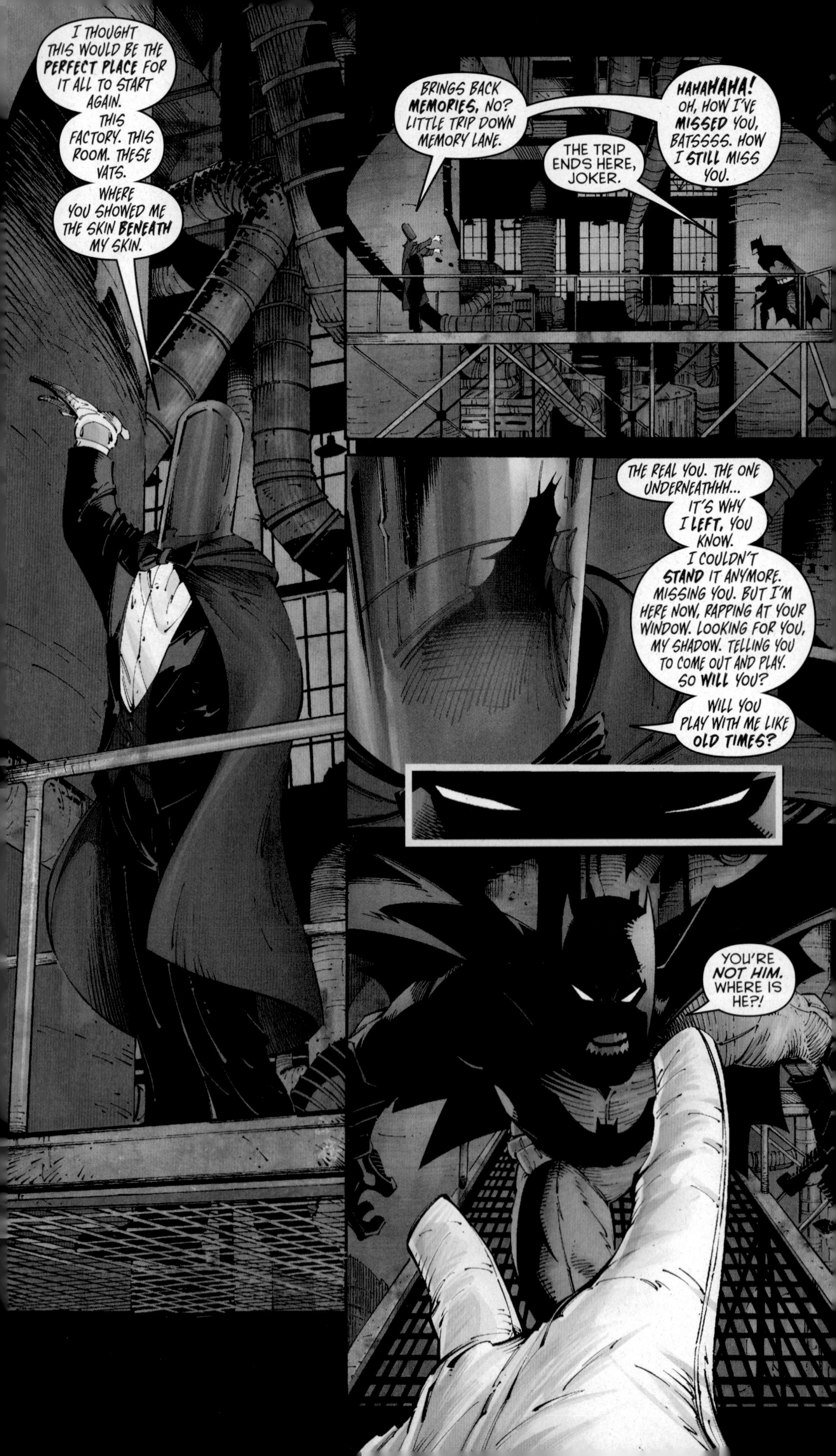

I THOUGHT THIS WOULD BE THE PERFECT PLACE FOR IT ALL TO START AGAIN.
THIS FACTORY. THIS ROOM. THESE VATS.
WHERE YOU SHOWED ME THE SKIN BENEATH MY SKIN.
BRINGS BACK MEMORIES, NO? LITTLE TRIP DOWN MEMORY LANE.
THE TRIP ENDS HERE, JOKER.
HAHAHAHA! OH, HOW I'VE MISSED YOU, BATSSSS. HOW I STILL MISS YOU.
THE REAL YOU. THE ONE UNDERNEATHHH...
IT'S WHY I LEFT, YOU KNOW.
I COULDN'T STAND IT ANYMORE. MISSING YOU. BUT I'M HERE NOW, RAPPING AT YOUR WINDOW. LOOKING FOR YOU, MY SHADOW. TELLING YOU TO COME OUT AND PLAY. SO WILL YOU?
WILL YOU PLAY WITH ME LIKE OLD TIMES?
YOU'RE NOT HIM. WHERE IS HE?!

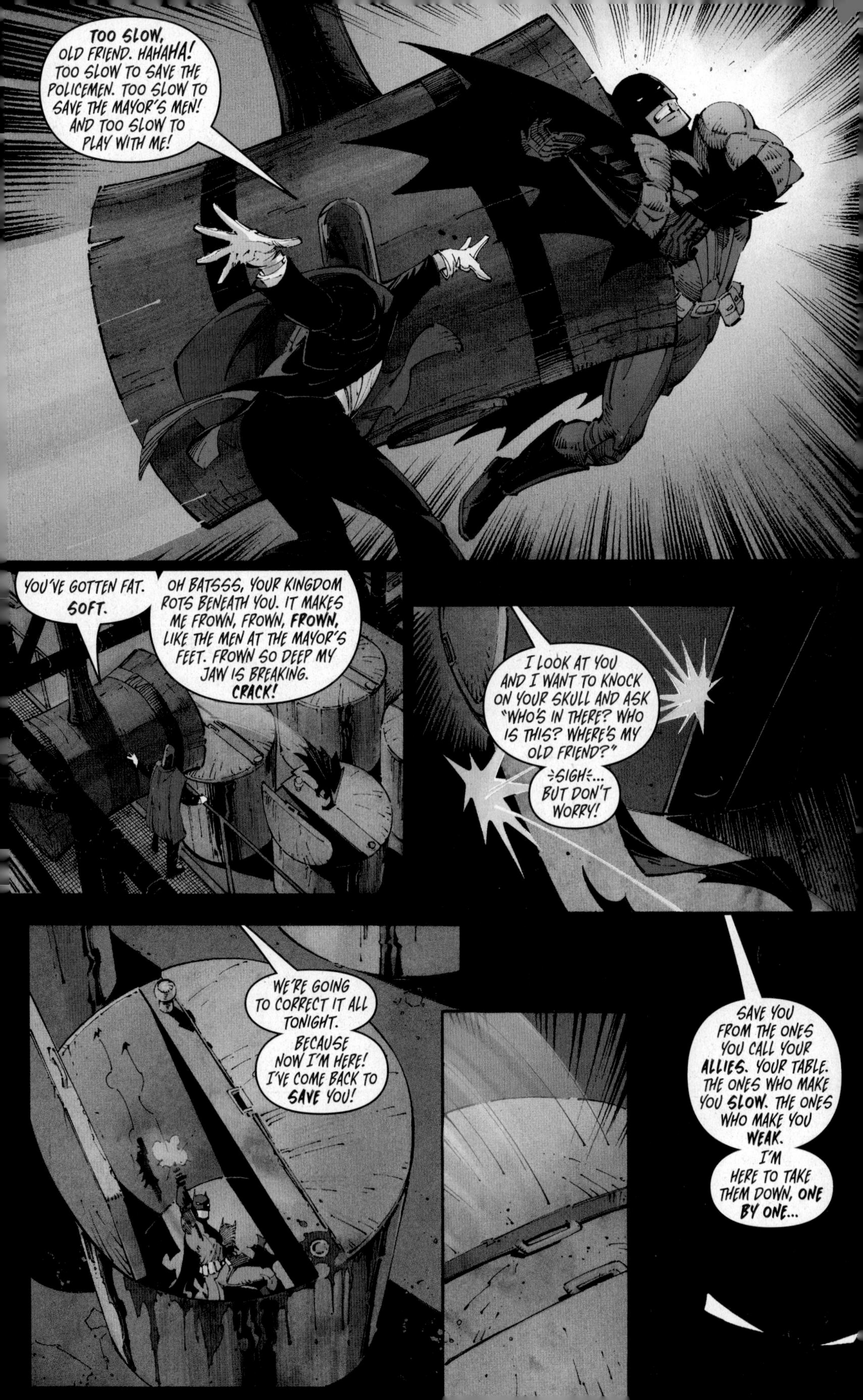
TOO SLOW, OLD FRIEND. HAHAHA! TOO SLOW TO SAVE THE POLICEMEN. TOO SLOW TO SAVE THE MAYOR'S MEN! AND TOO SLOW TO PLAY WITH ME!
YOU'VE GOTTEN FAT. SOFT.
OH BATSSS, YOUR KINGDOM ROTS BENEATH YOU. IT MAKES ME FROWN, FROWN, FROWN, LIKE THE MEN AT THE MAYOR'S FEET. FROWN SO DEEP MY JAW IS BREAKING. CRACK!
I LOOK AT YOU AND I WANT TO KNOCK ON YOUR SKULL AND ASK "WHO'S IN THERE? WHO IS THIS? WHERE'S MY OLD FRIEND?"
SIGH... BUT DON'T WORRY!
WE'RE GOING TO CORRECT IT ALL TONIGHT.
BECAUSE NOW I'M HERE! I'VE COME BACK TO SAVE YOU!
SAVE YOU FROM THE ONES YOU CALL YOUR ALLIES. YOUR TABLE. THE ONES WHO MAKE YOU SLOW. THE ONES WHO MAKE YOU WEAK.
I'M HERE TO TAKE THEM DOWN, ONE BY ONE...

...SO THAT YOU MAY BE REBORN AS THE *BAT-MAN* THIS CITY DESERVES!

REBORN IN GLORY! HOPE YOU BROUGHT YOUR SWIM TRUNKS! HAHAHA*HAHA!*

HARLEY! I KNOW YOU'RE UP THERE!

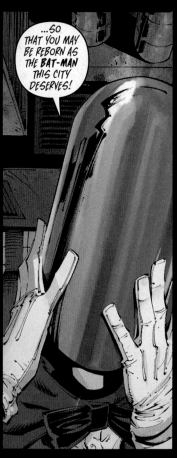

HE'S NOT THE SAME, BATS. HE'S NOT MY *MR. J* ANYMORE...

...AND WHAT HE'S GOING TO DO TO YOU...HIS PLAN... I CAN'T...

WHERE *IS* HE, HARLEY?!

TELL ME!

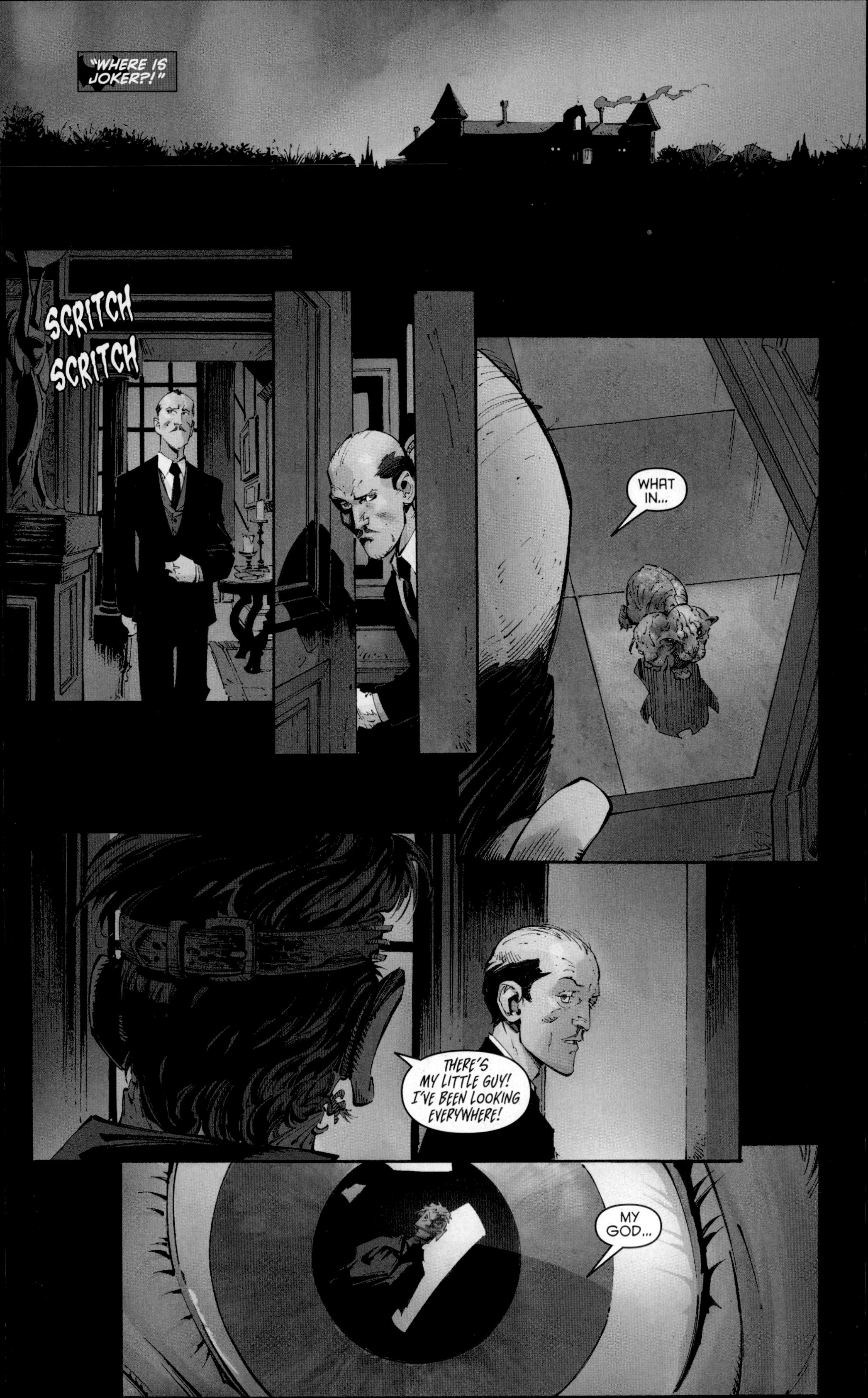
"WHERE IS JOKER?!"
SCRITCH
SCRITCH
WHAT IN...
THERE'S MY LITTLE GUY! I'VE BEEN LOOKING EVERYWHERE!
MY GOD...

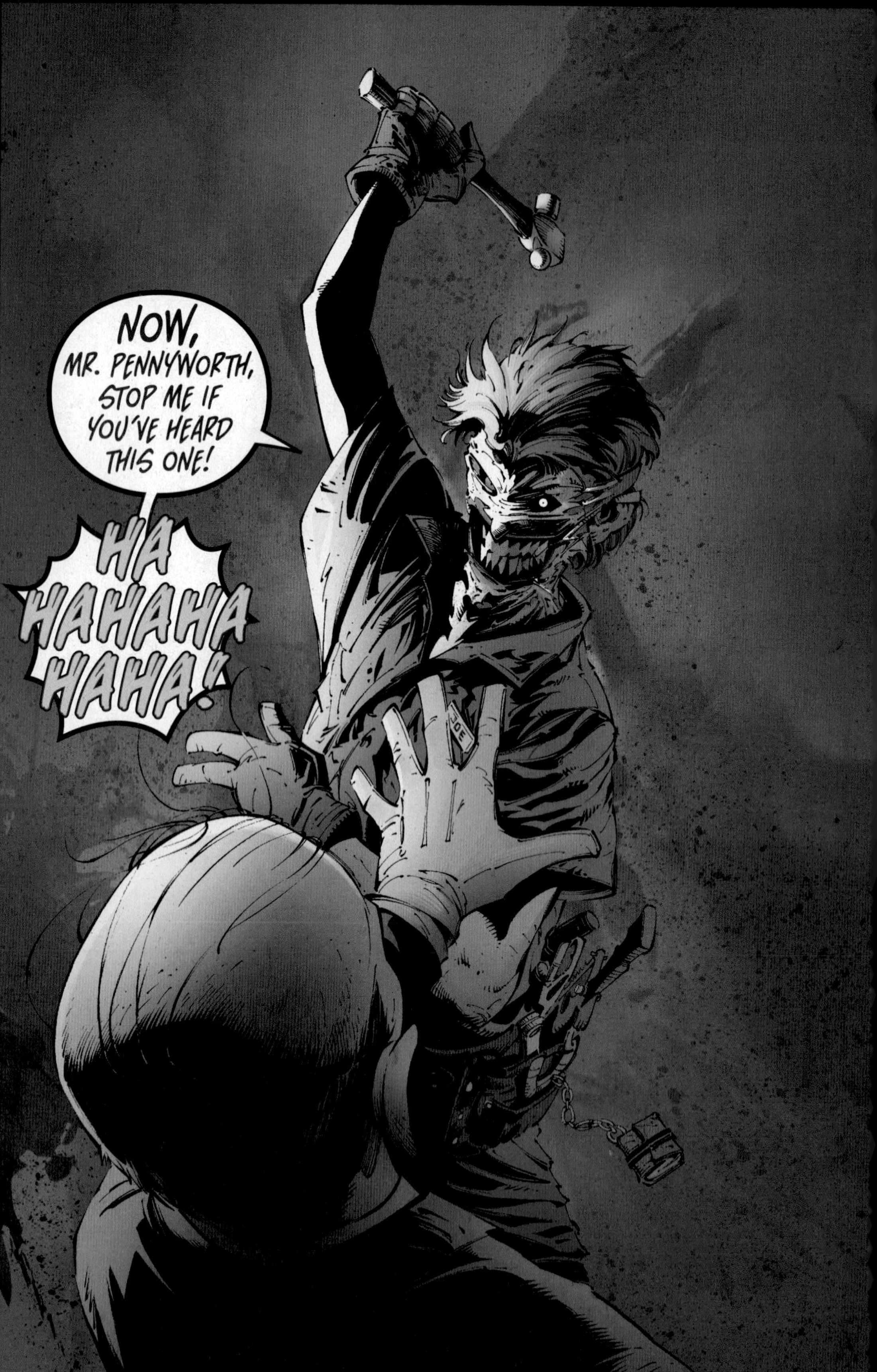
NOW, MR. PENNYWORTH, STOP ME IF YOU'VE HEARD THIS ONE!
HA HAHAHA HAHA!
JOE

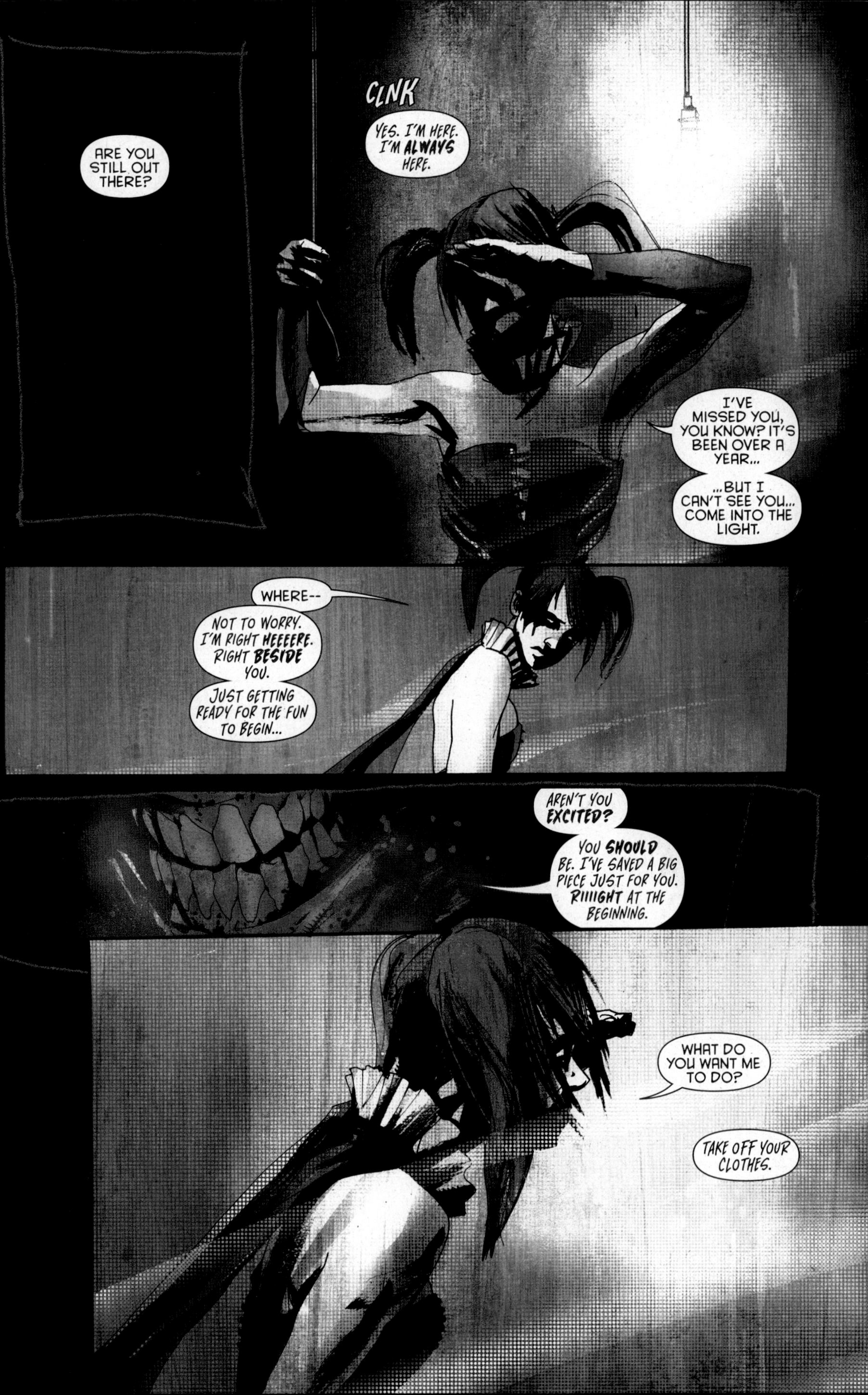
ARE YOU STILL OUT THERE?
CLNK
YES. I'M HERE. I'M ALWAYS HERE.
I'VE MISSED YOU, YOU KNOW? IT'S BEEN OVER A YEAR...
...BUT I CAN'T SEE YOU... COME INTO THE LIGHT.
WHERE--
NOT TO WORRY. I'M RIGHT HEEEERE. RIGHT BESIDE YOU.
JUST GETTING READY FOR THE FUN TO BEGIN...
AREN'T YOU EXCITED?
YOU SHOULD BE. I'VE SAVED A BIG PIECE JUST FOR YOU. RIIIIGHT AT THE BEGINNING.
WHAT DO YOU WANT ME TO DO?
TAKE OFF YOUR CLOTHES.

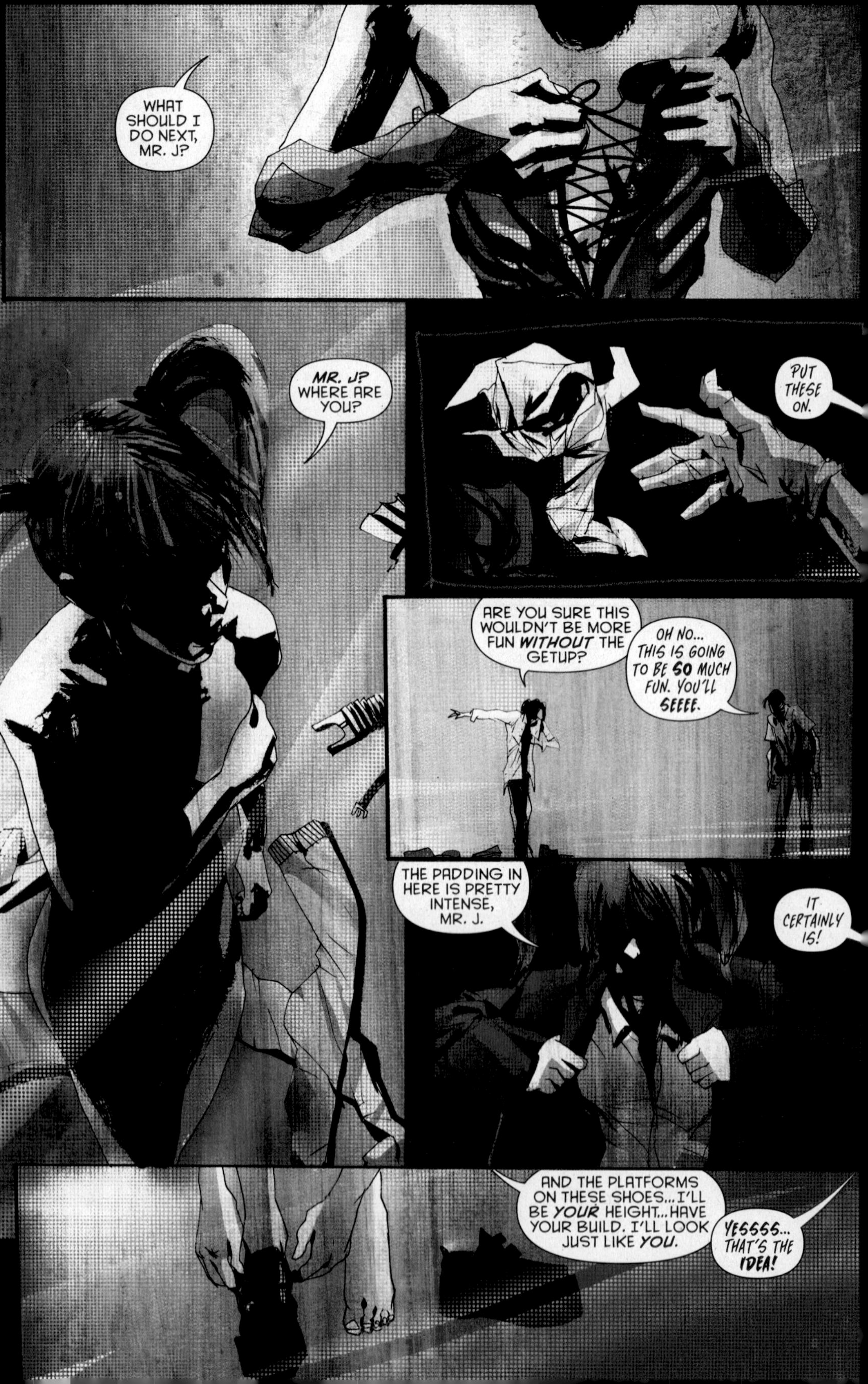
WHAT SHOULD I DO NEXT, MR. J?
MR. J? WHERE ARE YOU?
PUT THESE ON.
ARE YOU SURE THIS WOULDN'T BE MORE FUN WITHOUT THE GETUP?
OH NO... THIS IS GOING TO BE SO MUCH FUN. YOU'LL SEEEE.
THE PADDING IN HERE IS PRETTY INTENSE, MR. J.
IT CERTAINLY IS!
AND THE PLATFORMS ON THESE SHOES... I'LL BE YOUR HEIGHT... HAVE YOUR BUILD. I'LL LOOK JUST LIKE YOU.
YESSSS... THAT'S THE IDEA!

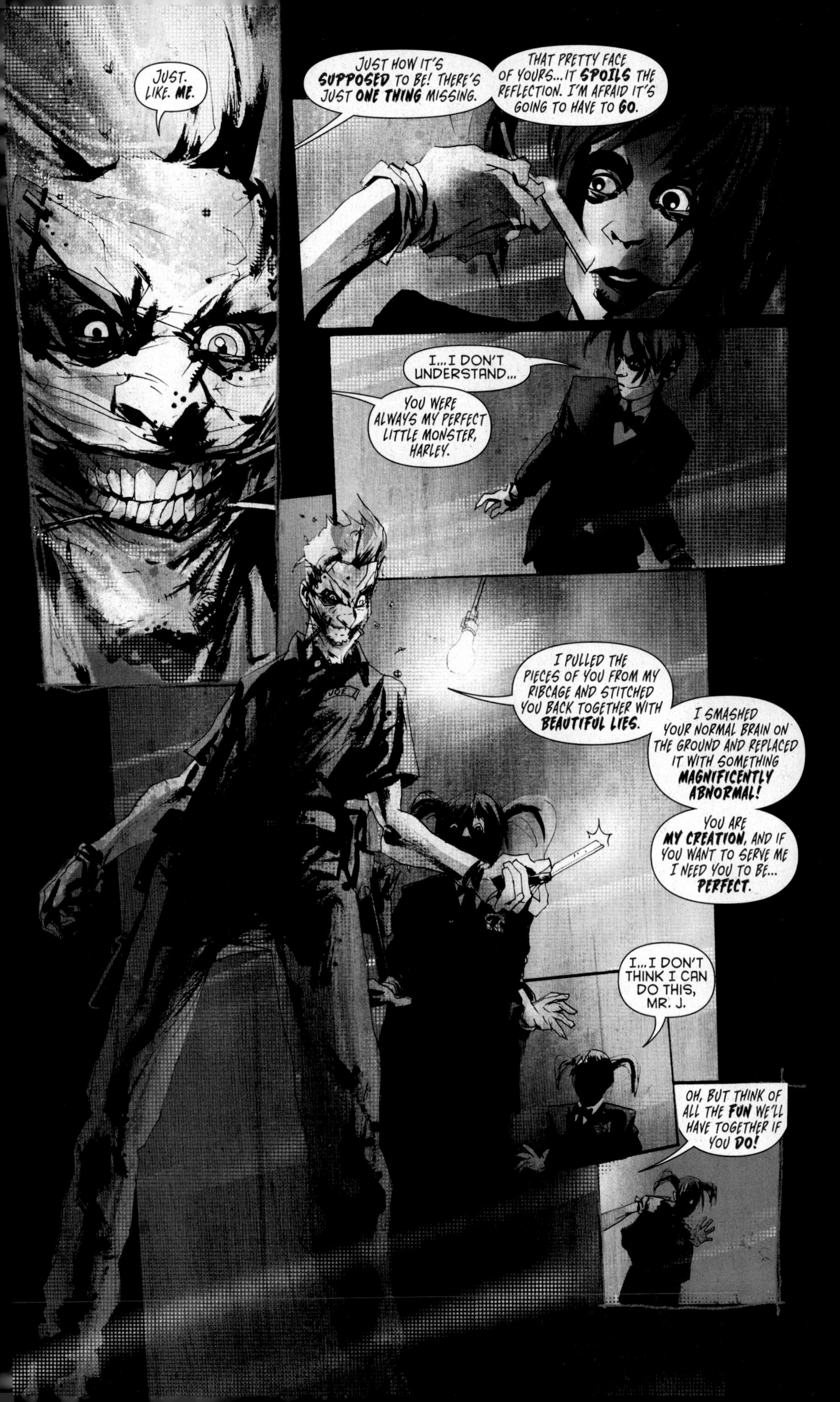
JUST. LIKE. ME.
JUST HOW IT'S SUPPOSED TO BE! THERE'S JUST ONE THING MISSING.
THAT PRETTY FACE OF YOURS... IT SPOILS THE REFLECTION. I'M AFRAID IT'S GOING TO HAVE TO GO.
I... I DON'T UNDERSTAND...
YOU WERE ALWAYS MY PERFECT LITTLE MONSTER, HARLEY.
I PULLED THE PIECES OF YOU FROM MY RIBCAGE AND STITCHED YOU BACK TOGETHER WITH BEAUTIFUL LIES.
I SMASHED YOUR NORMAL BRAIN ON THE GROUND AND REPLACED IT WITH SOMETHING MAGNIFICENTLY ABNORMAL!
YOU ARE MY CREATION, AND IF YOU WANT TO SERVE ME I NEED YOU TO BE... PERFECT.
I... I DON'T THINK I CAN DO THIS, MR. J.
OH, BUT THINK OF ALL THE FUN WE'LL HAVE TOGETHER IF YOU DO!

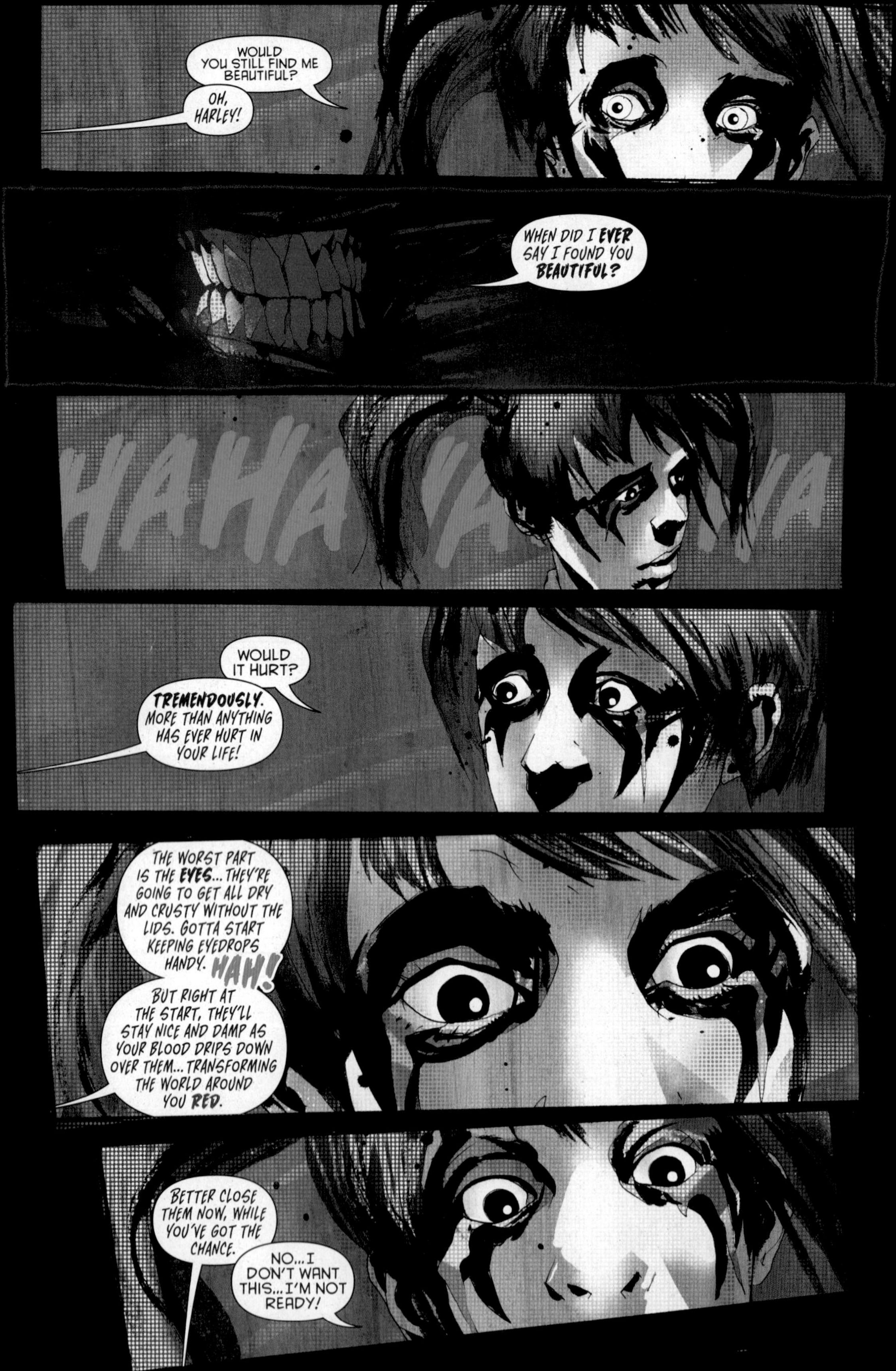
WOULD YOU STILL FIND ME BEAUTIFUL?
OH, HARLEY!
WHEN DID I EVER SAY I FOUND YOU BEAUTIFUL?
HAHA HAHA
WOULD IT HURT?
TREMENDOUSLY. MORE THAN ANYTHING HAS EVER HURT IN YOUR LIFE!
THE WORST PART IS THE EYES... THEY'RE GOING TO GET ALL DRY AND CRUSTY WITHOUT THE LIDS. GOTTA START KEEPING EYEDROPS HANDY. HAH!
BUT RIGHT AT THE START, THEY'LL STAY NICE AND DAMP AS YOUR BLOOD DRIPS DOWN OVER THEM... TRANSFORMING THE WORLD AROUND YOU RED.
BETTER CLOSE THEM NOW, WHILE YOU'VE GOT THE CHANCE.
NO... I DON'T WANT THIS... I'M NOT READY!

AAAHHH!
SHUNK
THERE...
...IT'S DONE.
BUT...I DIDN'T FEEL ANYTHING...
...YOU SAID IT WAS GOING TO HURT.
HEHEH...GOT YOU GOOD, DIDN'T I?
YOURS IS STILL ON.
WHEN HE COMES, YOU RUN UNTIL HE'S IN FRONT OF THE HAMMER. THEN YOU ACTIVATE IT.
SHOULDN'T BE LONG NOW...HAVE FUUUN...

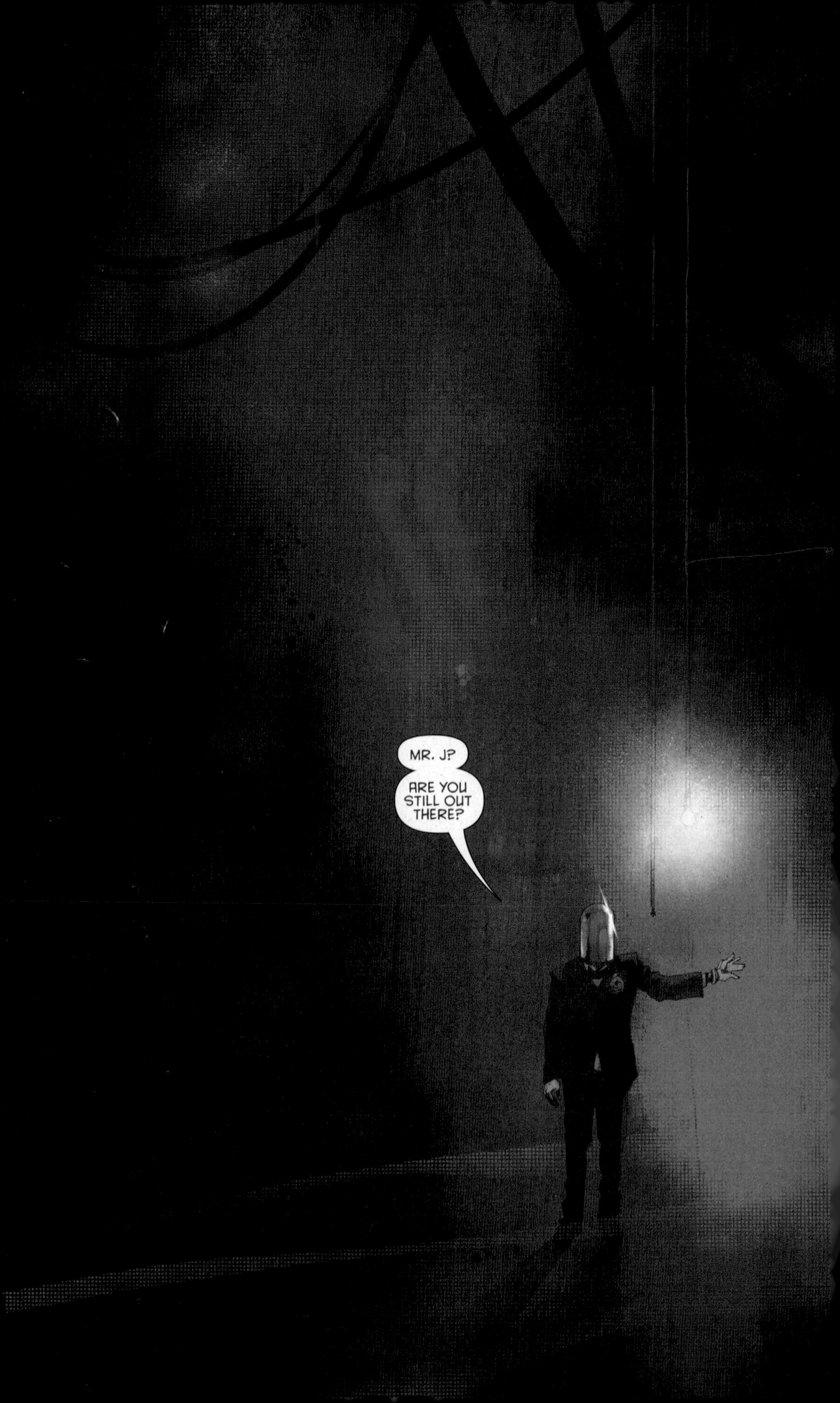
MR. J?
ARE YOU STILL OUT THERE?

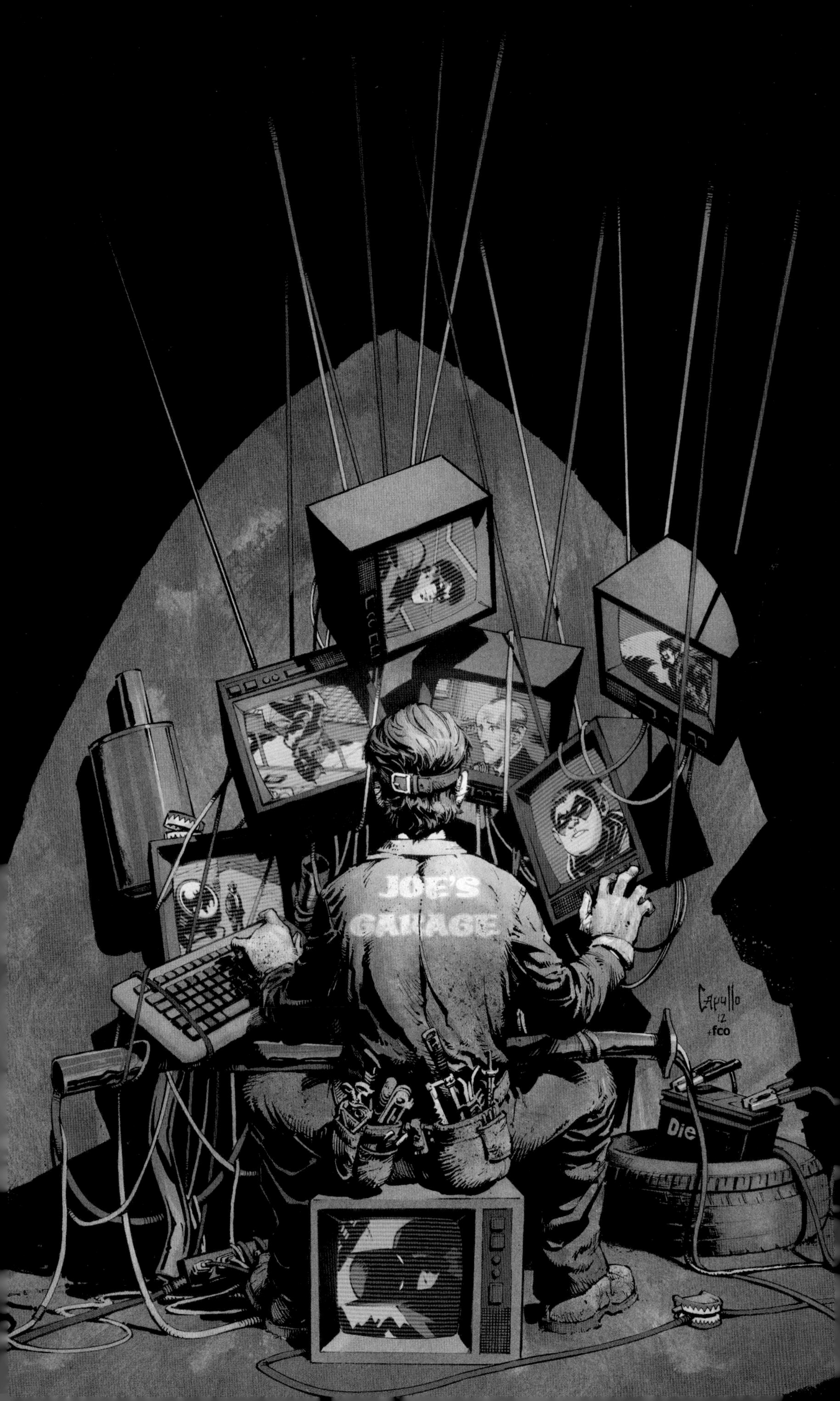
JOE'S GARAGE
Capullo '12 +fco
Die

FUNNY BONES SCOTT SNYDER writer GREG CAPULLO penciller JONATHAN GLAPION inker
MEN OF WORSHIP SCOTT SNYDER & JAMES TYNION IV writers JOCK artist

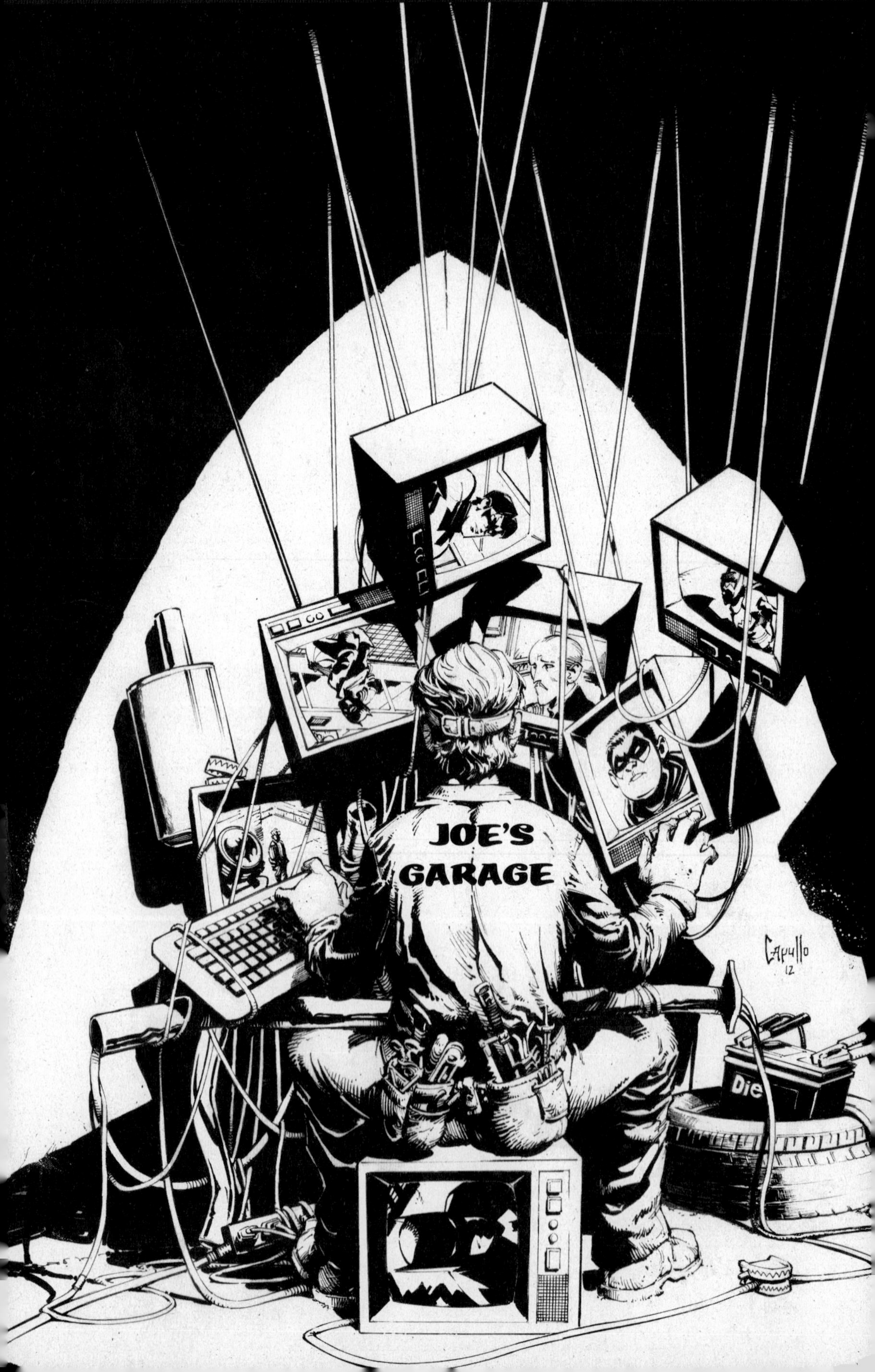
JOE'S GARAGE
Die
CAPULLO 12

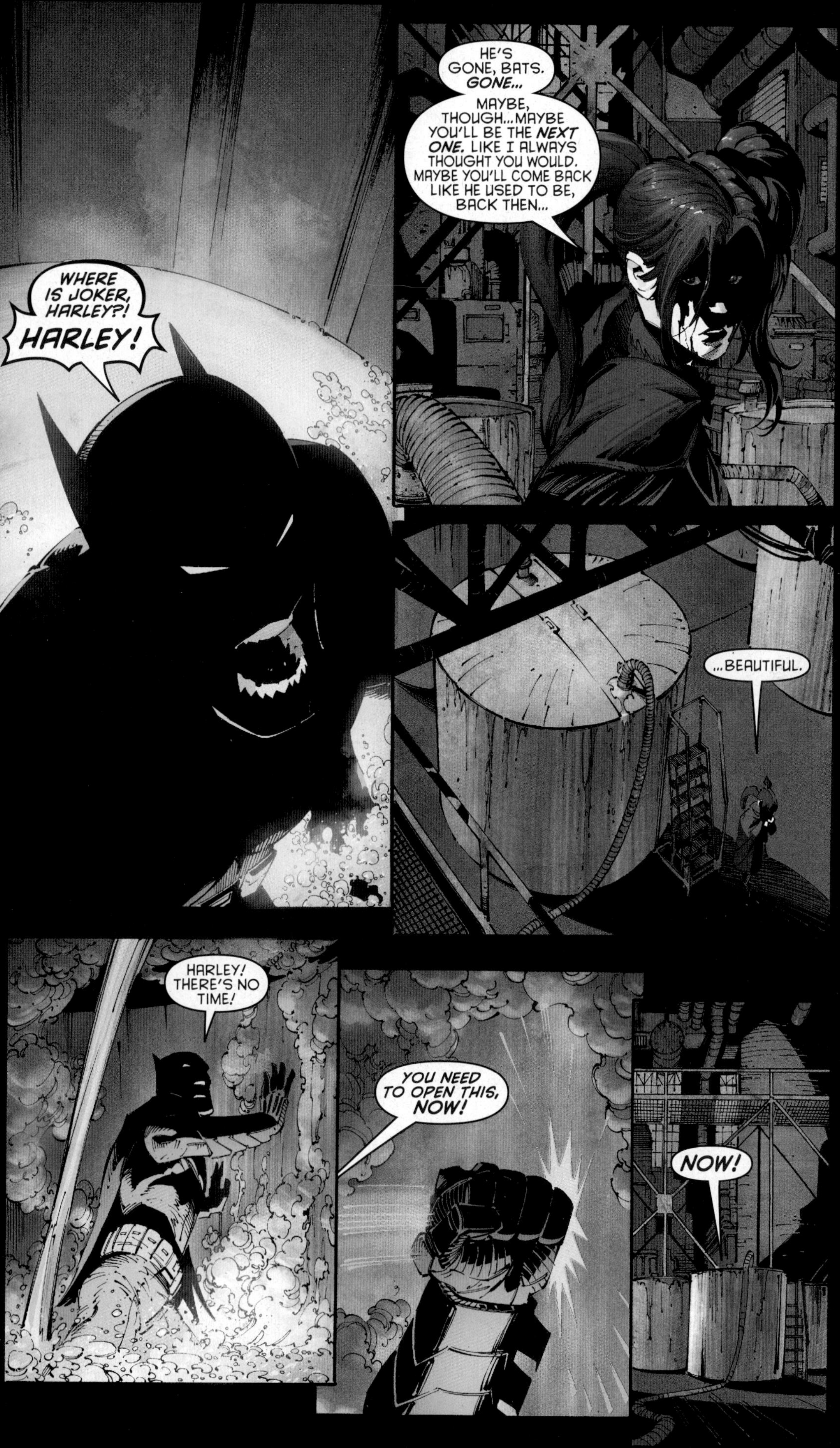

WHERE IS JOKER, HARLEY?! HARLEY!
HE'S GONE, BATS. GONE...
MAYBE, THOUGH...MAYBE YOU'LL BE THE NEXT ONE. LIKE I ALWAYS THOUGHT YOU WOULD. MAYBE YOU'LL COME BACK LIKE HE USED TO BE, BACK THEN...
...BEAUTIFUL.
HARLEY! THERE'S NO TIME!
YOU NEED TO OPEN THIS, NOW!
NOW!

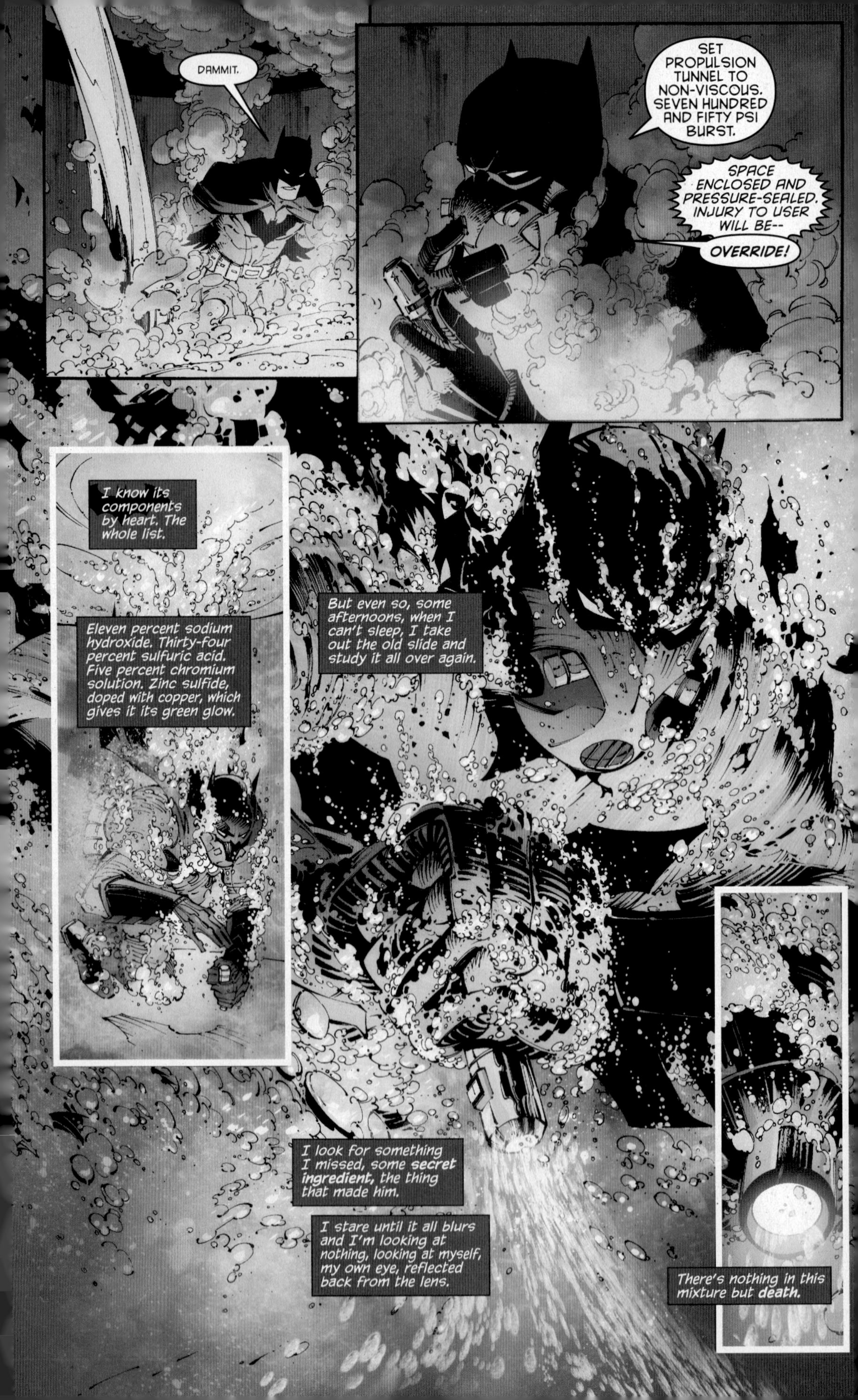
DAMMIT.
SET PROPULSION TUNNEL TO NON-VISCOUS. SEVEN HUNDRED AND FIFTY PSI BURST.
SPACE ENCLOSED AND PRESSURE-SEALED. INJURY TO USER WILL BE--
OVERRIDE!
I know its components by heart. The whole list.
Eleven percent sodium hydroxide. Thirty-four percent sulfuric acid. Five percent chromium solution. Zinc sulfide, doped with copper, which gives it its green glow.
But even so, some afternoons, when I can't sleep, I take out the old slide and study it all over again.
I look for something I missed, some **secret ingredient**, the thing that made him.
I stare until it all blurs and I'm looking at nothing, looking at myself, my own eye, reflected back from the lens.
There's nothing in this mixture but **death.**

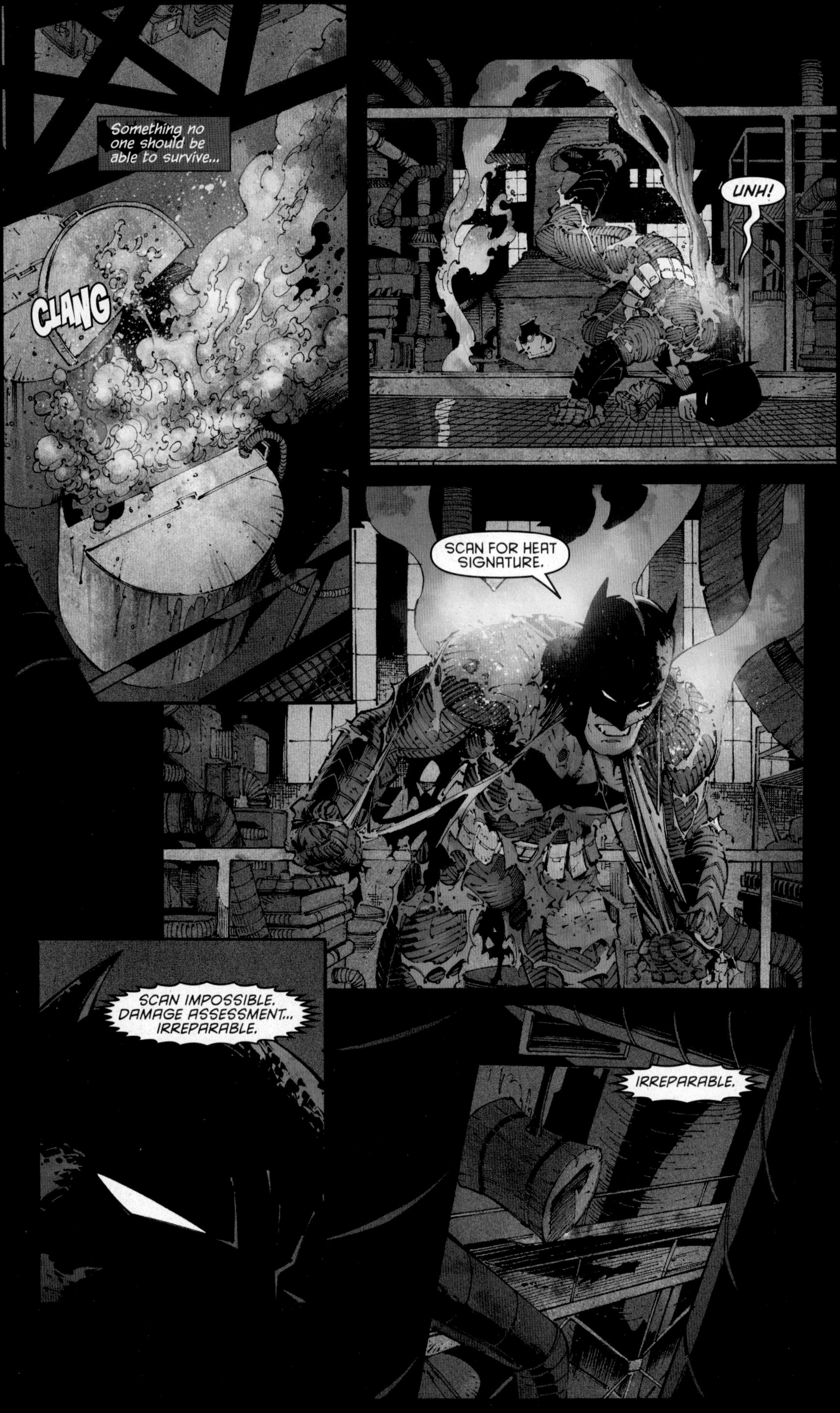

Something no one should be able to survive...
CLANG
UNH!
SCAN FOR HEAT SIGNATURE.
SCAN IMPOSSIBLE. DAMAGE ASSESSMENT... IRREPARABLE.
IRREPARABLE.

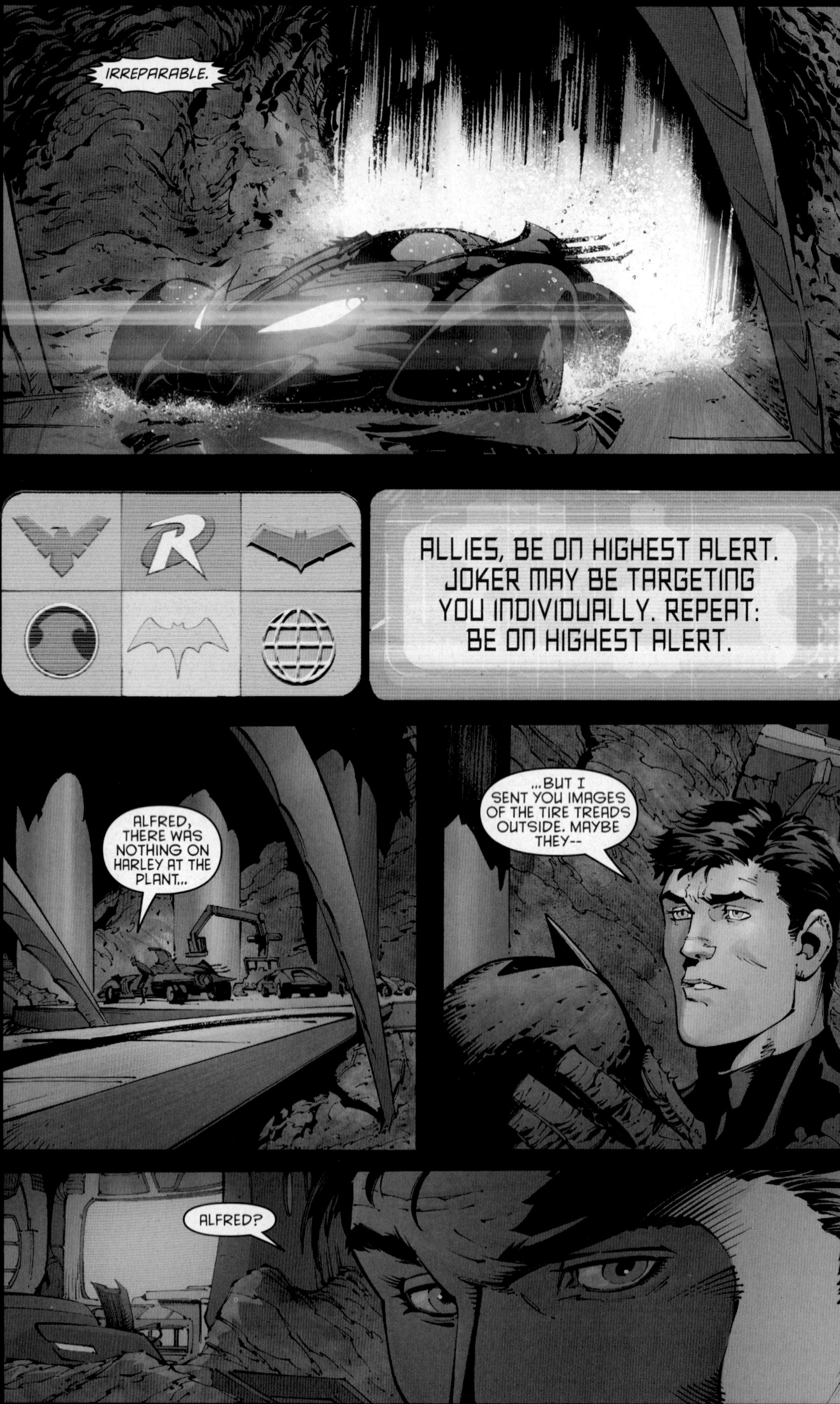
IRREPARABLE.
ALLIES, BE ON HIGHEST ALERT. JOKER MAY BE TARGETING YOU INDIVIDUALLY. REPEAT: BE ON HIGHEST ALERT.
ALFRED, THERE WAS NOTHING ON HARLEY AT THE PLANT...
...BUT I SENT YOU IMAGES OF THE TIRE TREADS OUTSIDE. MAYBE THEY--
ALFRED?

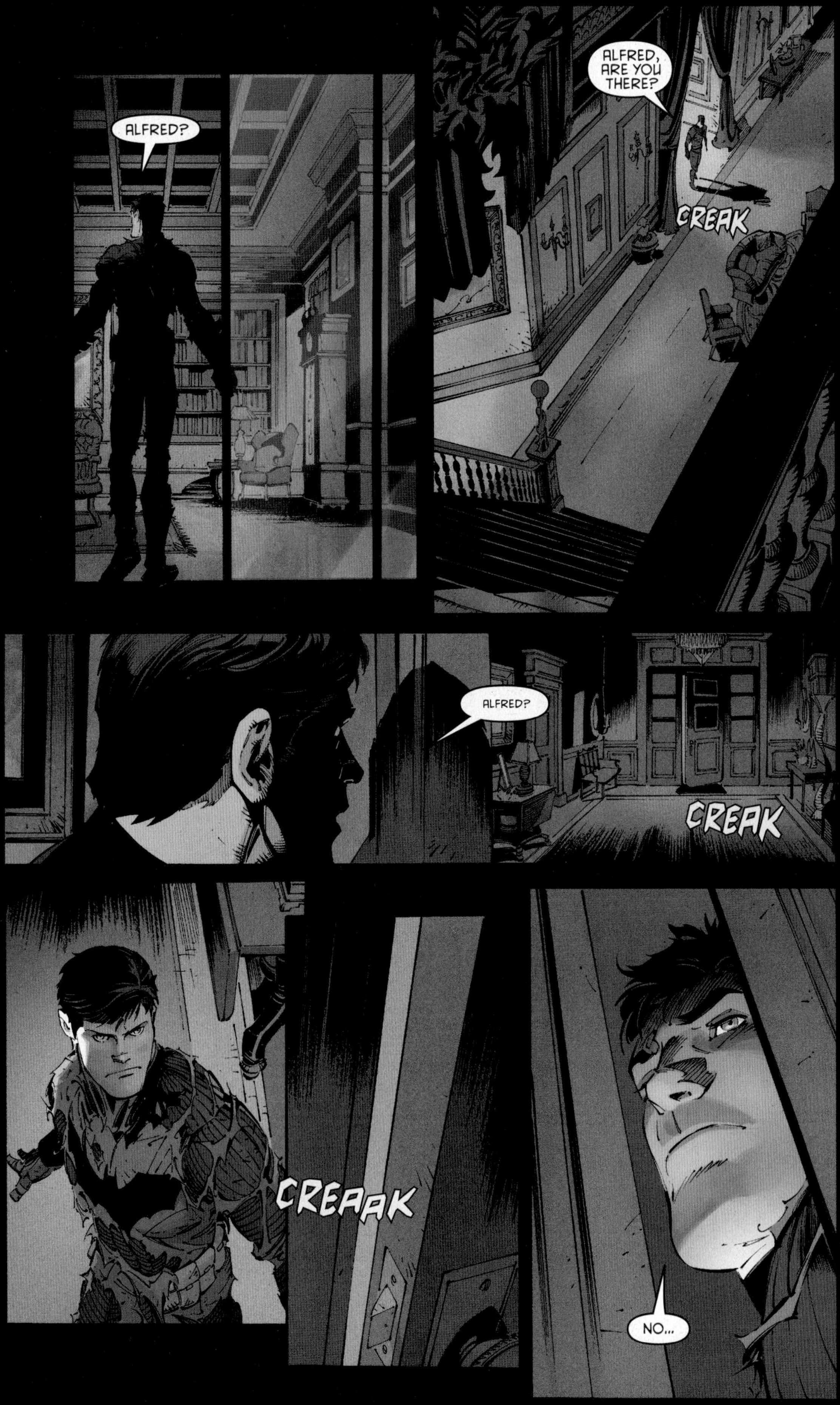
ALFRED?
ALFRED, ARE YOU THERE?
CREAK
ALFRED?
CREAK
CREAAK
NO...

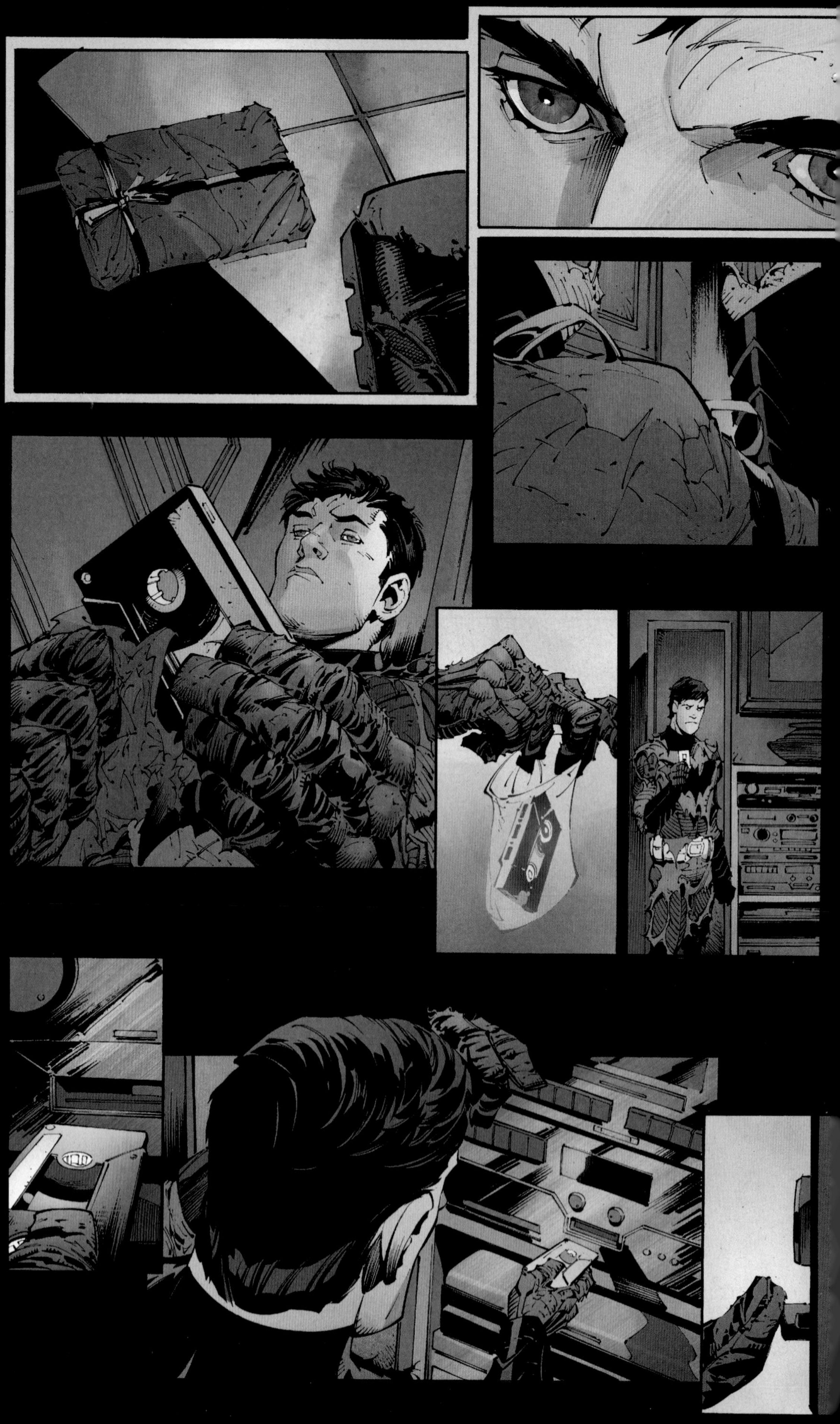

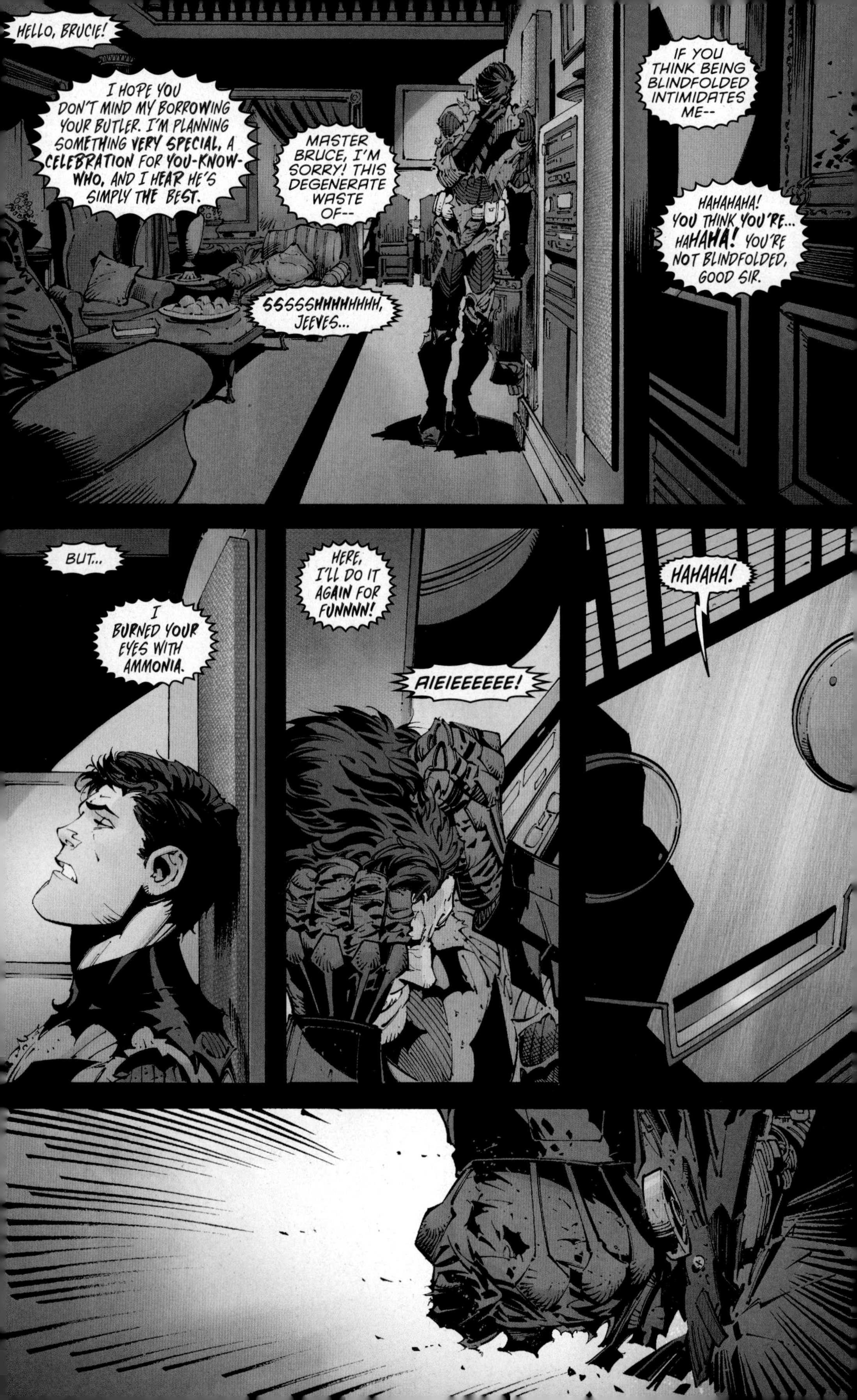
HELLO, BRUCIE!
I HOPE YOU DON'T MIND MY BORROWING YOUR BUTLER. I'M PLANNING SOMETHING VERY SPECIAL, A CELEBRATION FOR YOU-KNOW-WHO, AND I HEAR HE'S SIMPLY THE BEST.
MASTER BRUCE, I'M SORRY! THIS DEGENERATE WASTE OF--
SSSSSHHHHHHHH, JEEVES...
IF YOU THINK BEING BLINDFOLDED INTIMIDATES ME--
HAHAHAHA! YOU THINK YOU'RE... HAHAHA! YOU'RE NOT BLINDFOLDED, GOOD SIR.
BUT...
I BURNED YOUR EYES WITH AMMONIA.
HERE, I'LL DO IT AGAIN FOR FUNNNN!
AIEIEEEEEE!
HAHAHA!

JIM.

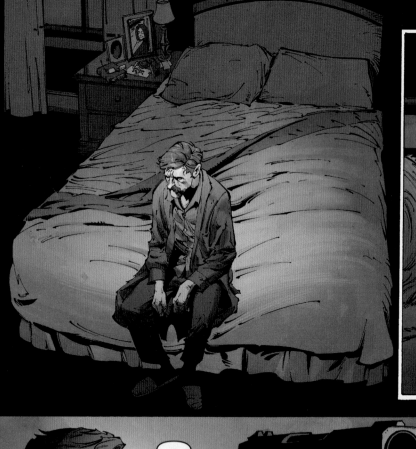

...

I'M SORRY.

BATMAN-- COME IN. WHAT DO YOU HAVE?

LAST NIGHT JOKER KIDNAPPED BRUCE WAYNE'S BUTLER.

HE ALSO SAID HE WAS *PLANNING* SOMETHING... A CELEBRATION, AND NEEDED SOMEONE TO HELP HIM SERVE.

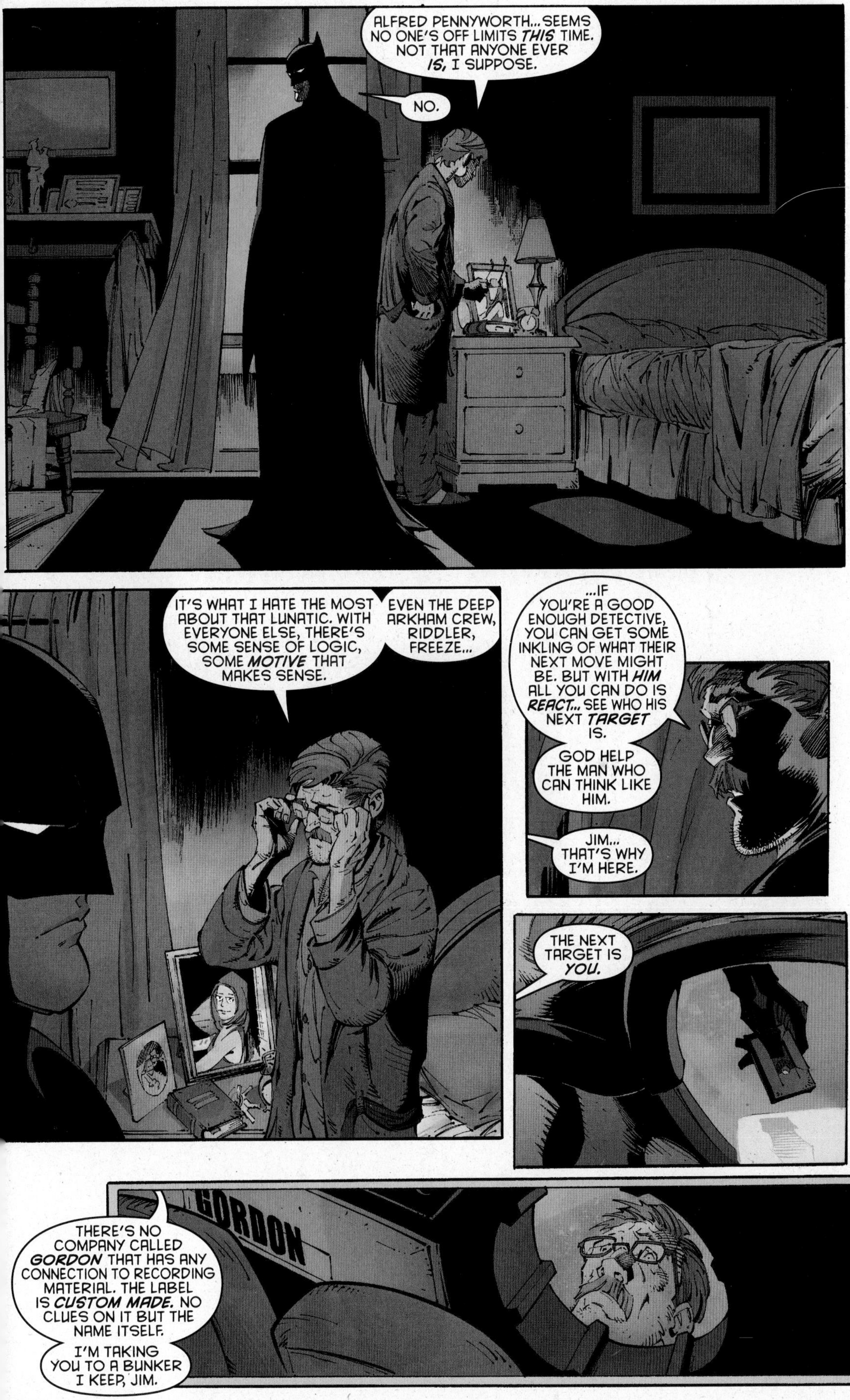

ALFRED PENNYWORTH... SEEMS NO ONE'S OFF LIMITS THIS TIME. NOT THAT ANYONE EVER IS, I SUPPOSE.
NO.
IT'S WHAT I HATE THE MOST ABOUT THAT LUNATIC. WITH EVERYONE ELSE, THERE'S SOME SENSE OF LOGIC, SOME MOTIVE THAT MAKES SENSE.
EVEN THE DEEP ARKHAM CREW, RIDDLER, FREEZE...
...IF YOU'RE A GOOD ENOUGH DETECTIVE, YOU CAN GET SOME INKLING OF WHAT THEIR NEXT MOVE MIGHT BE. BUT WITH HIM ALL YOU CAN DO IS REACT... SEE WHO HIS NEXT TARGET IS.
GOD HELP THE MAN WHO CAN THINK LIKE HIM.
JIM... THAT'S WHY I'M HERE.
THE NEXT TARGET IS YOU.
GORDON
THERE'S NO COMPANY CALLED GORDON THAT HAS ANY CONNECTION TO RECORDING MATERIAL. THE LABEL IS CUSTOM MADE. NO CLUES ON IT BUT THE NAME ITSELF.
I'M TAKING YOU TO A BUNKER I KEEP, JIM.

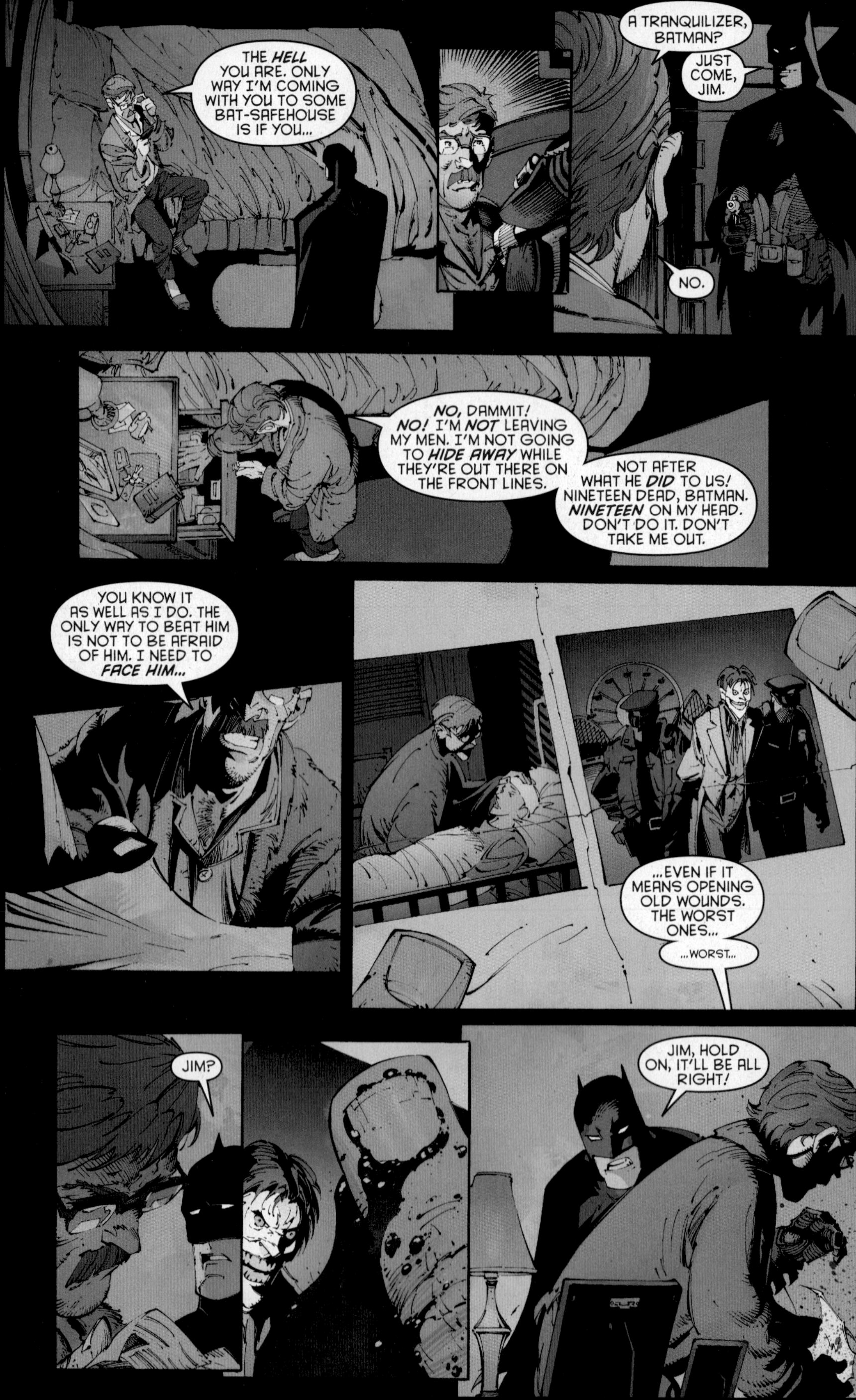
THE **HELL** YOU ARE. ONLY WAY I'M COMING WITH YOU TO SOME BAT-SAFEHOUSE IS IF YOU...
A TRANQUILIZER, BATMAN?
JUST COME, JIM.
NO.
NO, DAMMIT! **NO!** I'M **NOT** LEAVING MY MEN. I'M NOT GOING TO **HIDE AWAY** WHILE THEY'RE OUT THERE ON THE FRONT LINES.
NOT AFTER WHAT HE **DID** TO US! NINETEEN DEAD, BATMAN. **NINETEEN** ON MY HEAD. DON'T DO IT. DON'T TAKE ME OUT.
YOU KNOW IT AS WELL AS I DO. THE ONLY WAY TO BEAT HIM IS NOT TO BE AFRAID OF HIM. I NEED TO **FACE HIM...**
...EVEN IF IT MEANS OPENING OLD WOUNDS. THE WORST ONES...
...WORST...
JIM?
JIM, HOLD ON, IT'LL BE ALL RIGHT!

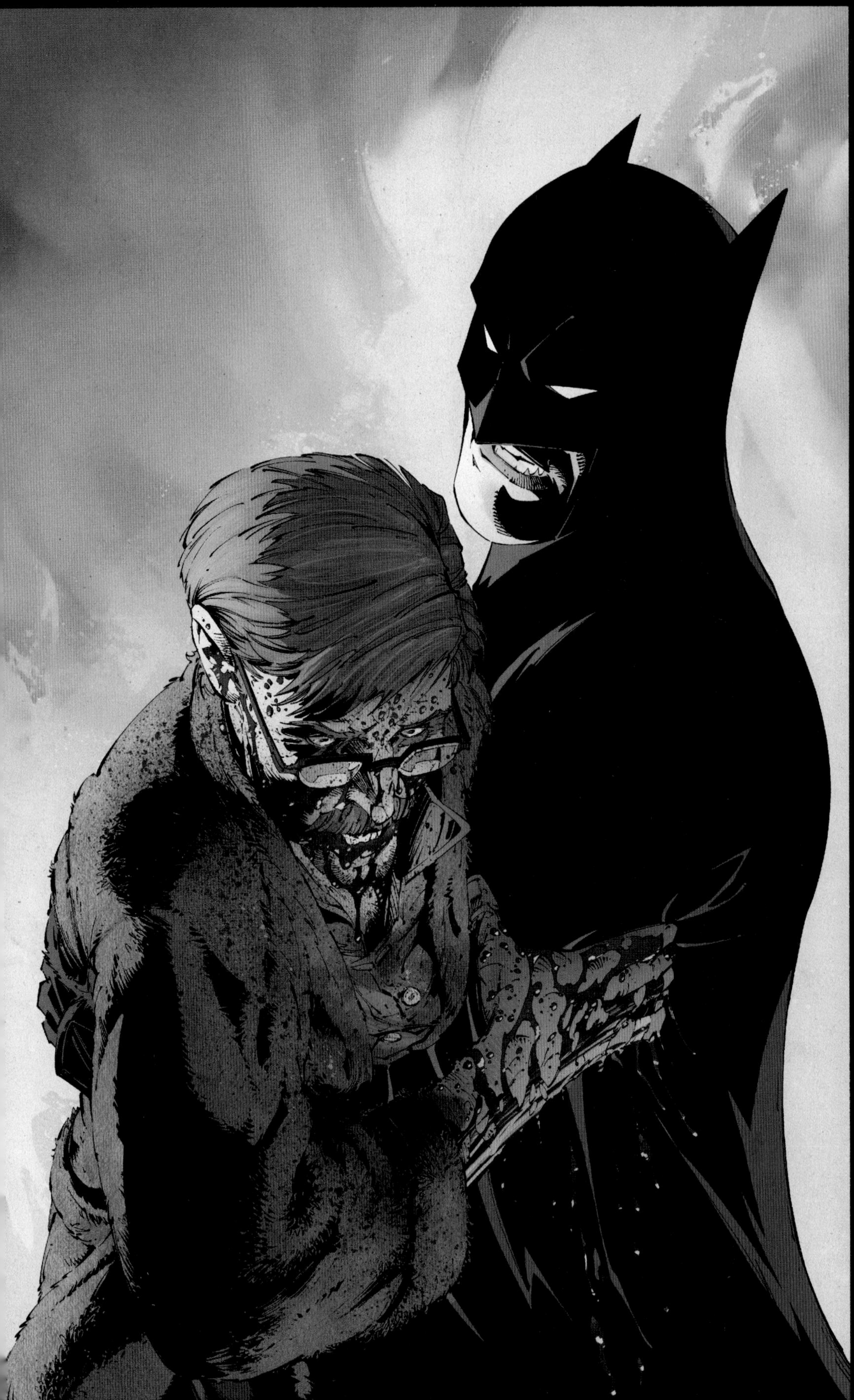

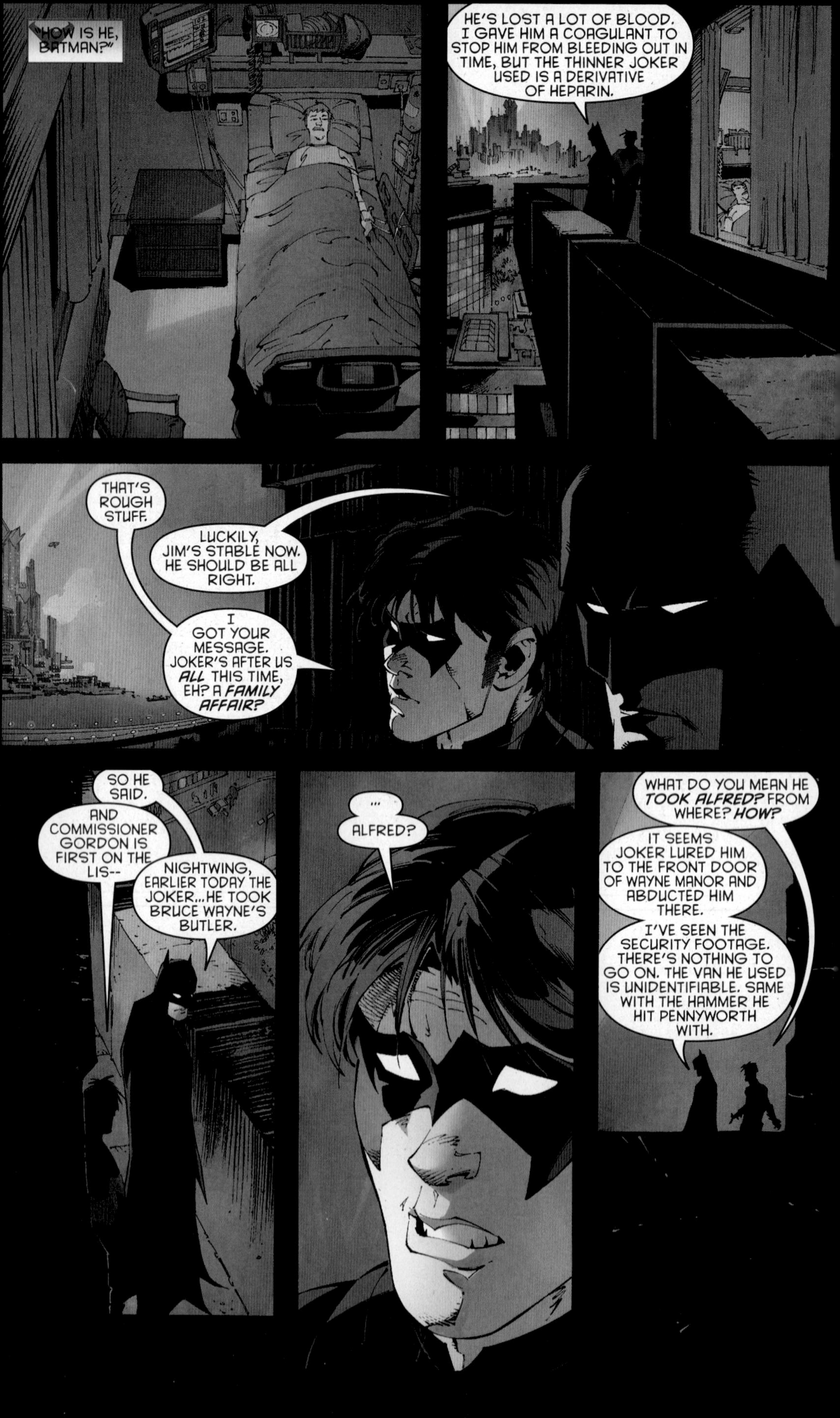
"HOW IS HE, BATMAN?"
HE'S LOST A LOT OF BLOOD. I GAVE HIM A COAGULANT TO STOP HIM FROM BLEEDING OUT IN TIME, BUT THE THINNER JOKER USED IS A DERIVATIVE OF HEPARIN.
THAT'S ROUGH STUFF.
LUCKILY, JIM'S STABLE NOW. HE SHOULD BE ALL RIGHT.
I GOT YOUR MESSAGE. JOKER'S AFTER US ALL THIS TIME, EH? A FAMILY AFFAIR?
SO HE SAID.
AND COMMISSIONER GORDON IS FIRST ON THE LIS--
NIGHTWING, EARLIER TODAY THE JOKER...HE TOOK BRUCE WAYNE'S BUTLER.
...
ALFRED?
WHAT DO YOU MEAN HE TOOK ALFRED? FROM WHERE? HOW?
IT SEEMS JOKER LURED HIM TO THE FRONT DOOR OF WAYNE MANOR AND ABDUCTED HIM THERE.
I'VE SEEN THE SECURITY FOOTAGE. THERE'S NOTHING TO GO ON. THE VAN HE USED IS UNIDENTIFIABLE. SAME WITH THE HAMMER HE HIT PENNYWORTH WITH.

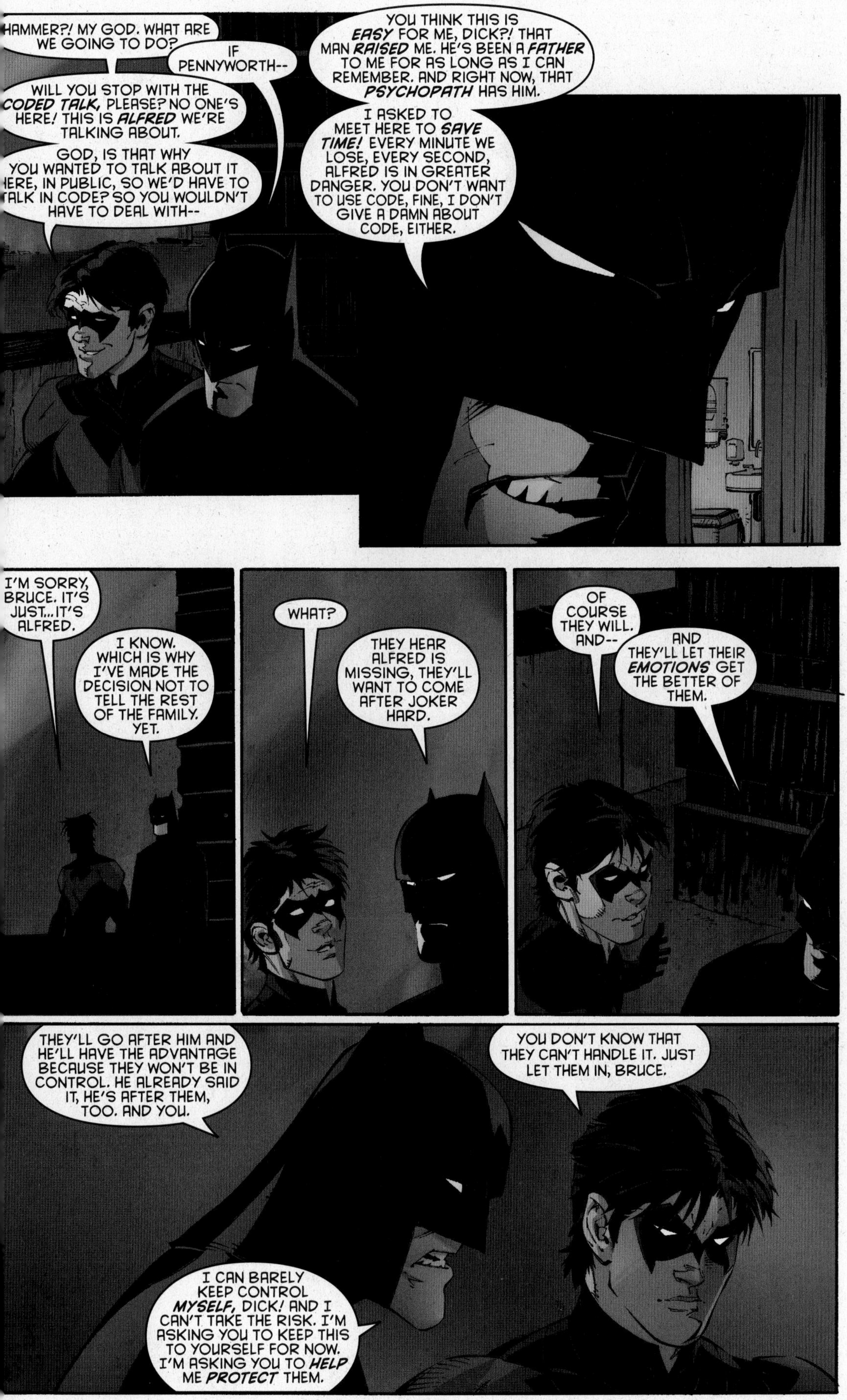
HAMMER?! MY GOD. WHAT ARE WE GOING TO DO?
IF PENNYWORTH--
WILL YOU STOP WITH THE CODED TALK, PLEASE? NO ONE'S HERE! THIS IS ALFRED WE'RE TALKING ABOUT.
GOD, IS THAT WHY YOU WANTED TO TALK ABOUT IT HERE, IN PUBLIC, SO WE'D HAVE TO TALK IN CODE? SO YOU WOULDN'T HAVE TO DEAL WITH--
YOU THINK THIS IS EASY FOR ME, DICK?! THAT MAN RAISED ME. HE'S BEEN A FATHER TO ME FOR AS LONG AS I CAN REMEMBER. AND RIGHT NOW, THAT PSYCHOPATH HAS HIM.
I ASKED TO MEET HERE TO SAVE TIME! EVERY MINUTE WE LOSE, EVERY SECOND, ALFRED IS IN GREATER DANGER. YOU DON'T WANT TO USE CODE, FINE, I DON'T GIVE A DAMN ABOUT CODE, EITHER.
I'M SORRY, BRUCE. IT'S JUST...IT'S ALFRED.
I KNOW. WHICH IS WHY I'VE MADE THE DECISION NOT TO TELL THE REST OF THE FAMILY. YET.
WHAT?
THEY HEAR ALFRED IS MISSING, THEY'LL WANT TO COME AFTER JOKER HARD.
OF COURSE THEY WILL. AND--
AND THEY'LL LET THEIR EMOTIONS GET THE BETTER OF THEM.
THEY'LL GO AFTER HIM AND HE'LL HAVE THE ADVANTAGE BECAUSE THEY WON'T BE IN CONTROL. HE ALREADY SAID IT, HE'S AFTER THEM, TOO. AND YOU.
YOU DON'T KNOW THAT THEY CAN'T HANDLE IT. JUST LET THEM IN, BRUCE.
I CAN BARELY KEEP CONTROL MYSELF, DICK! AND I CAN'T TAKE THE RISK. I'M ASKING YOU TO KEEP THIS TO YOURSELF FOR NOW. I'M ASKING YOU TO HELP ME PROTECT THEM.

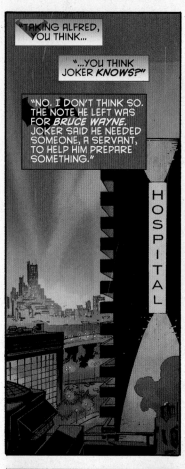

"TAKING ALFRED, YOU THINK...

"...YOU THINK JOKER *KNOWS?*"

"NO. I DON'T THINK SO. THE NOTE HE LEFT WAS FOR *BRUCE WAYNE.* JOKER SAID HE NEEDED SOMEONE, A SERVANT, TO HELP HIM PREPARE SOMETHING."

HOSPITAL

ALFRED IS WELL KNOWN AS MY BUTLER...ESPECIALLY SINCE WE BEGAN THE GOTHAM INITIATIVE. AND WITH BRUCE WAYNE'S CONNECTION TO *BATMAN, INCORPORATED,* IF JOKER WANTS SOMEONE IN THE WAY OF A SERVANT, ALFRED'S THE ONE HE'D GO FOR.

YOU REALLY THINK THAT'S ALL IT IS? THE CONNECTION TO *INC.* AT MOST?

I DO.

BRUCE, IS THERE SOMETHING YOU'RE NOT TELLING ME?

...I KNOW WHERE HE'S GOING TO BE NEXT. JOKER.

WELL WHY DIDN'T YOU SAY SO? LET'S *GO.*

NO. I'M GOING ALONE.

LIKE *HELL* YOU ARE. IF YOU THINK--

"I NEED YOU TO GO TO THE AQUEDUCT, DICK. HE'S REENACTING HIS CRIMES.

"HE'S PICKING AND CHOOSING FROM OUR EARLY ENCOUNTERS, REDOING THEM, BUT IN NEW WAYS. *INVERTING* THEM."

"YOU THINK HE'S GOING TO *POISON THE RESERVOIR?*"

"I DON'T KNOW, BUT I NEED YOU AT THE PIPELINE."

"HOW DO YOU KNOW HE'LL BE AT THE RESERVOIR?"

"BECAUSE I KNOW. CALL ME WHEN YOU'RE IN PLACE."

"ALL RIGHT, JUST BE CAREFUL..."

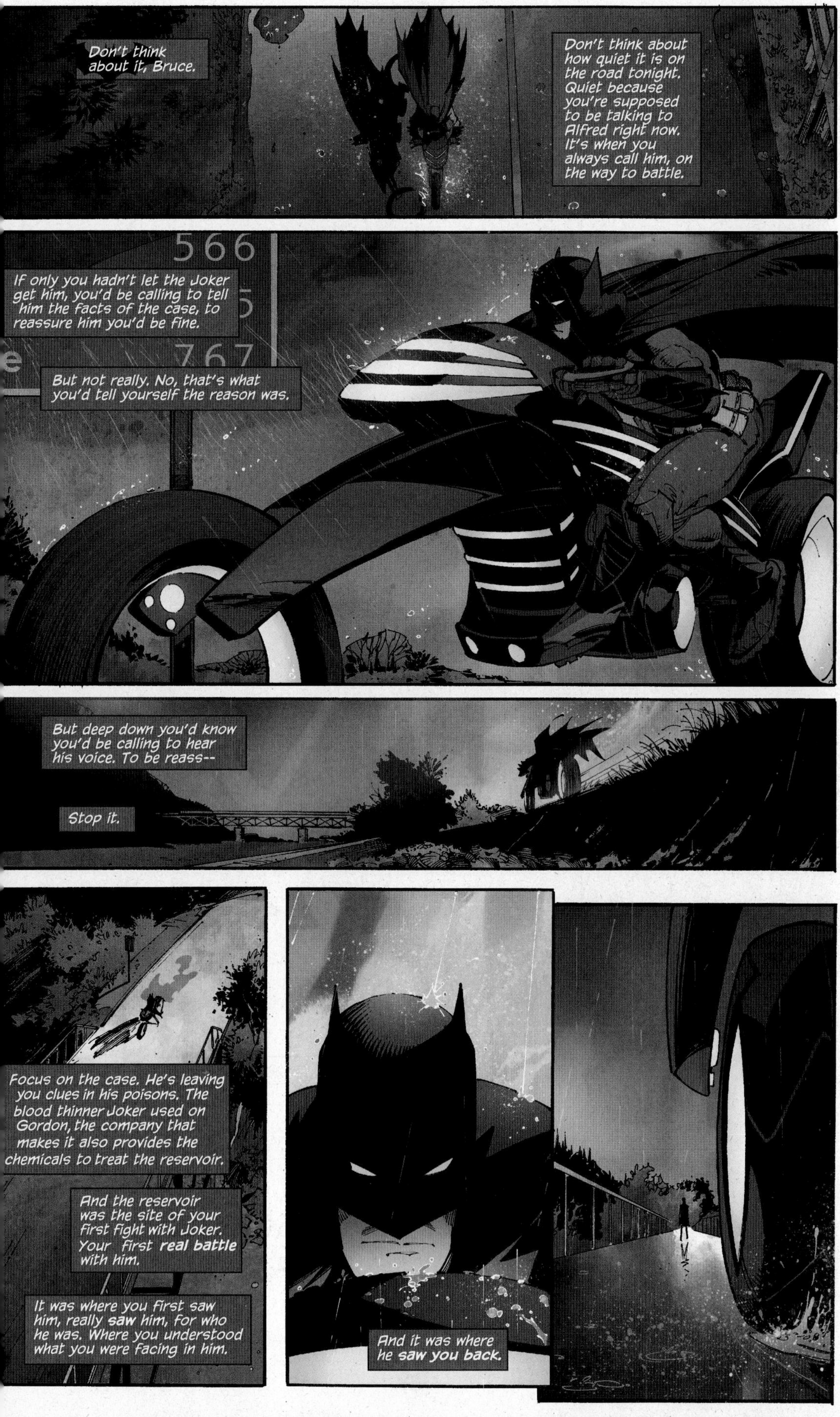
Don't think about it, Bruce.
Don't think about how quiet it is on the road tonight. Quiet because you're supposed to be talking to Alfred right now. It's when you always call him, on the way to battle.
566
767
If only you hadn't let the Joker get him, you'd be calling to tell him the facts of the case, to reassure him you'd be fine.
But not really. No, that's what you'd tell yourself the reason was.
But deep down you'd know you'd be calling to hear his voice. To be reass--
Stop it.
Focus on the case. He's leaving you clues in his poisons. The blood thinner Joker used on Gordon, the company that makes it also provides the chemicals to treat the reservoir.
And the reservoir was the site of your first fight with Joker. Your first **real battle** with him.
It was where you first saw him, really **saw him**, for who he was. Where you understood what you were facing in him.
And it was where he **saw you back.**

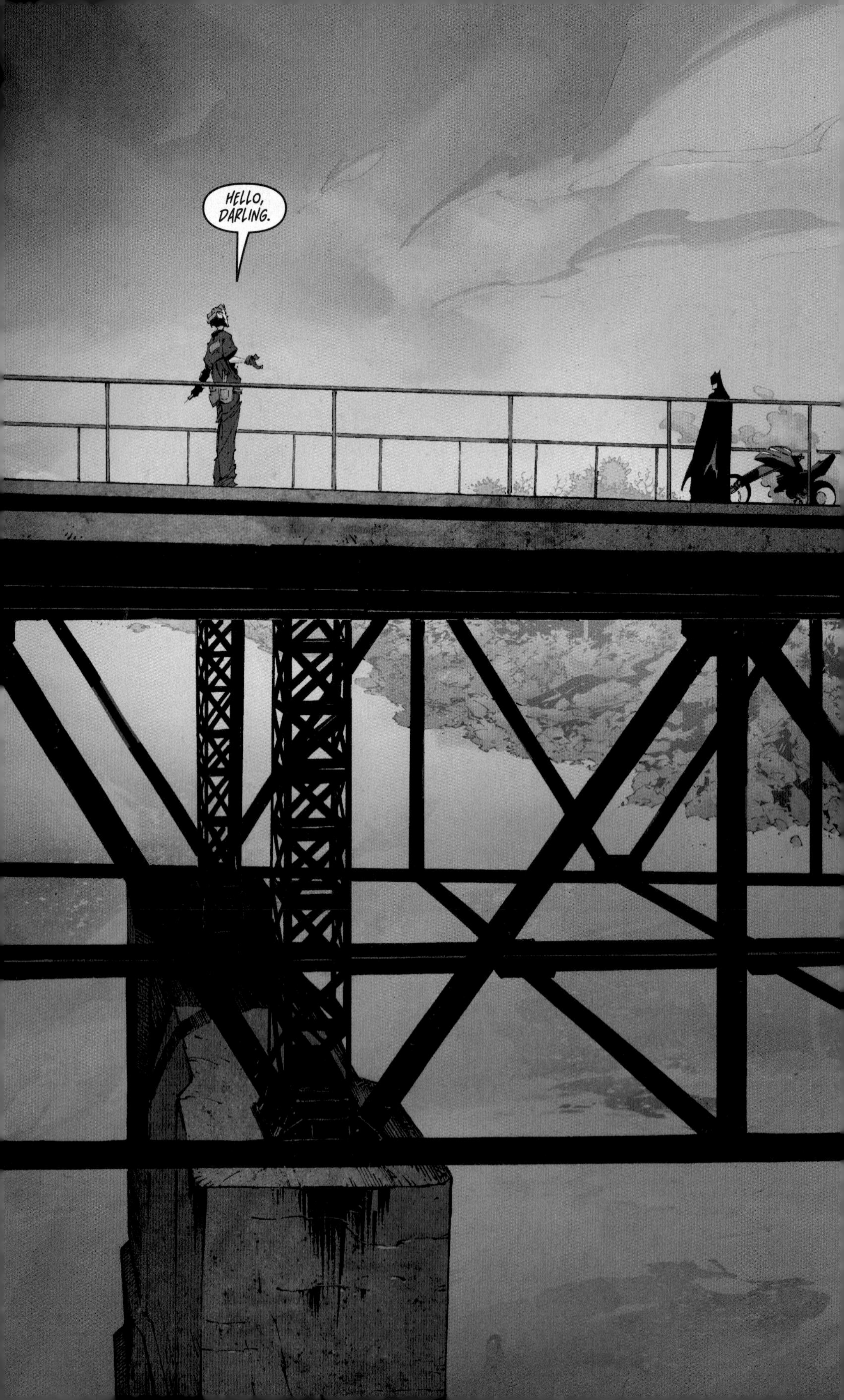
HELLO, DARLING.

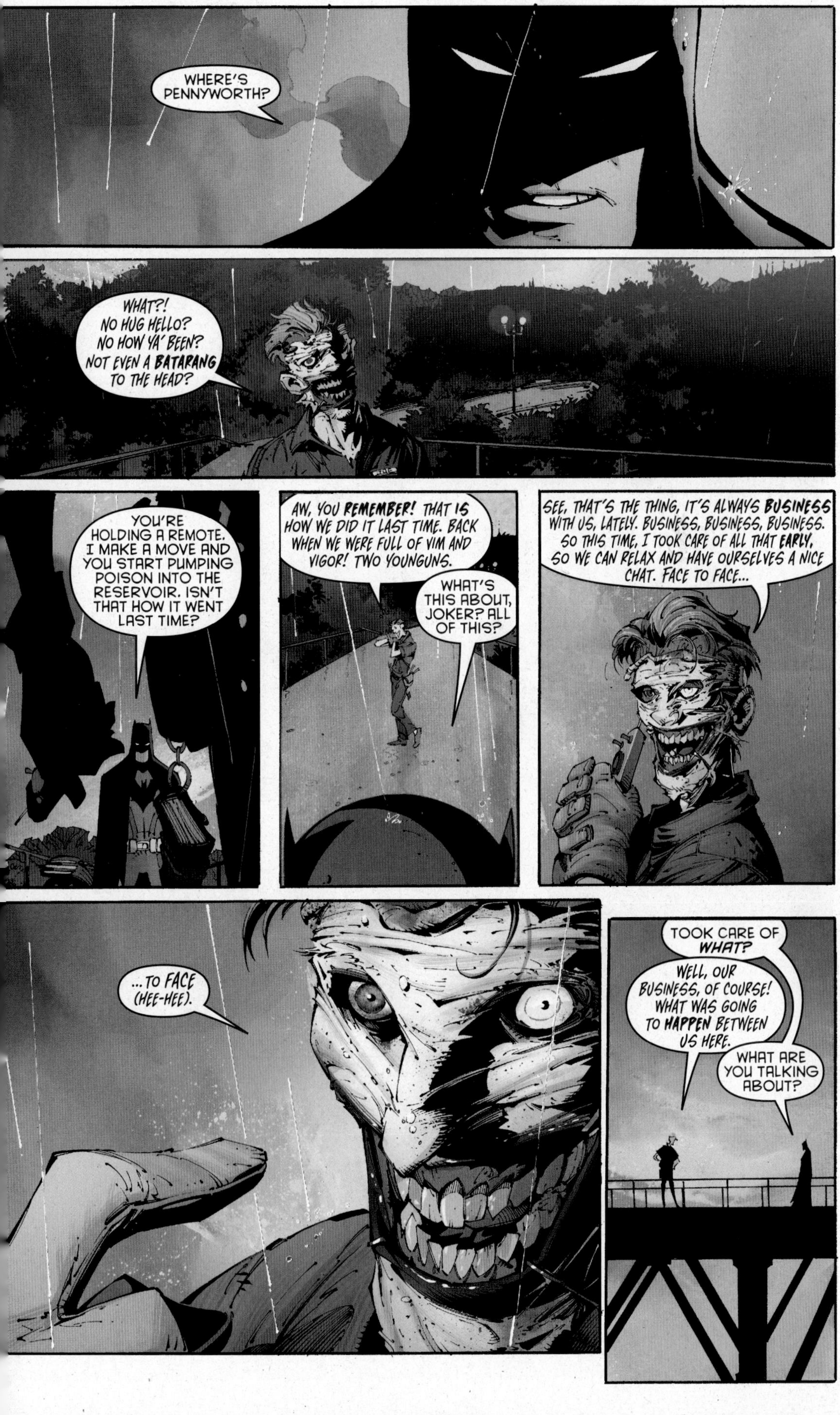
WHERE'S PENNYWORTH?
WHAT?! NO HUG HELLO? NO HOW YA' BEEN? NOT EVEN A BATARANG TO THE HEAD?
YOU'RE HOLDING A REMOTE. I MAKE A MOVE AND YOU START PUMPING POISON INTO THE RESERVOIR. ISN'T THAT HOW IT WENT LAST TIME?
AW, YOU REMEMBER! THAT IS HOW WE DID IT LAST TIME. BACK WHEN WE WERE FULL OF VIM AND VIGOR! TWO YOUNGUNS.
WHAT'S THIS ABOUT, JOKER? ALL OF THIS?
SEE, THAT'S THE THING, IT'S ALWAYS BUSINESS WITH US, LATELY. BUSINESS, BUSINESS, BUSINESS. SO THIS TIME, I TOOK CARE OF ALL THAT EARLY, SO WE CAN RELAX AND HAVE OURSELVES A NICE CHAT. FACE TO FACE...
...TO FACE (HEE-HEE).
TOOK CARE OF WHAT?
WELL, OUR BUSINESS, OF COURSE! WHAT WAS GOING TO HAPPEN BETWEEN US HERE.
WHAT ARE YOU TALKING ABOUT?

SEE, IN A MOMENT, YOU'D GET THE CALL YOU'RE WAITING FOR AND YOU'D MAKE YOUR DECISION...

...YOU'D DECIDE TO MAKE YOUR MOVE WOULDN'T YOU? YOU'D THROW THAT BATARANG FROM BEHIND YOUR BACK JUST LIKE LAST TIME!

AND WHAM! I'D GET HIT. OWWW! BUT BEING FAST, FAST FASSST, I'D PUSH MY REMOTE! AND POISON THE WATER! AND YOU'D CALL TO YOUR LITTLE FRIEND, THE ONE WHO USED TO BE ROBIN...NIGHTWING, ISN'T IT...?

"...AND HE'D BLOW THE AQUEDUCT."

BATMAN, I'M ARRIVING AT--

UNH!

BOOM

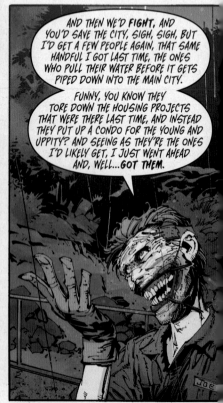

AND THEN WE'D FIGHT, AND YOU'D SAVE THE CITY, SIGH, SIGH, BUT I'D GET A FEW PEOPLE AGAIN, THAT SAME HANDFUL I GOT LAST TIME, THE ONES WHO PULL THEIR WATER BEFORE IT GETS PIPED DOWN INTO THE MAIN CITY.

FUNNY, YOU KNOW THEY TORE DOWN THE HOUSING PROJECTS THAT WERE THERE LAST TIME, AND INSTEAD THEY PUT UP A CONDO FOR THE YOUNG AND UPPITY? AND SEEING AS THEY'RE THE ONES I'D LIKELY GET, I JUST WENT AHEAD AND, WELL...GOT THEM.

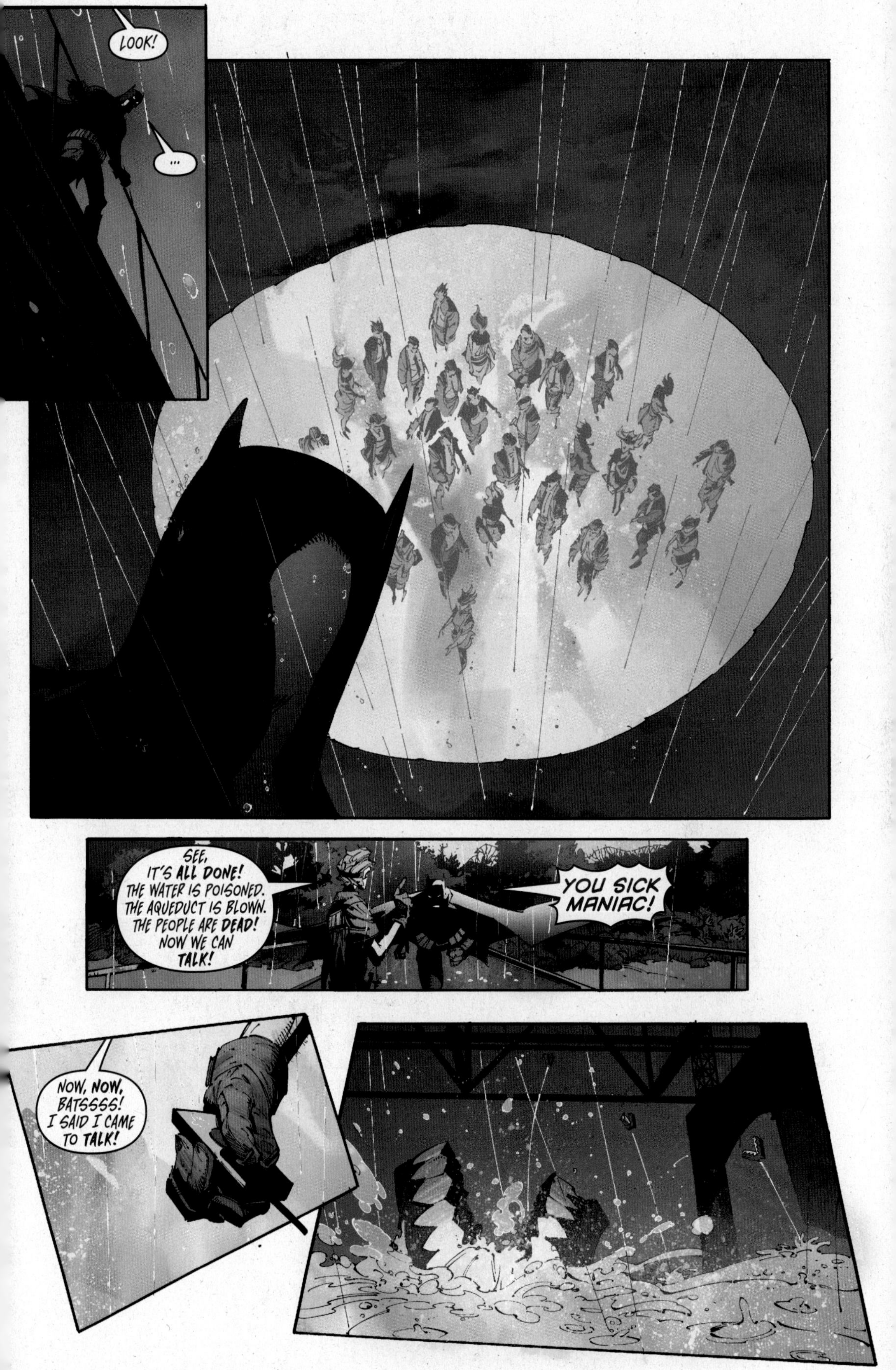
LOOK!
...
SEE, IT'S ALL DONE! THE WATER IS POISONED. THE AQUEDUCT IS BLOWN. THE PEOPLE ARE DEAD! NOW WE CAN TALK!
YOU SICK MANIAC!
NOW, NOW, BATSSSS! I SAID I CAME TO TALK!

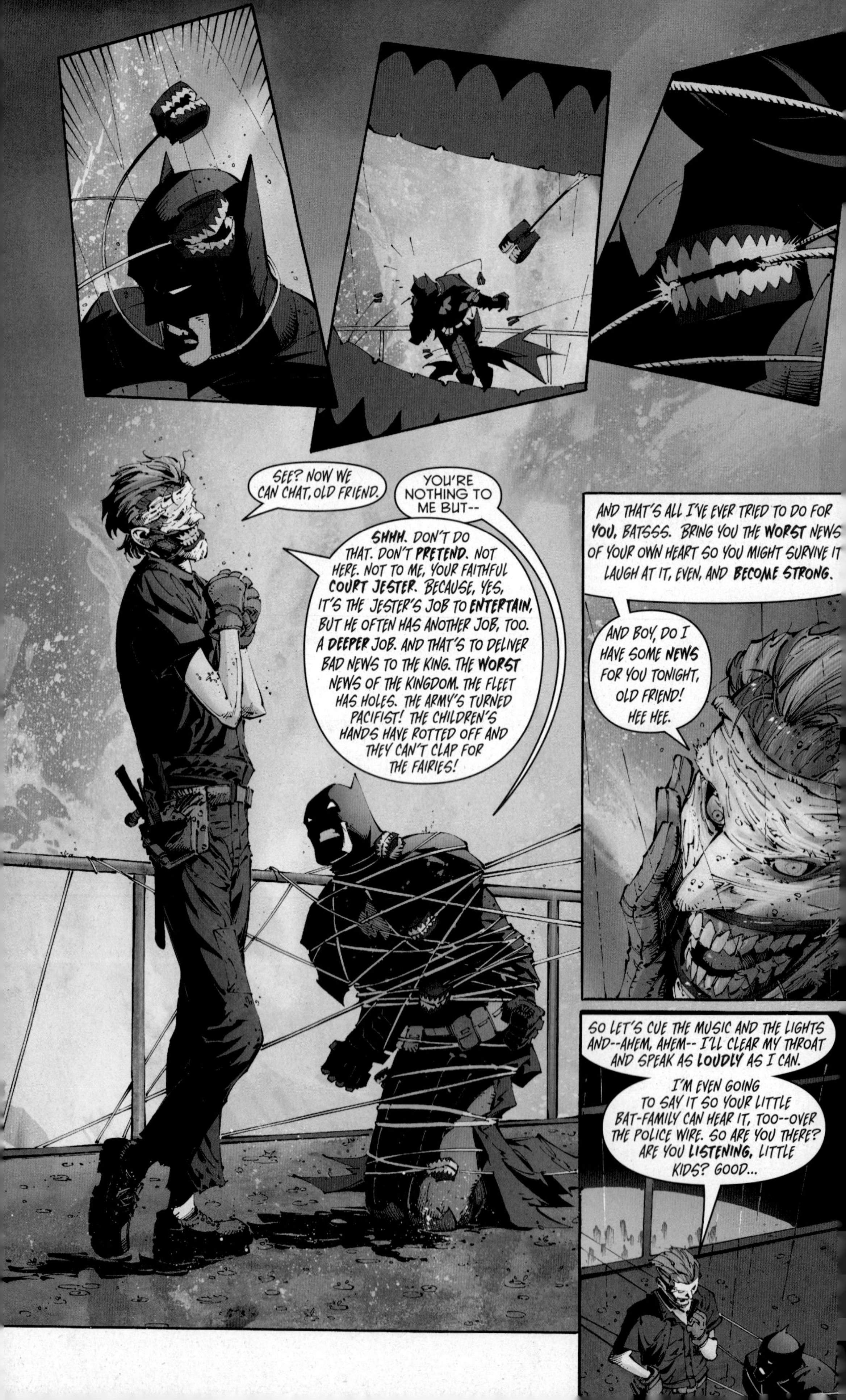

SEE? NOW WE CAN CHAT, OLD FRIEND.
YOU'RE NOTHING TO ME BUT--
SHHH. DON'T DO THAT. DON'T PRETEND. NOT HERE. NOT TO ME, YOUR FAITHFUL COURT JESTER. BECAUSE, YES, IT'S THE JESTER'S JOB TO ENTERTAIN, BUT HE OFTEN HAS ANOTHER JOB, TOO. A DEEPER JOB. AND THAT'S TO DELIVER BAD NEWS TO THE KING. THE WORST NEWS OF THE KINGDOM. THE FLEET HAS HOLES. THE ARMY'S TURNED PACIFIST! THE CHILDREN'S HANDS HAVE ROTTED OFF AND THEY CAN'T CLAP FOR THE FAIRIES!
AND THAT'S ALL I'VE EVER TRIED TO DO FOR YOU, BATSSS. BRING YOU THE WORST NEWS OF YOUR OWN HEART SO YOU MIGHT SURVIVE IT. LAUGH AT IT, EVEN, AND BECOME STRONG.
AND BOY, DO I HAVE SOME NEWS FOR YOU TONIGHT, OLD FRIEND! HEE HEE.
SO LET'S CUE THE MUSIC AND THE LIGHTS AND--AHEM, AHEM-- I'LL CLEAR MY THROAT AND SPEAK AS LOUDLY AS I CAN.
I'M EVEN GOING TO SAY IT SO YOUR LITTLE BAT-FAMILY CAN HEAR IT, TOO--OVER THE POLICE WIRE. SO ARE YOU THERE? ARE YOU LISTENING, LITTLE KIDS? GOOD...

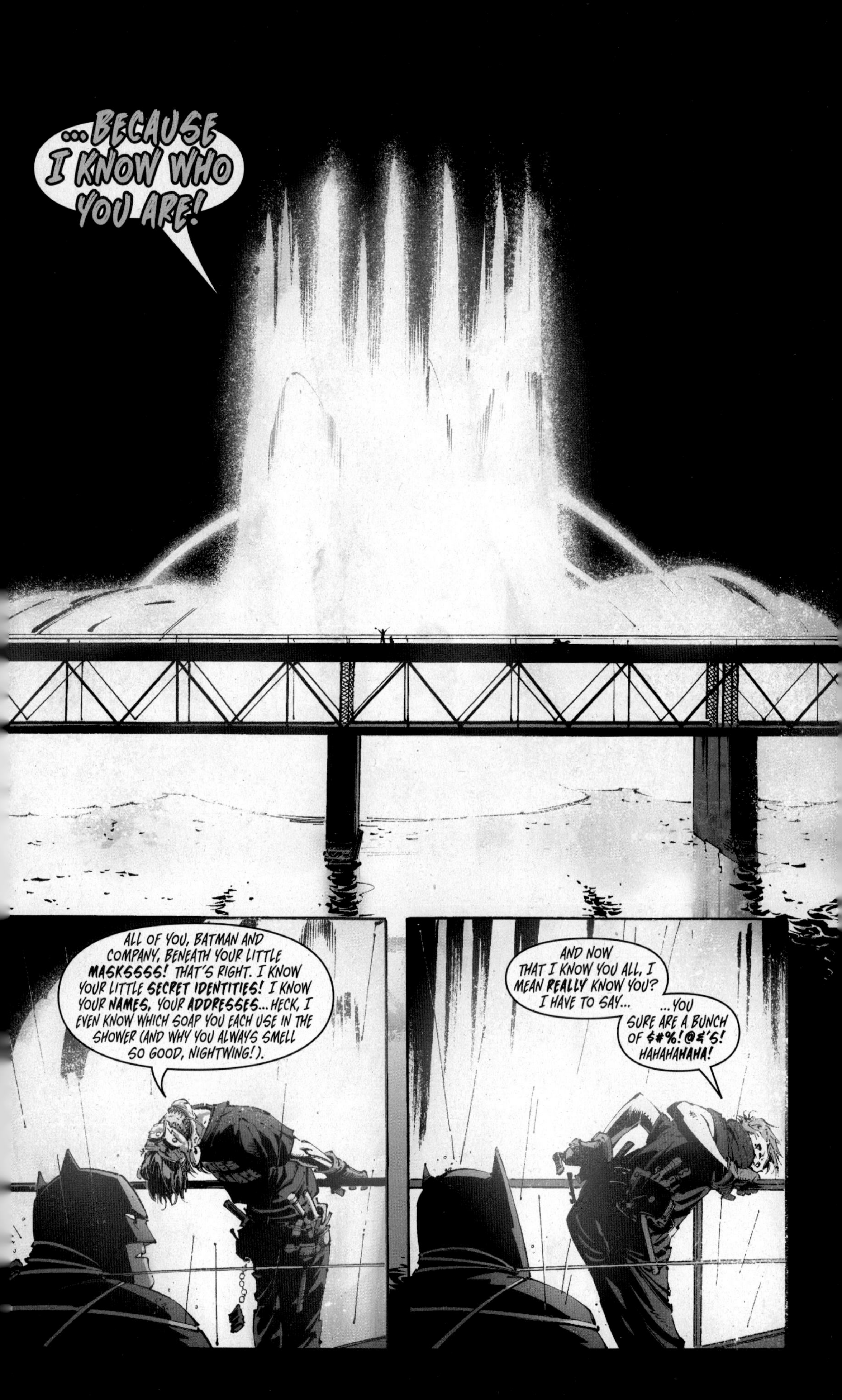
...BECAUSE I KNOW WHO YOU ARE!
ALL OF YOU, BATMAN AND COMPANY, BENEATH YOUR LITTLE MASKSSSS! THAT'S RIGHT. I KNOW YOUR LITTLE SECRET IDENTITIES! I KNOW YOUR NAMES, YOUR ADDRESSES... HECK, I EVEN KNOW WHICH SOAP YOU EACH USE IN THE SHOWER (AND WHY YOU ALWAYS SMELL SO GOOD, NIGHTWING!).
AND NOW THAT I KNOW YOU ALL, I MEAN REALLY KNOW YOU? I HAVE TO SAY...
...YOU SURE ARE A BUNCH OF $#%!@&'S! HAHAHAHAHA!

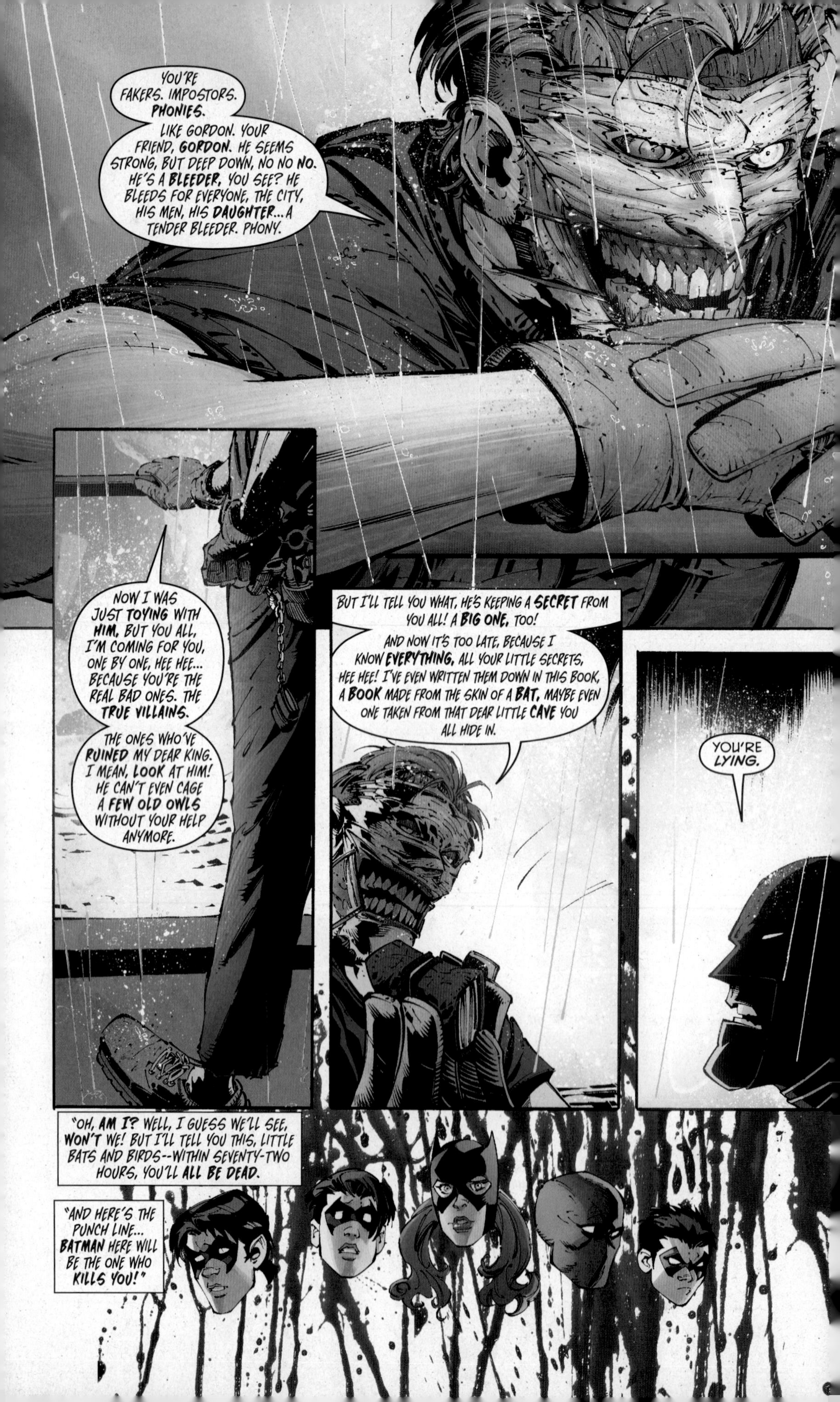

YOU'RE FAKERS. IMPOSTORS. PHONIES.
LIKE GORDON. YOUR FRIEND, GORDON. HE SEEMS STRONG, BUT DEEP DOWN, NO NO NO. HE'S A BLEEDER, YOU SEE? HE BLEEDS FOR EVERYONE, THE CITY, HIS MEN, HIS DAUGHTER... A TENDER BLEEDER. PHONY.
NOW I WAS JUST TOYING WITH HIM. BUT YOU ALL, I'M COMING FOR YOU, ONE BY ONE, HEE HEE... BECAUSE YOU'RE THE REAL BAD ONES. THE TRUE VILLAINS.
THE ONES WHO'VE RUINED MY DEAR KING. I MEAN, LOOK AT HIM! HE CAN'T EVEN CAGE A FEW OLD OWLS WITHOUT YOUR HELP ANYMORE.
BUT I'LL TELL YOU WHAT, HE'S KEEPING A SECRET FROM YOU ALL! A BIG ONE, TOO!
AND NOW IT'S TOO LATE, BECAUSE I KNOW EVERYTHING, ALL YOUR LITTLE SECRETS, HEE HEE! I'VE EVEN WRITTEN THEM DOWN IN THIS BOOK, A BOOK MADE FROM THE SKIN OF A BAT, MAYBE EVEN ONE TAKEN FROM THAT DEAR LITTLE CAVE YOU ALL HIDE IN.
YOU'RE LYING.
"OH, AM I? WELL, I GUESS WE'LL SEE, WON'T WE! BUT I'LL TELL YOU THIS, LITTLE BATS AND BIRDS--WITHIN SEVENTY-TWO HOURS, YOU'LL ALL BE DEAD.
"AND HERE'S THE PUNCH LINE... BATMAN HERE WILL BE THE ONE WHO KILLS YOU!"

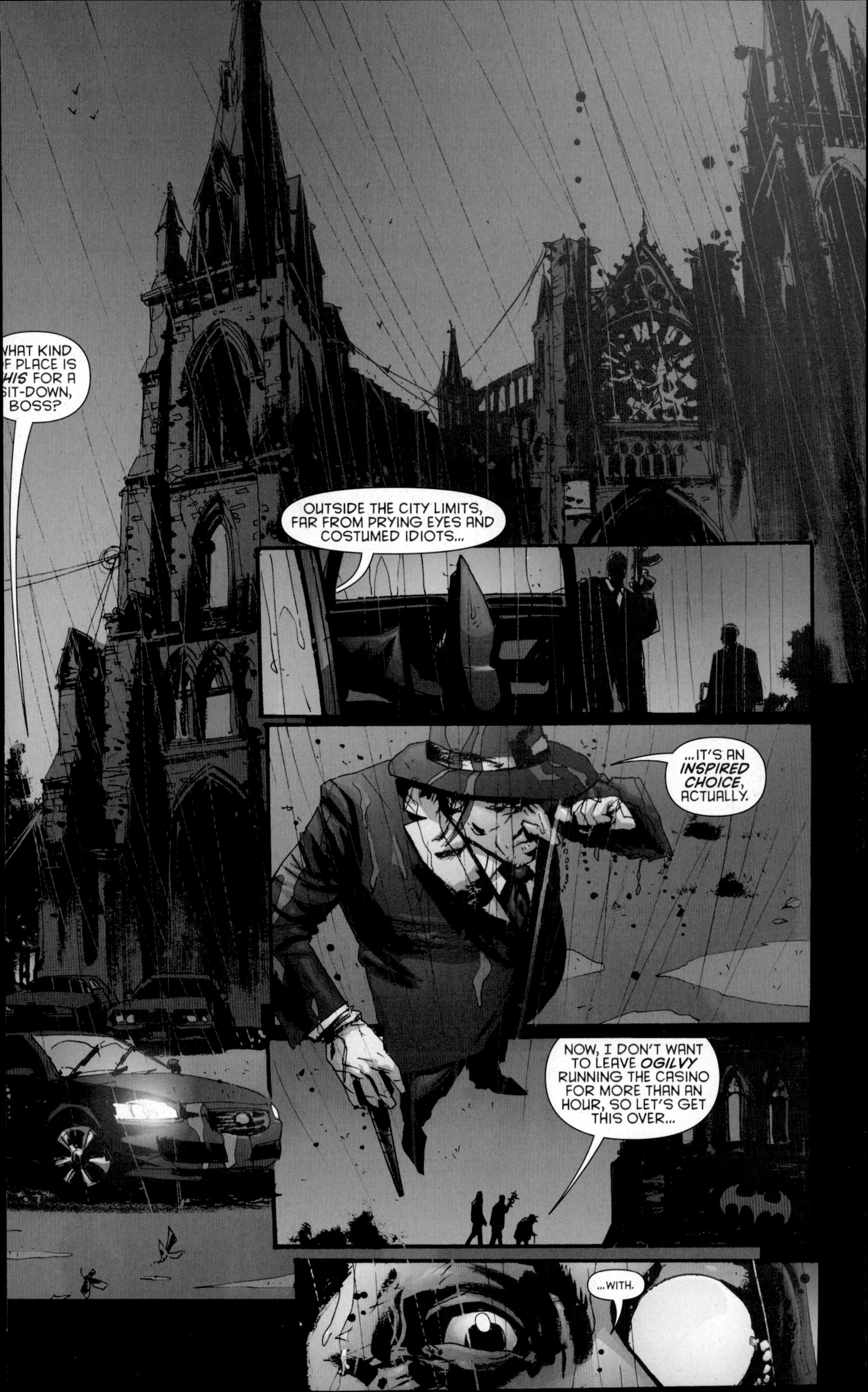
WHAT KIND
F PLACE IS
HIS FOR A
SIT-DOWN,
BOSS?
OUTSIDE THE CITY LIMITS, FAR FROM PRYING EYES AND COSTUMED IDIOTS...
...IT'S AN INSPIRED CHOICE, ACTUALLY.
NOW, I DON'T WANT TO LEAVE OGILVY RUNNING THE CASINO FOR MORE THAN AN HOUR, SO LET'S GET THIS OVER...
...WITH.

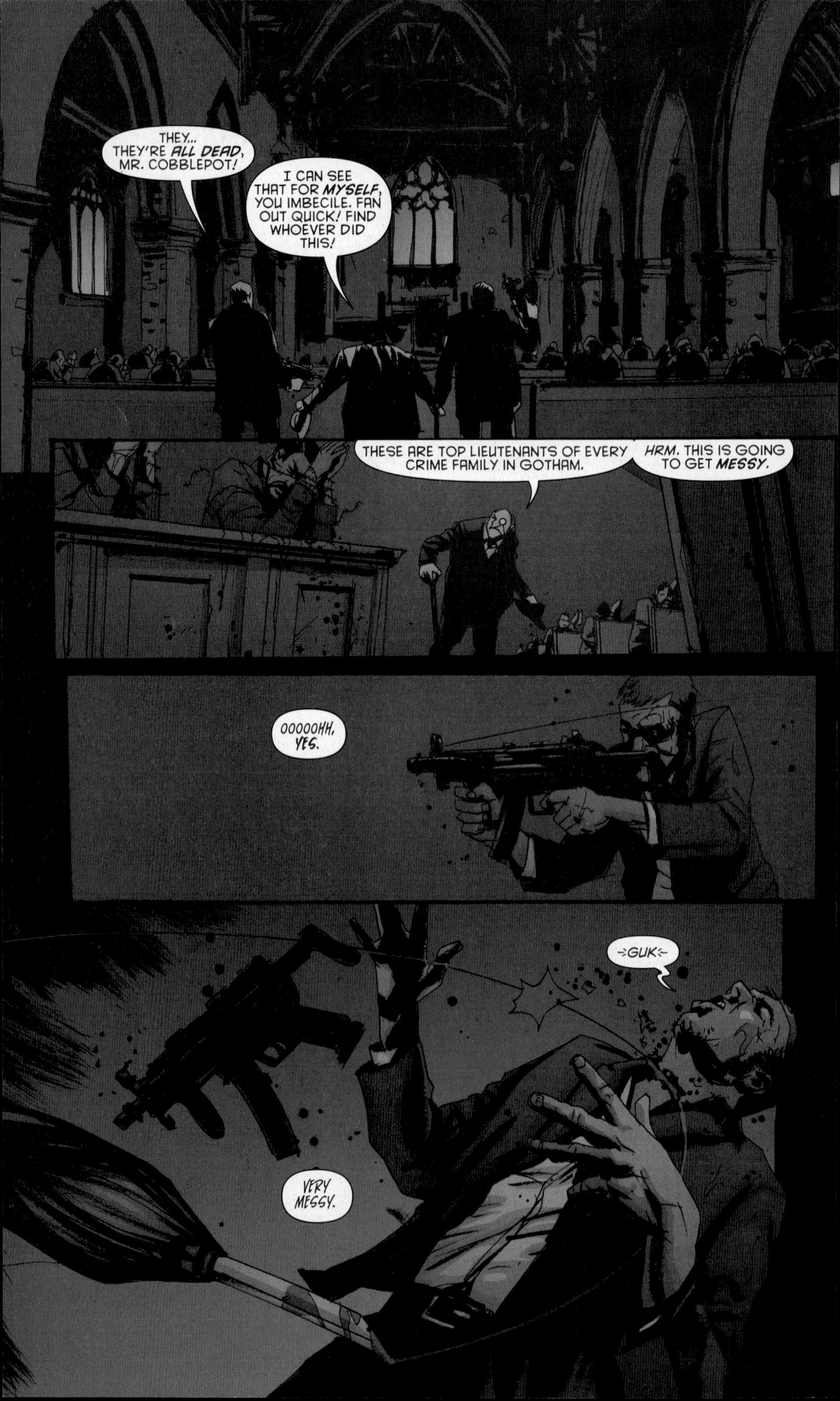
THEY... THEY'RE ALL DEAD, MR. COBBLEPOT!
I CAN SEE THAT FOR MYSELF, YOU IMBECILE. FAN OUT QUICK! FIND WHOEVER DID THIS!
THESE ARE TOP LIEUTENANTS OF EVERY CRIME FAMILY IN GOTHAM.
HRM. THIS IS GOING TO GET MESSY.
OOOOOHH, YES.
-GUK-
VERY MESSY.

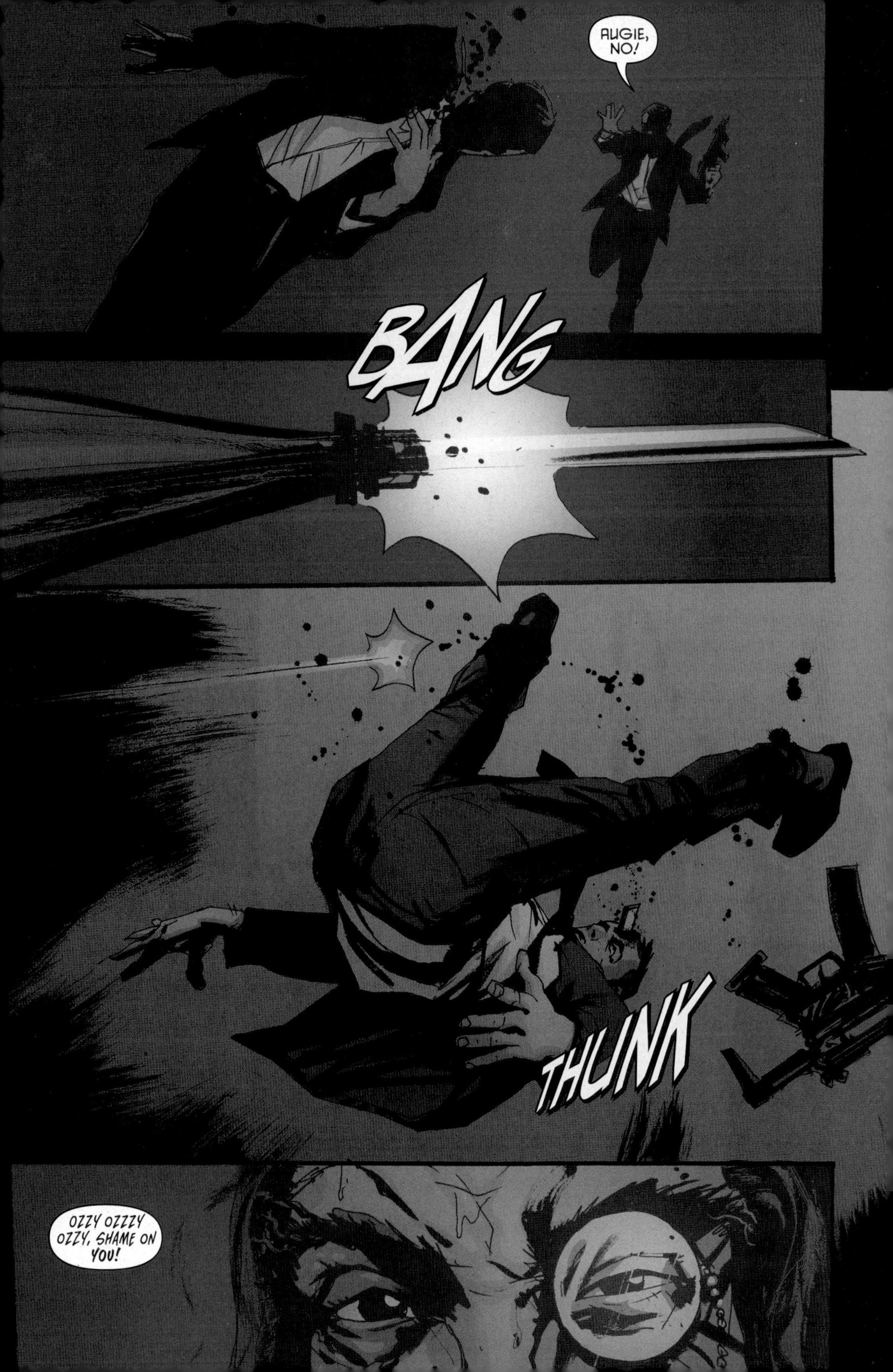
AUGIE, NO!
BANG
THUNK
OZZY OZZZY OZZY, SHAME ON YOU!

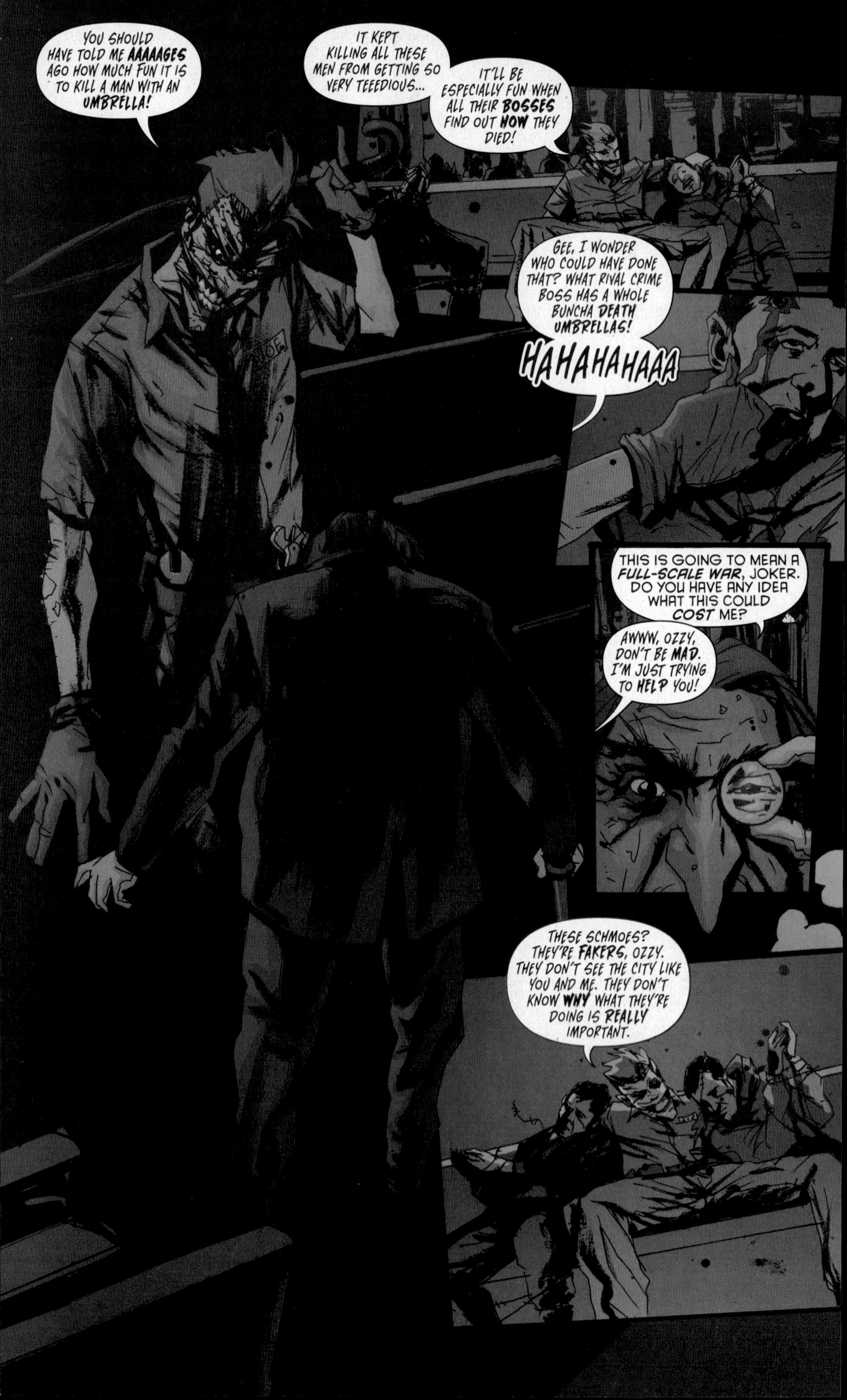
YOU SHOULD HAVE TOLD ME AAAAAGES AGO HOW MUCH FUN IT IS TO KILL A MAN WITH AN UMBRELLA!
IT KEPT KILLING ALL THESE MEN FROM GETTING SO VERY TEEEDIOUS...
IT'LL BE ESPECIALLY FUN WHEN ALL THEIR BOSSES FIND OUT HOW THEY DIED!
GEE, I WONDER WHO COULD HAVE DONE THAT? WHAT RIVAL CRIME BOSS HAS A WHOLE BUNCHA DEATH UMBRELLAS!
HAHAHAHAAA
THIS IS GOING TO MEAN A FULL-SCALE WAR, JOKER. DO YOU HAVE ANY IDEA WHAT THIS COULD COST ME?
AWWW, OZZY, DON'T BE MAD. I'M JUST TRYING TO HELP YOU!
THESE SCHMOES? THEY'RE FAKERS, OZZY. THEY DON'T SEE THE CITY LIKE YOU AND ME. THEY DON'T KNOW WHY WHAT THEY'RE DOING IS REALLY IMPORTANT.

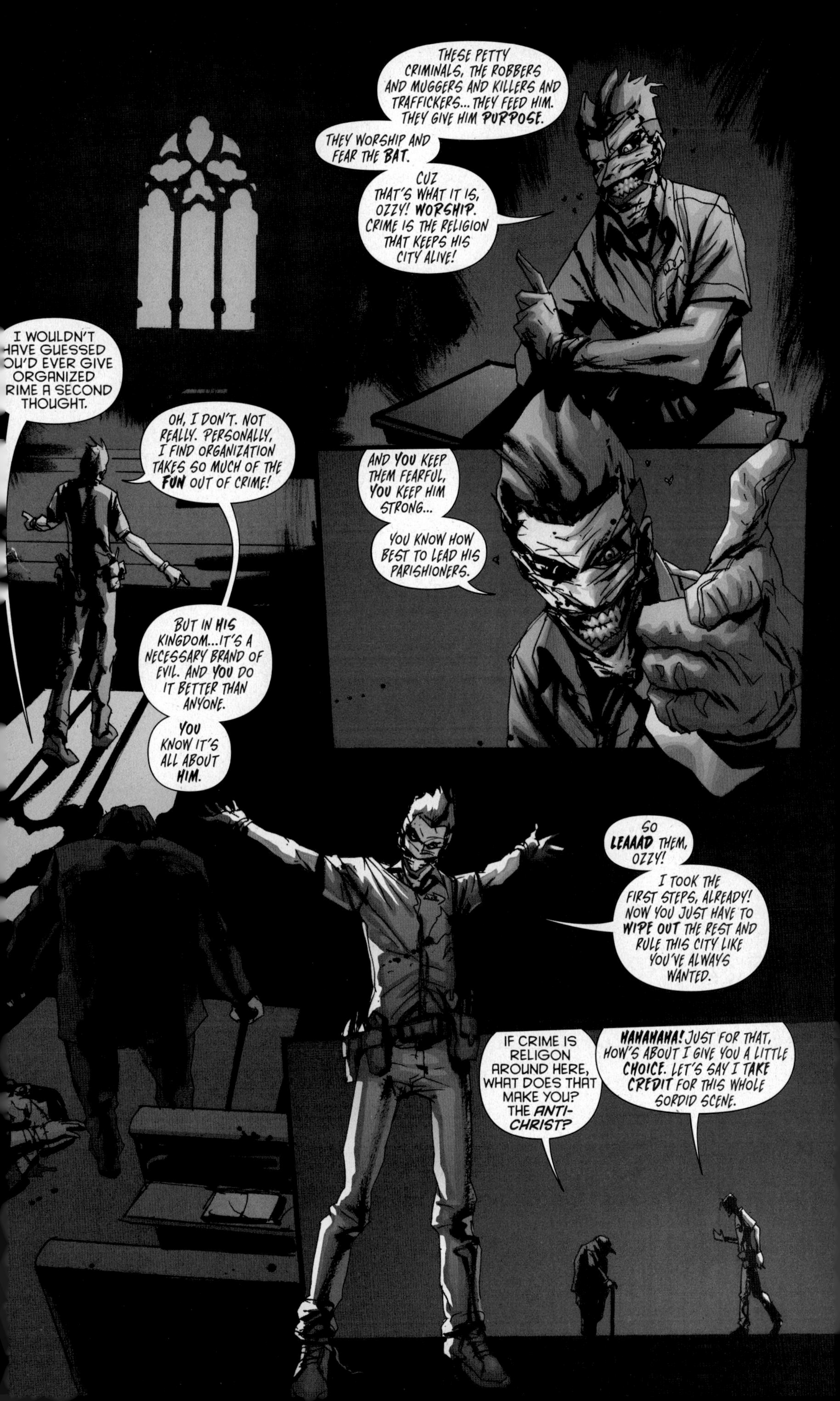
THESE PETTY CRIMINALS, THE ROBBERS AND MUGGERS AND KILLERS AND TRAFFICKERS... THEY FEED HIM. THEY GIVE HIM PURPOSE.
THEY WORSHIP AND FEAR THE BAT.
CUZ THAT'S WHAT IT IS, OZZY! WORSHIP. CRIME IS THE RELIGION THAT KEEPS HIS CITY ALIVE!
I WOULDN'T HAVE GUESSED YOU'D EVER GIVE ORGANIZED CRIME A SECOND THOUGHT.
OH, I DON'T. NOT REALLY. PERSONALLY, I FIND ORGANIZATION TAKES SO MUCH OF THE FUN OUT OF CRIME!
BUT IN HIS KINGDOM...IT'S A NECESSARY BRAND OF EVIL. AND YOU DO IT BETTER THAN ANYONE.
YOU KNOW IT'S ALL ABOUT HIM.
AND YOU KEEP THEM FEARFUL, YOU KEEP HIM STRONG...
YOU KNOW HOW BEST TO LEAD HIS PARISHIONERS.
SO LEAAAD THEM, OZZY!
I TOOK THE FIRST STEPS, ALREADY! NOW YOU JUST HAVE TO WIPE OUT THE REST AND RULE THIS CITY LIKE YOU'VE ALWAYS WANTED.
IF CRIME IS RELIGON AROUND HERE, WHAT DOES THAT MAKE YOU? THE ANTI-CHRIST?
HAHAHAHA! JUST FOR THAT, HOW'S ABOUT I GIVE YOU A LITTLE CHOICE. LET'S SAY I TAKE CREDIT FOR THIS WHOLE SORDID SCENE.

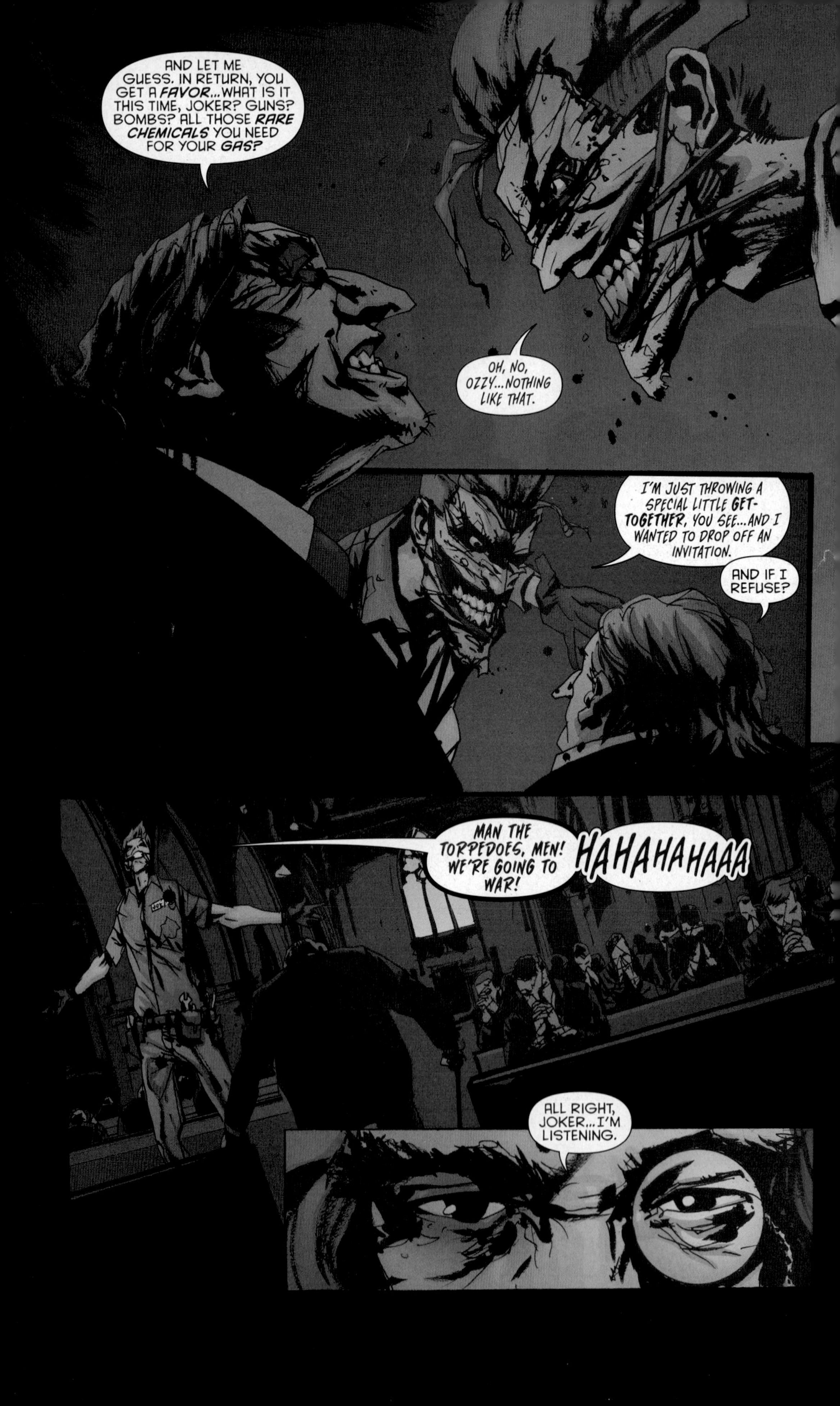

AND LET ME GUESS. IN RETURN, YOU GET A *FAVOR*... WHAT IS IT THIS TIME, JOKER? GUNS? BOMBS? ALL THOSE *RARE CHEMICALS* YOU NEED FOR YOUR *GAS?*
OH, NO, OZZY... NOTHING LIKE THAT.
I'M JUST THROWING A SPECIAL LITTLE **GET-TOGETHER**, YOU SEE... AND I WANTED TO DROP OFF AN INVITATION.
AND IF I REFUSE?
MAN THE TORPEDOES, MEN! WE'RE GOING TO WAR!
HAHAHAHAHAAA
ALL RIGHT, JOKER... I'M LISTENING.

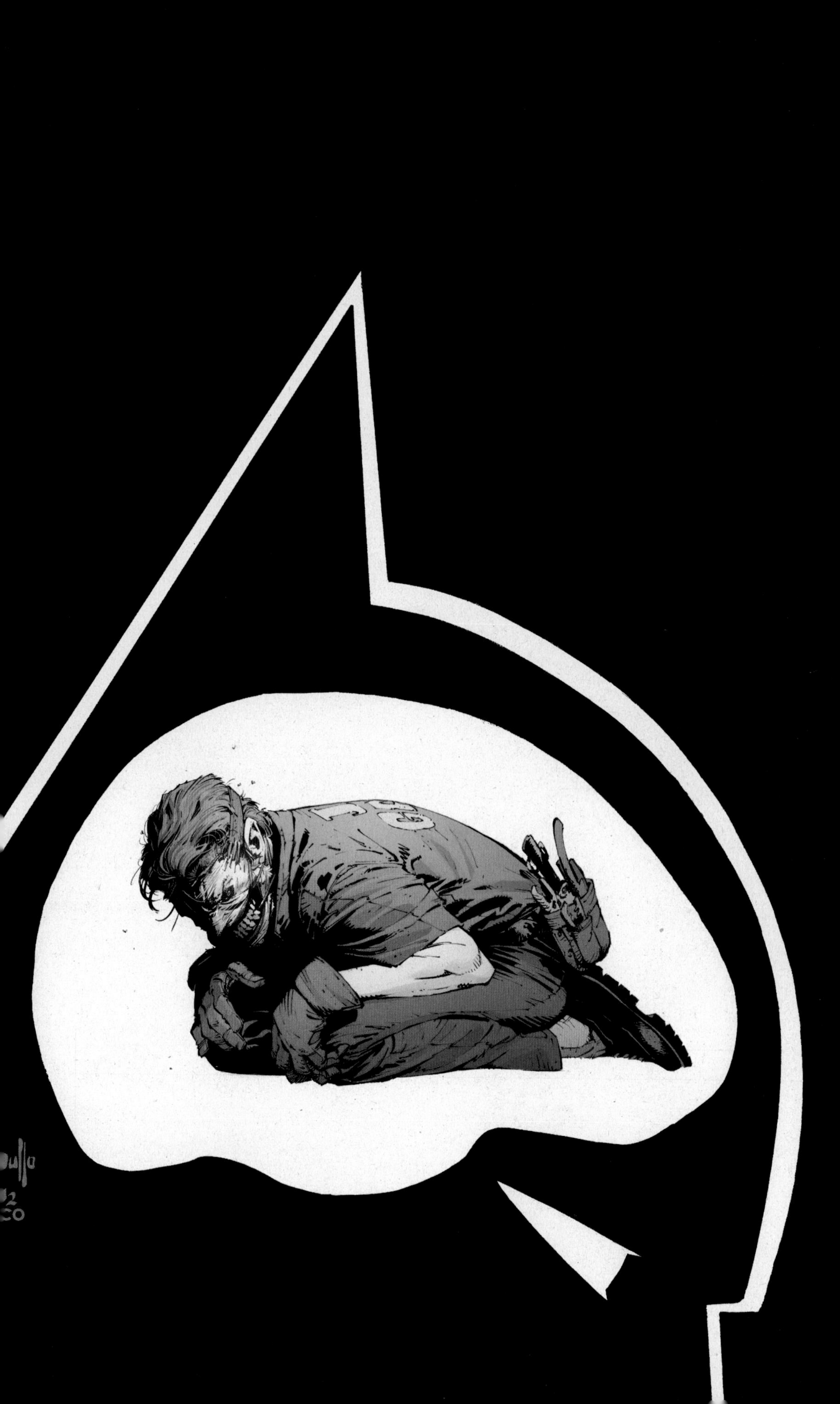

BUT HERE'S THE KICKER SCOTT SNYDER writer GREG CAPULLO penciller JONATHAN GLAPION inker
RED LIGHT, GREEN LIGHT SCOTT SNYDER & JAMES TYNION IV writers JOCK artist

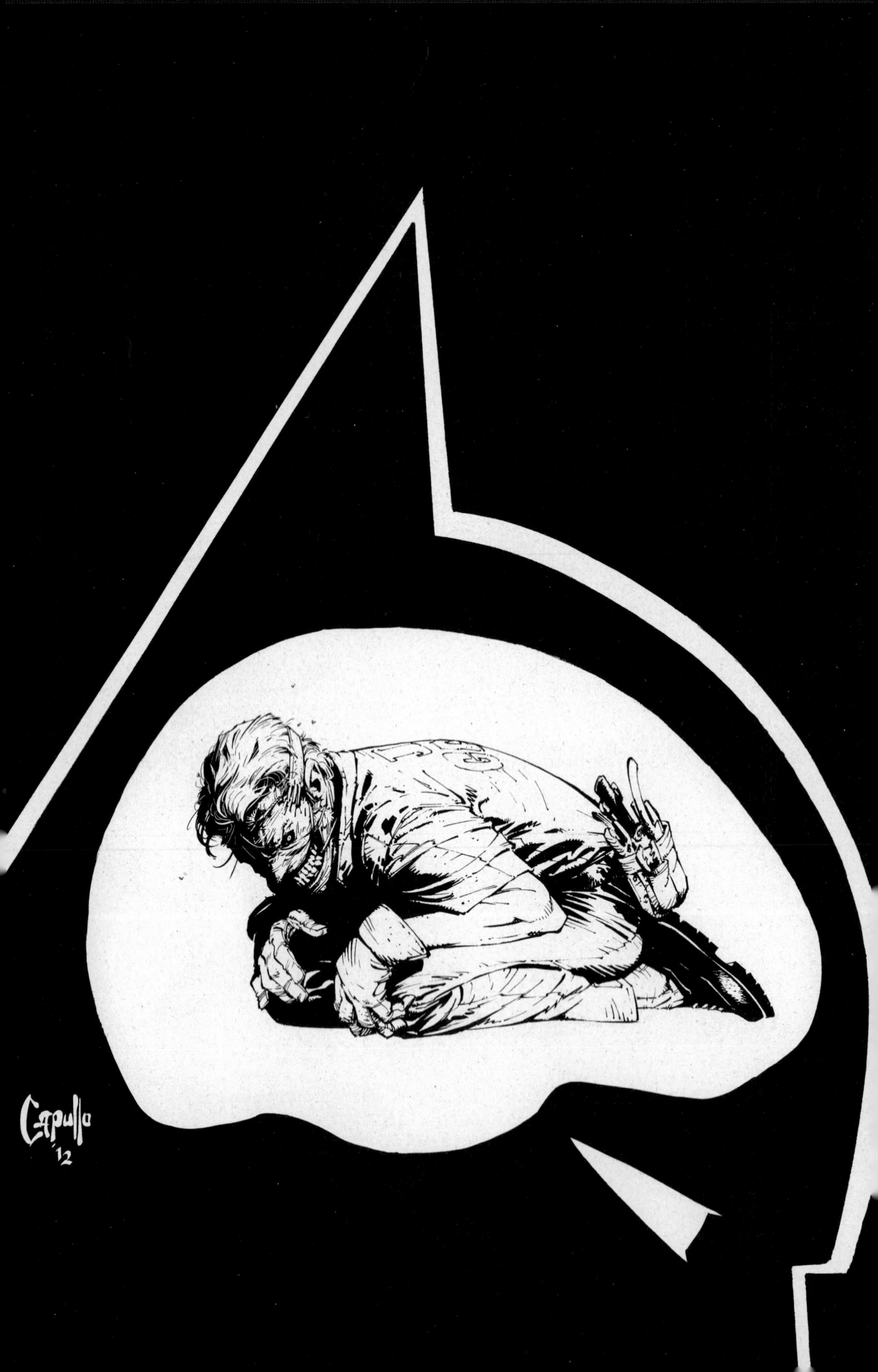
Capullo '12

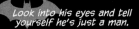 Look into his eyes and tell yourself he's just a man.

Tell yourself he can't know the things he says he does. He can't know your fears. But he has **Alfred**. He has your friend. And his eyes...

...you have studied the human eye. There are six eye movements that reveal motive, then fifteen variations of each one.

On everyone else you face--even the most hardened criminals--the pupils contract or expand depending on emotion.

Happiness, laughter, affection. The pupils **open**.

Fear, anger, hatred, the pupils **close**.

But not his. His pupils stay **fixed**, tiny points of blackness, the eyes of someone who hates everything, everyone.

Eyes that let in no light, that see through the darkness, stare into you, each pupil a tiny black pearl fixed in space.

A bullet coming at you. Eyes that say he's more than a man, eyes that say he **knows you**.

No...you know what he is. Tell yourself the truth. He's just a man who fell in a vat of chemical waste. He's just a man...

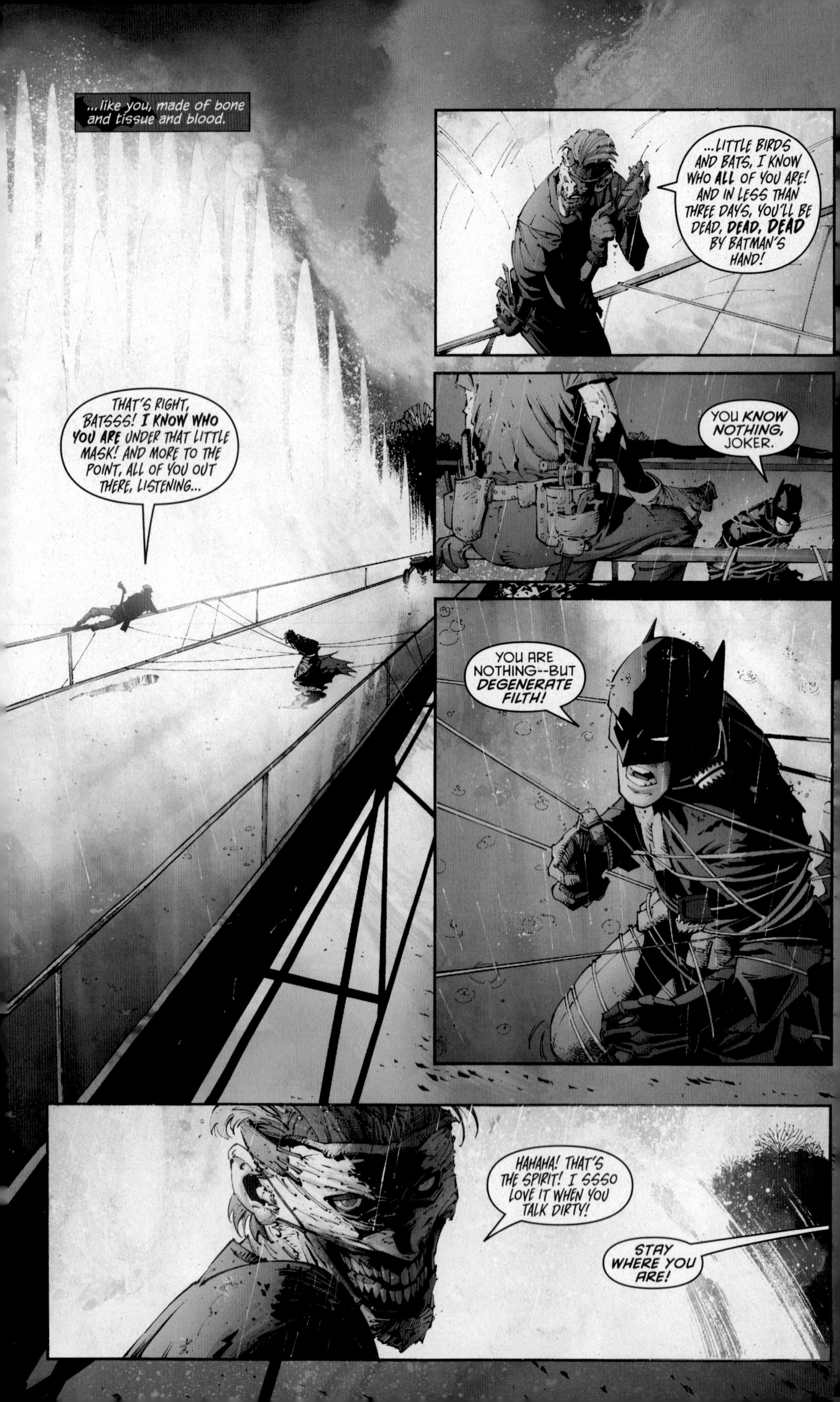

...like you, made of bone and tissue and blood.
...LITTLE BIRDS AND BATS, I KNOW WHO ALL OF YOU ARE! AND IN LESS THAN THREE DAYS, YOU'LL BE DEAD, DEAD, DEAD BY BATMAN'S HAND!
THAT'S RIGHT, BATSSS! I KNOW WHO YOU ARE UNDER THAT LITTLE MASK! AND MORE TO THE POINT, ALL OF YOU OUT THERE, LISTENING...
YOU KNOW NOTHING, JOKER.
YOU ARE NOTHING--BUT DEGENERATE FILTH!
HAHAHA! THAT'S THE SPIRIT! I SSSO LOVE IT WHEN YOU TALK DIRTY!
STAY WHERE YOU ARE!

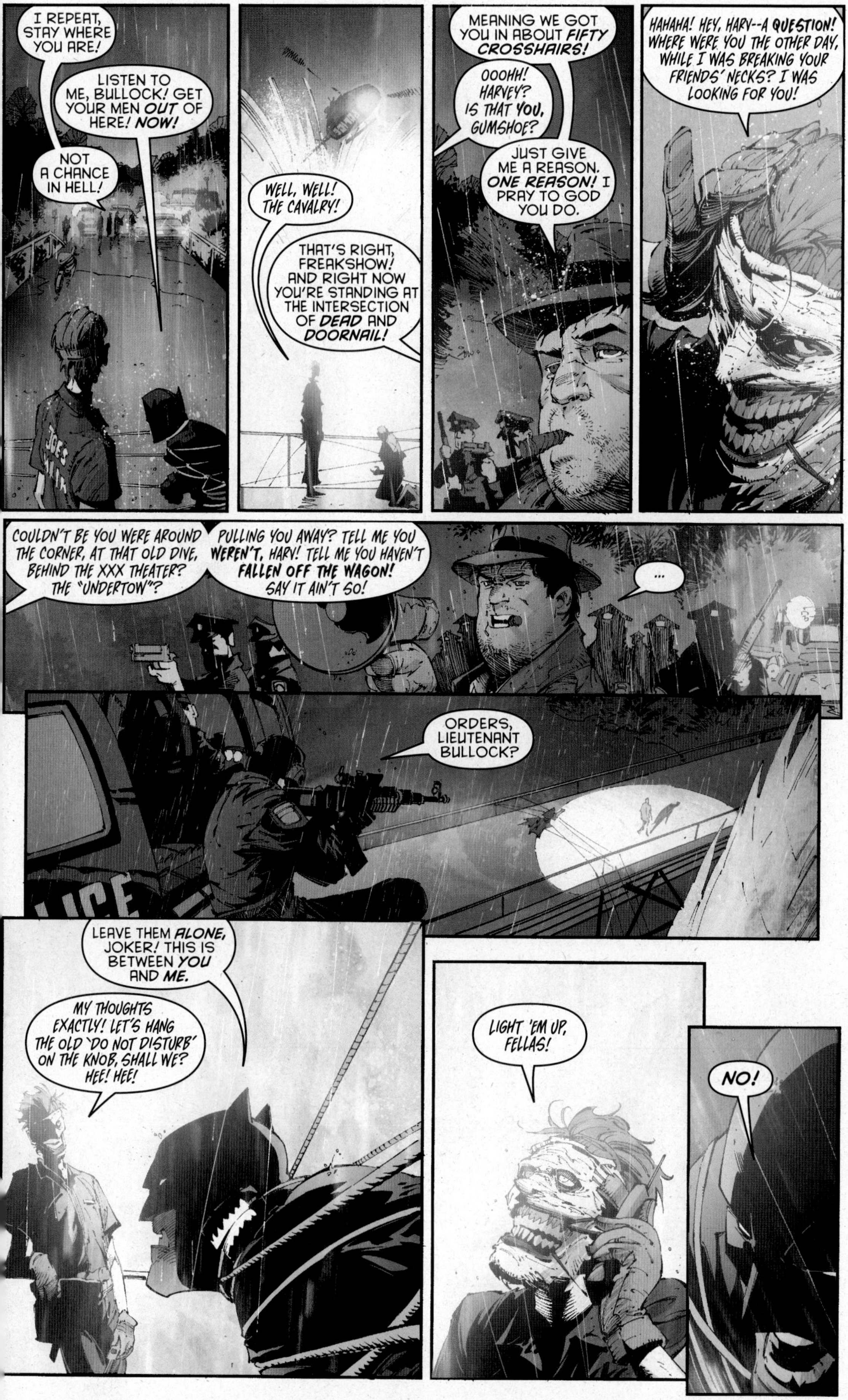
I REPEAT, STAY WHERE YOU ARE!
LISTEN TO ME, BULLOCK! GET YOUR MEN OUT OF HERE! NOW!
NOT A CHANCE IN HELL!
WELL, WELL! THE CAVALRY!
THAT'S RIGHT, FREAKSHOW! AND RIGHT NOW YOU'RE STANDING AT THE INTERSECTION OF DEAD AND DOORNAIL!
MEANING WE GOT YOU IN ABOUT FIFTY CROSSHAIRS!
OOOHH! HARVEY? IS THAT YOU, GUMSHOE?
JUST GIVE ME A REASON. ONE REASON! I PRAY TO GOD YOU DO.
HAHAHA! HEY, HARV--A QUESTION! WHERE WERE YOU THE OTHER DAY, WHILE I WAS BREAKING YOUR FRIENDS' NECKS? I WAS LOOKING FOR YOU!
COULDN'T BE YOU WERE AROUND THE CORNER, AT THAT OLD DIVE, BEHIND THE XXX THEATER? THE "UNDERTOW"?
PULLING YOU AWAY? TELL ME YOU WEREN'T, HARV! TELL ME YOU HAVEN'T FALLEN OFF THE WAGON! SAY IT AIN'T SO!
...
ORDERS, LIEUTENANT BULLOCK?
LEAVE THEM ALONE, JOKER! THIS IS BETWEEN YOU AND ME.
MY THOUGHTS EXACTLY! LET'S HANG THE OLD 'DO NOT DISTURB' ON THE KNOB, SHALL WE? HEE! HEE!
LIGHT 'EM UP, FELLAS!
NO!

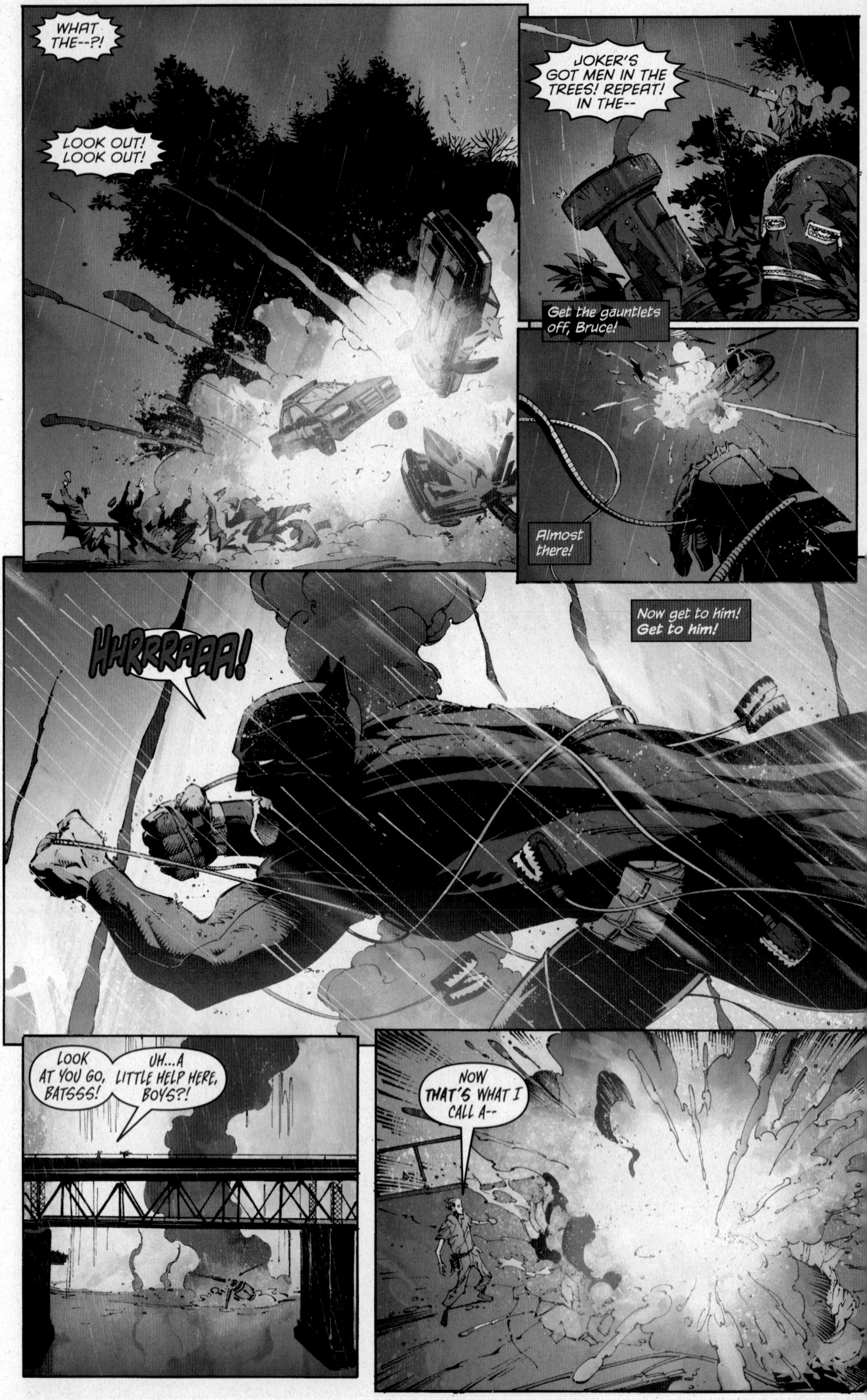

WHAT THE--?!
LOOK OUT! LOOK OUT!
JOKER'S GOT MEN IN THE TREES! REPEAT! IN THE--
Get the gauntlets off, Bruce!
Almost there!
Now get to him! Get to him!
HHRRRAAAA!
LOOK AT YOU GO, BATSSS!
UH...A LITTLE HELP HERE, BOYS?!
NOW THAT'S WHAT I CALL A--

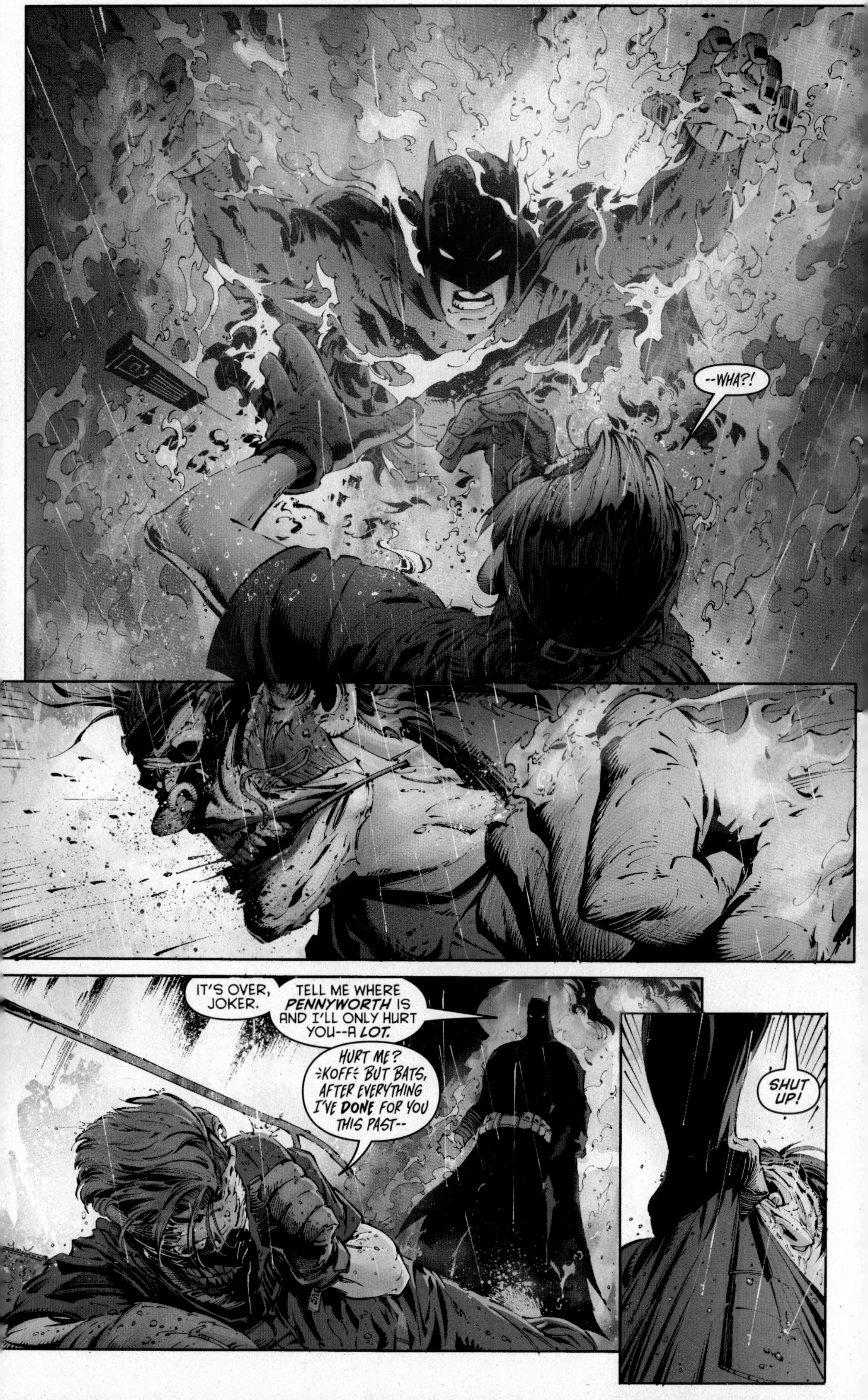
--WHA?!
IT'S OVER, JOKER.
TELL ME WHERE PENNYWORTH IS AND I'LL ONLY HURT YOU--A LOT.
HURT ME? *KOFF* BUT BATS, AFTER EVERYTHING I'VE DONE FOR YOU THIS PAST--
SHUT UP!

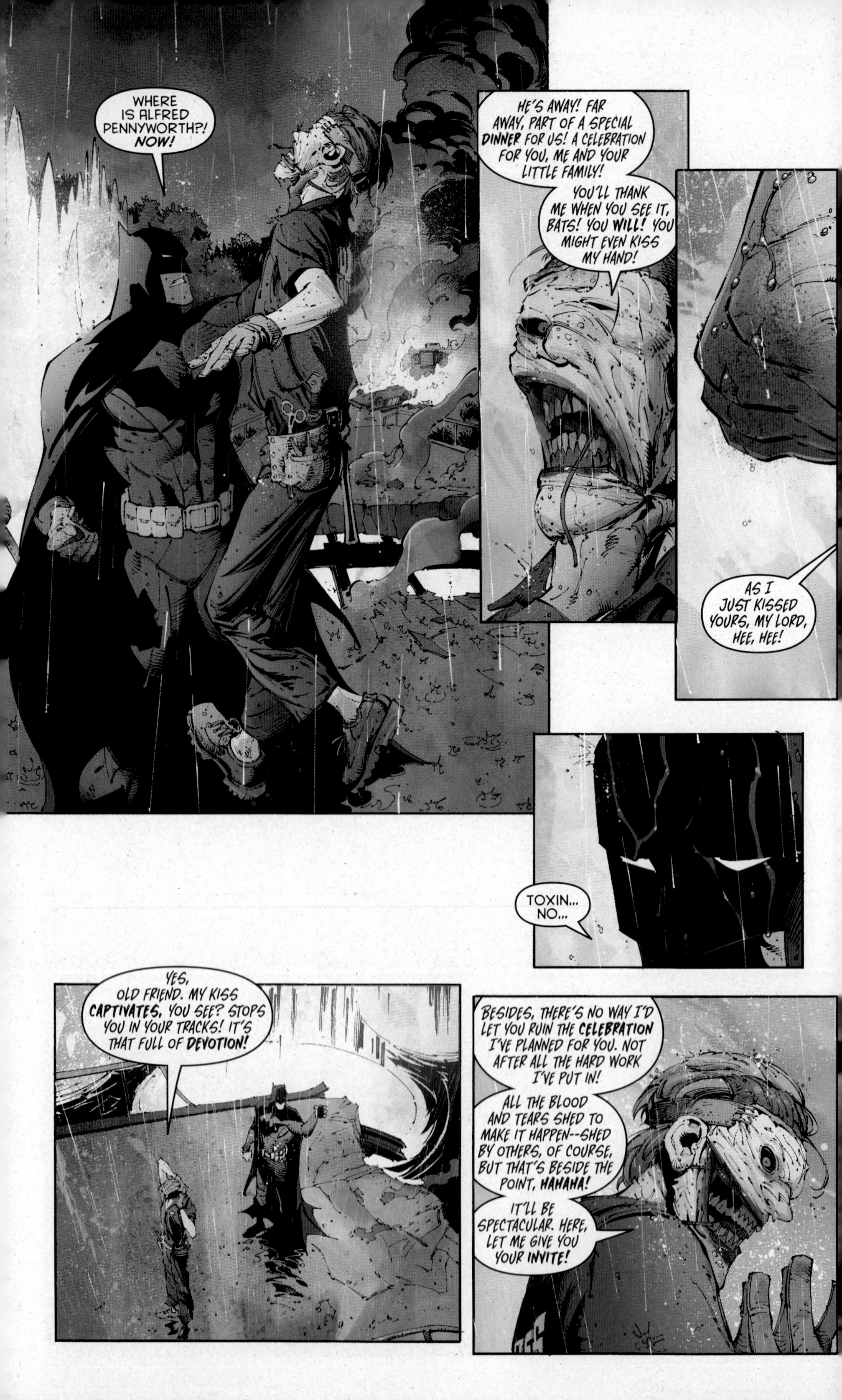
WHERE IS ALFRED PENNYWORTH?! NOW!
HE'S AWAY! FAR AWAY, PART OF A SPECIAL DINNER FOR US! A CELEBRATION FOR YOU, ME AND YOUR LITTLE FAMILY!
YOU'LL THANK ME WHEN YOU SEE IT, BATS! YOU WILL! YOU MIGHT EVEN KISS MY HAND!
AS I JUST KISSED YOURS, MY LORD, HEE, HEE!
TOXIN... NO...
YES, OLD FRIEND. MY KISS CAPTIVATES, YOU SEE? STOPS YOU IN YOUR TRACKS! IT'S THAT FULL OF DEVOTION!
BESIDES, THERE'S NO WAY I'D LET YOU RUIN THE CELEBRATION I'VE PLANNED FOR YOU. NOT AFTER ALL THE HARD WORK I'VE PUT IN!
ALL THE BLOOD AND TEARS SHED TO MAKE IT HAPPEN--SHED BY OTHERS, OF COURSE, BUT THAT'S BESIDE THE POINT, HAHAHA!
IT'LL BE SPECTACULAR. HERE, LET ME GIVE YOU YOUR INVITE!

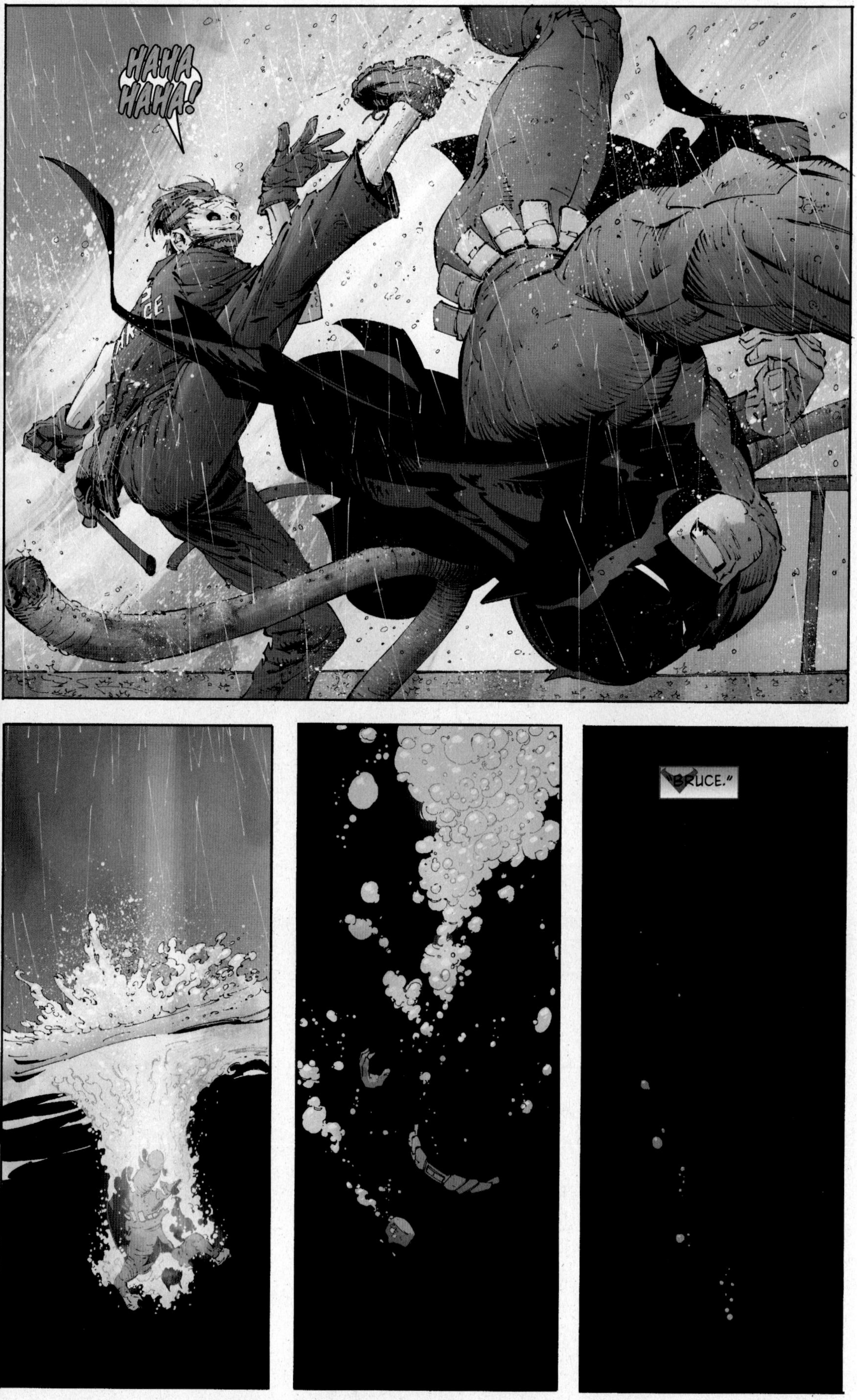
HAHA HAHA!
"BRUCE."

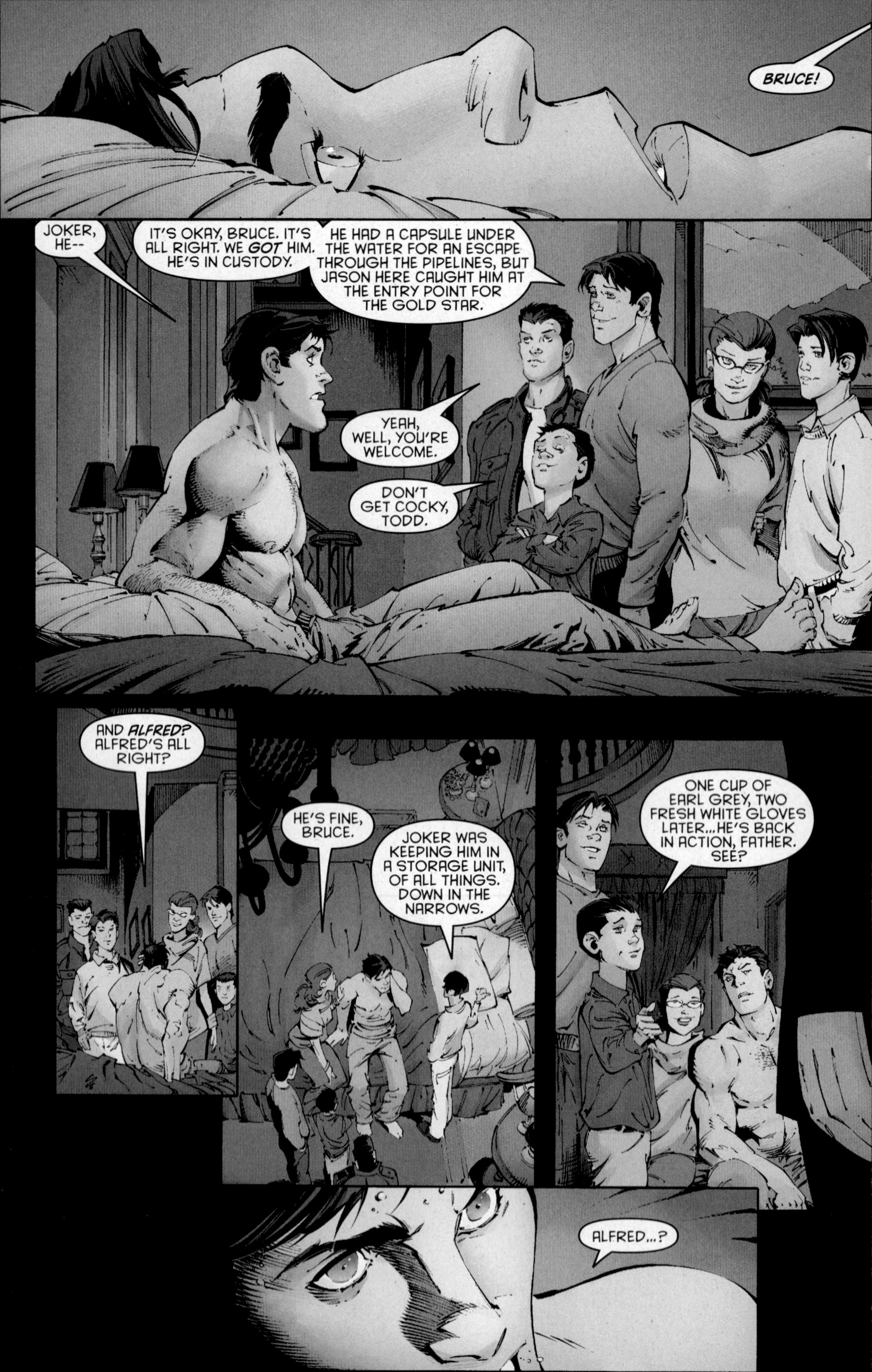
BRUCE!
JOKER, HE--
IT'S OKAY, BRUCE. IT'S ALL RIGHT. WE GOT HIM. HE'S IN CUSTODY.
HE HAD A CAPSULE UNDER THE WATER FOR AN ESCAPE THROUGH THE PIPELINES, BUT JASON HERE CAUGHT HIM AT THE ENTRY POINT FOR THE GOLD STAR.
YEAH, WELL, YOU'RE WELCOME.
DON'T GET COCKY, TODD.
AND ALFRED? ALFRED'S ALL RIGHT?
HE'S FINE, BRUCE.
JOKER WAS KEEPING HIM IN A STORAGE UNIT, OF ALL THINGS. DOWN IN THE NARROWS.
ONE CUP OF EARL GREY, TWO FRESH WHITE GLOVES LATER...HE'S BACK IN ACTION, FATHER. SEE?
ALFRED...?

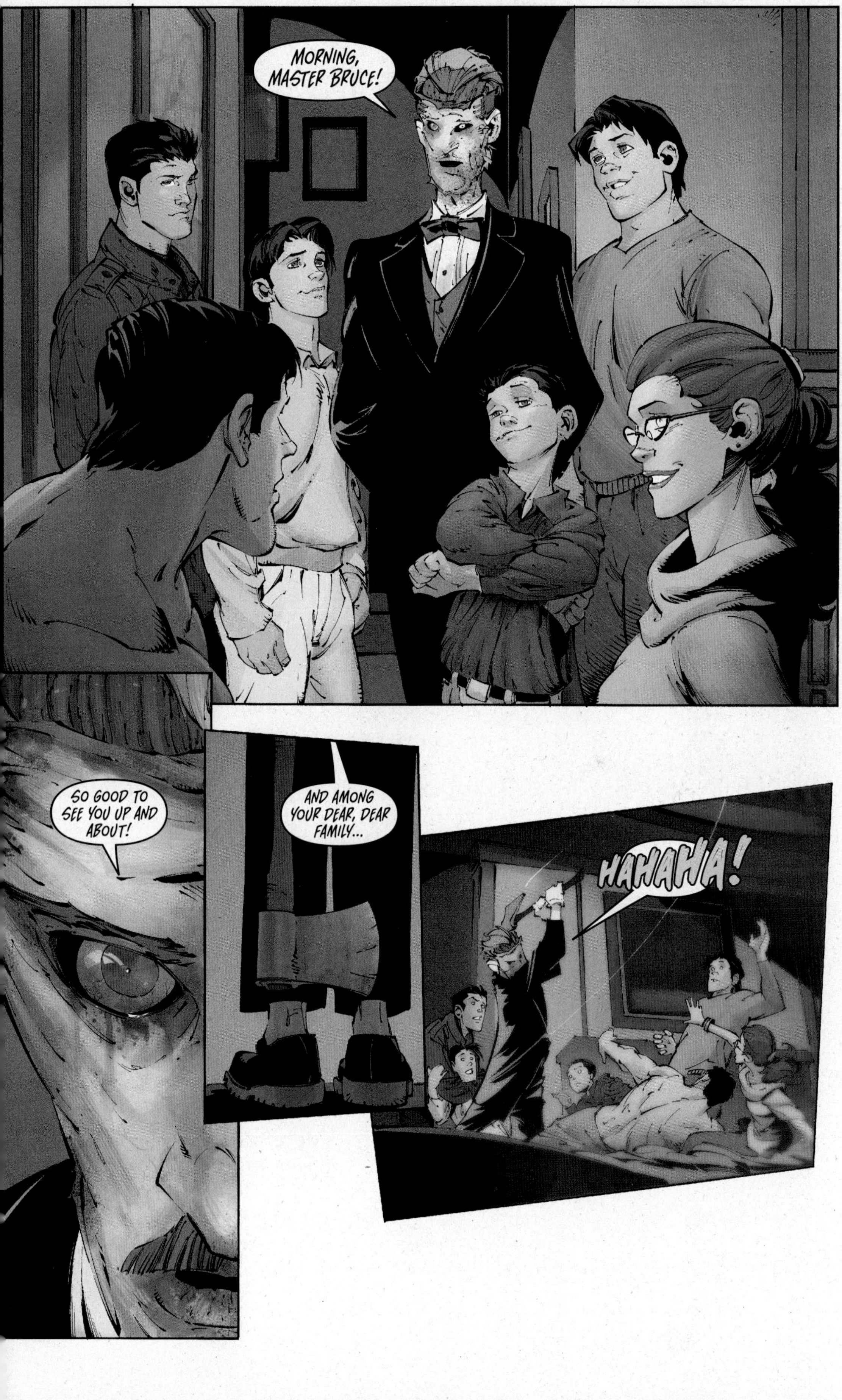
MORNING, MASTER BRUCE!
SO GOOD TO SEE YOU UP AND ABOUT!
AND AMONG YOUR DEAR, DEAR FAMILY...
HAHAHA!

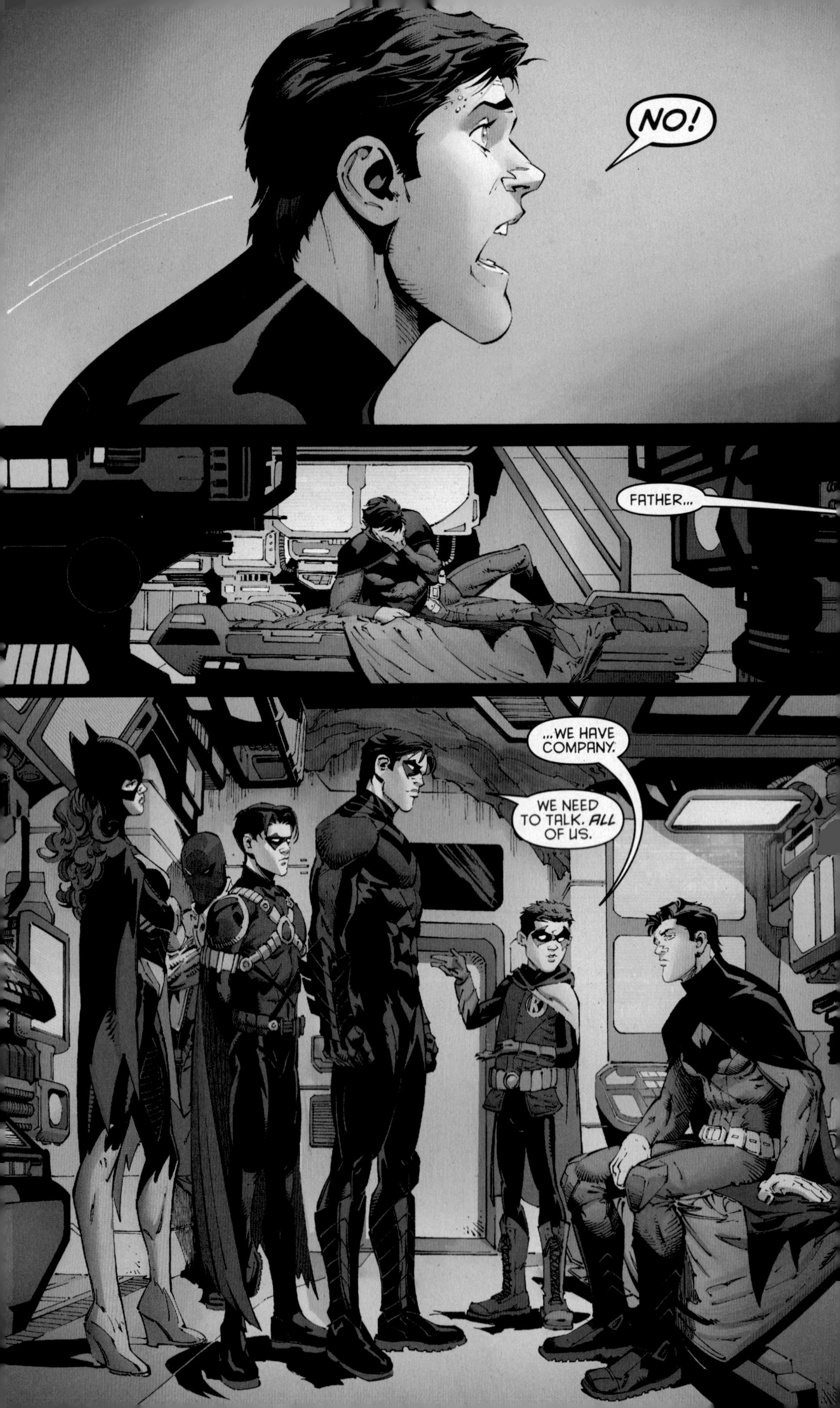
NO!
FATHER...
...WE HAVE COMPANY.
WE NEED TO TALK. ALL OF US.

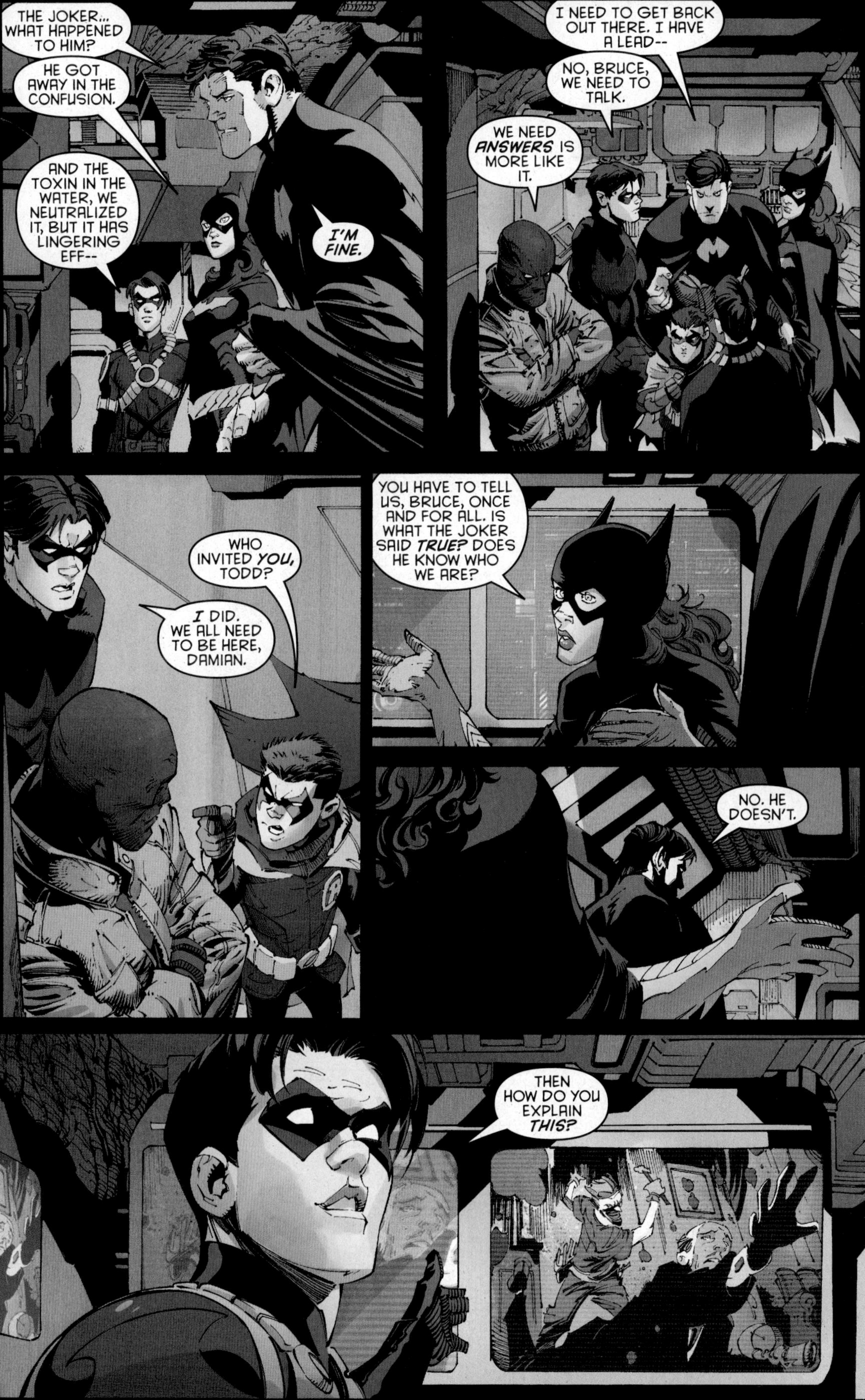
THE JOKER... WHAT HAPPENED TO HIM?
HE GOT AWAY IN THE CONFUSION.
AND THE TOXIN IN THE WATER, WE NEUTRALIZED IT, BUT IT HAS LINGERING EFF--
I'M FINE.
I NEED TO GET BACK OUT THERE. I HAVE A LEAD--
NO, BRUCE, WE NEED TO TALK.
WE NEED ANSWERS IS MORE LIKE IT.
WHO INVITED YOU, TODD?
I DID. WE ALL NEED TO BE HERE, DAMIAN.
YOU HAVE TO TELL US, BRUCE, ONCE AND FOR ALL. IS WHAT THE JOKER SAID TRUE? DOES HE KNOW WHO WE ARE?
NO. HE DOESN'T.
THEN HOW DO YOU EXPLAIN THIS?

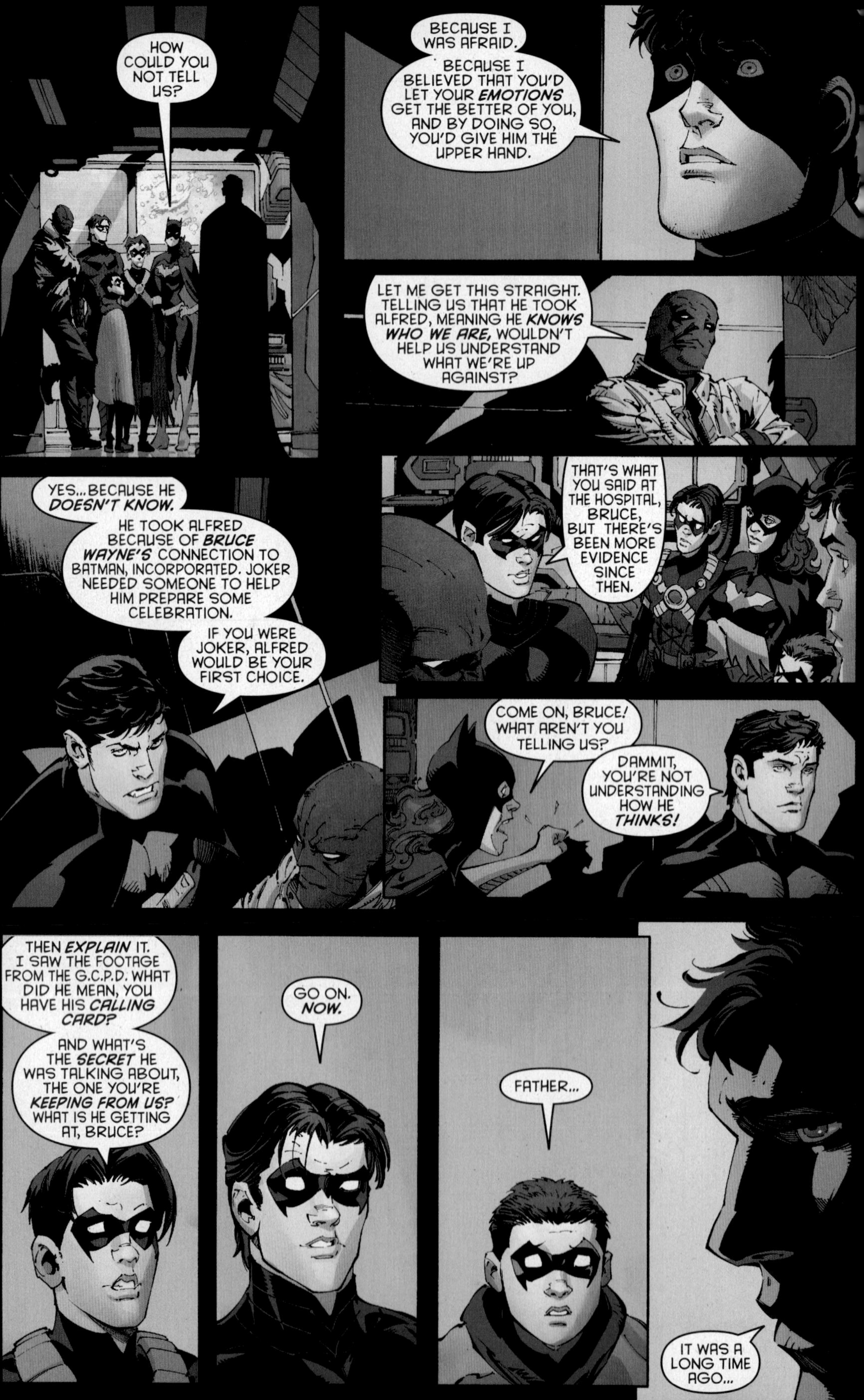
HOW COULD YOU NOT TELL US?
BECAUSE I WAS AFRAID.
BECAUSE I BELIEVED THAT YOU'D LET YOUR EMOTIONS GET THE BETTER OF YOU, AND BY DOING SO, YOU'D GIVE HIM THE UPPER HAND.
LET ME GET THIS STRAIGHT. TELLING US THAT HE TOOK ALFRED, MEANING HE KNOWS WHO WE ARE, WOULDN'T HELP US UNDERSTAND WHAT WE'RE UP AGAINST?
YES... BECAUSE HE DOESN'T KNOW.
HE TOOK ALFRED BECAUSE OF BRUCE WAYNE'S CONNECTION TO BATMAN, INCORPORATED. JOKER NEEDED SOMEONE TO HELP HIM PREPARE SOME CELEBRATION.
IF YOU WERE JOKER, ALFRED WOULD BE YOUR FIRST CHOICE.
THAT'S WHAT YOU SAID AT THE HOSPITAL, BRUCE, BUT THERE'S BEEN MORE EVIDENCE SINCE THEN.
COME ON, BRUCE! WHAT AREN'T YOU TELLING US?
DAMMIT, YOU'RE NOT UNDERSTANDING HOW HE THINKS!
THEN EXPLAIN IT. I SAW THE FOOTAGE FROM THE G.C.P.D. WHAT DID HE MEAN, YOU HAVE HIS CALLING CARD?
AND WHAT'S THE SECRET HE WAS TALKING ABOUT, THE ONE YOU'RE KEEPING FROM US? WHAT IS HE GETTING AT, BRUCE?
GO ON. NOW.
FATHER...
IT WAS A LONG TIME AGO...

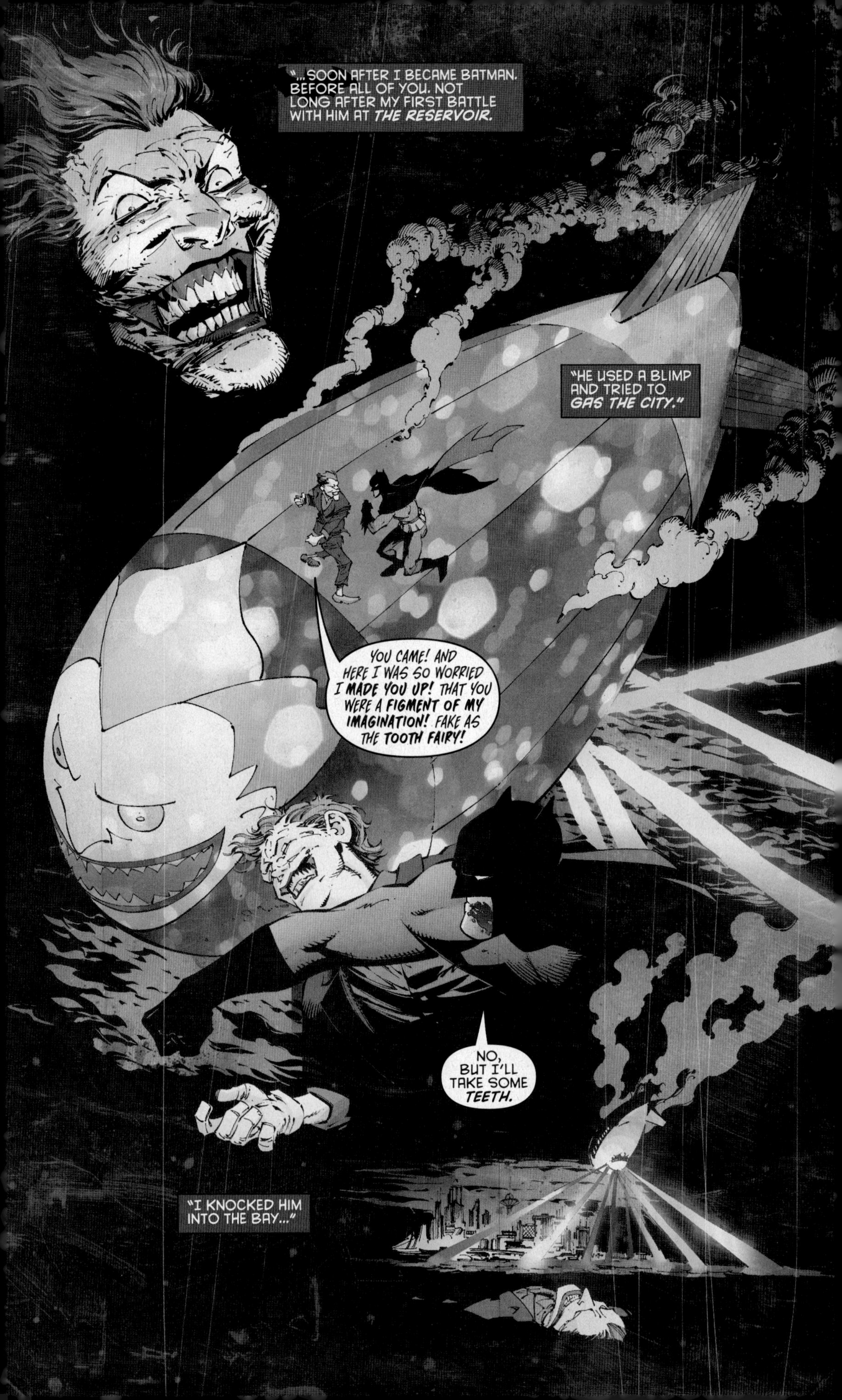
"...SOON AFTER I BECAME BATMAN. BEFORE ALL OF YOU. NOT LONG AFTER MY FIRST BATTLE WITH HIM AT THE RESERVOIR.
"HE USED A BLIMP AND TRIED TO GAS THE CITY."
YOU CAME! AND HERE I WAS SO WORRIED I MADE YOU UP! THAT YOU WERE A FIGMENT OF MY IMAGINATION! FAKE AS THE TOOTH FAIRY!
NO, BUT I'LL TAKE SOME TEETH.
"I KNOCKED HIM INTO THE BAY..."

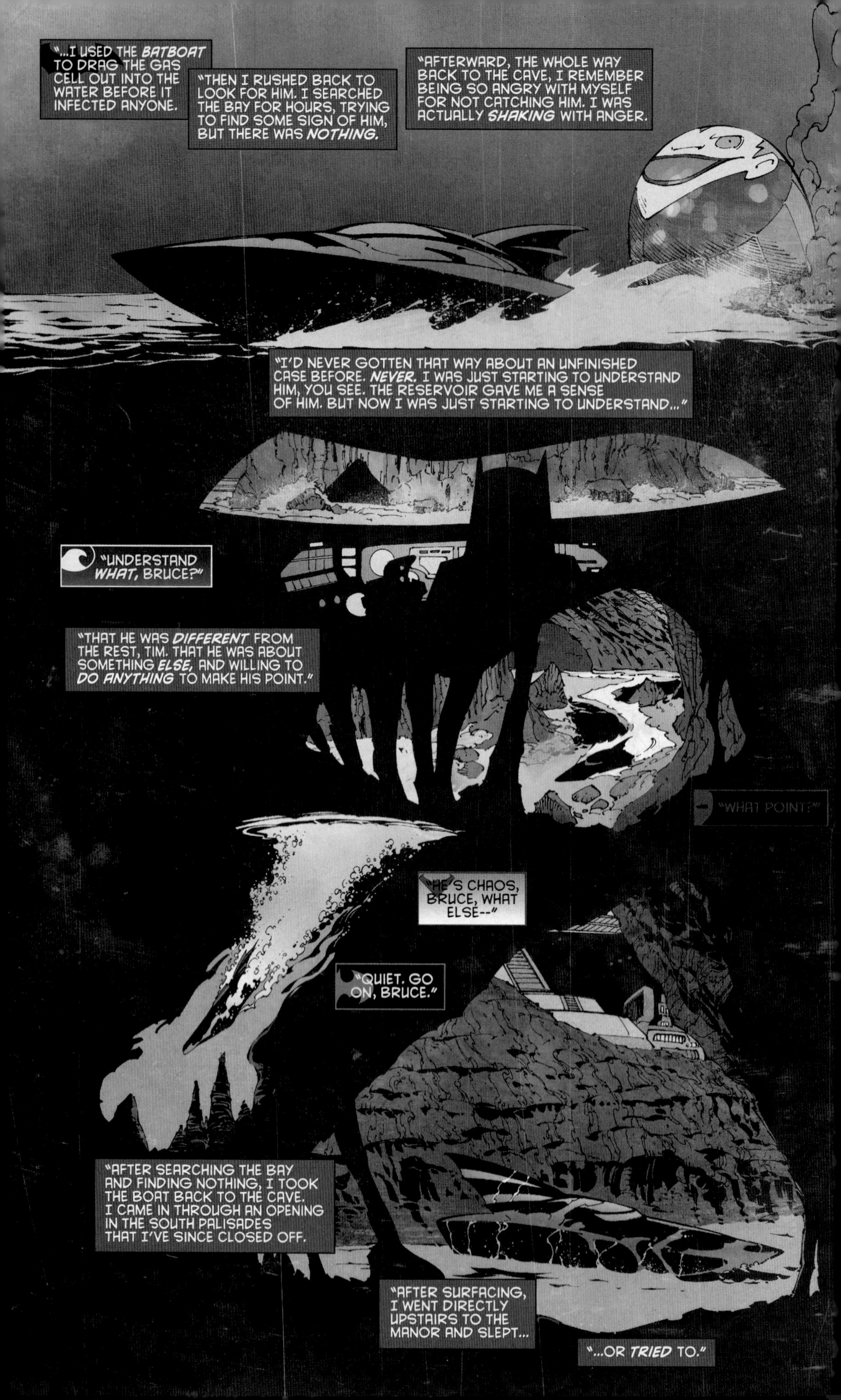
"...I USED THE BATBOAT TO DRAG THE GAS CELL OUT INTO THE WATER BEFORE IT INFECTED ANYONE.
"THEN I RUSHED BACK TO LOOK FOR HIM. I SEARCHED THE BAY FOR HOURS, TRYING TO FIND SOME SIGN OF HIM, BUT THERE WAS NOTHING.
"AFTERWARD, THE WHOLE WAY BACK TO THE CAVE, I REMEMBER BEING SO ANGRY WITH MYSELF FOR NOT CATCHING HIM. I WAS ACTUALLY SHAKING WITH ANGER.
"I'D NEVER GOTTEN THAT WAY ABOUT AN UNFINISHED CASE BEFORE. NEVER. I WAS JUST STARTING TO UNDERSTAND HIM, YOU SEE. THE RESERVOIR GAVE ME A SENSE OF HIM. BUT NOW I WAS JUST STARTING TO UNDERSTAND..."
"UNDERSTAND WHAT, BRUCE?"
"THAT HE WAS DIFFERENT FROM THE REST, TIM. THAT HE WAS ABOUT SOMETHING ELSE, AND WILLING TO DO ANYTHING TO MAKE HIS POINT."
"WHAT POINT?"
"HE'S CHAOS, BRUCE, WHAT ELSE--"
"QUIET. GO ON, BRUCE."
"AFTER SEARCHING THE BAY AND FINDING NOTHING, I TOOK THE BOAT BACK TO THE CAVE. I CAME IN THROUGH AN OPENING IN THE SOUTH PALISADES THAT I'VE SINCE CLOSED OFF.
"AFTER SURFACING, I WENT DIRECTLY UPSTAIRS TO THE MANOR AND SLEPT...
"...OR TRIED TO."

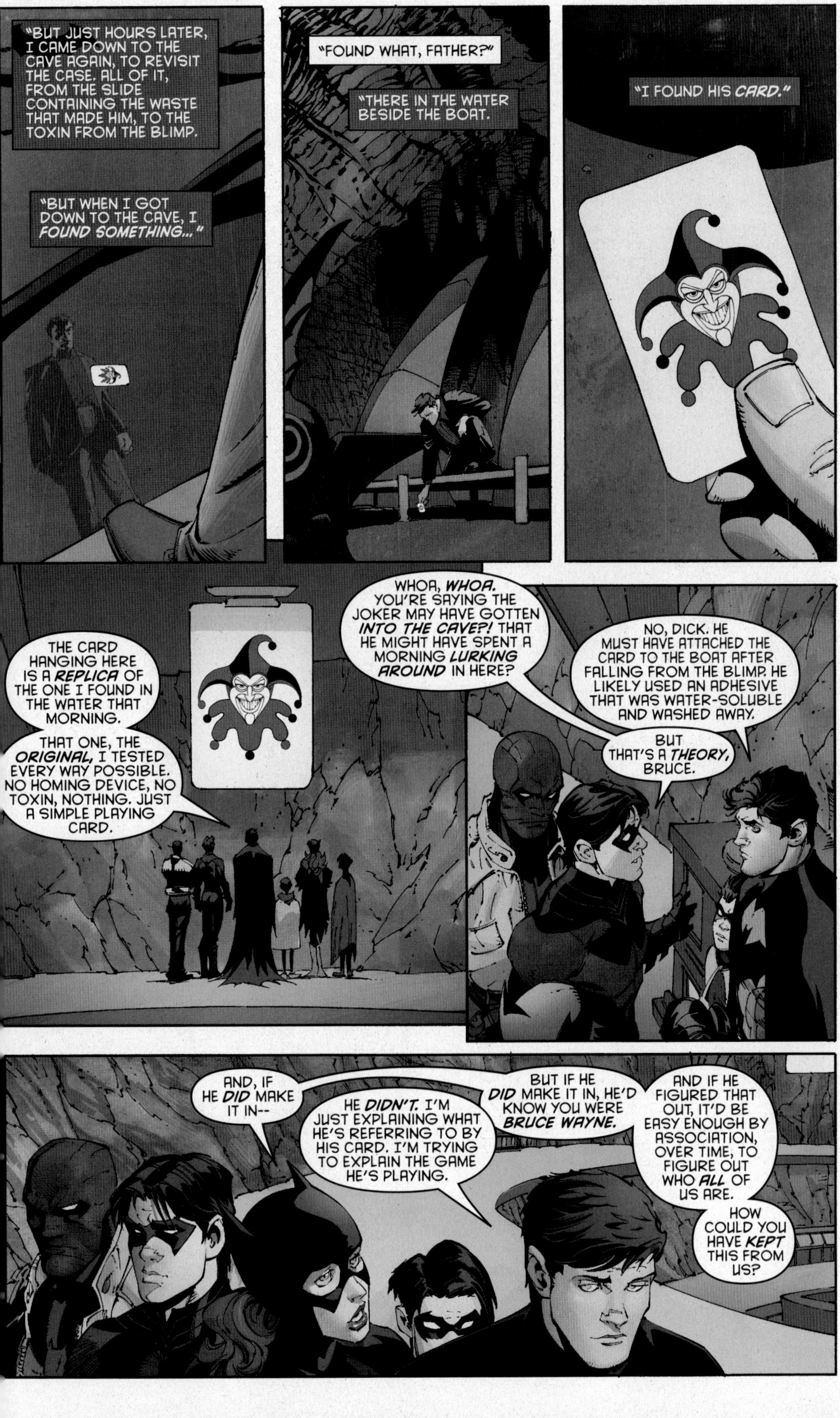

"BUT JUST HOURS LATER, I CAME DOWN TO THE CAVE AGAIN, TO REVISIT THE CASE. ALL OF IT, FROM THE SLIDE CONTAINING THE WASTE THAT MADE HIM, TO THE TOXIN FROM THE BLIMP.
"BUT WHEN I GOT DOWN TO THE CAVE, I FOUND SOMETHING..."
"FOUND WHAT, FATHER?"
"THERE IN THE WATER BESIDE THE BOAT.
"I FOUND HIS CARD."
THE CARD HANGING HERE IS A REPLICA OF THE ONE I FOUND IN THE WATER THAT MORNING.
THAT ONE, THE ORIGINAL, I TESTED EVERY WAY POSSIBLE. NO HOMING DEVICE, NO TOXIN, NOTHING. JUST A SIMPLE PLAYING CARD.
WHOA, WHOA. YOU'RE SAYING THE JOKER MAY HAVE GOTTEN INTO THE CAVE?! THAT HE MIGHT HAVE SPENT A MORNING LURKING AROUND IN HERE?
NO, DICK. HE MUST HAVE ATTACHED THE CARD TO THE BOAT AFTER FALLING FROM THE BLIMP. HE LIKELY USED AN ADHESIVE THAT WAS WATER-SOLUBLE AND WASHED AWAY.
BUT THAT'S A THEORY, BRUCE.
AND, IF HE DID MAKE IT IN--
HE DIDN'T. I'M JUST EXPLAINING WHAT HE'S REFERRING TO BY HIS CARD. I'M TRYING TO EXPLAIN THE GAME HE'S PLAYING.
BUT IF HE DID MAKE IT IN, HE'D KNOW YOU WERE BRUCE WAYNE.
AND IF HE FIGURED THAT OUT, IT'D BE EASY ENOUGH BY ASSOCIATION, OVER TIME, TO FIGURE OUT WHO ALL OF US ARE.
HOW COULD YOU HAVE KEPT THIS FROM US?

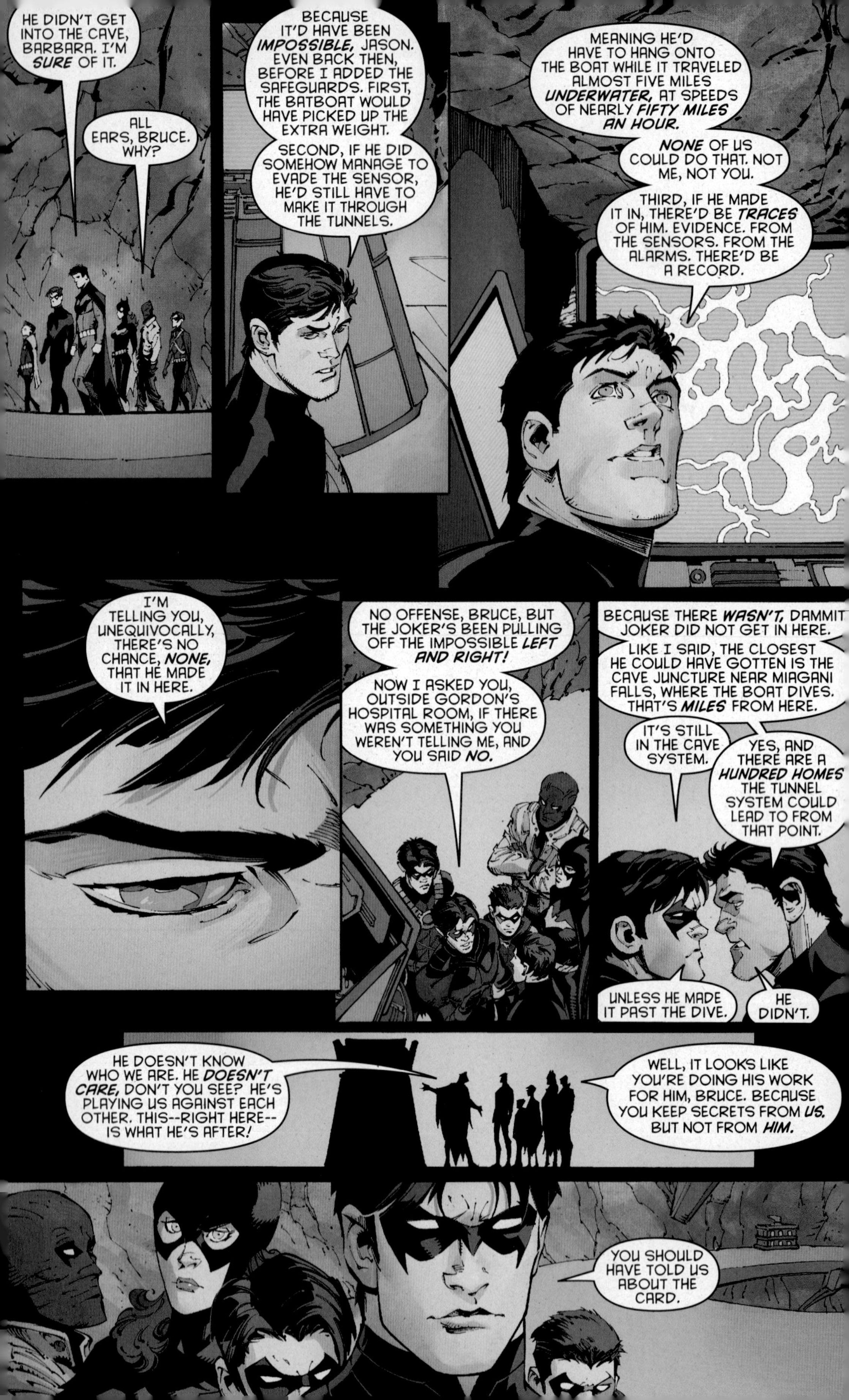
HE DIDN'T GET INTO THE CAVE, BARBARA. I'M *SURE* OF IT.
ALL EARS, BRUCE. WHY?
BECAUSE IT'D HAVE BEEN *IMPOSSIBLE,* JASON. EVEN BACK THEN, BEFORE I ADDED THE SAFEGUARDS. FIRST, THE BATBOAT WOULD HAVE PICKED UP THE EXTRA WEIGHT.
SECOND, IF HE DID SOMEHOW MANAGE TO EVADE THE SENSOR, HE'D STILL HAVE TO MAKE IT THROUGH THE TUNNELS.
MEANING HE'D HAVE TO HANG ONTO THE BOAT WHILE IT TRAVELED ALMOST FIVE MILES *UNDERWATER,* AT SPEEDS OF NEARLY *FIFTY MILES AN HOUR.*
NONE OF US COULD DO THAT. NOT ME, NOT YOU.
THIRD, IF HE MADE IT IN, THERE'D BE *TRACES* OF HIM. EVIDENCE. FROM THE SENSORS. FROM THE ALARMS. THERE'D BE A RECORD.
I'M TELLING YOU, UNEQUIVOCALLY, THERE'S NO CHANCE, *NONE,* THAT HE MADE IT IN HERE.
NO OFFENSE, BRUCE, BUT THE JOKER'S BEEN PULLING OFF THE IMPOSSIBLE *LEFT AND RIGHT!*
NOW I ASKED YOU, OUTSIDE GORDON'S HOSPITAL ROOM, IF THERE WAS SOMETHING YOU WEREN'T TELLING ME, AND YOU SAID *NO.*
BECAUSE THERE *WASN'T,* DAMMIT JOKER DID NOT GET IN HERE.
LIKE I SAID, THE CLOSEST HE COULD HAVE GOTTEN IS THE CAVE JUNCTURE NEAR MIAGANI FALLS, WHERE THE BOAT DIVES. THAT'S *MILES* FROM HERE.
IT'S STILL IN THE CAVE SYSTEM.
YES, AND THERE ARE A *HUNDRED HOMES* THE TUNNEL SYSTEM COULD LEAD TO FROM THAT POINT.
UNLESS HE MADE IT PAST THE DIVE.
HE DIDN'T.
HE DOESN'T KNOW WHO WE ARE. HE *DOESN'T CARE,* DON'T YOU SEE? HE'S PLAYING US AGAINST EACH OTHER. THIS--RIGHT HERE-- IS WHAT HE'S AFTER!
WELL, IT LOOKS LIKE YOU'RE DOING HIS WORK FOR HIM, BRUCE. BECAUSE YOU KEEP SECRETS FROM *US.* BUT NOT FROM *HIM.*
YOU SHOULD HAVE TOLD US ABOUT THE CARD.

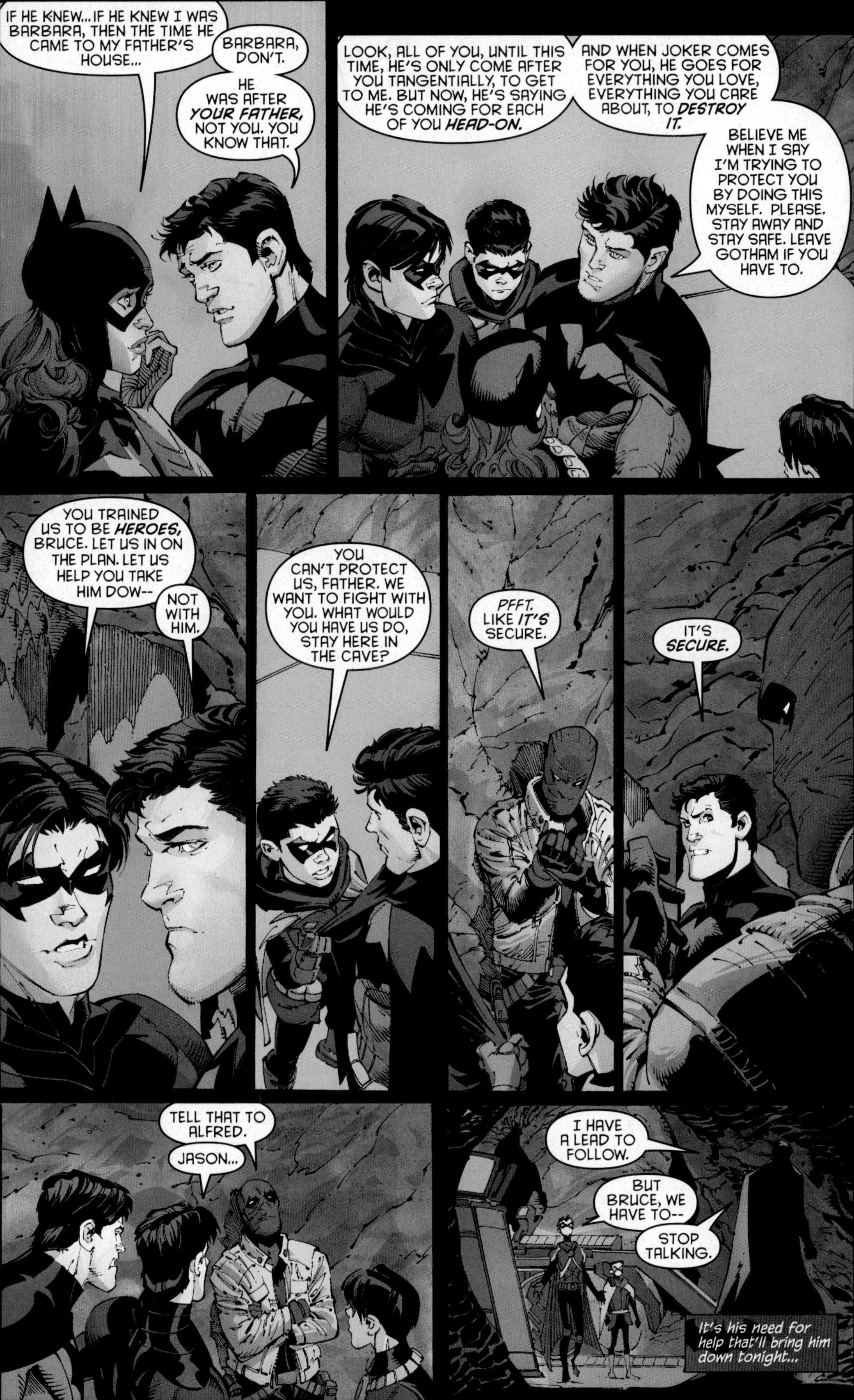
IF HE KNEW... IF HE KNEW I WAS BARBARA, THEN THE TIME HE CAME TO MY FATHER'S HOUSE...
BARBARA, DON'T.
HE WAS AFTER *YOUR FATHER,* NOT YOU. YOU KNOW THAT.
LOOK, ALL OF YOU, UNTIL THIS TIME, HE'S ONLY COME AFTER YOU TANGENTIALLY, TO GET TO ME. BUT NOW, HE'S SAYING HE'S COMING FOR EACH OF YOU *HEAD-ON.*
AND WHEN JOKER COMES FOR YOU, HE GOES FOR EVERYTHING YOU LOVE, EVERYTHING YOU CARE ABOUT, TO *DESTROY IT.*
BELIEVE ME WHEN I SAY I'M TRYING TO PROTECT YOU BY DOING THIS MYSELF. PLEASE. STAY AWAY AND STAY SAFE. LEAVE GOTHAM IF YOU HAVE TO.
YOU TRAINED US TO BE *HEROES,* BRUCE. LET US IN ON THE PLAN. LET US HELP YOU TAKE HIM DOW--
NOT WITH HIM.
YOU CAN'T PROTECT US, FATHER. WE WANT TO FIGHT WITH YOU. WHAT WOULD YOU HAVE US DO, STAY HERE IN THE CAVE?
PFFT. LIKE *IT'S* SECURE.
IT'S *SECURE.*
TELL THAT TO ALFRED.
JASON...
I HAVE A LEAD TO FOLLOW.
BUT BRUCE, WE HAVE TO--
STOP TALKING.
It's his need for help that'll bring him down tonight...

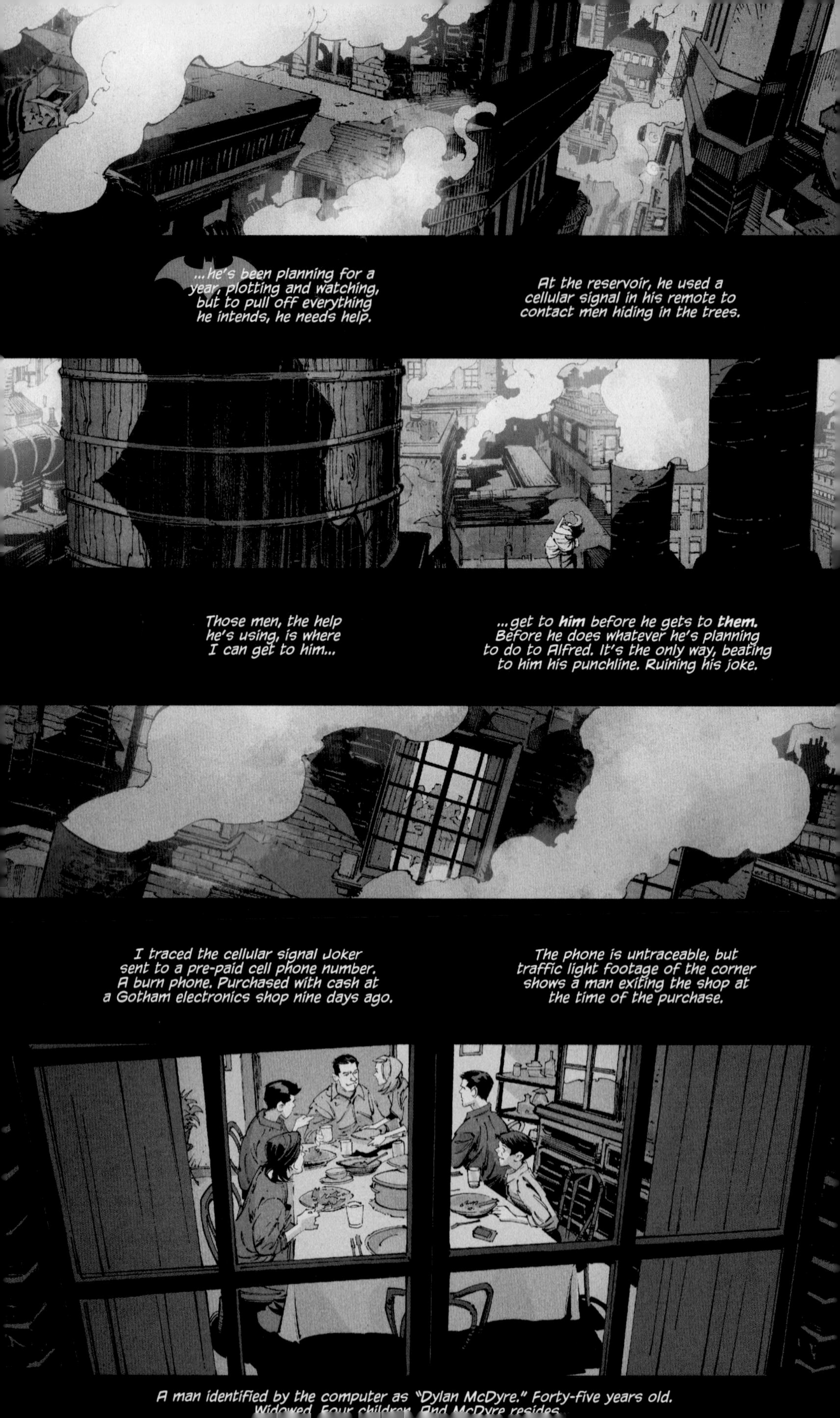
...he's been planning for a year, plotting and watching, but to pull off everything he intends, he needs help.
At the reservoir, he used a cellular signal in his remote to contact men hiding in the trees.
Those men, the help he's using, is where I can get to him...
...get to **him** before he gets to **them.** Before he does whatever he's planning to do to Alfred. It's the only way, beating to him his punchline. Ruining his joke.
I traced the cellular signal Joker sent to a pre-paid cell phone number. A burn phone. Purchased with cash at a Gotham electronics shop nine days ago.
The phone is untraceable, but traffic light footage of the corner shows a man exiting the shop at the time of the purchase.
A man identified by the computer as "Dylan McDyre." Forty-five years old.
Widowed. Four children. And McDyre resides

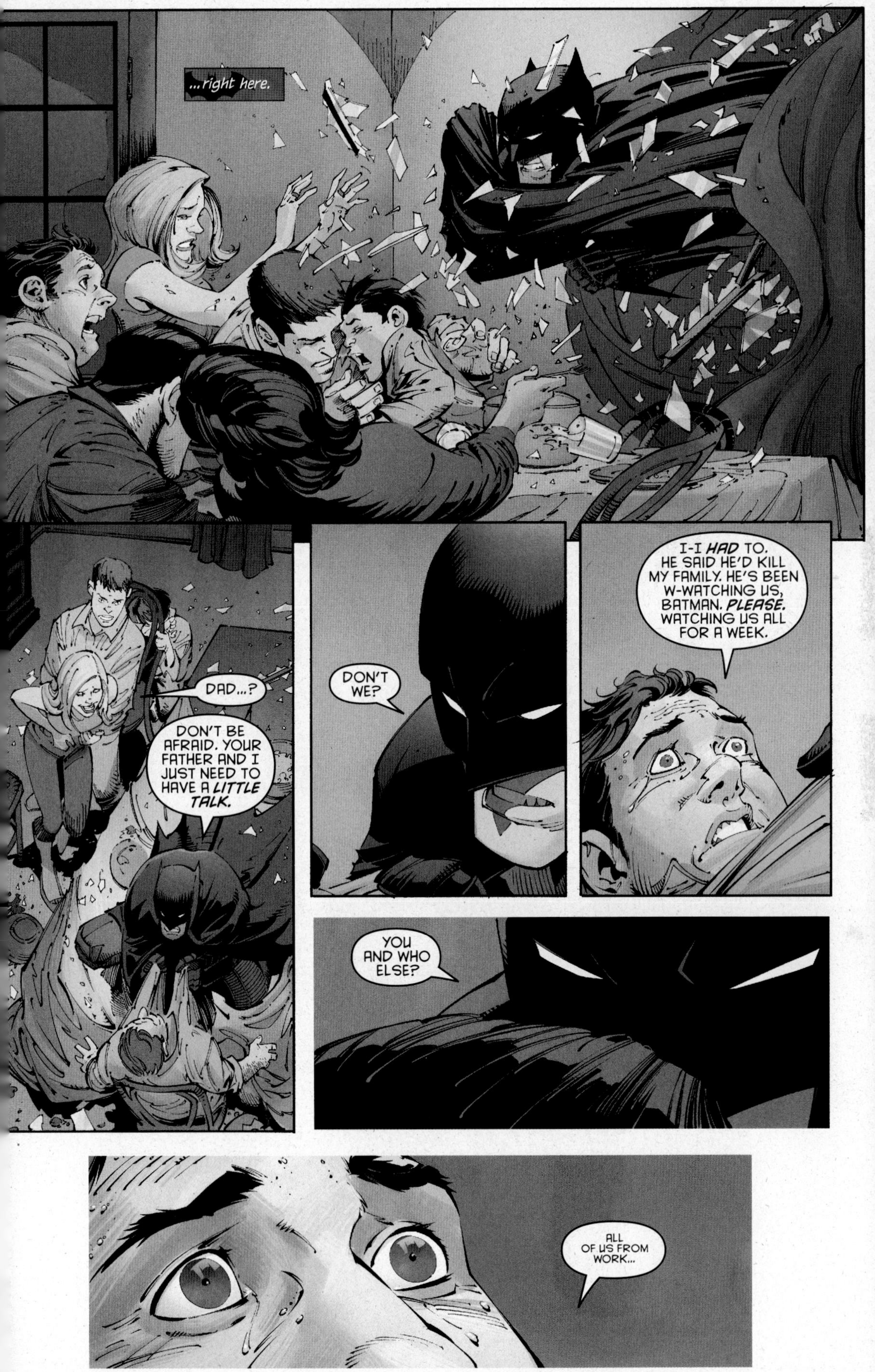
...right here.
DAD...?
DON'T BE AFRAID. YOUR FATHER AND I JUST NEED TO HAVE A *LITTLE TALK.*
DON'T WE?
I-I *HAD* TO. HE SAID HE'D KILL MY FAMILY. HE'S BEEN W-WATCHING US, BATMAN. *PLEASE.* WATCHING US ALL FOR A WEEK.
YOU AND WHO ELSE?
ALL OF US FROM WORK...

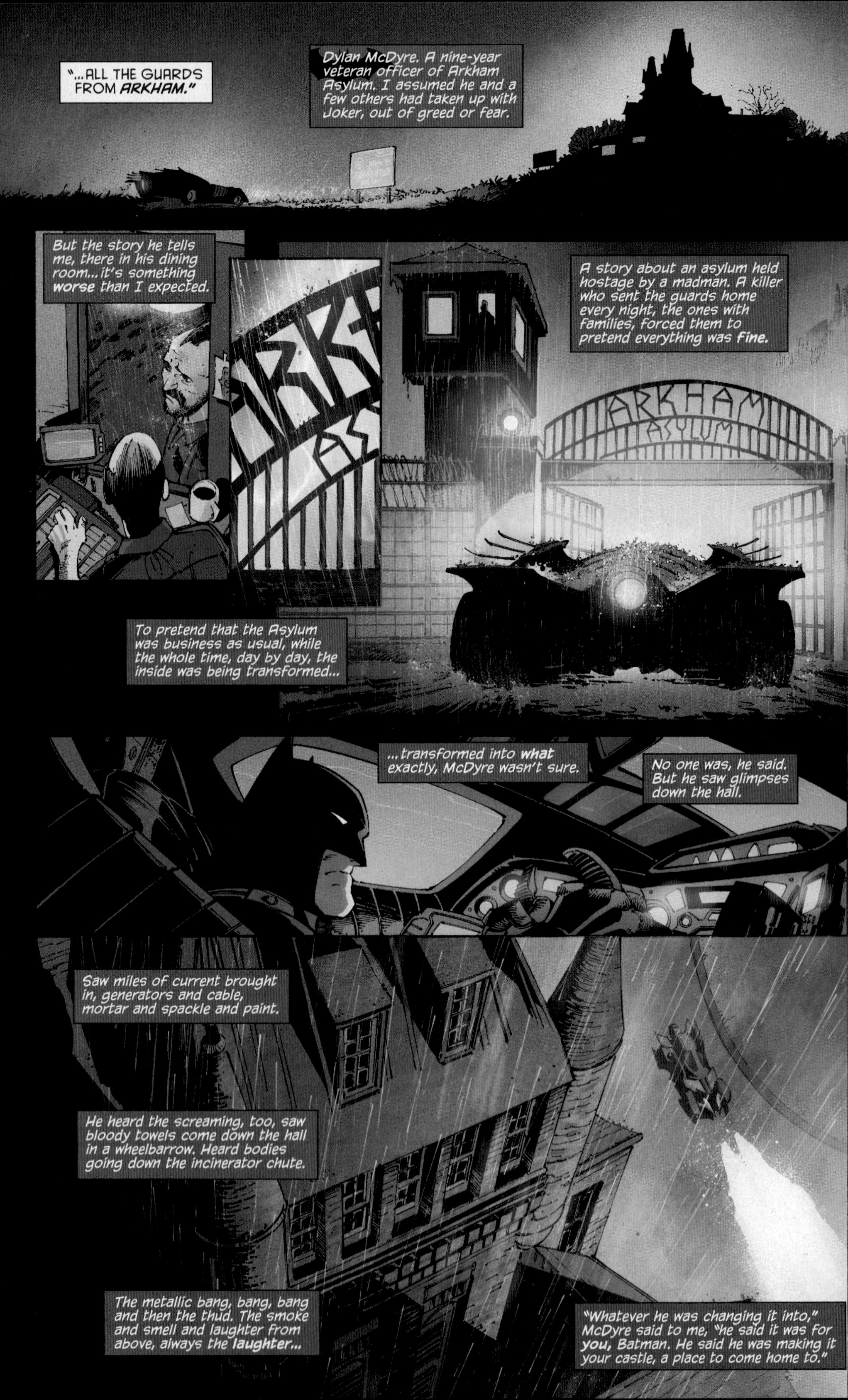
"...ALL THE GUARDS FROM ARKHAM."
Dylan McDyre. A nine-year veteran officer of Arkham Asylum. I assumed he and a few others had taken up with Joker, out of greed or fear.
But the story he tells me, there in his dining room... it's something worse than I expected.
A story about an asylum held hostage by a madman. A killer who sent the guards home every night, the ones with families, forced them to pretend everything was fine.
ARKHAM ASYLUM
To pretend that the Asylum was business as usual, while the whole time, day by day, the inside was being transformed...
...transformed into what exactly, McDyre wasn't sure.
No one was, he said. But he saw glimpses down the hall.
Saw miles of current brought in, generators and cable, mortar and spackle and paint.
He heard the screaming, too, saw bloody towels come down the hall in a wheelbarrow. Heard bodies going down the incinerator chute.
The metallic bang, bang, bang and then the thud. The smoke and smell and laughter from above, always the laughter...
"Whatever he was changing it into," McDyre said to me, "he said it was for you, Batman. He said he was making it your castle, a place to come home to."

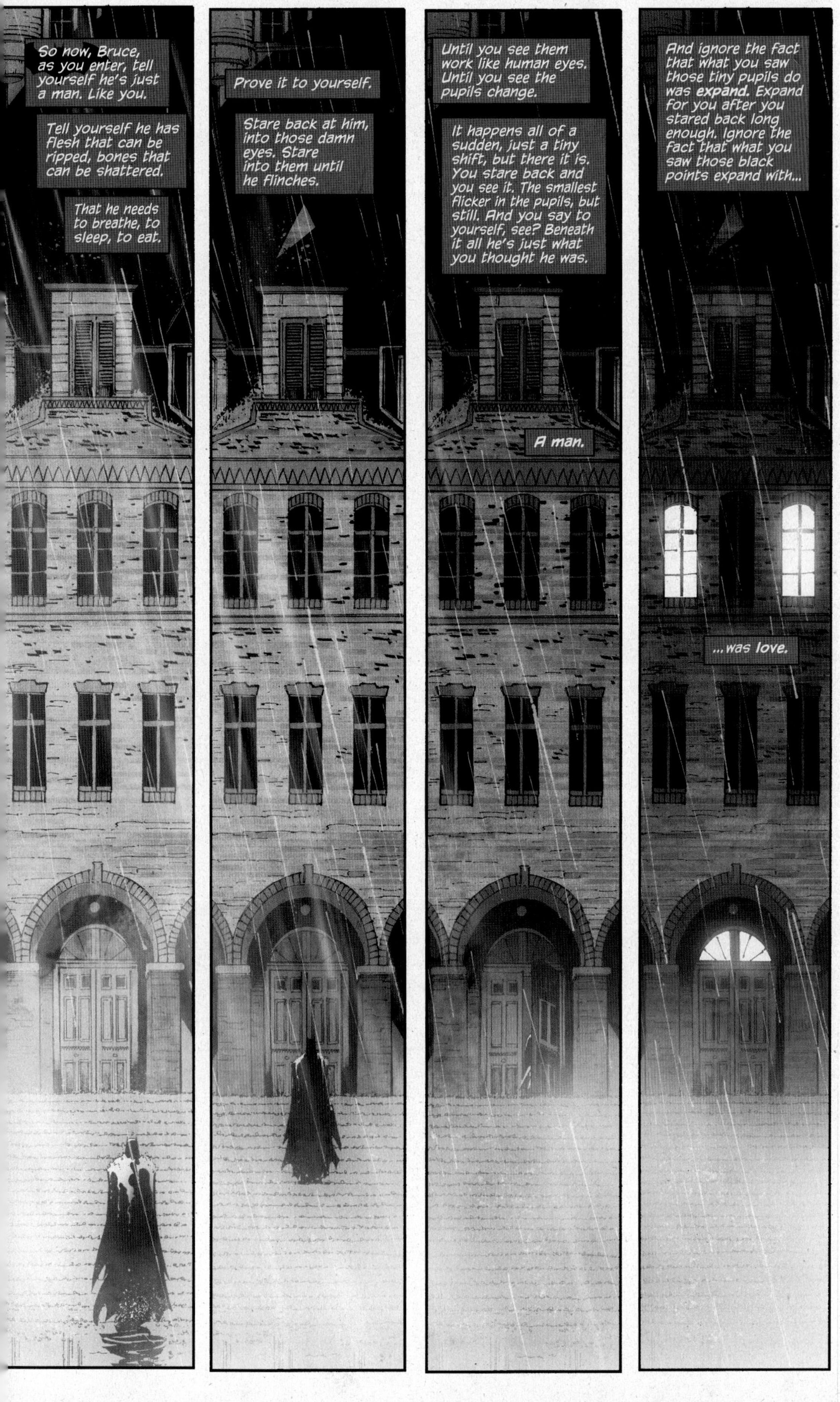

So now, Bruce, as you enter, tell yourself he's just a man. Like you.
Tell yourself he has flesh that can be ripped, bones that can be shattered.
That he needs to breathe, to sleep, to eat.
Prove it to yourself.
Stare back at him, into those damn eyes. Stare into them until he flinches.
Until you see them work like human eyes. Until you see the pupils change.
It happens all of a sudden, just a tiny shift, but there it is. You stare back and you see it. The smallest flicker in the pupils, but still. And you say to yourself, see? Beneath it all he's just what you thought he was.
A man.
And ignore the fact that what you saw those tiny pupils do was **expand.** Expand for you after you stared back long enough. Ignore the fact that what you saw those black points expand with...
...was **love.**

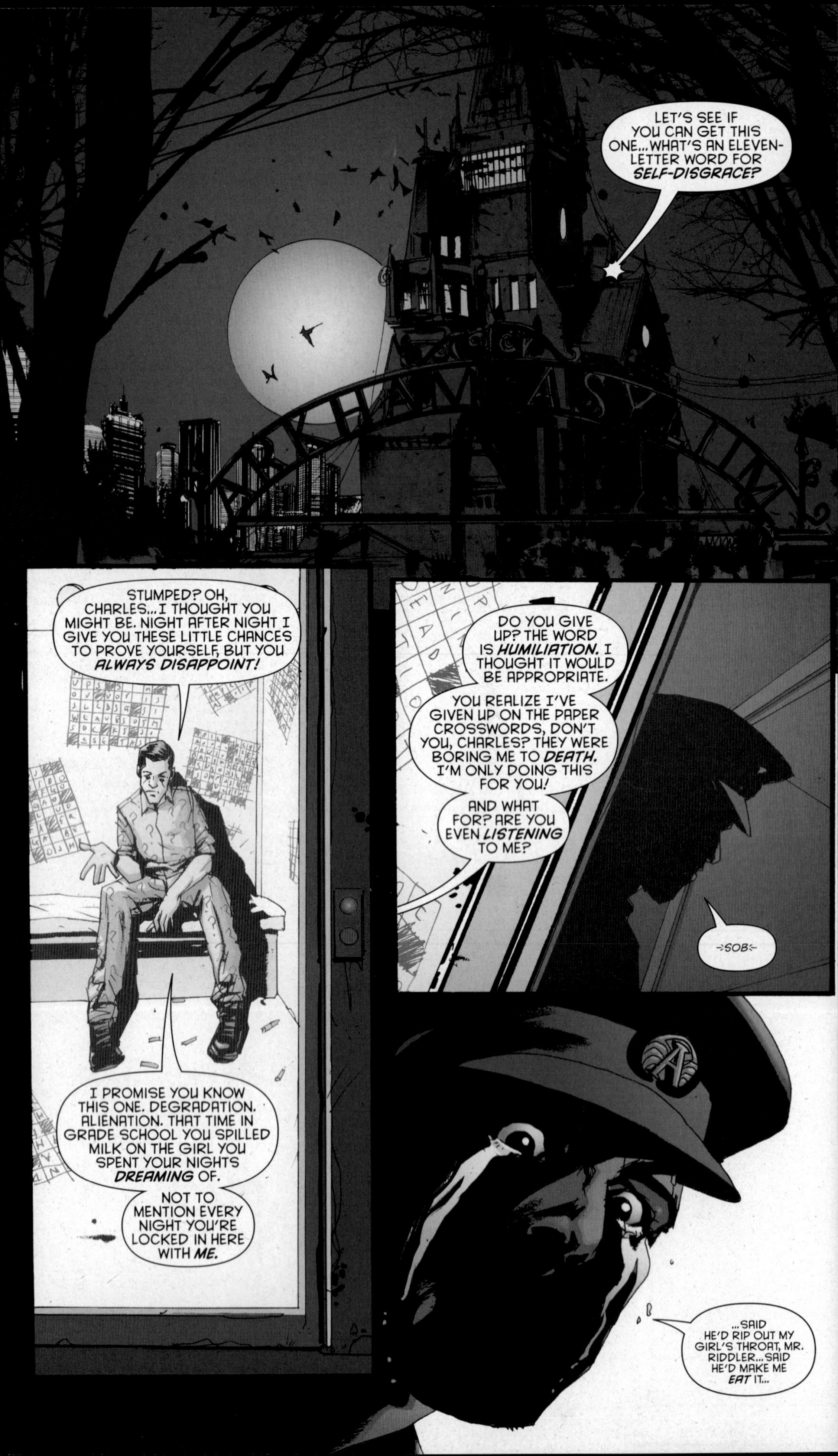
LET'S SEE IF YOU CAN GET THIS ONE... WHAT'S AN ELEVEN-LETTER WORD FOR SELF-DISGRACE?
STUMPED? OH, CHARLES... I THOUGHT YOU MIGHT BE. NIGHT AFTER NIGHT I GIVE YOU THESE LITTLE CHANCES TO PROVE YOURSELF, BUT YOU ALWAYS DISAPPOINT!
I PROMISE YOU KNOW THIS ONE. DEGRADATION. ALIENATION. THAT TIME IN GRADE SCHOOL YOU SPILLED MILK ON THE GIRL YOU SPENT YOUR NIGHTS DREAMING OF.
NOT TO MENTION EVERY NIGHT YOU'RE LOCKED IN HERE WITH ME.
DO YOU GIVE UP? THE WORD IS HUMILIATION. I THOUGHT IT WOULD BE APPROPRIATE.
YOU REALIZE I'VE GIVEN UP ON THE PAPER CROSSWORDS, DON'T YOU, CHARLES? THEY WERE BORING ME TO DEATH. I'M ONLY DOING THIS FOR YOU!
AND WHAT FOR? ARE YOU EVEN LISTENING TO ME?
SOB
...SAID HE'D RIP OUT MY GIRL'S THROAT, MR. RIDDLER... SAID HE'D MAKE ME EAT IT...

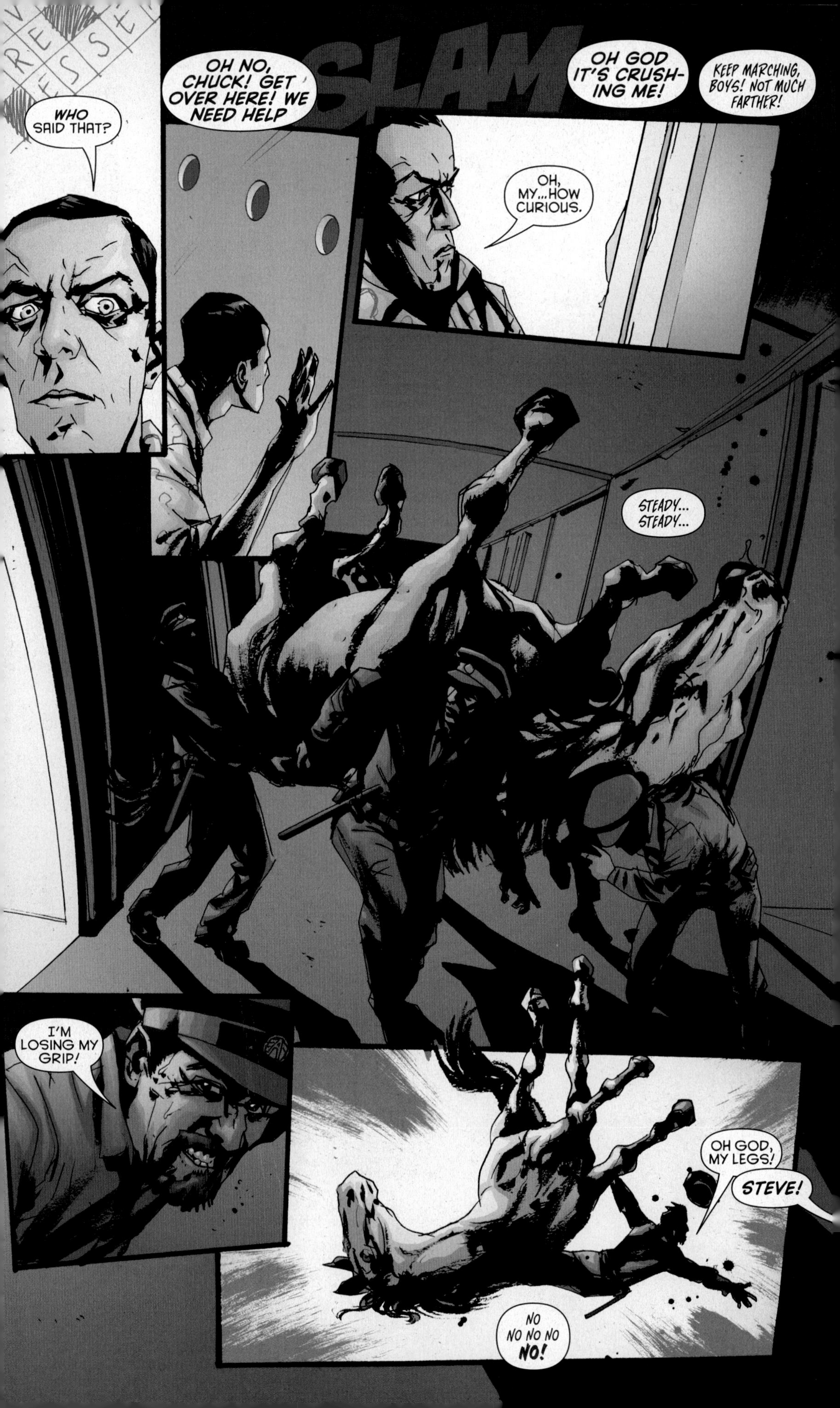

WHO SAID THAT?
OH NO, CHUCK! GET OVER HERE! WE NEED HELP
SLAM
OH GOD IT'S CRUSHING ME!
KEEP MARCHING, BOYS! NOT MUCH FARTHER!
OH, MY...HOW CURIOUS.
STEADY... STEADY...
I'M LOSING MY GRIP!
OH GOD, MY LEGS!
STEVE!
NO NO NO NO NO!

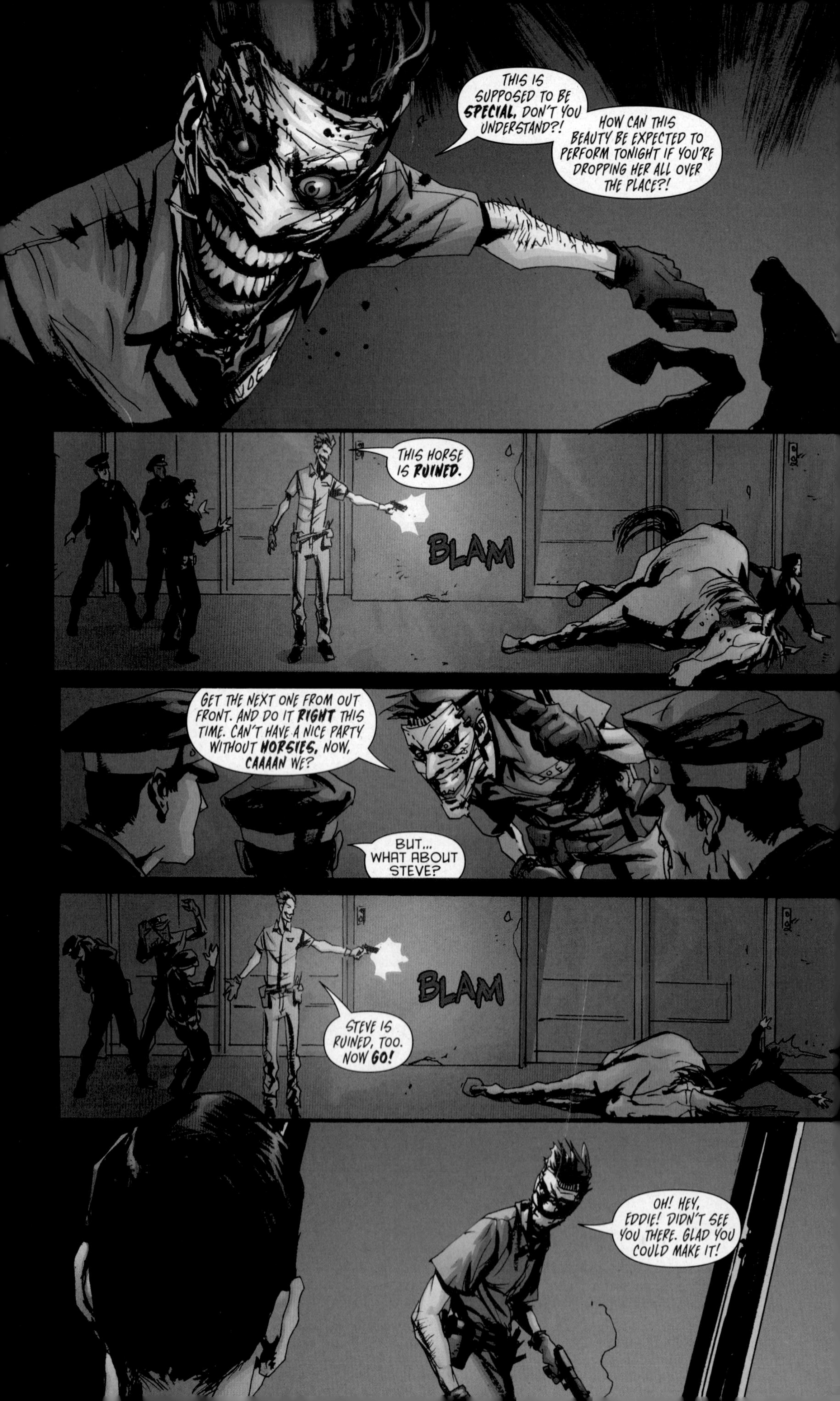
THIS IS SUPPOSED TO BE SPECIAL. DON'T YOU UNDERSTAND?!
HOW CAN THIS BEAUTY BE EXPECTED TO PERFORM TONIGHT IF YOU'RE DROPPING HER ALL OVER THE PLACE?!
THIS HORSE IS RUINED.
BLAM
GET THE NEXT ONE FROM OUT FRONT. AND DO IT RIGHT THIS TIME. CAN'T HAVE A NICE PARTY WITHOUT HORSIES. NOW, CAAAAN WE?
BUT... WHAT ABOUT STEVE?
BLAM
STEVE IS RUINED, TOO. NOW GO!
OH! HEY, EDDIE! DIDN'T SEE YOU THERE. GLAD YOU COULD MAKE IT!

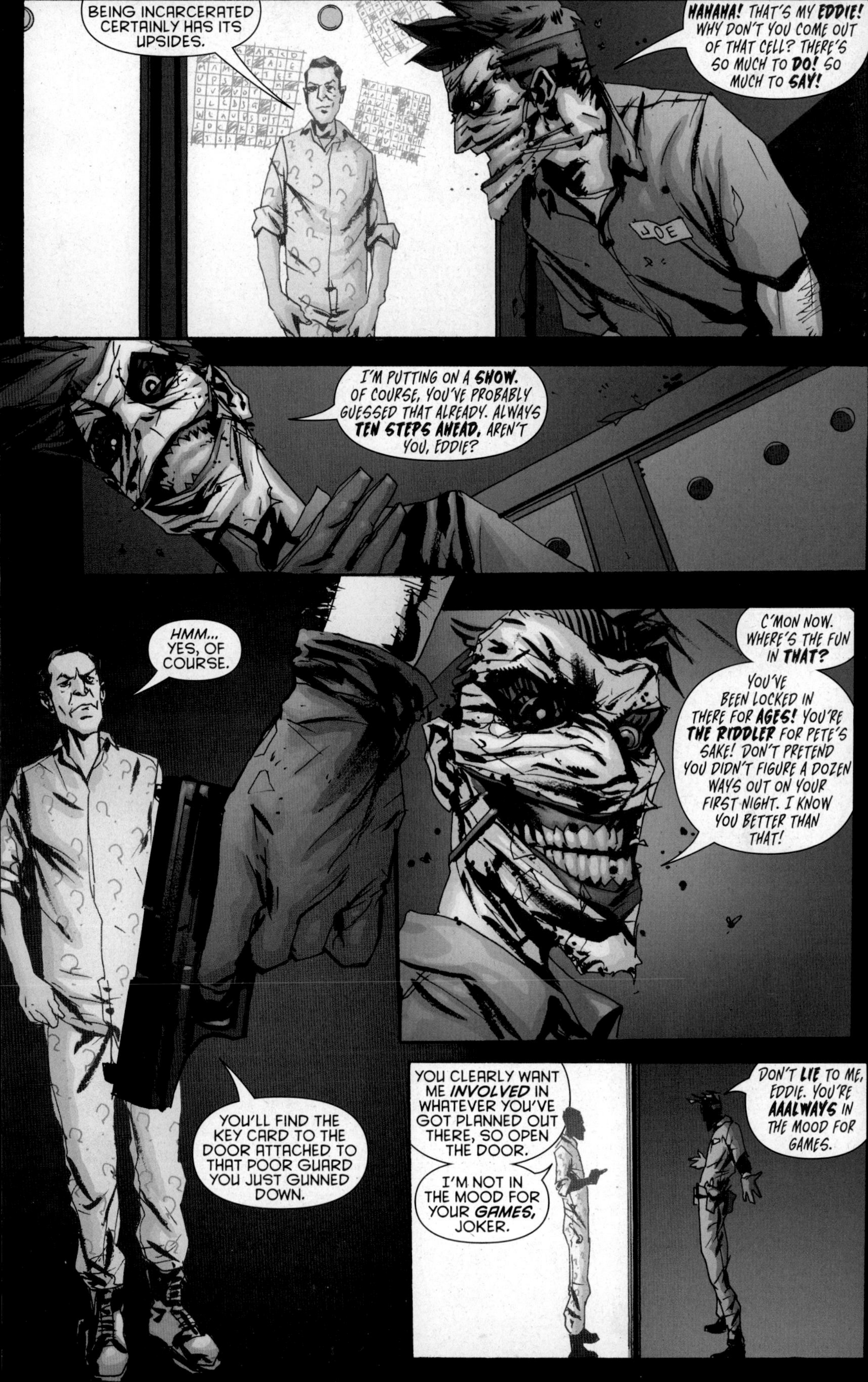
BEING INCARCERATED CERTAINLY HAS ITS UPSIDES.
HAHAHA! THAT'S MY EDDIE! WHY DON'T YOU COME OUT OF THAT CELL? THERE'S SO MUCH TO DO! SO MUCH TO SAY!
JOE
I'M PUTTING ON A SHOW. OF COURSE, YOU'VE PROBABLY GUESSED THAT ALREADY. ALWAYS TEN STEPS AHEAD, AREN'T YOU, EDDIE?
HMM... YES, OF COURSE.
C'MON NOW. WHERE'S THE FUN IN THAT?
YOU'VE BEEN LOCKED IN THERE FOR AGES! YOU'RE THE RIDDLER FOR PETE'S SAKE! DON'T PRETEND YOU DIDN'T FIGURE A DOZEN WAYS OUT ON YOUR FIRST NIGHT. I KNOW YOU BETTER THAN THAT!
YOU'LL FIND THE KEY CARD TO THE DOOR ATTACHED TO THAT POOR GUARD YOU JUST GUNNED DOWN.
YOU CLEARLY WANT ME INVOLVED IN WHATEVER YOU'VE GOT PLANNED OUT THERE, SO OPEN THE DOOR.
I'M NOT IN THE MOOD FOR YOUR GAMES, JOKER.
DON'T LIE TO ME, EDDIE. YOU'RE AAALWAYS IN THE MOOD FOR GAMES.

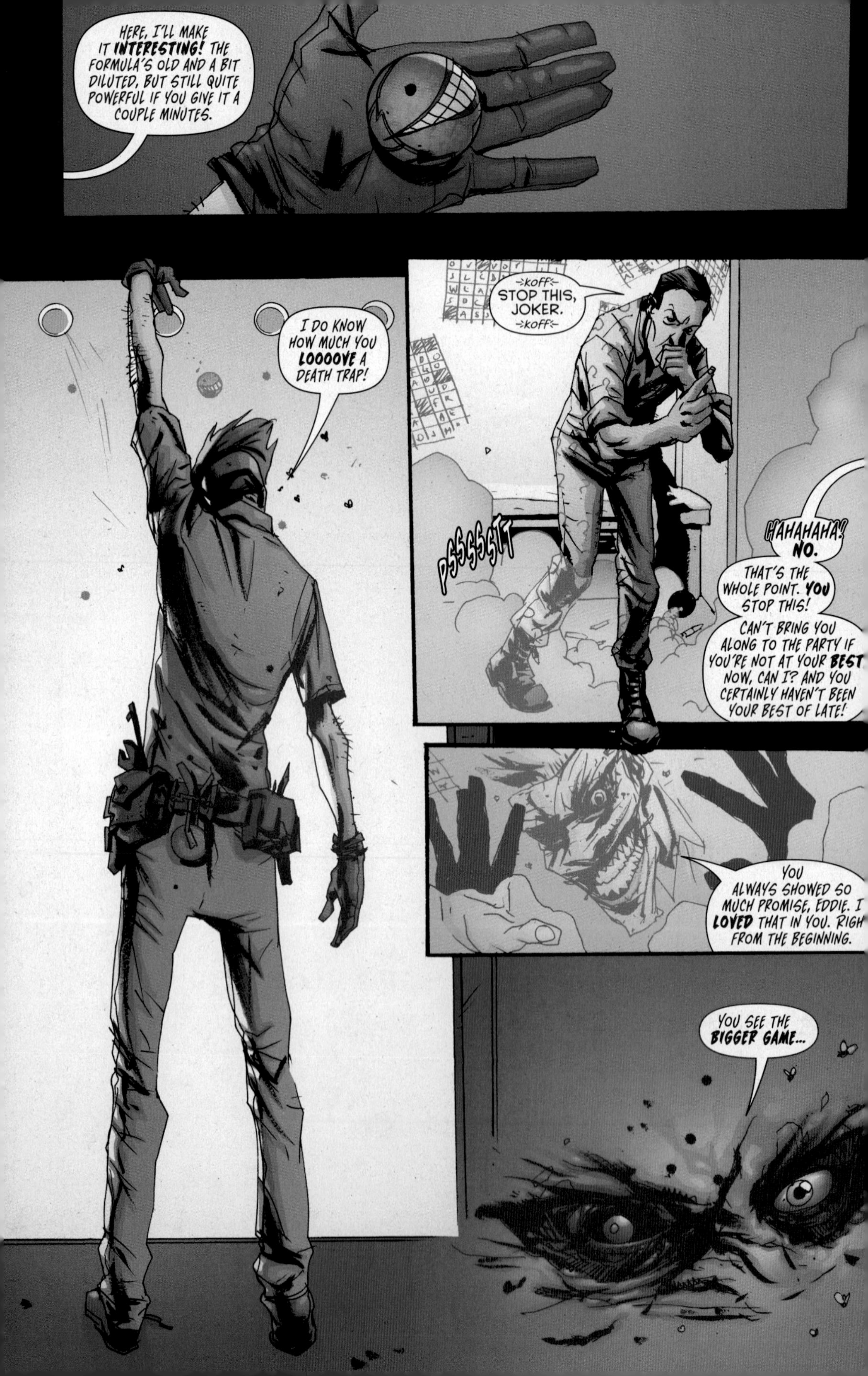
HERE, I'LL MAKE IT INTERESTING! THE FORMULA'S OLD AND A BIT DILUTED, BUT STILL QUITE POWERFUL IF YOU GIVE IT A COUPLE MINUTES.
I DO KNOW HOW MUCH YOU LOOOOVE A DEATH TRAP!
-koff- STOP THIS, JOKER. -koff-
PSSSSSTT
HAHAHAHA! NO.
THAT'S THE WHOLE POINT. YOU STOP THIS!
CAN'T BRING YOU ALONG TO THE PARTY IF YOU'RE NOT AT YOUR BEST NOW, CAN I? AND YOU CERTAINLY HAVEN'T BEEN YOUR BEST OF LATE!
YOU ALWAYS SHOWED SO MUCH PROMISE, EDDIE. I LOVED THAT IN YOU. RIGH FROM THE BEGINNING.
YOU SEE THE BIGGER GAME...

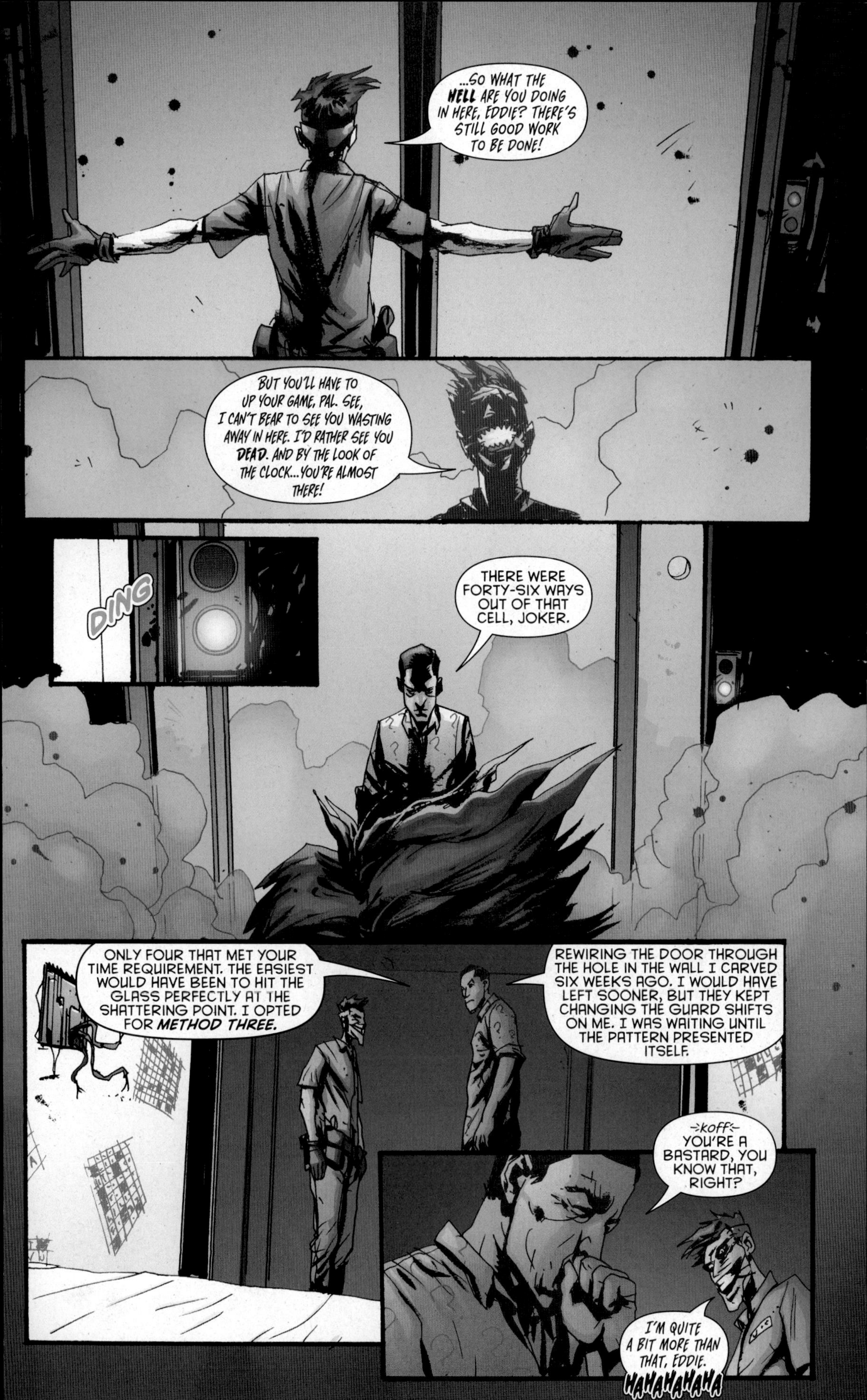
...SO WHAT THE **HELL** ARE YOU DOING IN HERE, EDDIE? THERE'S STILL GOOD WORK TO BE DONE!
BUT YOU'LL HAVE TO UP YOUR GAME, PAL. SEE, I CAN'T BEAR TO SEE YOU WASTING AWAY IN HERE. I'D RATHER SEE YOU **DEAD**. AND BY THE LOOK OF THE CLOCK...YOU'RE ALMOST THERE!
DING
THERE WERE FORTY-SIX WAYS OUT OF THAT CELL, JOKER.
ONLY FOUR THAT MET YOUR TIME REQUIREMENT. THE EASIEST WOULD HAVE BEEN TO HIT THE GLASS PERFECTLY AT THE SHATTERING POINT. I OPTED FOR ***METHOD THREE.***
REWIRING THE DOOR THROUGH THE HOLE IN THE WALL I CARVED SIX WEEKS AGO. I WOULD HAVE LEFT SOONER, BUT THEY KEPT CHANGING THE GUARD SHIFTS ON ME. I WAS WAITING UNTIL THE PATTERN PRESENTED ITSELF.
-koff- YOU'RE A BASTARD, YOU KNOW THAT, RIGHT?
I'M QUITE A BIT MORE THAN THAT, EDDIE.
HAHAHAHAHA

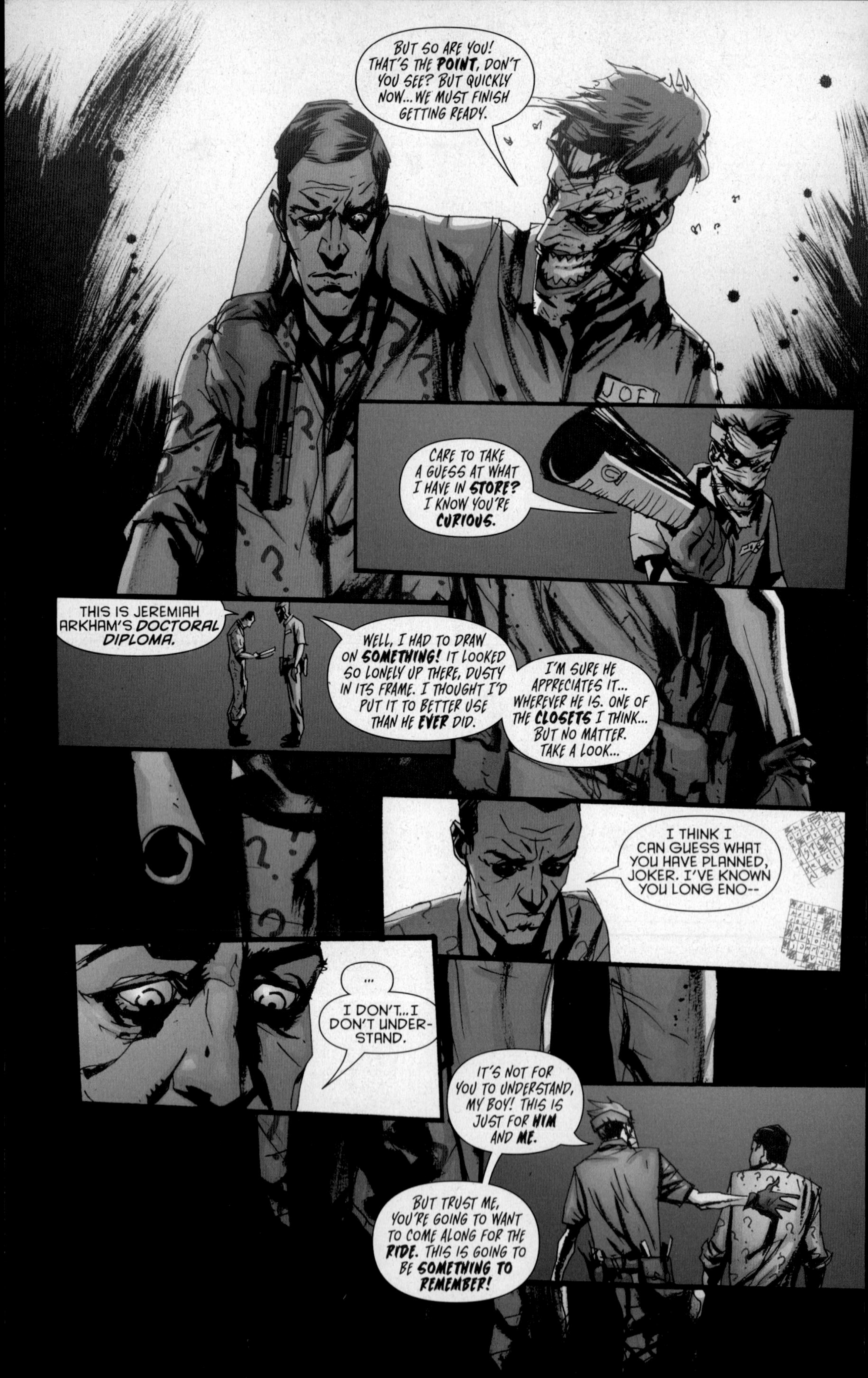
BUT SO ARE YOU! THAT'S THE POINT, DON'T YOU SEE? BUT QUICKLY NOW... WE MUST FINISH GETTING READY.
JOE
CARE TO TAKE A GUESS AT WHAT I HAVE IN STORE? I KNOW YOU'RE CURIOUS.
THIS IS JEREMIAH ARKHAM'S DOCTORAL DIPLOMA.
WELL, I HAD TO DRAW ON SOMETHING! IT LOOKED SO LONELY UP THERE, DUSTY IN ITS FRAME. I THOUGHT I'D PUT IT TO BETTER USE THAN HE EVER DID.
I'M SURE HE APPRECIATES IT... WHEREVER HE IS. ONE OF THE CLOSETS I THINK... BUT NO MATTER. TAKE A LOOK...
I THINK I CAN GUESS WHAT YOU HAVE PLANNED, JOKER. I'VE KNOWN YOU LONG ENO--
...
I DON'T... I DON'T UNDER-STAND.
IT'S NOT FOR YOU TO UNDERSTAND, MY BOY! THIS IS JUST FOR HIM AND ME.
BUT TRUST ME, YOU'RE GOING TO WANT TO COME ALONG FOR THE RIDE. THIS IS GOING TO BE SOMETHING TO REMEMBER!

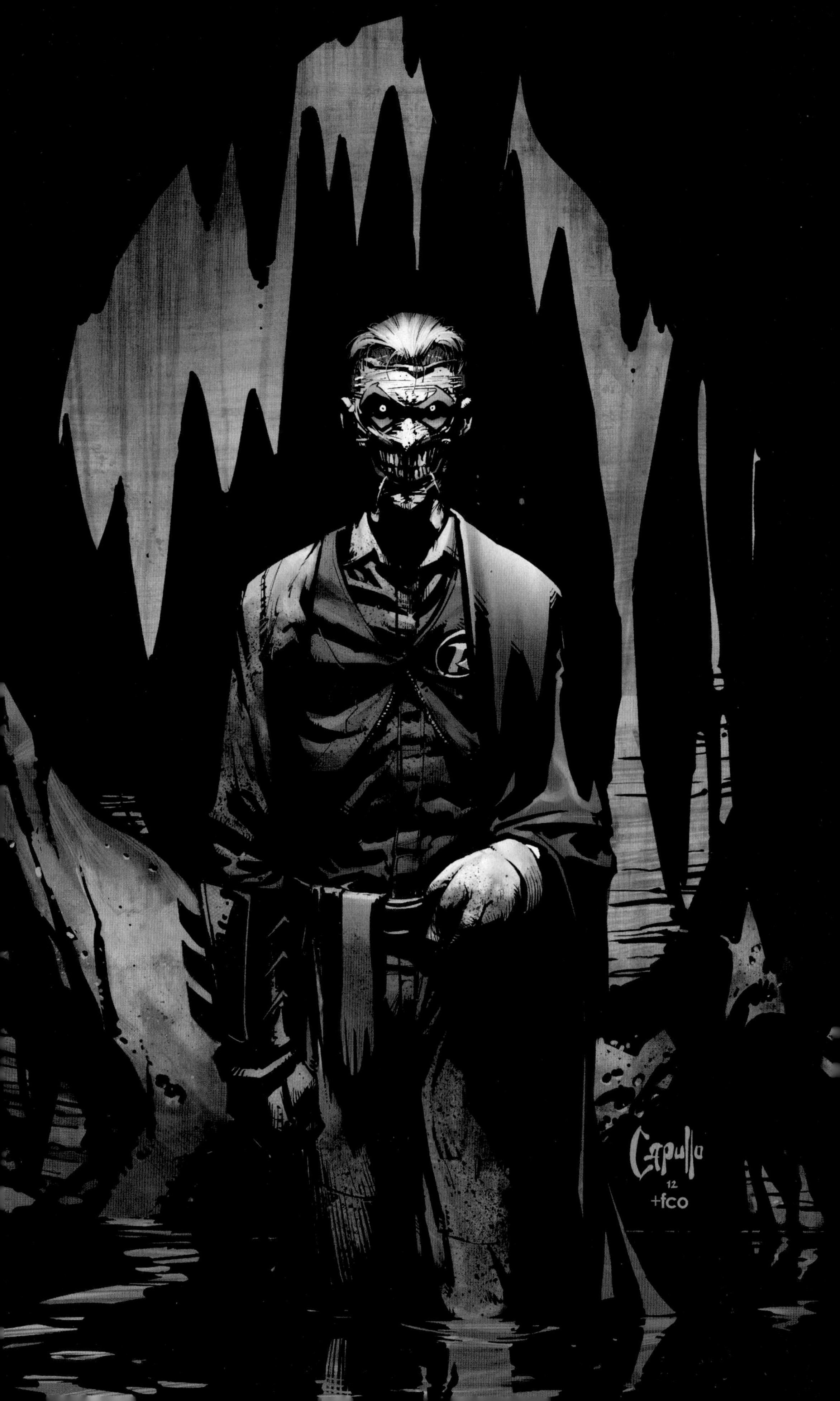
Capullo
12
+fco

CASTLE OF CARDS SCOTT SNYDER writer GREG CAPULLO penciller JONATHAN GLAPION inker
JUDGMENT SCOTT SNYDER & JAMES TYNION IV writers JOCK artist

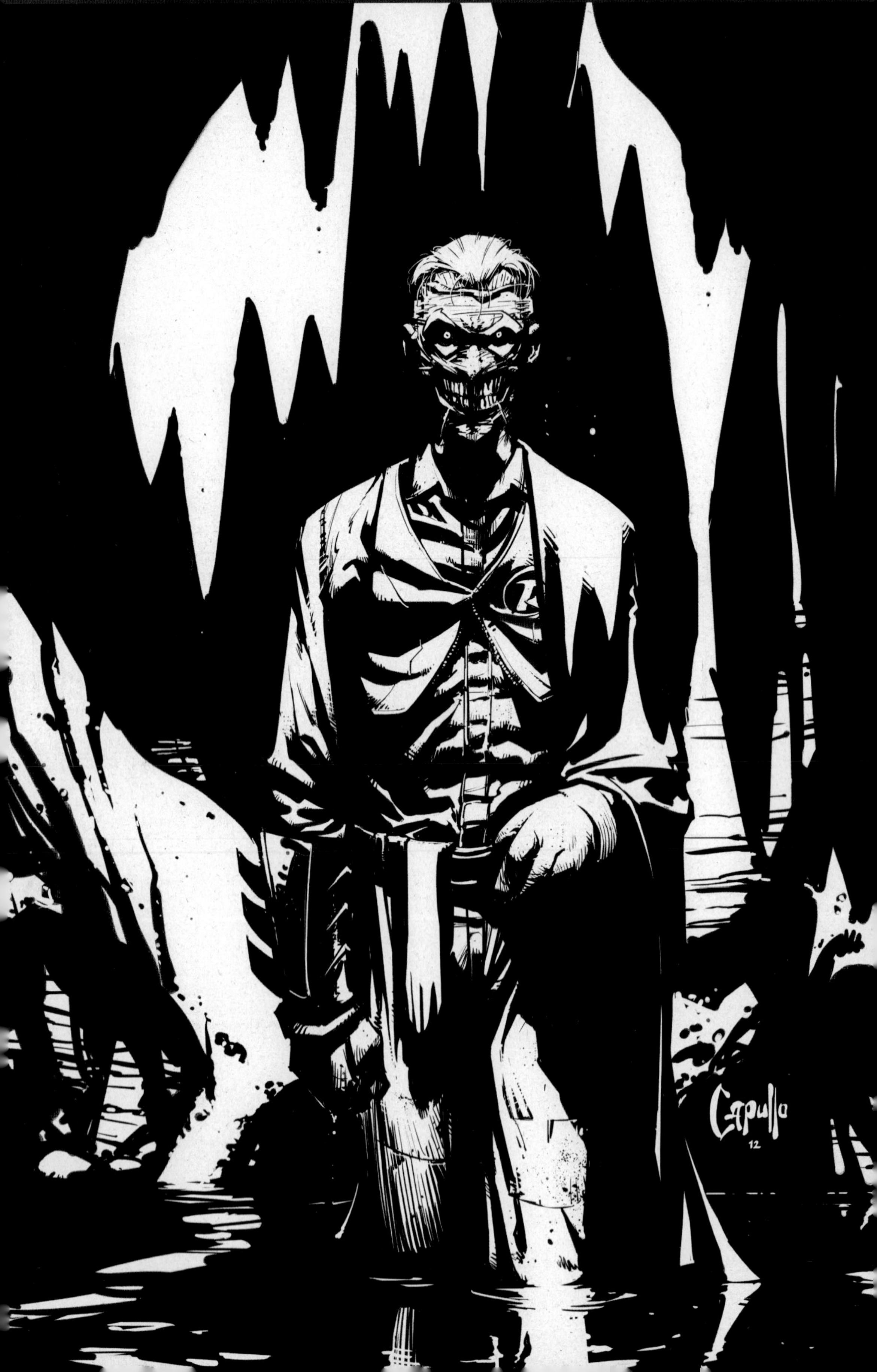

Capullo
12

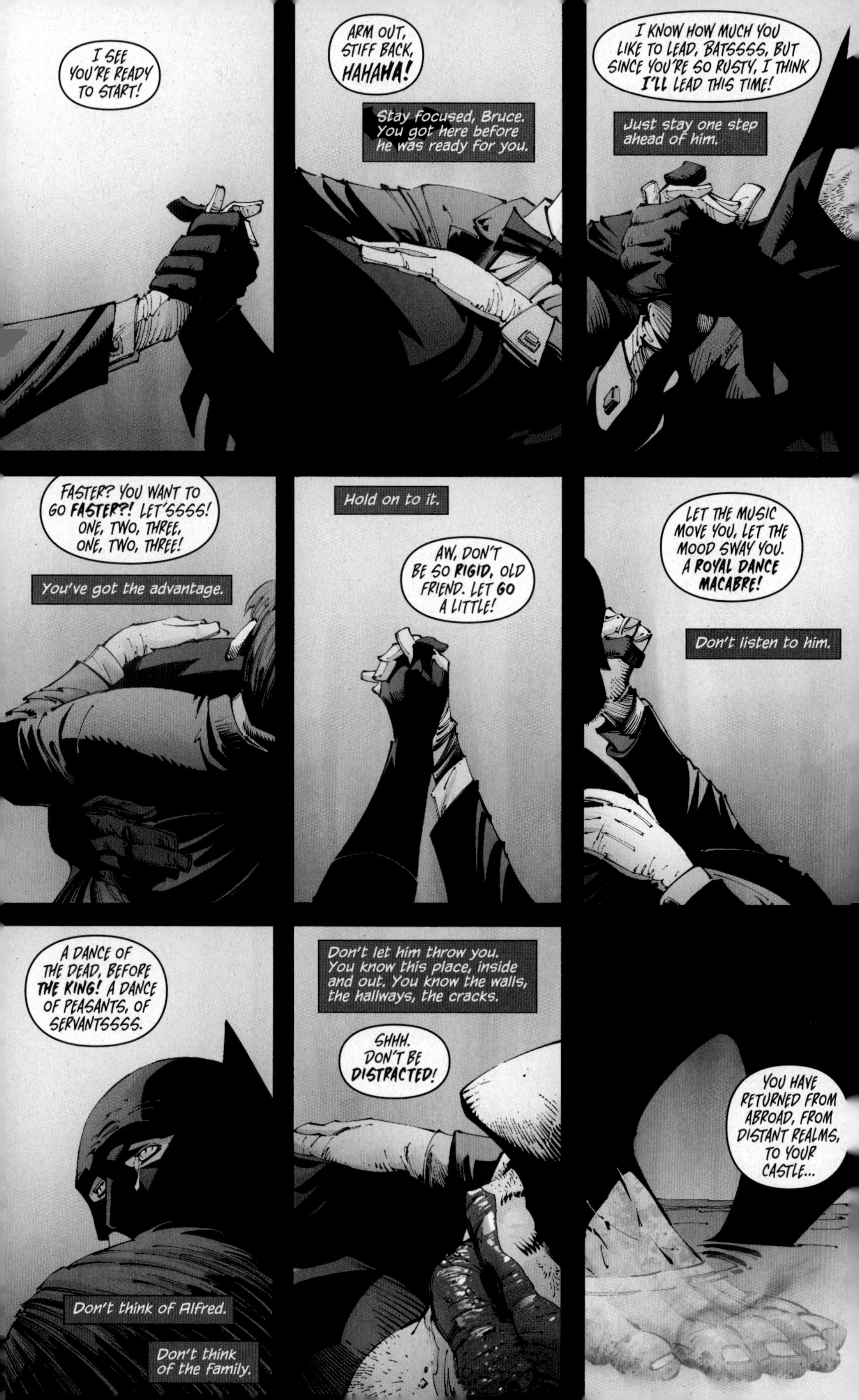
I SEE YOU'RE READY TO START!
ARM OUT, STIFF BACK, HAHAHA!
Stay focused, Bruce. You got here before he was ready for you.
I KNOW HOW MUCH YOU LIKE TO LEAD, BATSSSS, BUT SINCE YOU'RE SO RUSTY, I THINK I'LL LEAD THIS TIME!
Just stay one step ahead of him.
FASTER? YOU WANT TO GO FASTER?! LET'SSSS! ONE, TWO, THREE, ONE, TWO, THREE!
You've got the advantage.
Hold on to it.
AW, DON'T BE SO RIGID, OLD FRIEND. LET GO A LITTLE!
LET THE MUSIC MOVE YOU, LET THE MOOD SWAY YOU. A ROYAL DANCE MACABRE!
Don't listen to him.
A DANCE OF THE DEAD, BEFORE THE KING! A DANCE OF PEASANTS, OF SERVANTSSSS.
Don't think of Alfred.
Don't think of the family.
Don't let him throw you. You know this place, inside and out. You know the walls, the hallways, the cracks.
SHHH. DON'T BE DISTRACTED!
YOU HAVE RETURNED FROM ABROAD, FROM DISTANT REALMS, TO YOUR CASTLE...

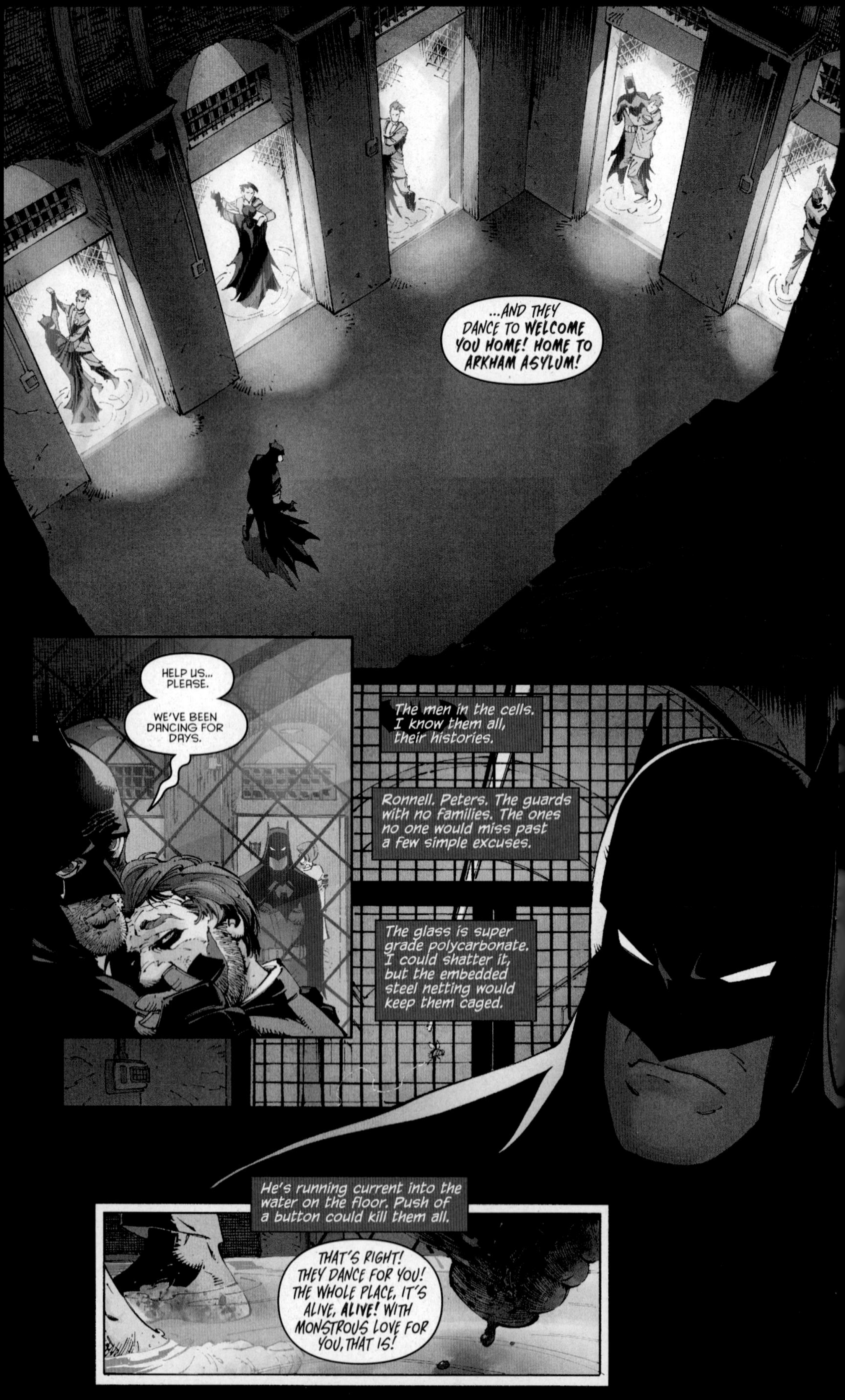

...AND THEY DANCE TO WELCOME YOU HOME! HOME TO ARKHAM ASYLUM!
HELP US... PLEASE.
WE'VE BEEN DANCING FOR DAYS.
The men in the cells. I know them all, their histories.
Ronnell. Peters. The guards with no families. The ones no one would miss past a few simple excuses.
The glass is super grade polycarbonate. I could shatter it, but the embedded steel netting would keep them caged.
He's running current into the water on the floor. Push of a button could kill them all.
THAT'S RIGHT! THEY DANCE FOR YOU! THE WHOLE PLACE, IT'S ALIVE, ALIVE! WITH MONSTROUS LOVE FOR YOU, THAT IS!

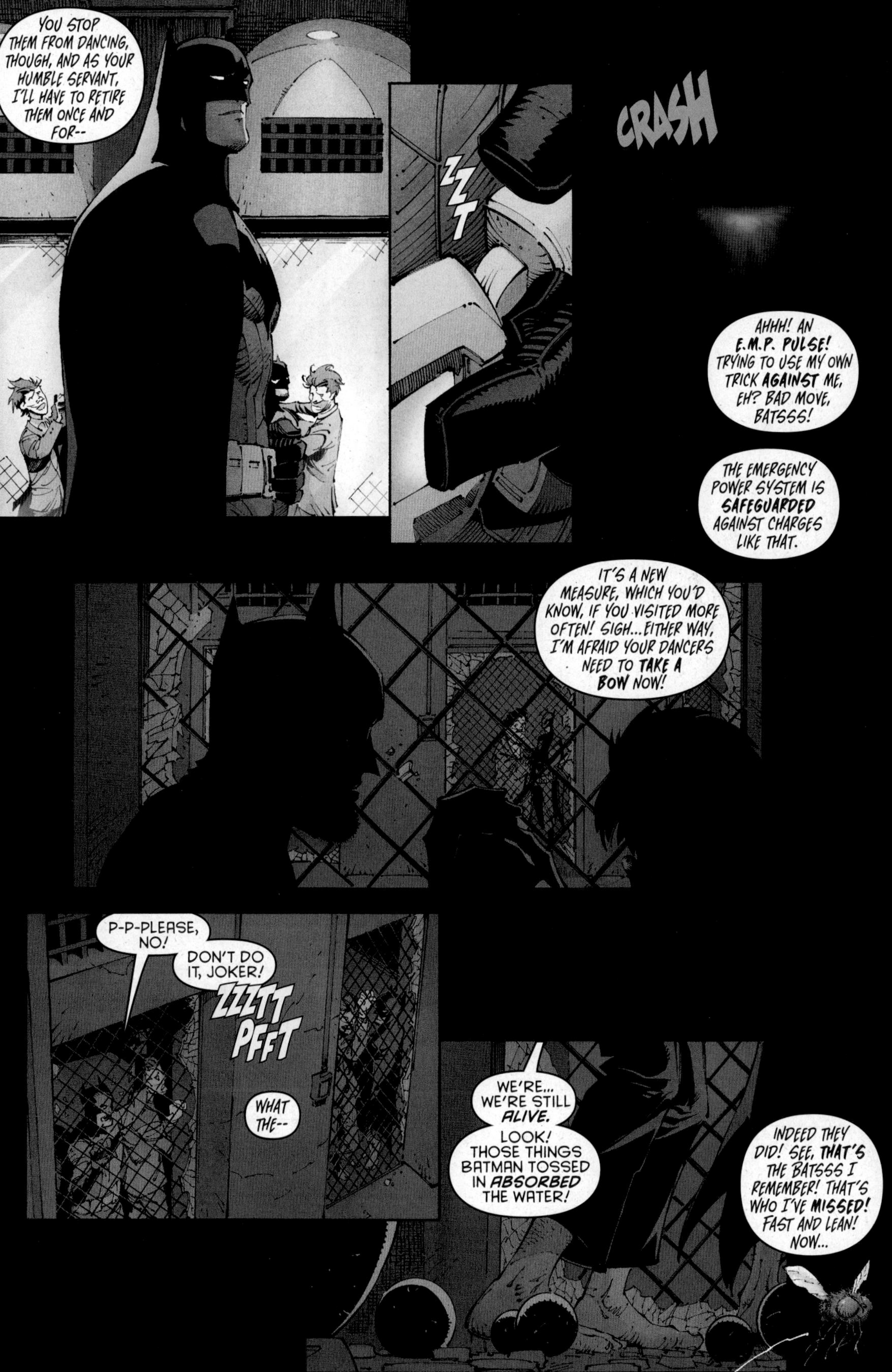
YOU STOP THEM FROM DANCING, THOUGH, AND AS YOUR HUMBLE SERVANT, I'LL HAVE TO RETIRE THEM ONCE AND FOR--
ZZT
CRASH
AHHH! AN E.M.P. PULSE! TRYING TO USE MY OWN TRICK AGAINST ME, EH? BAD MOVE, BATSSS!
THE EMERGENCY POWER SYSTEM IS SAFEGUARDED AGAINST CHARGES LIKE THAT.
IT'S A NEW MEASURE, WHICH YOU'D KNOW, IF YOU VISITED MORE OFTEN! SIGH...EITHER WAY, I'M AFRAID YOUR DANCERS NEED TO TAKE A BOW NOW!
P-P-PLEASE, NO!
DON'T DO IT, JOKER!
ZZZTT PFFT
WHAT THE--
WE'RE... WE'RE STILL ALIVE.
LOOK! THOSE THINGS BATMAN TOSSED IN ABSORBED THE WATER!
INDEED THEY DID! SEE, THAT'S THE BATSSS I REMEMBER! THAT'S WHO I'VE MISSED! FAST AND LEAN! NOW...

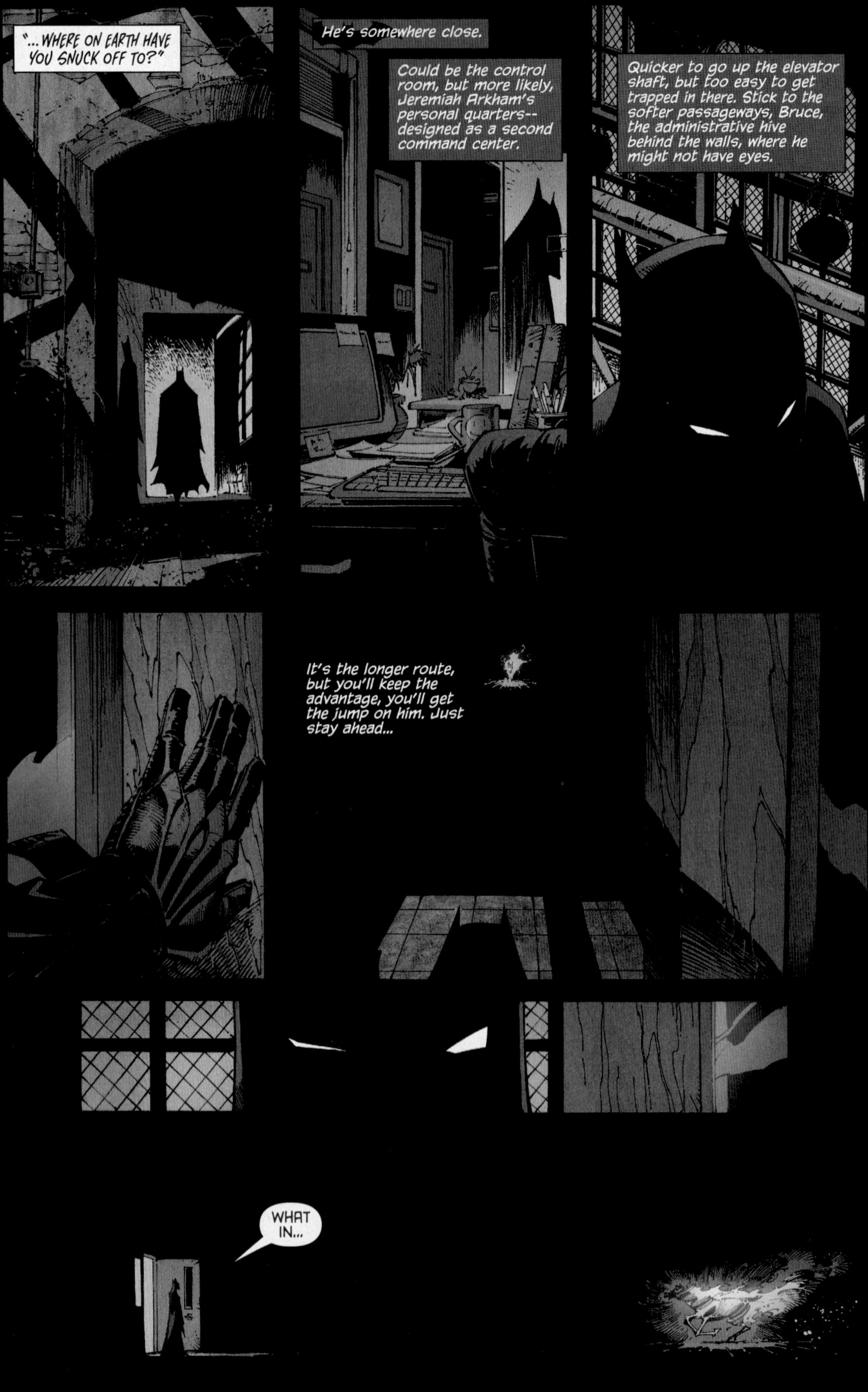
"...WHERE ON EARTH HAVE YOU SNUCK OFF TO?"
He's somewhere close.
Could be the control room, but more likely, Jeremiah Arkham's personal quarters-- designed as a second command center.
Quicker to go up the elevator shaft, but too easy to get trapped in there. Stick to the softer passageways, Bruce, the administrative hive behind the walls, where he might not have eyes.
It's the longer route, but you'll keep the advantage, you'll get the jump on him. Just stay ahead...
WHAT IN...

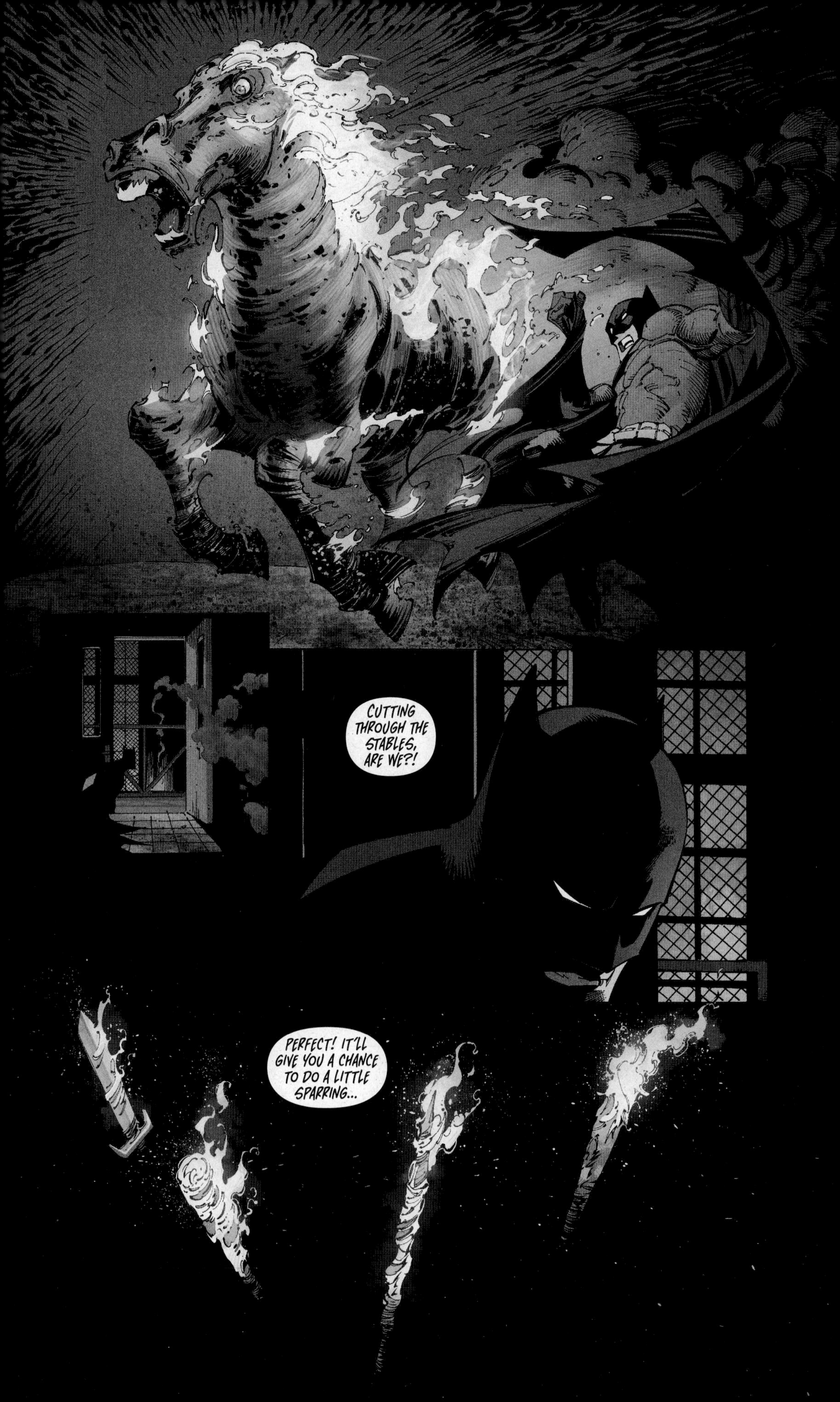
CUTTING THROUGH THE STABLES, ARE WE?!
PERFECT! IT'LL GIVE YOU A CHANCE TO DO A LITTLE SPARRING...

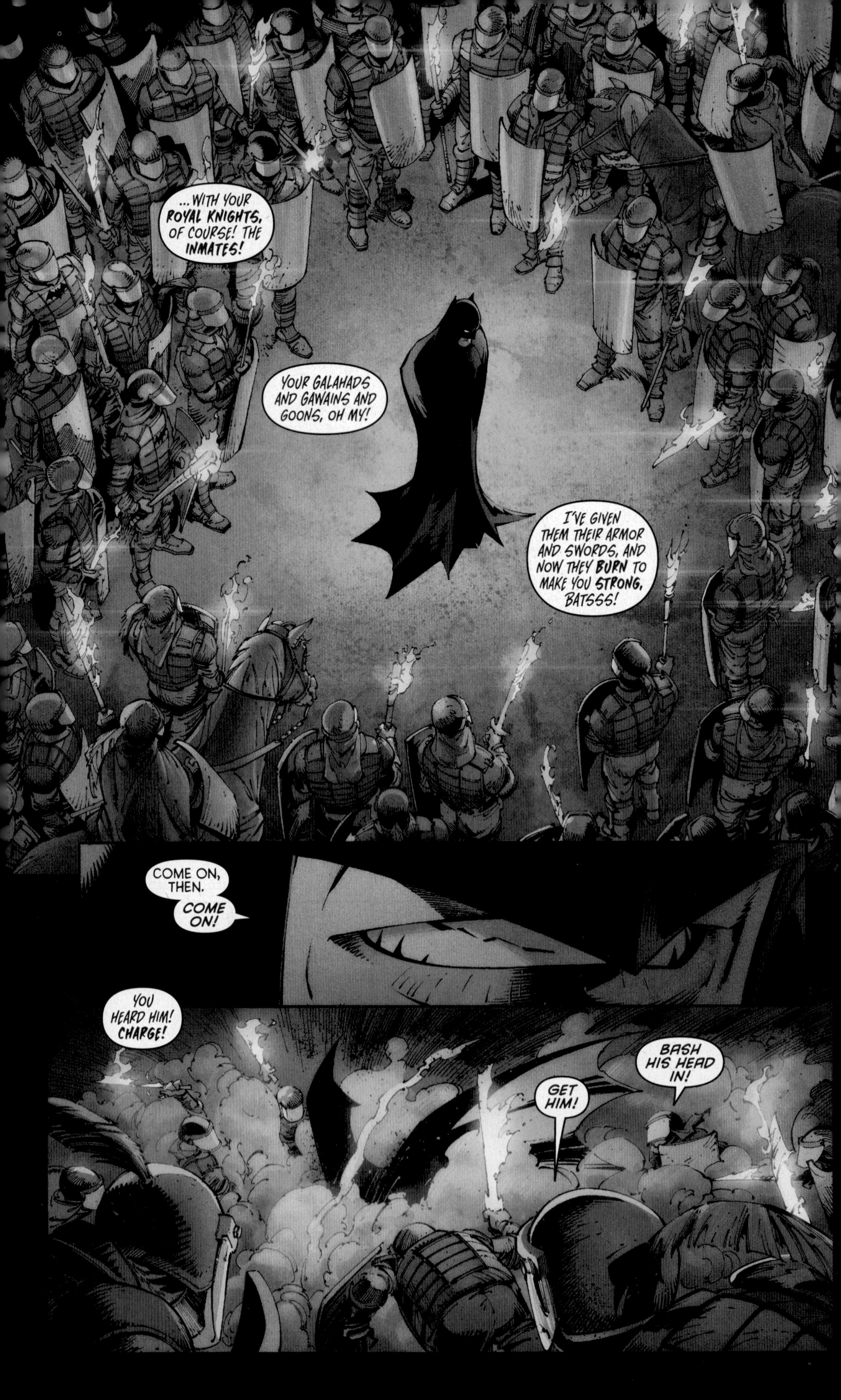
...WITH YOUR ROYAL KNIGHTS, OF COURSE! THE INMATES!
YOUR GALAHADS AND GAWAINS AND GOONS, OH MY!
I'VE GIVEN THEM THEIR ARMOR AND SWORDS, AND NOW THEY BURN TO MAKE YOU STRONG, BATSSS!
COME ON, THEN.
COME ON!
YOU HEARD HIM! CHARGE!
GET HIM!
BASH HIS HEAD IN!

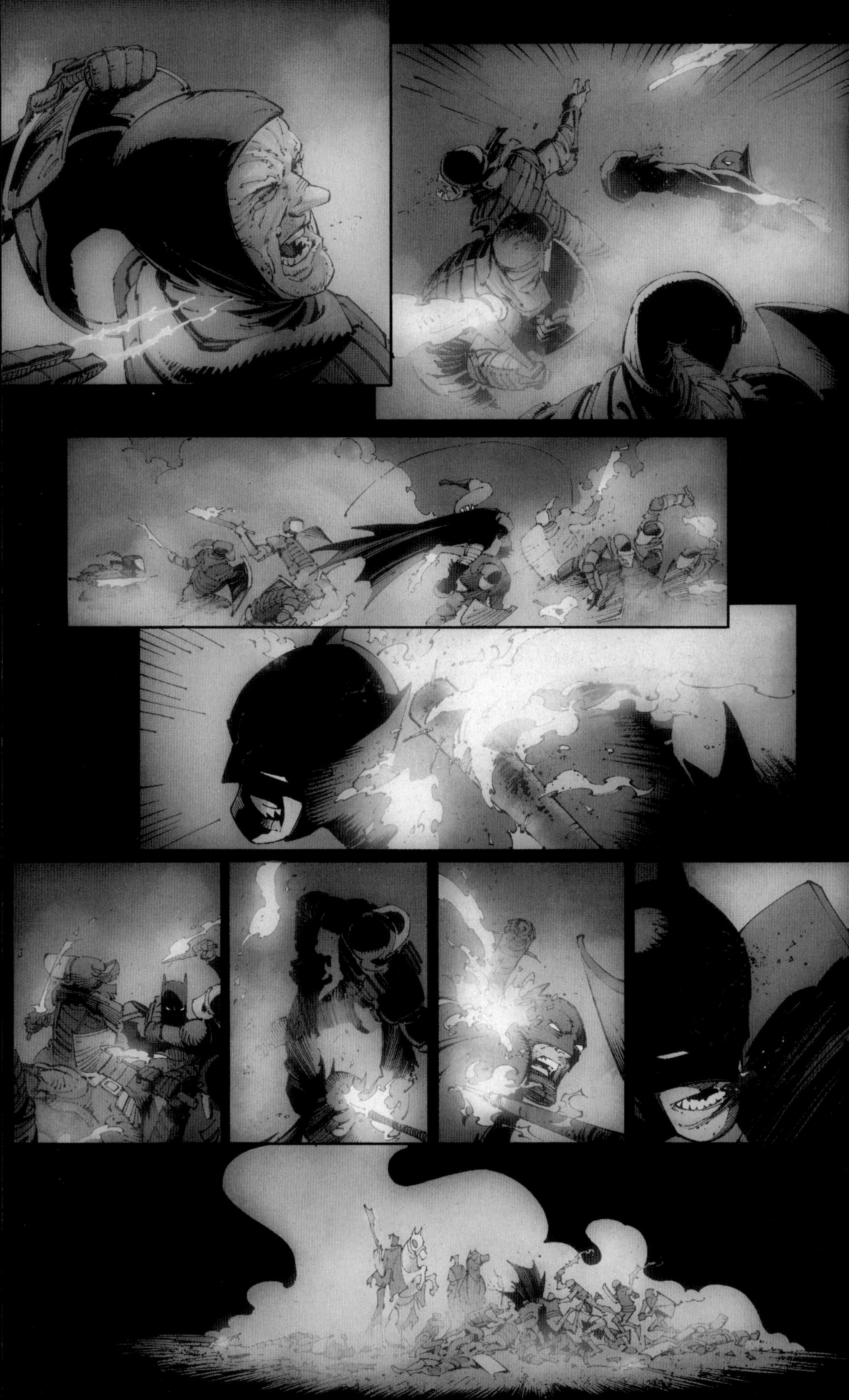

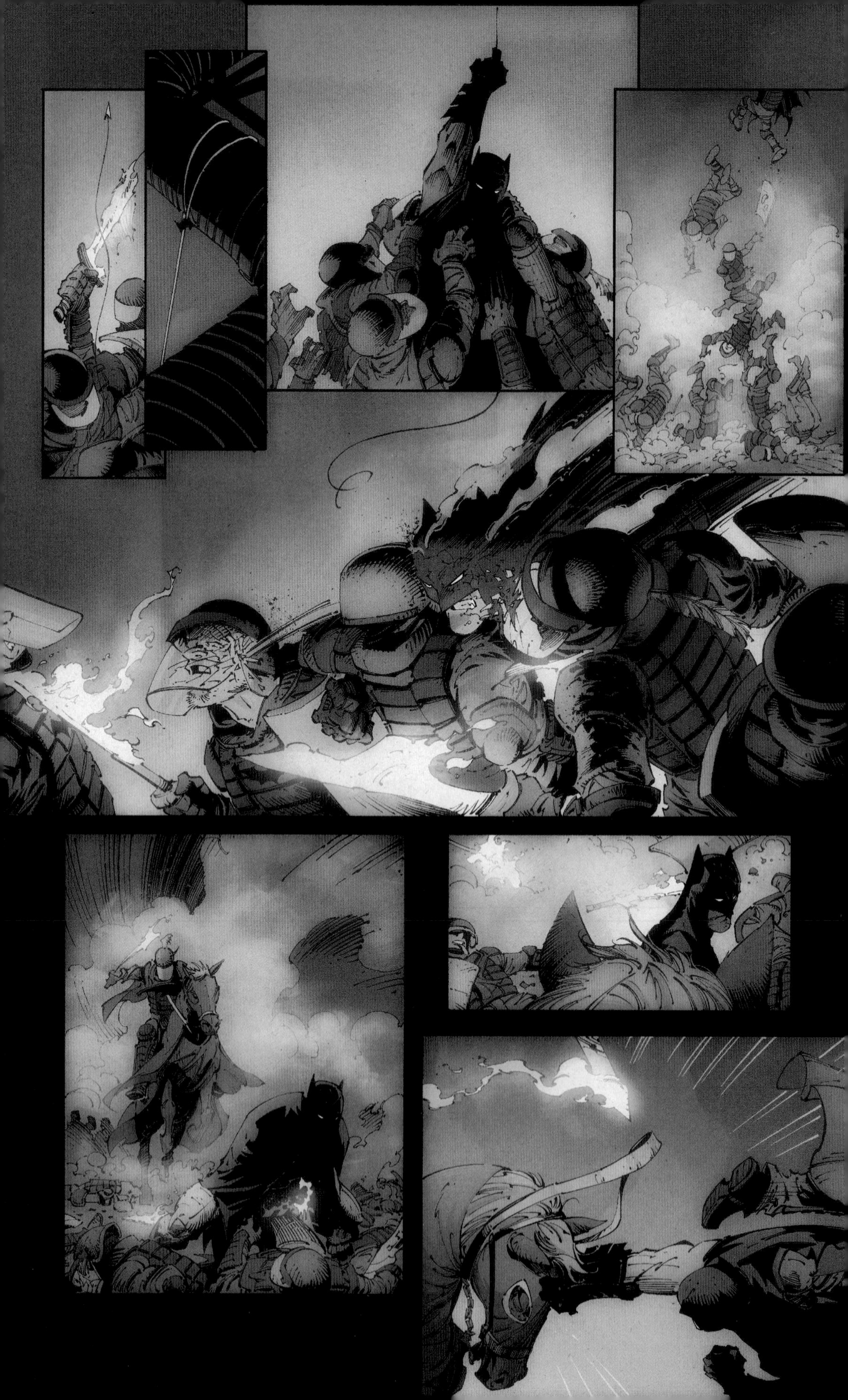

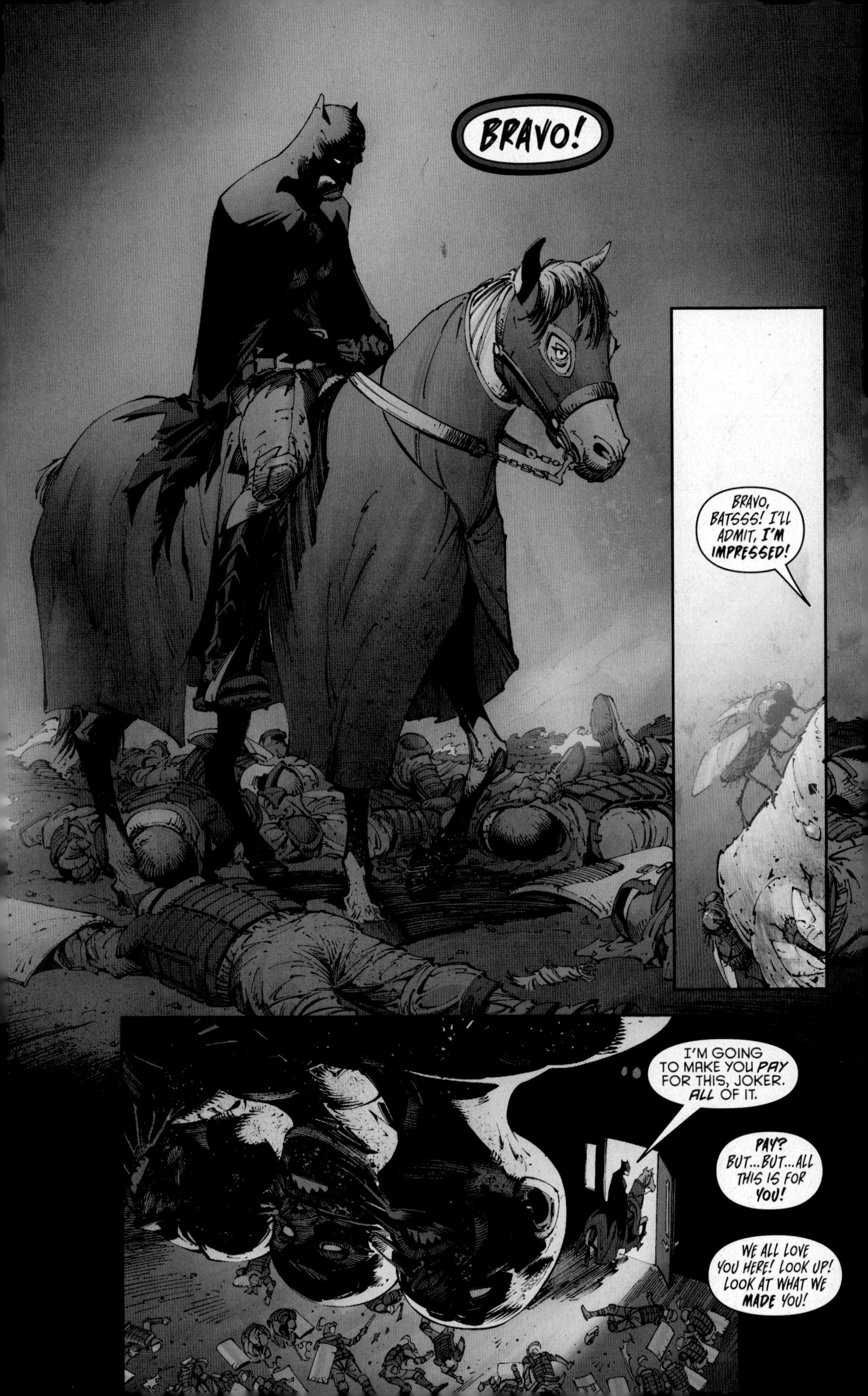
BRAVO!
BRAVO, BATSSS! I'LL ADMIT, I'M IMPRESSED!
...
I'M GOING TO MAKE YOU PAY FOR THIS, JOKER. ALL OF IT.
PAY? BUT...BUT...ALL THIS IS FOR YOU!
WE ALL LOVE YOU HERE! LOOK UP! LOOK AT WHAT WE MADE YOU!

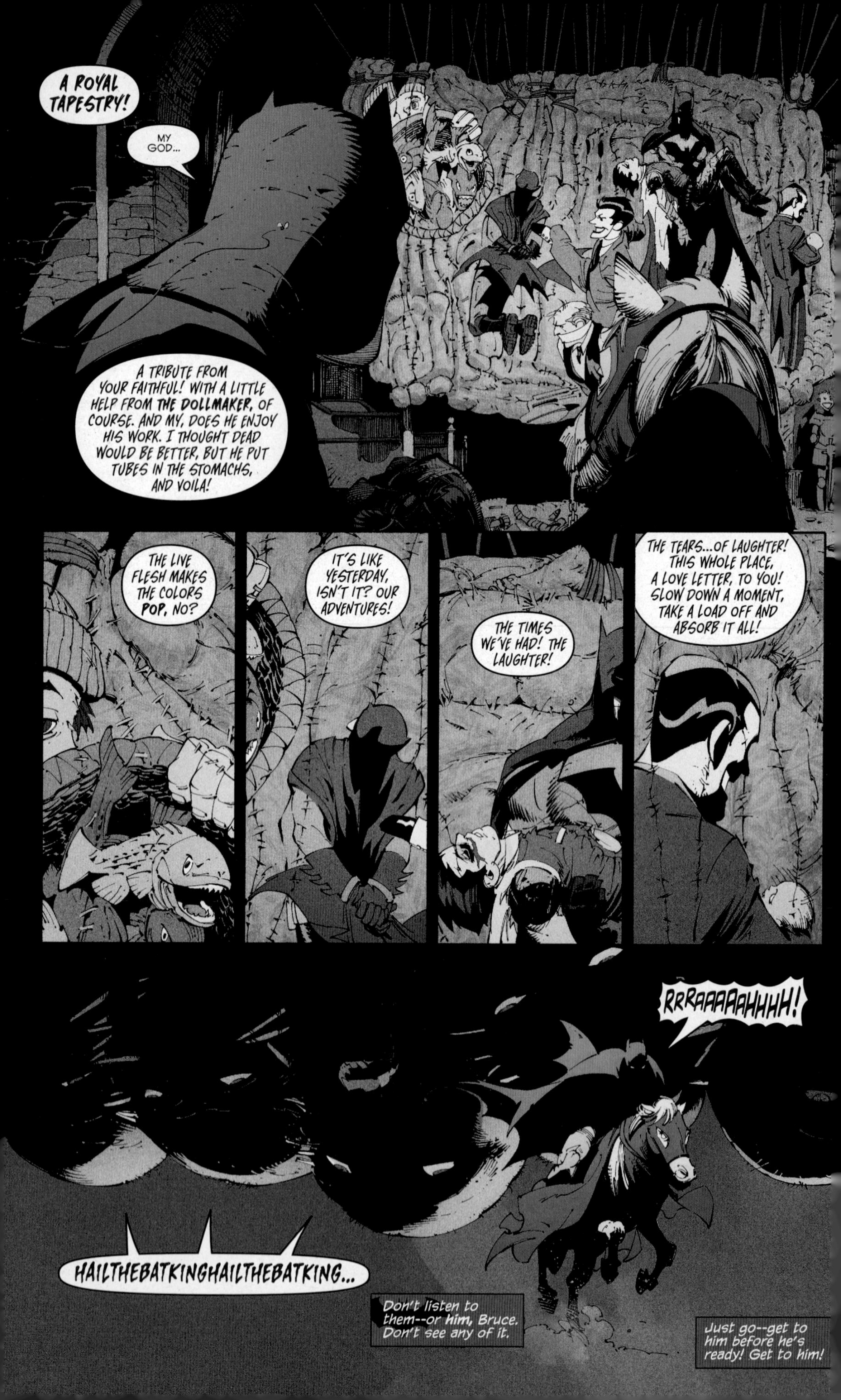
A ROYAL TAPESTRY!
MY GOD...
A TRIBUTE FROM YOUR FAITHFUL! WITH A LITTLE HELP FROM THE DOLLMAKER, OF COURSE. AND MY, DOES HE ENJOY HIS WORK. I THOUGHT DEAD WOULD BE BETTER, BUT HE PUT TUBES IN THE STOMACHS, AND VOILA!
THE LIVE FLESH MAKES THE COLORS POP, NO?
IT'S LIKE YESTERDAY, ISN'T IT? OUR ADVENTURES!
THE TIMES WE'VE HAD! THE LAUGHTER!
THE TEARS...OF LAUGHTER! THIS WHOLE PLACE, A LOVE LETTER, TO YOU! SLOW DOWN A MOMENT, TAKE A LOAD OFF AND ABSORB IT ALL!
RRRAAAAAHHHH!
HAILTHEBATKINGHAILTHEBATKING...
Don't listen to them--or him, Bruce. Don't see any of it.
Just go--get to him before he's ready! Get to him!

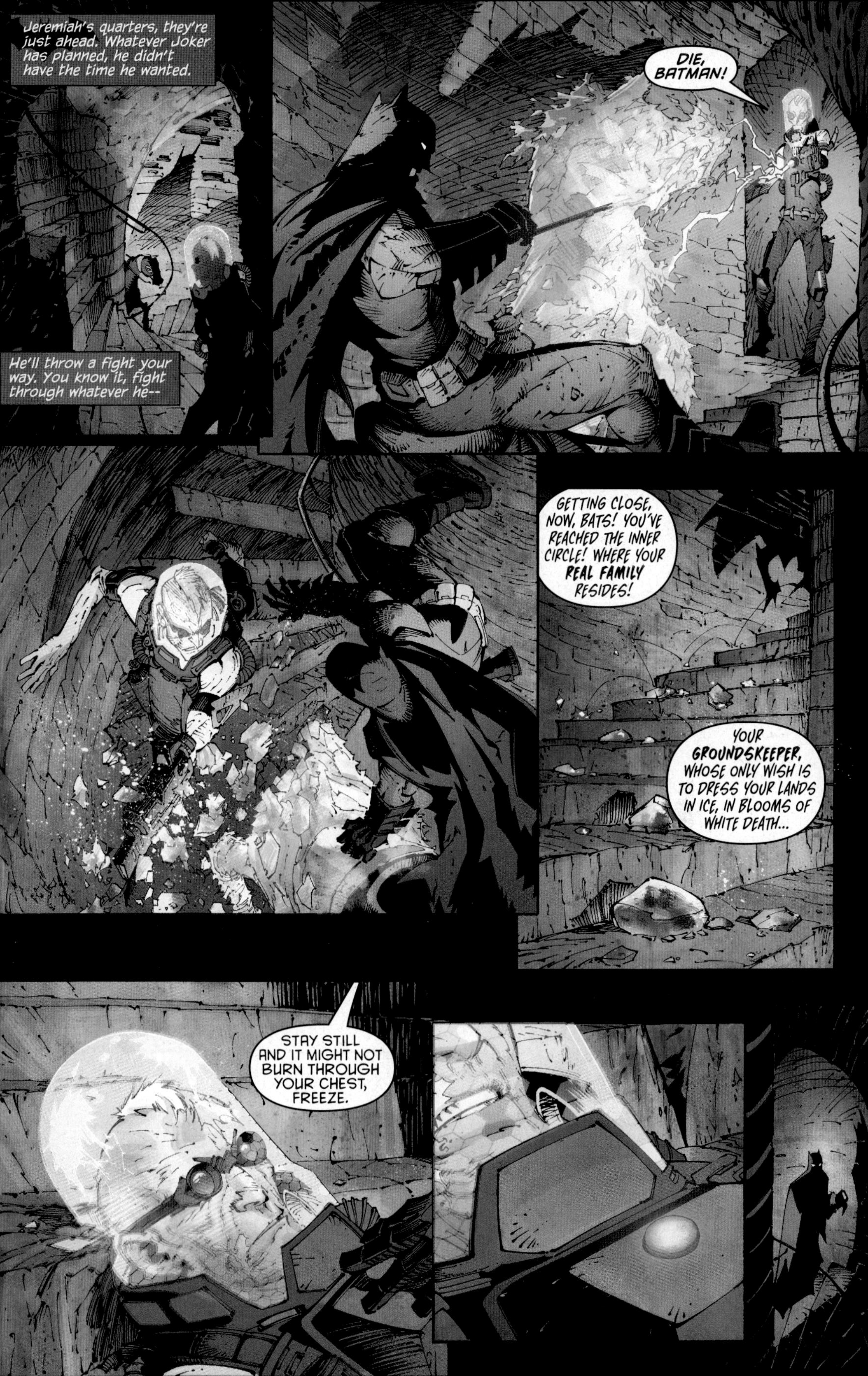
Jeremiah's quarters, they're just ahead. Whatever Joker has planned, he didn't have the time he wanted.
He'll throw a fight your way. You know it, fight through whatever he--
DIE, BATMAN!
GETTING CLOSE, NOW, BATS! YOU'VE REACHED THE INNER CIRCLE! WHERE YOUR REAL FAMILY RESIDES!
YOUR GROUNDSKEEPER, WHOSE ONLY WISH IS TO DRESS YOUR LANDS IN ICE, IN BLOOMS OF WHITE DEATH...
STAY STILL AND IT MIGHT NOT BURN THROUGH YOUR CHEST, FREEZE.

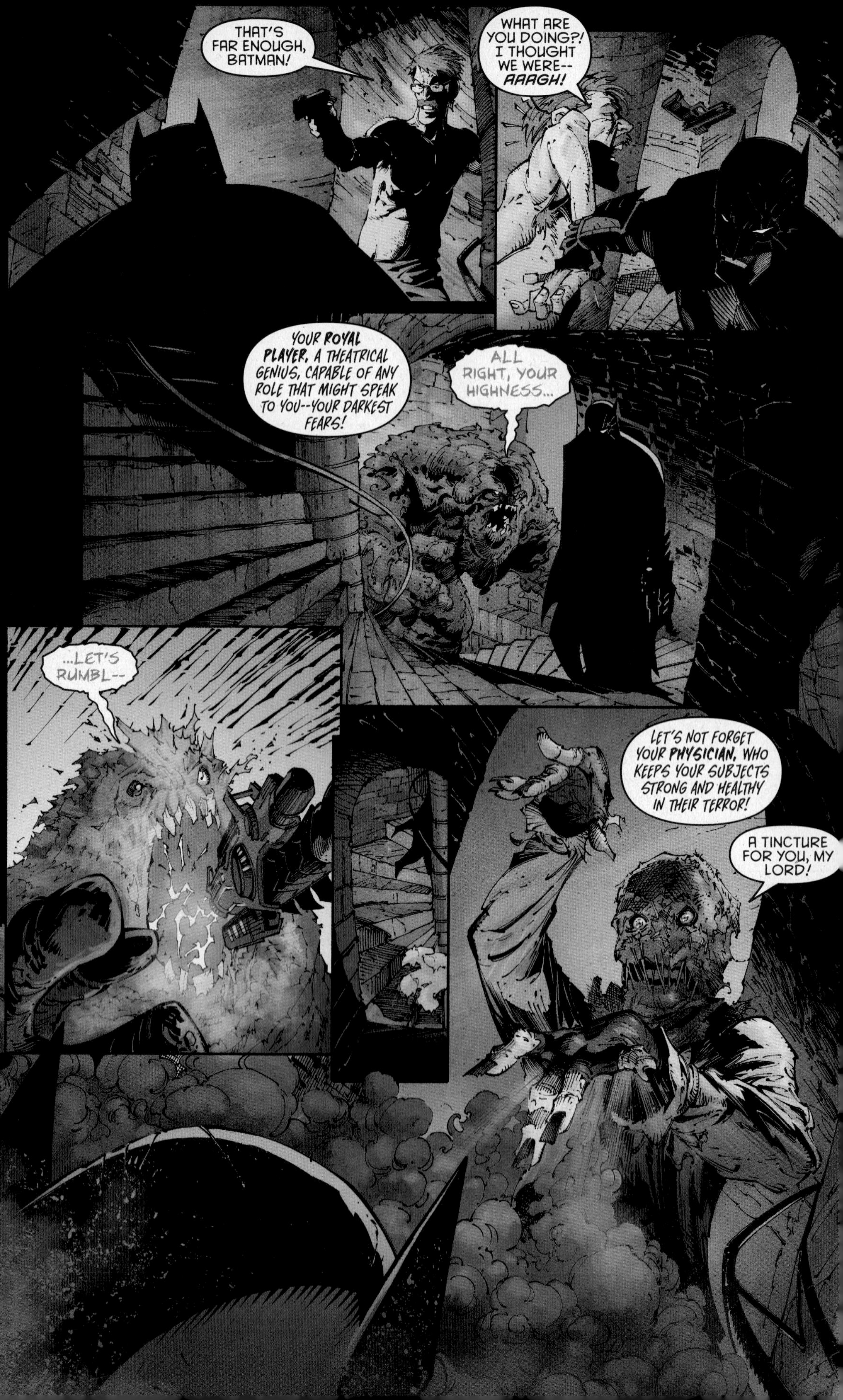
THAT'S FAR ENOUGH, BATMAN!
WHAT ARE YOU DOING?! I THOUGHT WE WERE-- AAAGH!
YOUR ROYAL PLAYER, A THEATRICAL GENIUS, CAPABLE OF ANY ROLE THAT MIGHT SPEAK TO YOU--YOUR DARKEST FEARS!
ALL RIGHT, YOUR HIGHNESS...
...LET'S RUMBL--
LET'S NOT FORGET YOUR PHYSICIAN, WHO KEEPS YOUR SUBJECTS STRONG AND HEALTHY IN THEIR TERROR!
A TINCTURE FOR YOU, MY LORD!

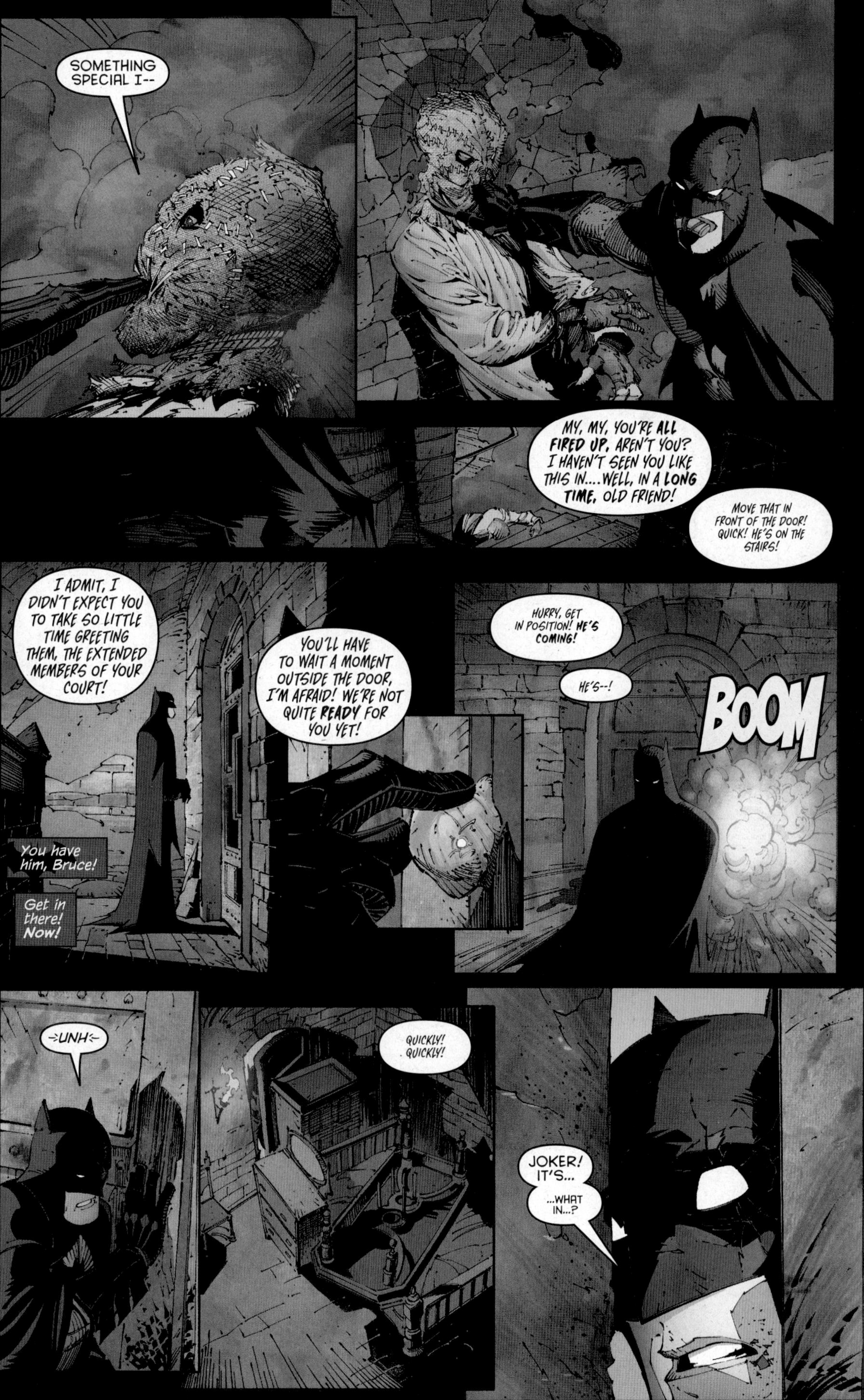
SOMETHING SPECIAL I--
MY, MY, YOU'RE ALL FIRED UP, AREN'T YOU? I HAVEN'T SEEN YOU LIKE THIS IN....WELL, IN A LONG TIME, OLD FRIEND!
Move that in front of the door! Quick! He's on the stairs!
I ADMIT, I DIDN'T EXPECT YOU TO TAKE SO LITTLE TIME GREETING THEM, THE EXTENDED MEMBERS OF YOUR COURT!
YOU'LL HAVE TO WAIT A MOMENT OUTSIDE THE DOOR, I'M AFRAID! WE'RE NOT QUITE READY FOR YOU YET!
You have him, Bruce!
Get in there! Now!
HURRY, GET IN POSITION! HE'S COMING!
HE'S--!
BOOM
UNH
QUICKLY! QUICKLY!
JOKER! IT'S...
...WHAT IN...?

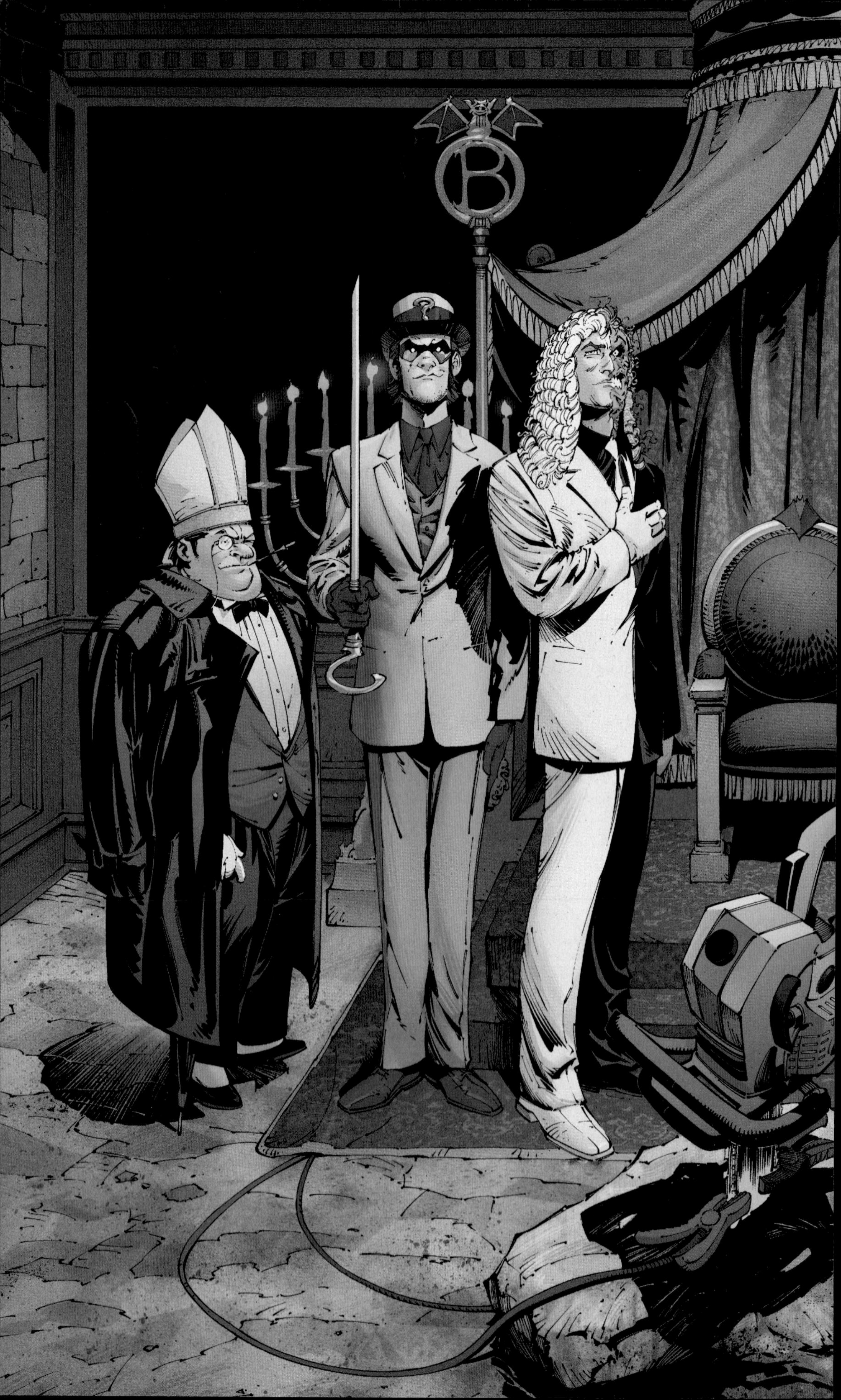

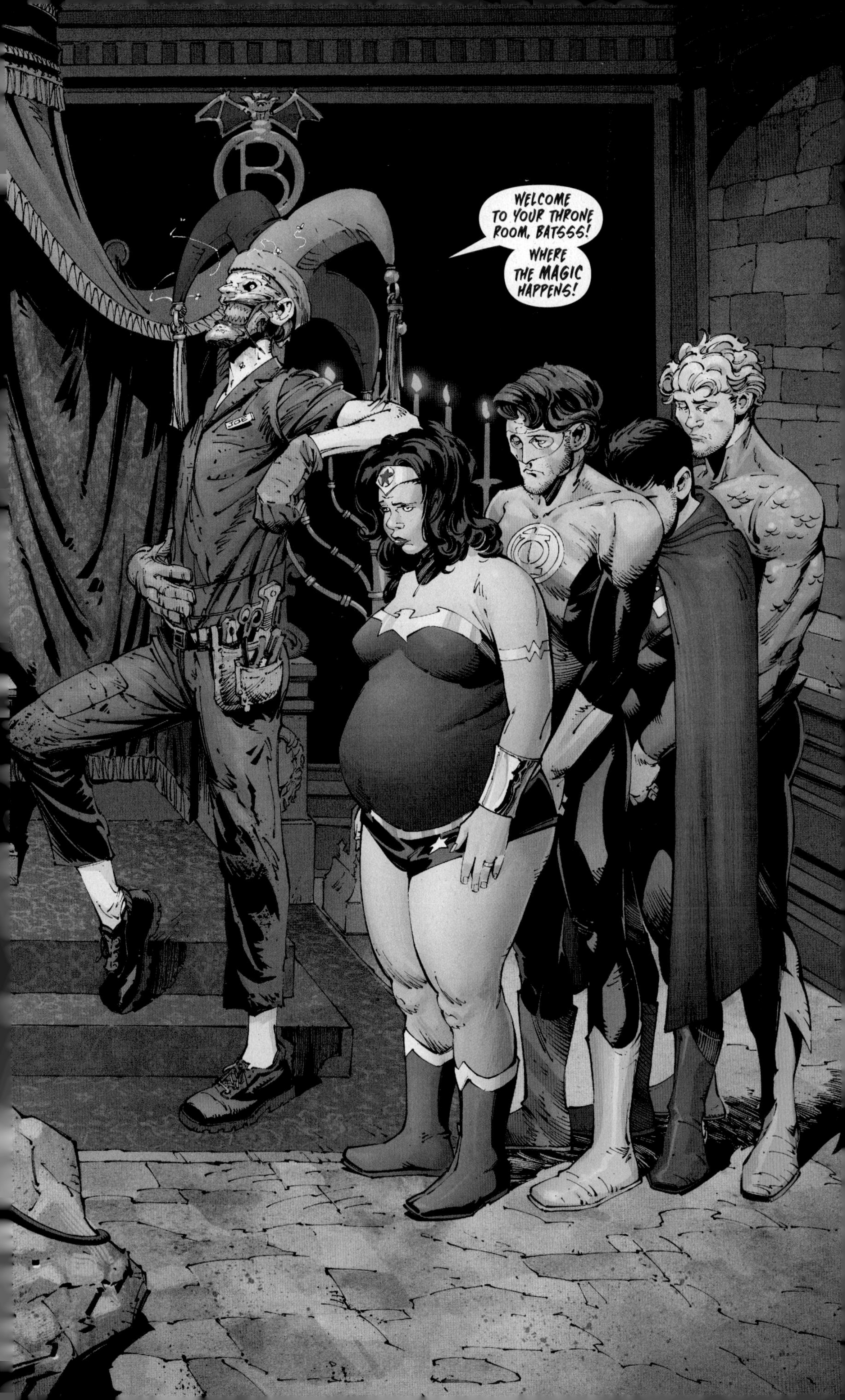
WELCOME TO YOUR THRONE ROOM, BATSSS!
WHERE THE MAGIC HAPPENS!
JOE

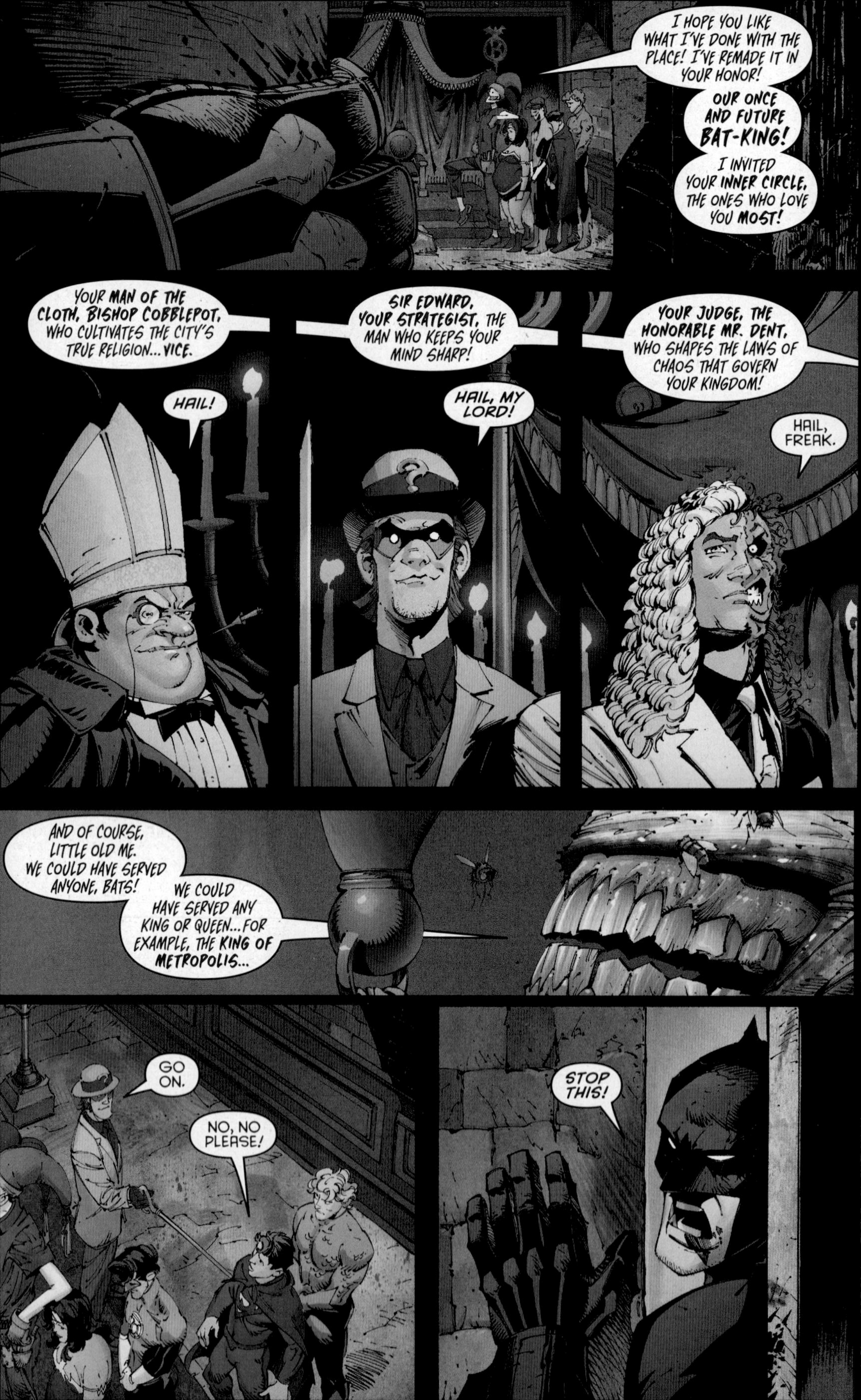
I HOPE YOU LIKE WHAT I'VE DONE WITH THE PLACE! I'VE REMADE IT IN YOUR HONOR!
OUR ONCE AND FUTURE BAT-KING!
I INVITED YOUR INNER CIRCLE, THE ONES WHO LOVE YOU MOST!
YOUR MAN OF THE CLOTH, BISHOP COBBLEPOT, WHO CULTIVATES THE CITY'S TRUE RELIGION... VICE.
HAIL!
SIR EDWARD, YOUR STRATEGIST, THE MAN WHO KEEPS YOUR MIND SHARP!
HAIL, MY LORD!
YOUR JUDGE, THE HONORABLE MR. DENT, WHO SHAPES THE LAWS OF CHAOS THAT GOVERN YOUR KINGDOM!
HAIL, FREAK.
AND OF COURSE, LITTLE OLD ME. WE COULD HAVE SERVED ANYONE, BATS!
WE COULD HAVE SERVED ANY KING OR QUEEN... FOR EXAMPLE, THE KING OF METROPOLIS...
GO ON.
NO, NO PLEASE!
STOP THIS!

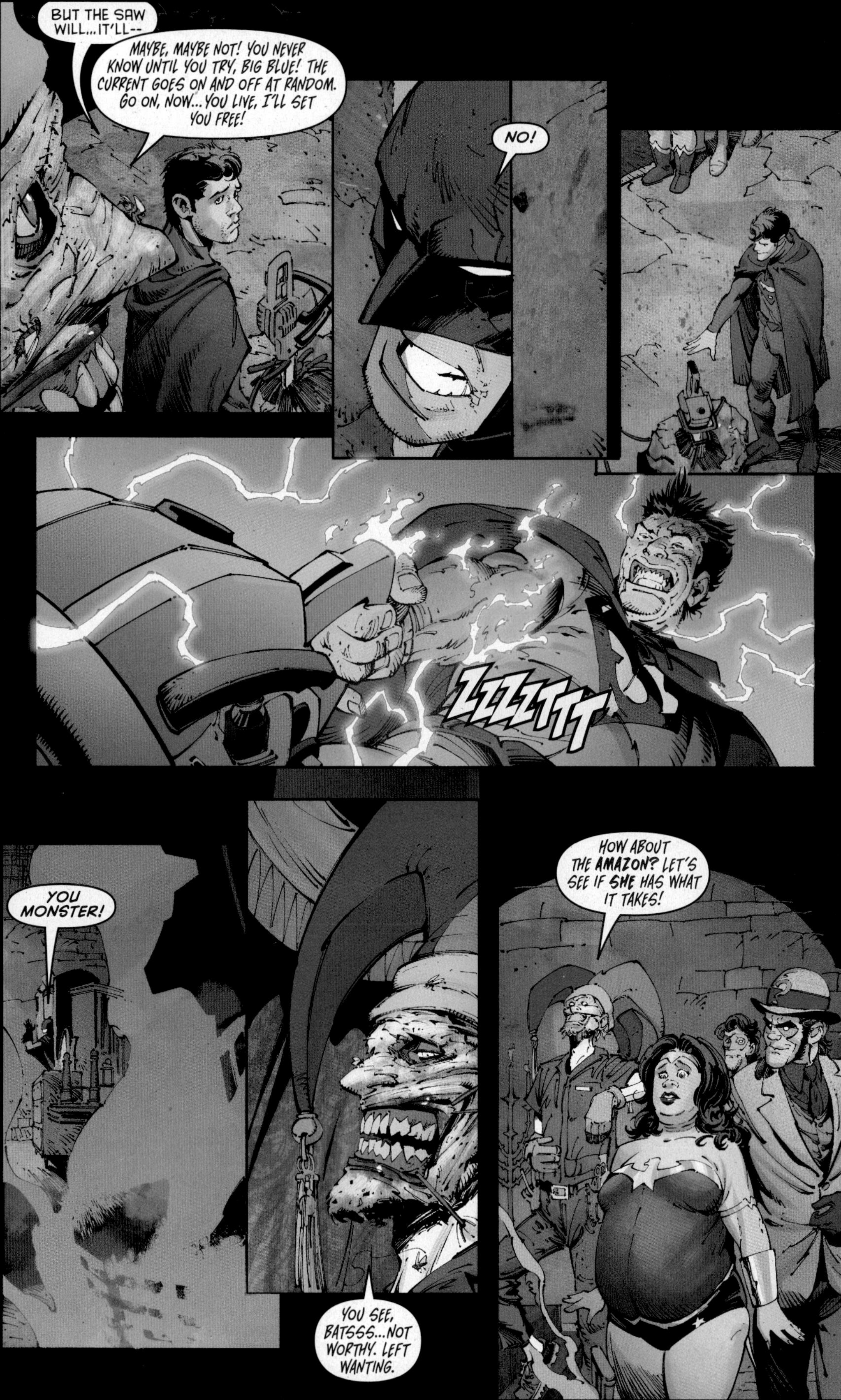

BUT THE SAW WILL...IT'LL--
MAYBE, MAYBE NOT! YOU NEVER KNOW UNTIL YOU TRY, BIG BLUE! THE CURRENT GOES ON AND OFF AT RANDOM. GO ON, NOW...YOU LIVE, I'LL SET YOU FREE!
NO!
ZZZZTTT
YOU MONSTER!
YOU SEE, BATSSS...NOT WORTHY. LEFT WANTING.
HOW ABOUT THE AMAZON? LET'S SEE IF SHE HAS WHAT IT TAKES!

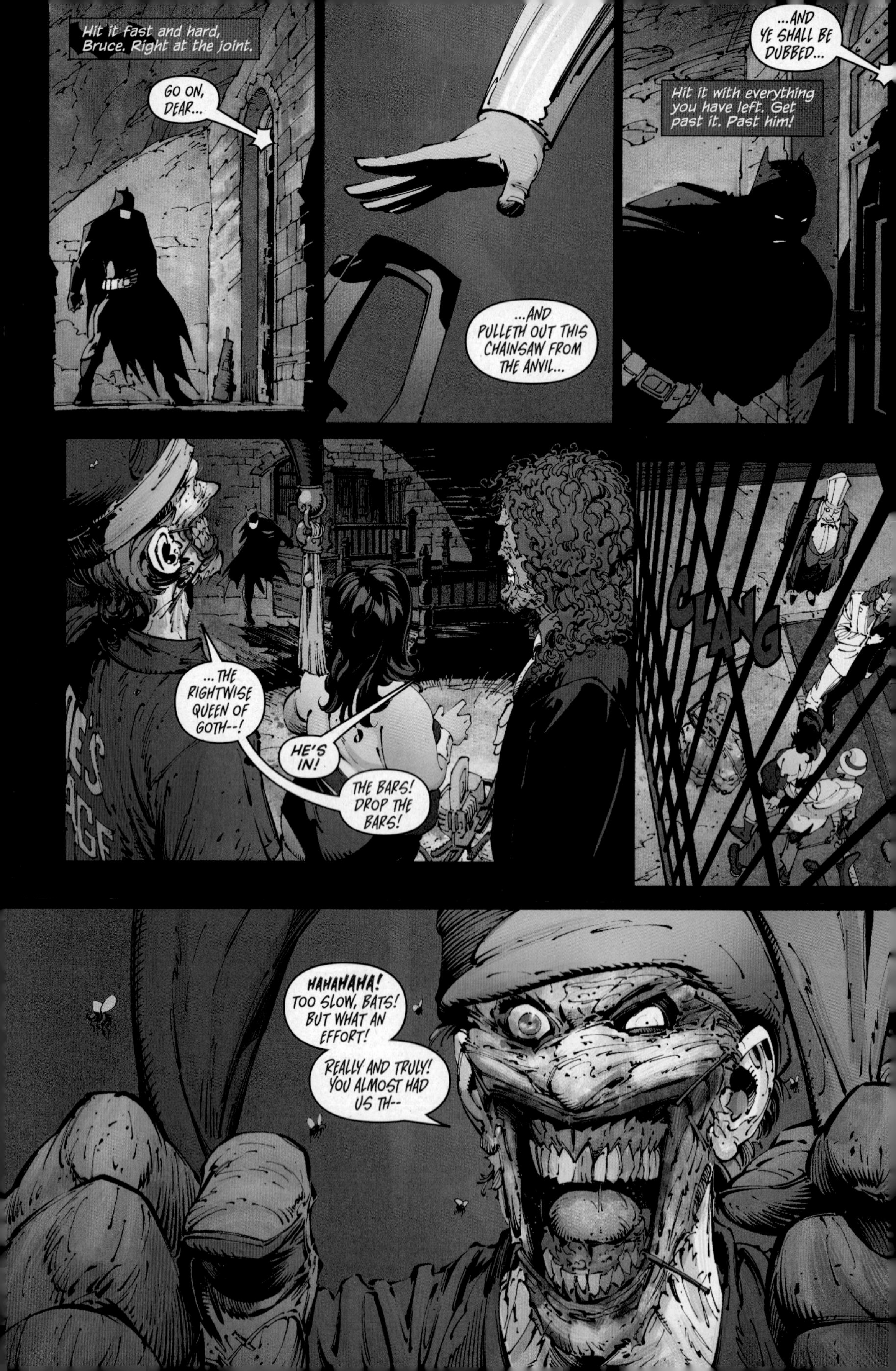

Hit it fast and hard, Bruce. Right at the joint.
GO ON, DEAR...
...AND PULLETH OUT THIS CHAINSAW FROM THE ANVIL...
...AND YE SHALL BE DUBBED...
Hit it with everything you have left. Get past it. Past him!
...THE RIGHTWISE QUEEN OF GOTH--!
HE'S IN!
THE BARS! DROP THE BARS!
CLANG
HAHAHAHA! TOO SLOW, BATS! BUT WHAT AN EFFORT!
REALLY AND TRULY! YOU ALMOST HAD US TH--

WHAT'S THE MATTER, JOKER? SO *QUIET* ALL OF A SUDDEN.

HE CUT THE POWER! WE GOT NOTHING!

GO ON, THROW IT! MAKE SURE YOU AIM FOR THE RIGHT GRIN, THOUGH!

I DON'T NEED TO THROW A DAMN THING. THE POLICE WILL BE HERE ANY MINUTE. UNTIL THEN, I'M JUST GOING TO STAND HERE AND ENJOY THE VIEW.

NOW LET GUARD FREEMAN GO.

WHAT THE HELL IS *HAPPENING,* JOKER?!

WHAT'S HAPPENING IS THE BAT JUST *WON,* YOU DAMN--

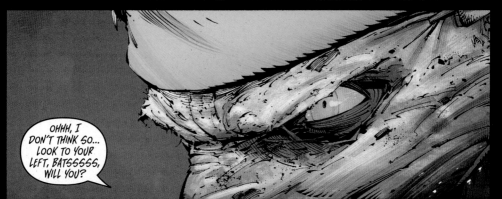

OHHH, I DON'T THINK SO... LOOK TO YOUR LEFT, BATSSSSS, WILL YOU?

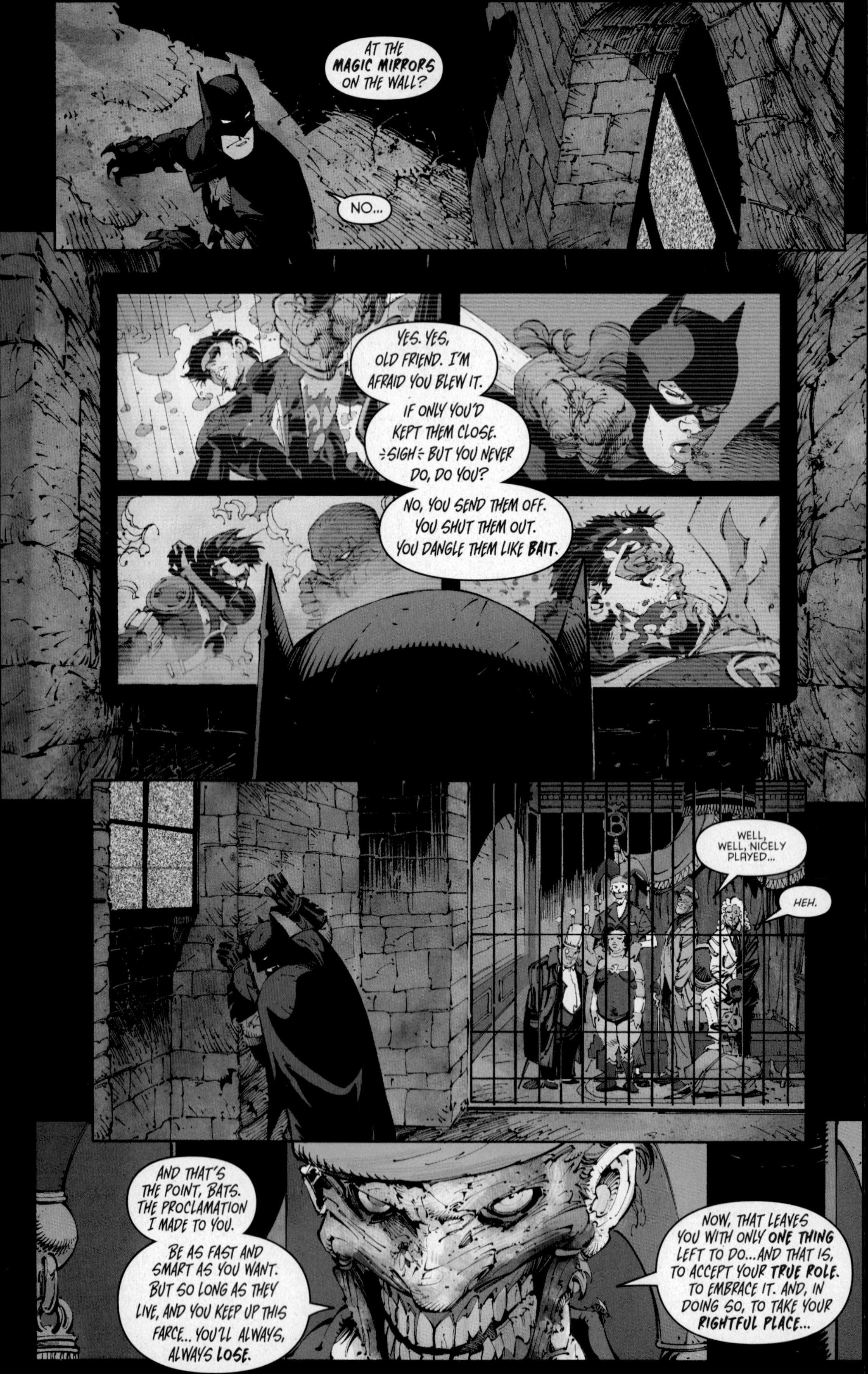
AT THE MAGIC MIRRORS ON THE WALL?
NO...
YES. YES, OLD FRIEND. I'M AFRAID YOU BLEW IT.
IF ONLY YOU'D KEPT THEM CLOSE. ÷SIGH÷ BUT YOU NEVER DO, DO YOU?
NO, YOU SEND THEM OFF. YOU SHUT THEM OUT. YOU DANGLE THEM LIKE BAIT.
WELL, WELL, NICELY PLAYED...
HEH.
AND THAT'S THE POINT, BATS. THE PROCLAMATION I MADE TO YOU.
BE AS FAST AND SMART AS YOU WANT. BUT SO LONG AS THEY LIVE, AND YOU KEEP UP THIS FARCE... YOU'LL ALWAYS, ALWAYS LOSE.
NOW, THAT LEAVES YOU WITH ONLY ONE THING LEFT TO DO...AND THAT IS, TO ACCEPT YOUR TRUE ROLE. TO EMBRACE IT. AND, IN DOING SO, TO TAKE YOUR RIGHTFUL PLACE...

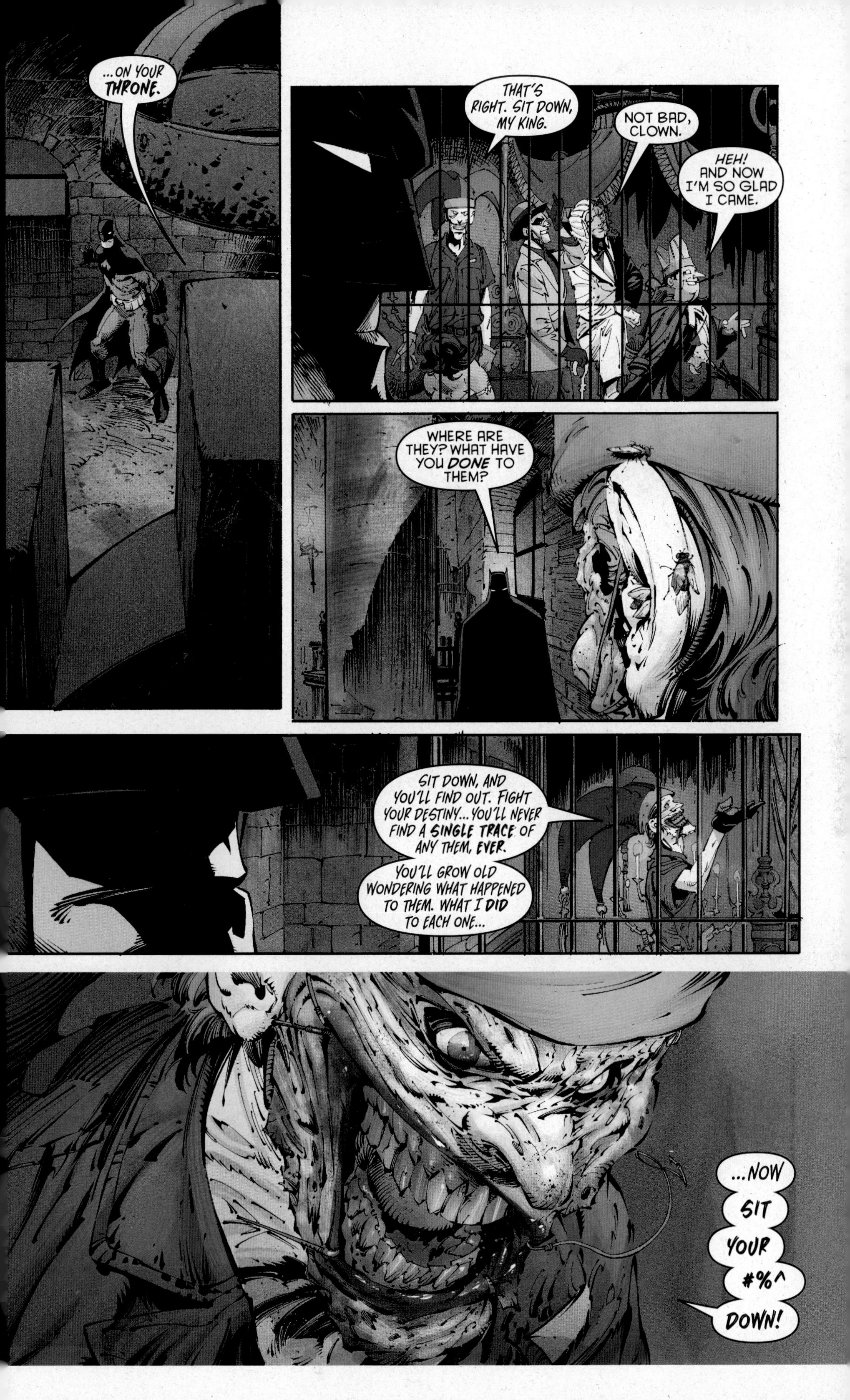
...ON YOUR THRONE.
THAT'S RIGHT. SIT DOWN, MY KING.
NOT BAD, CLOWN.
HEH! AND NOW I'M SO GLAD I CAME.
WHERE ARE THEY? WHAT HAVE YOU DONE TO THEM?
SIT DOWN, AND YOU'LL FIND OUT. FIGHT YOUR DESTINY... YOU'LL NEVER FIND A SINGLE TRACE OF ANY THEM, EVER.
YOU'LL GROW OLD WONDERING WHAT HAPPENED TO THEM. WHAT I DID TO EACH ONE...
...NOW SIT YOUR #%^ DOWN!

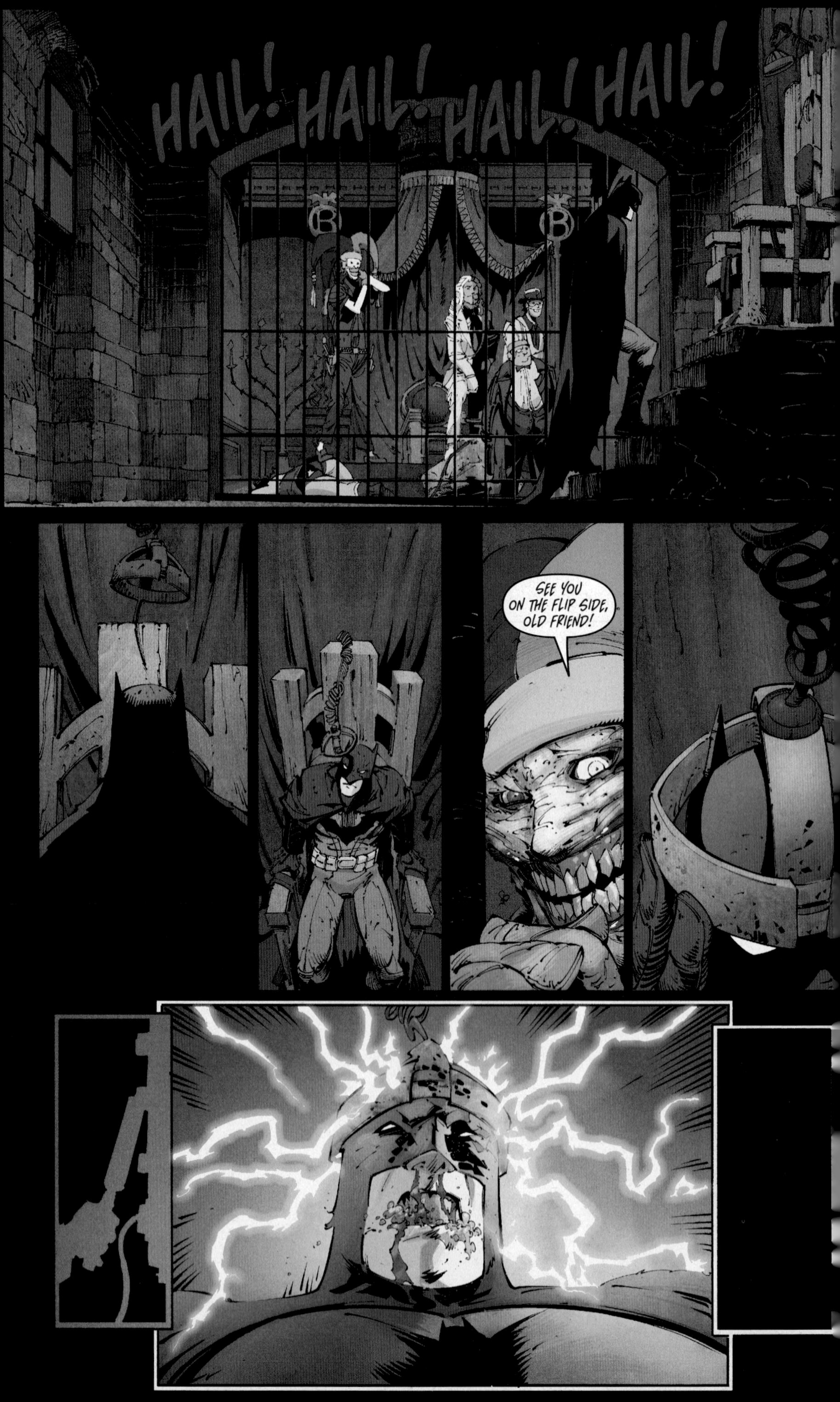
HAIL! HAIL! HAIL! HAIL!
SEE YOU ON THE FLIP SIDE, OLD FRIEND!

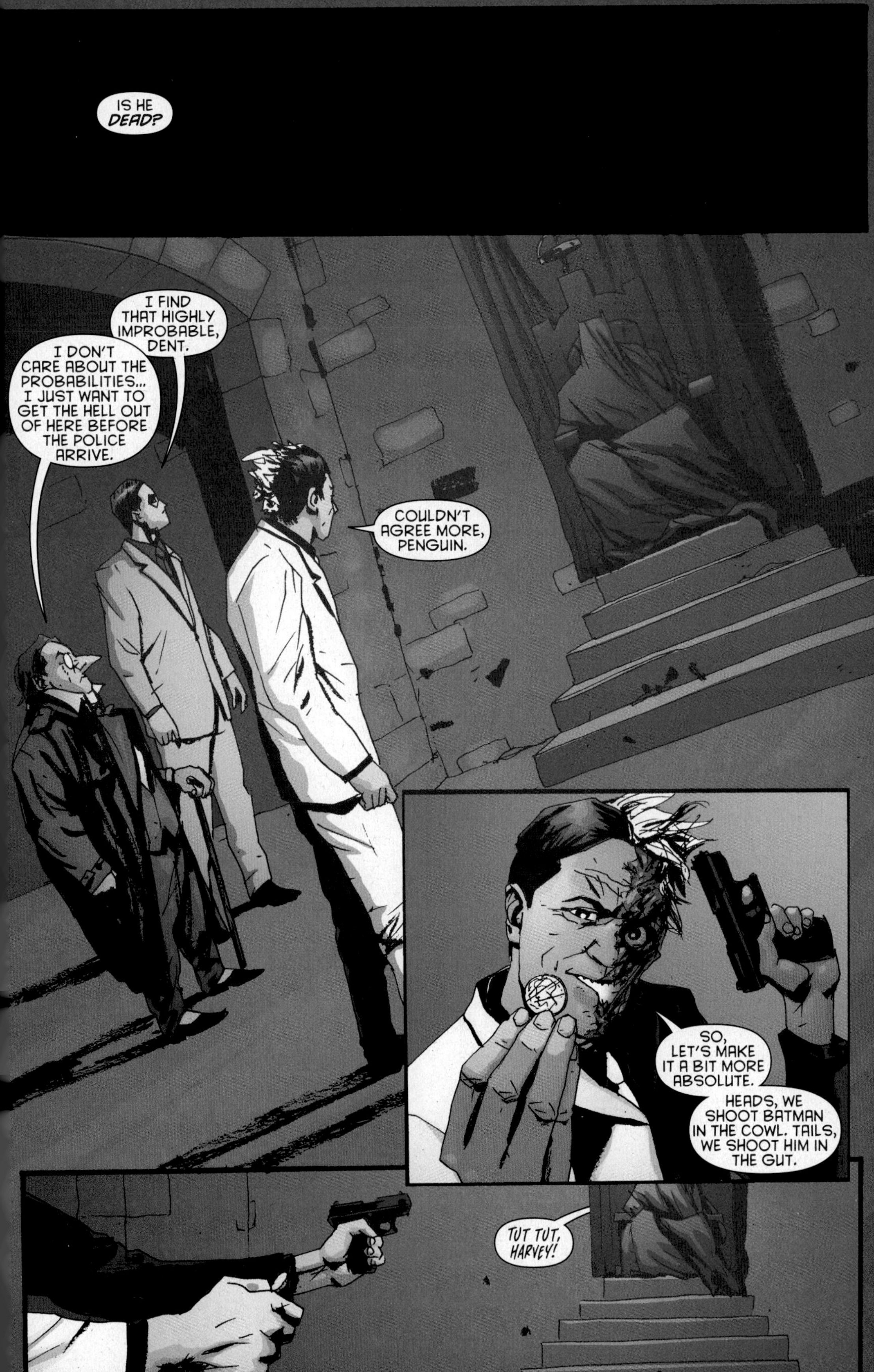
IS HE *DEAD?*
I FIND THAT HIGHLY IMPROBABLE, DENT.
I DON'T CARE ABOUT THE PROBABILITIES... I JUST WANT TO GET THE HELL OUT OF HERE BEFORE THE POLICE ARRIVE.
COULDN'T AGREE MORE, PENGUIN.
SO, LET'S MAKE IT A BIT MORE ABSOLUTE.
HEADS, WE SHOOT BATMAN IN THE COWL. TAILS, WE SHOOT HIM IN THE GUT.
TUT TUT, HARVEY!

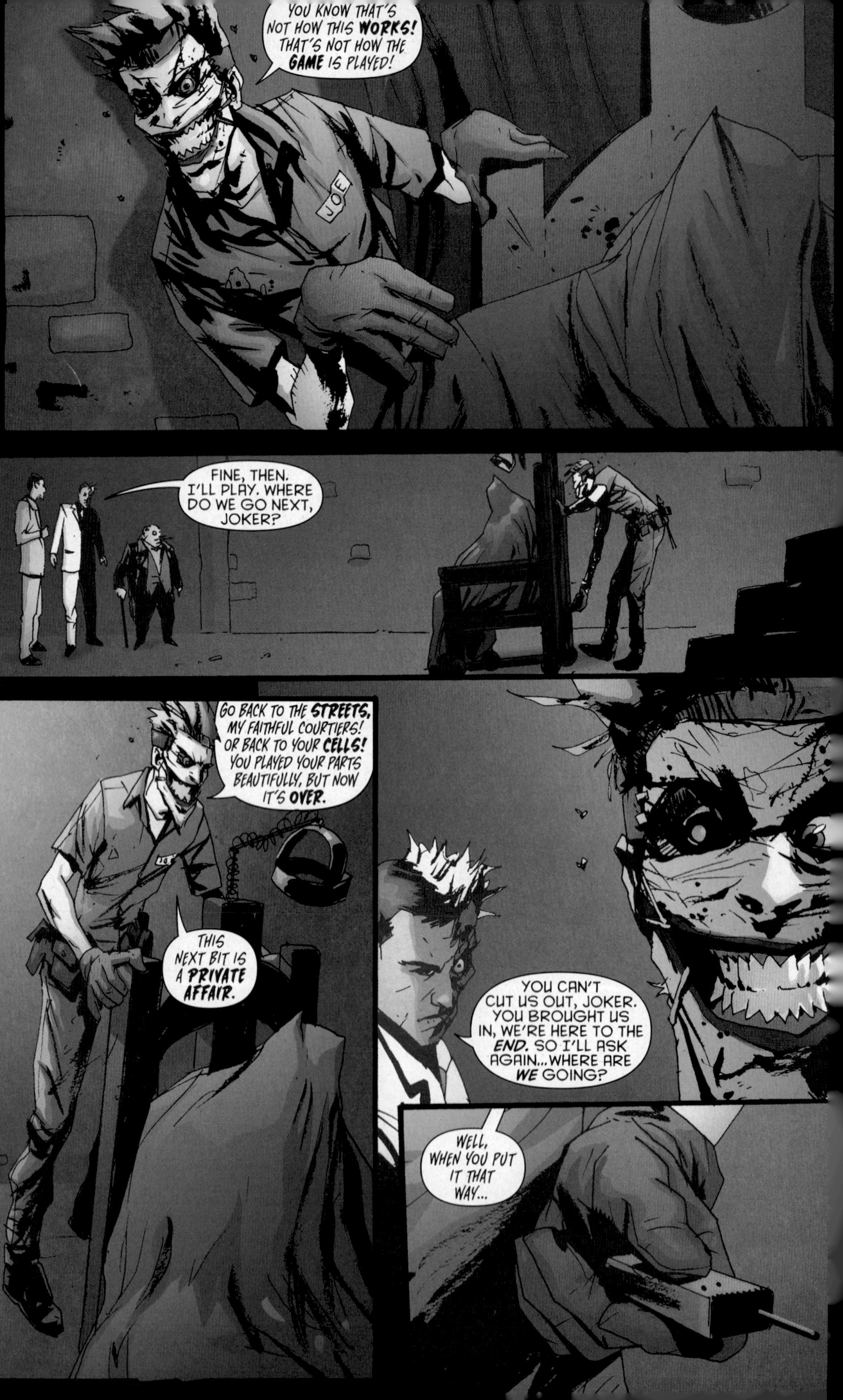
YOU KNOW THAT'S NOT HOW THIS WORKS! THAT'S NOT HOW THE GAME IS PLAYED!
JOE
FINE, THEN. I'LL PLAY. WHERE DO WE GO NEXT, JOKER?
GO BACK TO THE STREETS, MY FAITHFUL COURTIERS! OR BACK TO YOUR CELLS! YOU PLAYED YOUR PARTS BEAUTIFULLY, BUT NOW IT'S OVER.
THIS NEXT BIT IS A PRIVATE AFFAIR.
YOU CAN'T CUT US OUT, JOKER. YOU BROUGHT US IN, WE'RE HERE TO THE END. SO I'LL ASK AGAIN...WHERE ARE WE GOING?
WELL, WHEN YOU PUT IT THAT WAY...

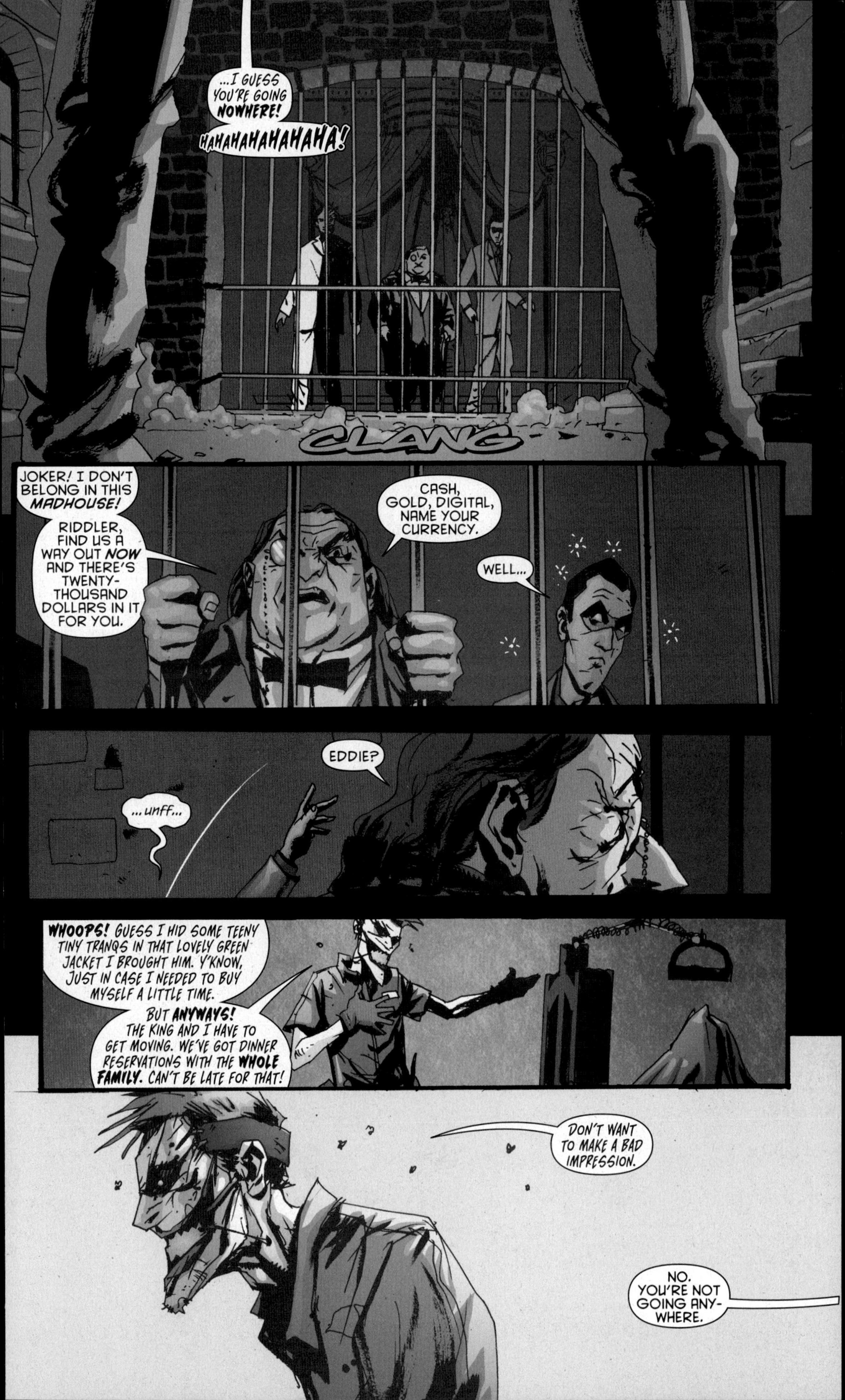
...I GUESS YOU'RE GOING NOWHERE!
HAHAHAHAHAHAHA!
CLANG
JOKER! I DON'T BELONG IN THIS MADHOUSE!
RIDDLER, FIND US A WAY OUT NOW AND THERE'S TWENTY-THOUSAND DOLLARS IN IT FOR YOU.
CASH, GOLD, DIGITAL, NAME YOUR CURRENCY.
WELL...
EDDIE?
...unff...
WHOOPS! GUESS I HID SOME TEENY TINY TRANQS IN THAT LOVELY GREEN JACKET I BROUGHT HIM. Y'KNOW, JUST IN CASE I NEEDED TO BUY MYSELF A LITTLE TIME.
BUT ANYWAYS! THE KING AND I HAVE TO GET MOVING. WE'VE GOT DINNER RESERVATIONS WITH THE WHOLE FAMILY. CAN'T BE LATE FOR THAT!
DON'T WANT TO MAKE A BAD IMPRESSION.
NO. YOU'RE NOT GOING ANY-WHERE.

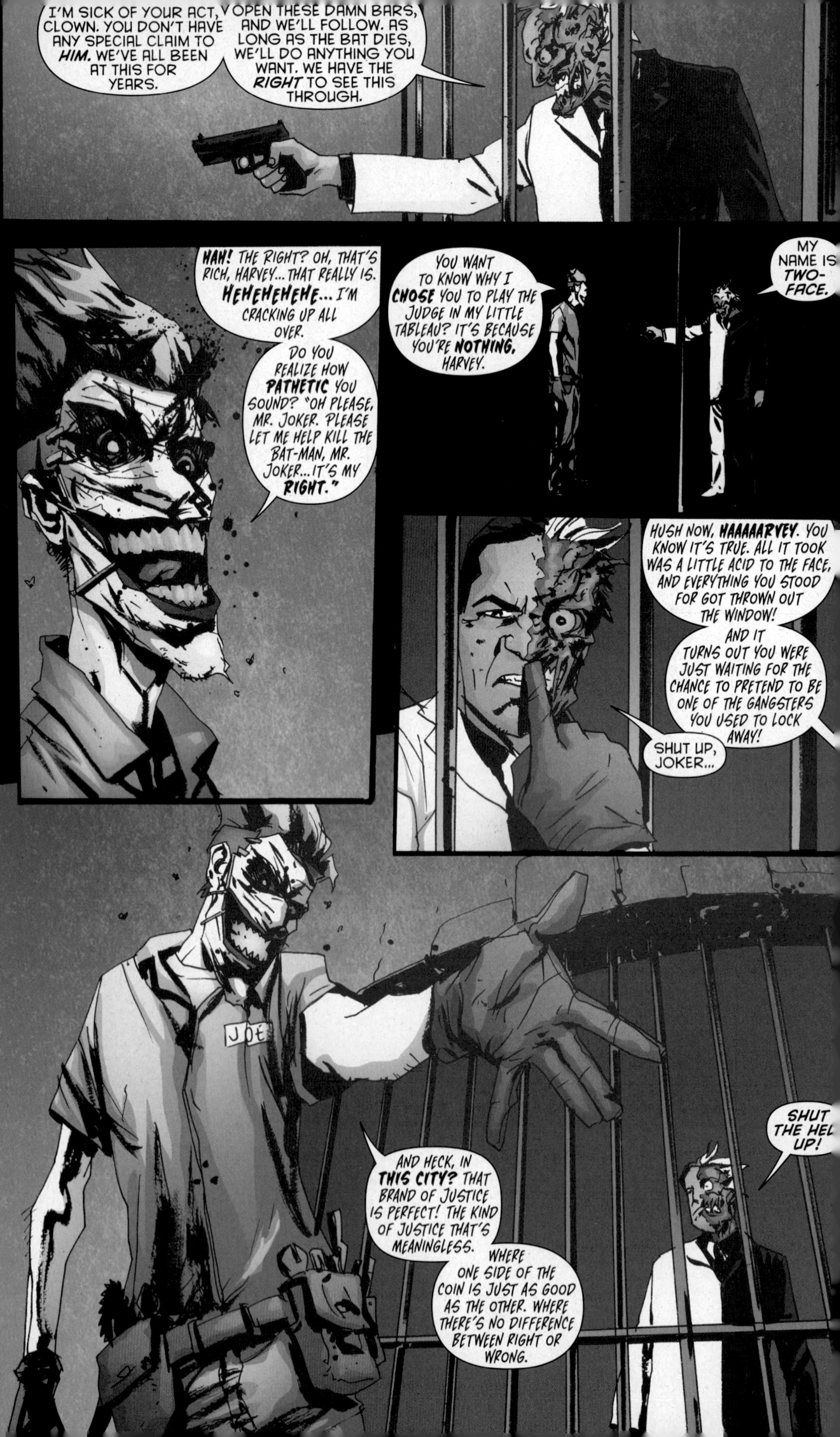
I'M SICK OF YOUR ACT, CLOWN. YOU DON'T HAVE ANY SPECIAL CLAIM TO HIM. WE'VE ALL BEEN AT THIS FOR YEARS.
OPEN THESE DAMN BARS, AND WE'LL FOLLOW. AS LONG AS THE BAT DIES, WE'LL DO ANYTHING YOU WANT. WE HAVE THE RIGHT TO SEE THIS THROUGH.
HAH! THE RIGHT? OH, THAT'S RICH, HARVEY... THAT REALLY IS. HEHEHEHEHE... I'M CRACKING UP ALL OVER.
DO YOU REALIZE HOW PATHETIC YOU SOUND? "OH PLEASE, MR. JOKER. PLEASE LET ME HELP KILL THE BAT-MAN, MR. JOKER... IT'S MY RIGHT."
YOU WANT TO KNOW WHY I CHOSE YOU TO PLAY THE JUDGE IN MY LITTLE TABLEAU? IT'S BECAUSE YOU'RE NOTHING, HARVEY.
MY NAME IS TWO-FACE.
HUSH NOW, HAAAAARVEY. YOU KNOW IT'S TRUE. ALL IT TOOK WAS A LITTLE ACID TO THE FACE, AND EVERYTHING YOU STOOD FOR GOT THROWN OUT THE WINDOW!
AND IT TURNS OUT YOU WERE JUST WAITING FOR THE CHANCE TO PRETEND TO BE ONE OF THE GANGSTERS YOU USED TO LOCK AWAY!
SHUT UP, JOKER...
JOE
AND HECK, IN THIS CITY? THAT BRAND OF JUSTICE IS PERFECT! THE KIND OF JUSTICE THAT'S MEANINGLESS.
WHERE ONE SIDE OF THE COIN IS JUST AS GOOD AS THE OTHER. WHERE THERE'S NO DIFFERENCE BETWEEN RIGHT OR WRONG.
SHUT THE HEL UP!

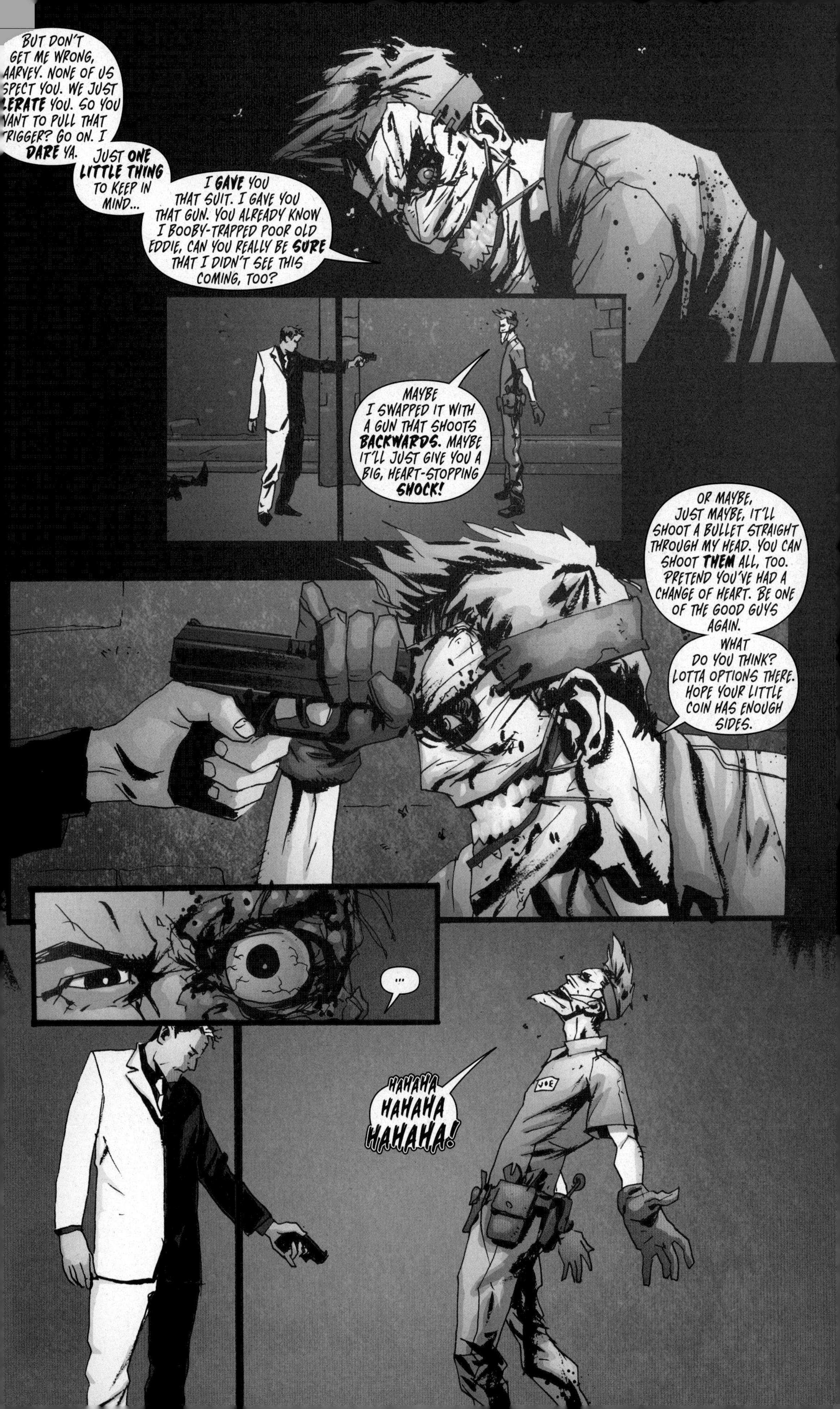

BUT DON'T GET ME WRONG, AARVEY. NONE OF US SPECT YOU. WE JUST LERATE YOU. SO YOU WANT TO PULL THAT TRIGGER? GO ON. I DARE YA.
JUST ONE LITTLE THING TO KEEP IN MIND...
I GAVE YOU THAT SUIT. I GAVE YOU THAT GUN. YOU ALREADY KNOW I BOOBY-TRAPPED POOR OLD EDDIE, CAN YOU REALLY BE SURE THAT I DIDN'T SEE THIS COMING, TOO?
MAYBE I SWAPPED IT WITH A GUN THAT SHOOTS BACKWARDS. MAYBE IT'LL JUST GIVE YOU A BIG, HEART-STOPPING SHOCK!
OR MAYBE, JUST MAYBE, IT'LL SHOOT A BULLET STRAIGHT THROUGH MY HEAD. YOU CAN SHOOT THEM ALL, TOO. PRETEND YOU'VE HAD A CHANGE OF HEART. BE ONE OF THE GOOD GUYS AGAIN.
WHAT DO YOU THINK? LOTTA OPTIONS THERE. HOPE YOUR LITTLE COIN HAS ENOUGH SIDES.
...
HAHAHA HAHAHA HAHAHA!
JOE

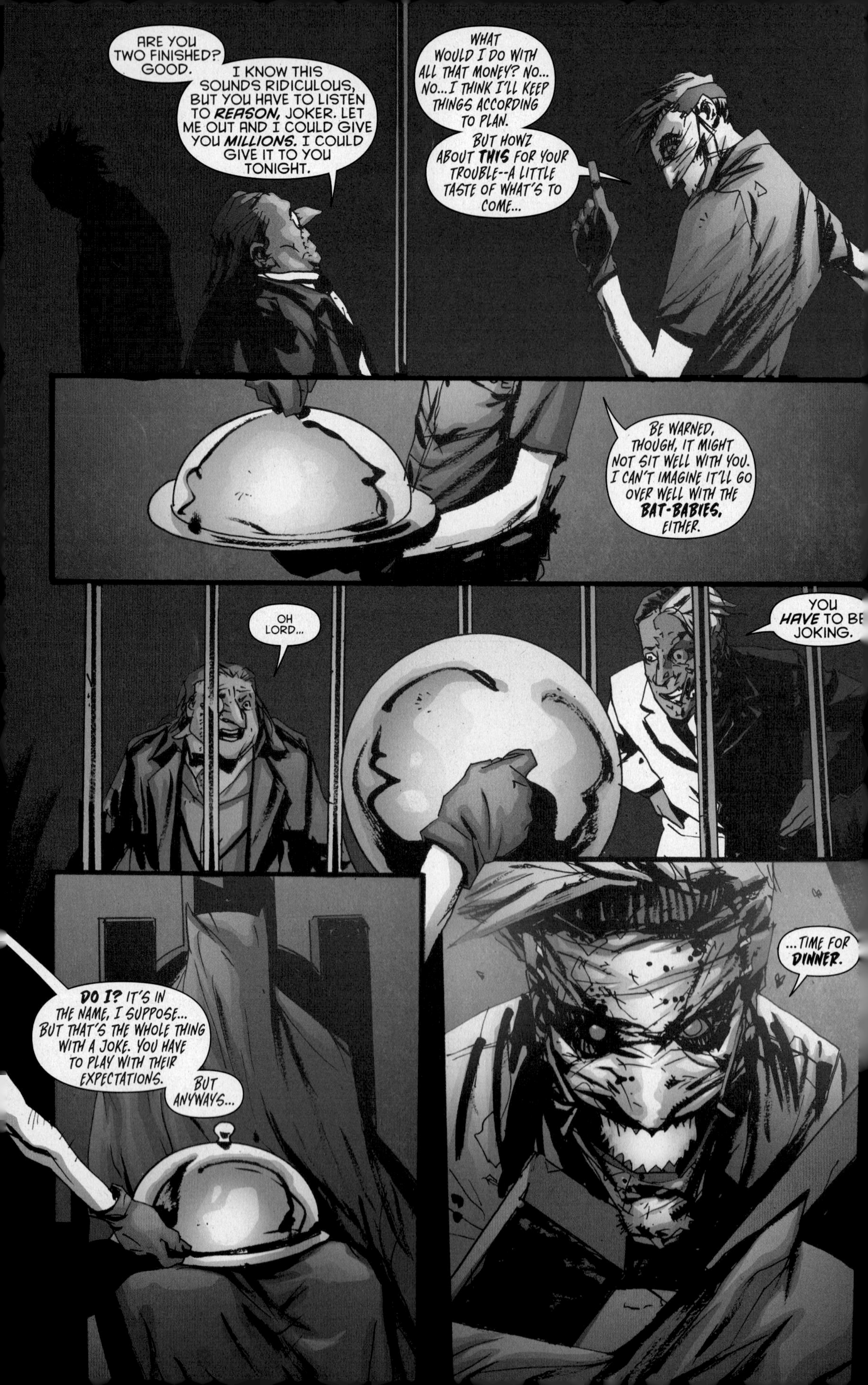
ARE YOU TWO FINISHED? GOOD.
I KNOW THIS SOUNDS RIDICULOUS, BUT YOU HAVE TO LISTEN TO REASON, JOKER. LET ME OUT AND I COULD GIVE YOU MILLIONS. I COULD GIVE IT TO YOU TONIGHT.
WHAT WOULD I DO WITH ALL THAT MONEY? NO... NO...I THINK I'LL KEEP THINGS ACCORDING TO PLAN.
BUT HOWZ ABOUT THIS FOR YOUR TROUBLE--A LITTLE TASTE OF WHAT'S TO COME...
BE WARNED, THOUGH, IT MIGHT NOT SIT WELL WITH YOU. I CAN'T IMAGINE IT'LL GO OVER WELL WITH THE BAT-BABIES, EITHER.
OH LORD...
YOU HAVE TO BE JOKING.
DO I? IT'S IN THE NAME, I SUPPOSE... BUT THAT'S THE WHOLE THING WITH A JOKE. YOU HAVE TO PLAY WITH THEIR EXPECTATIONS.
BUT ANYWAYS...
...TIME FOR DINNER.

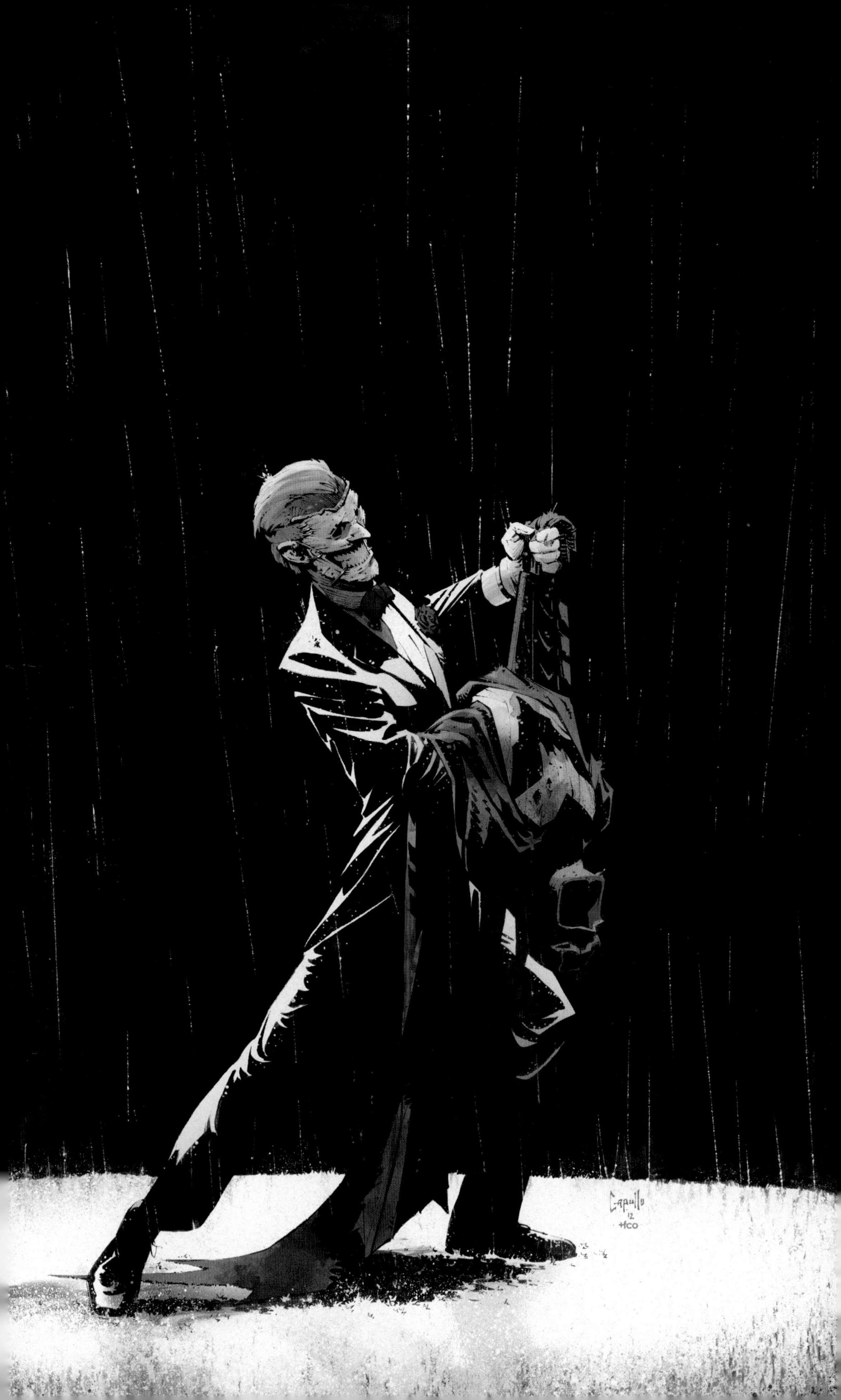

THE PUNCHLINE

SCOTT SNYDER writers GREG CAPULLO penciller JONATHAN GLAPION inker

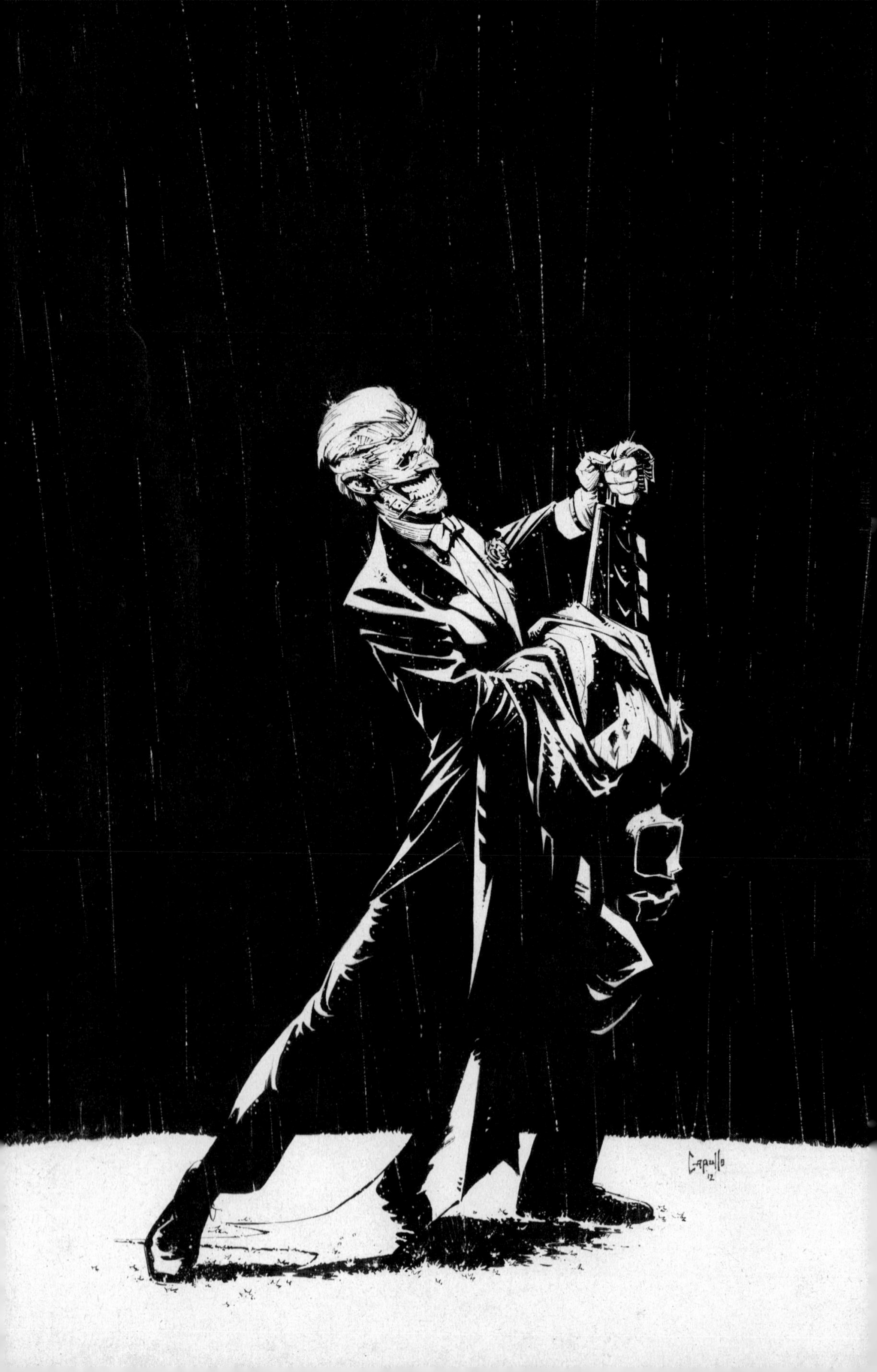

Capullo
'12

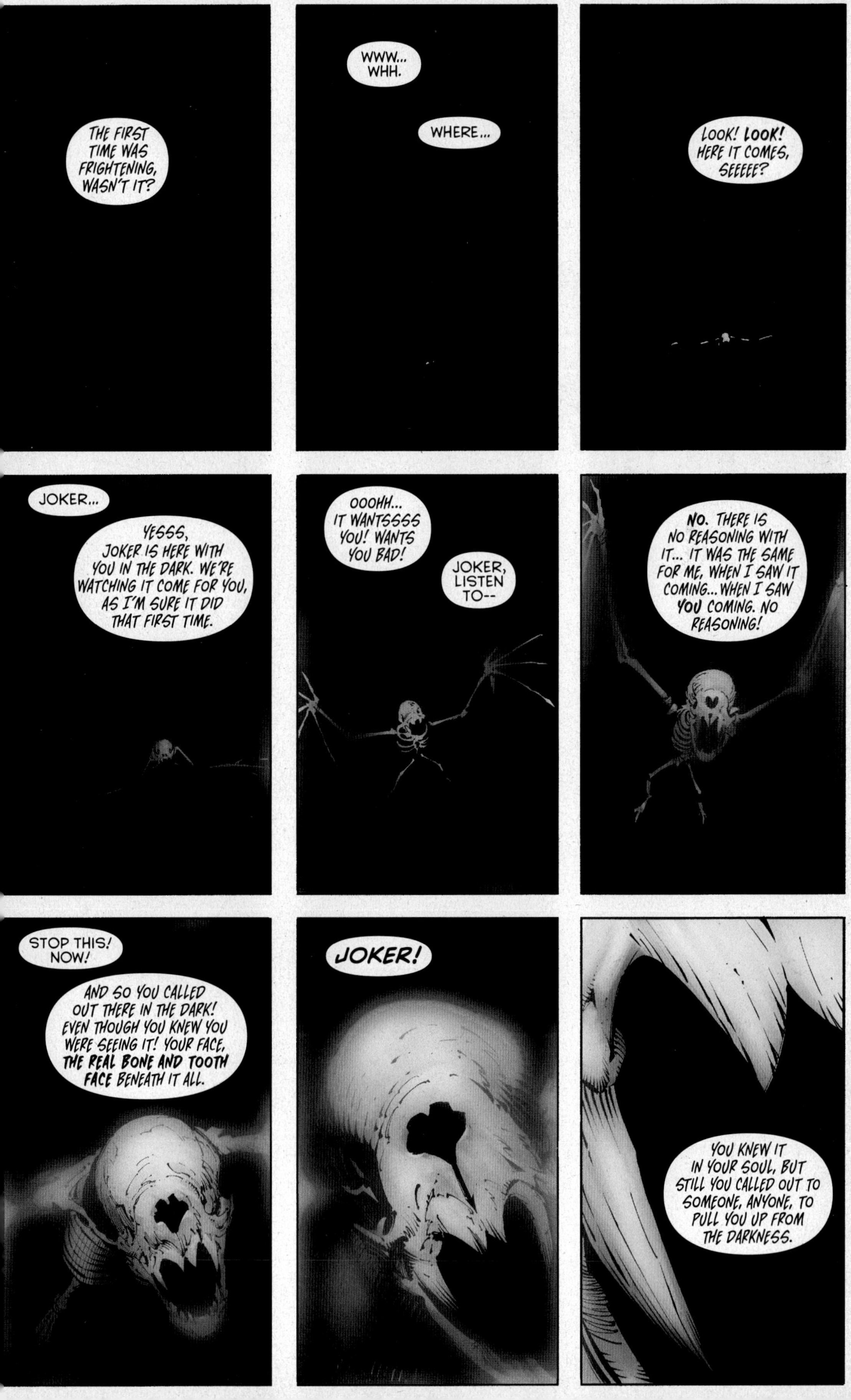
THE FIRST TIME WAS FRIGHTENING, WASN'T IT?
WWW... WHH.
WHERE...
LOOK! LOOK! HERE IT COMES, SEEEEE?
JOKER...
YESSS, JOKER IS HERE WITH YOU IN THE DARK. WE'RE WATCHING IT COME FOR YOU, AS I'M SURE IT DID THAT FIRST TIME.
OOOHH... IT WANTSSSS YOU! WANTS YOU BAD!
JOKER, LISTEN TO--
NO. THERE IS NO REASONING WITH IT... IT WAS THE SAME FOR ME, WHEN I SAW IT COMING... WHEN I SAW YOU COMING. NO REASONING!
STOP THIS! NOW!
AND SO YOU CALLED OUT THERE IN THE DARK! EVEN THOUGH YOU KNEW YOU WERE SEEING IT! YOUR FACE, THE REAL BONE AND TOOTH FACE BENEATH IT ALL.
JOKER!
YOU KNEW IT IN YOUR SOUL, BUT STILL YOU CALLED OUT TO SOMEONE, ANYONE, TO PULL YOU UP FROM THE DARKNESS.

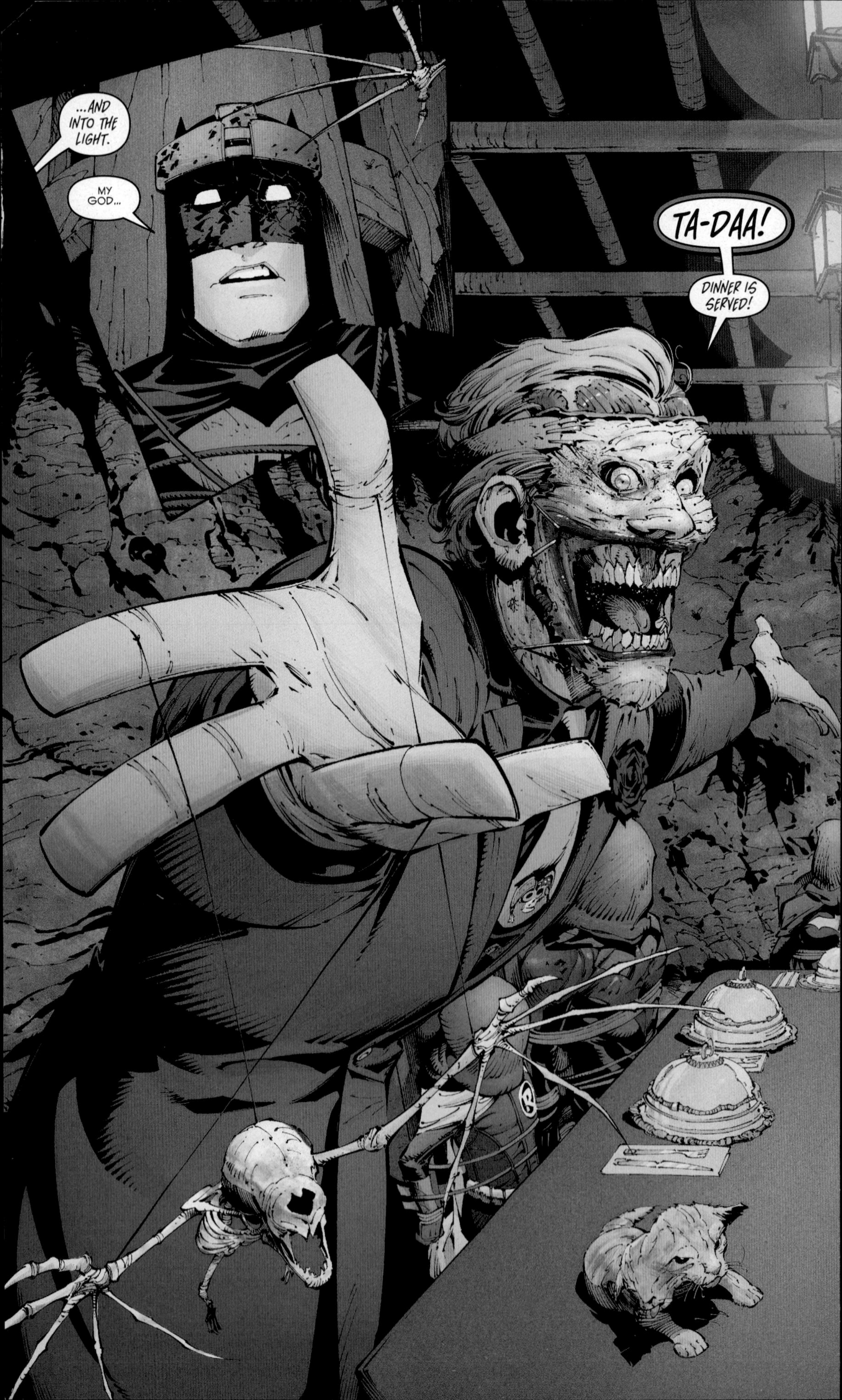
...AND INTO THE LIGHT.
MY GOD...
TA-DAA!
DINNER IS SERVED!

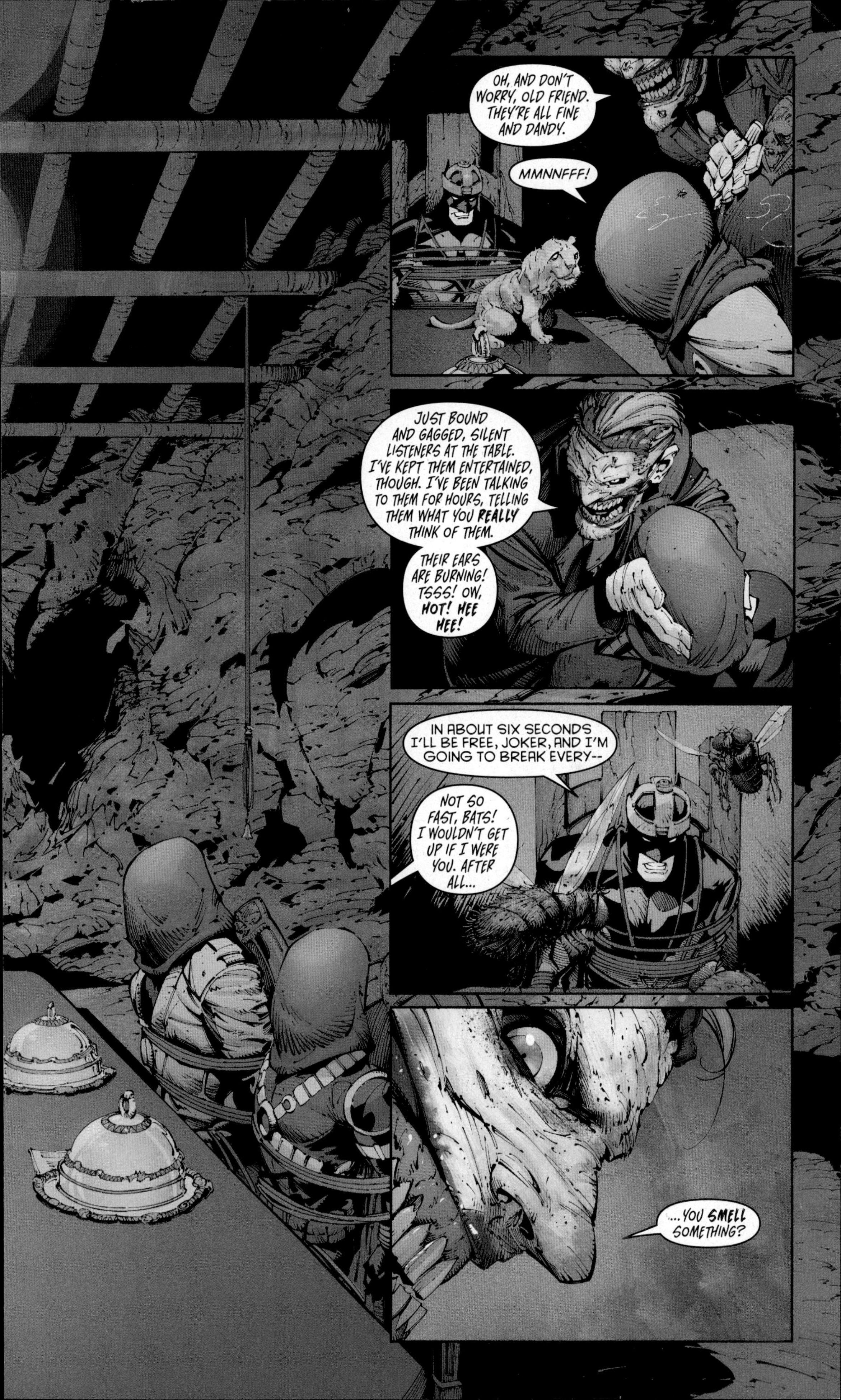
OH, AND DON'T WORRY, OLD FRIEND. THEY'RE ALL FINE AND DANDY.
MMNNFFF!
JUST BOUND AND GAGGED, SILENT LISTENERS AT THE TABLE. I'VE KEPT THEM ENTERTAINED, THOUGH. I'VE BEEN TALKING TO THEM FOR HOURS, TELLING THEM WHAT YOU REALLY THINK OF THEM.
THEIR EARS ARE BURNING! TSSS! OW, HOT! HEE HEE!
IN ABOUT SIX SECONDS I'LL BE FREE, JOKER, AND I'M GOING TO BREAK EVERY--
NOT SO FAST, BATS! I WOULDN'T GET UP IF I WERE YOU. AFTER ALL...
...YOU SMELL SOMETHING?

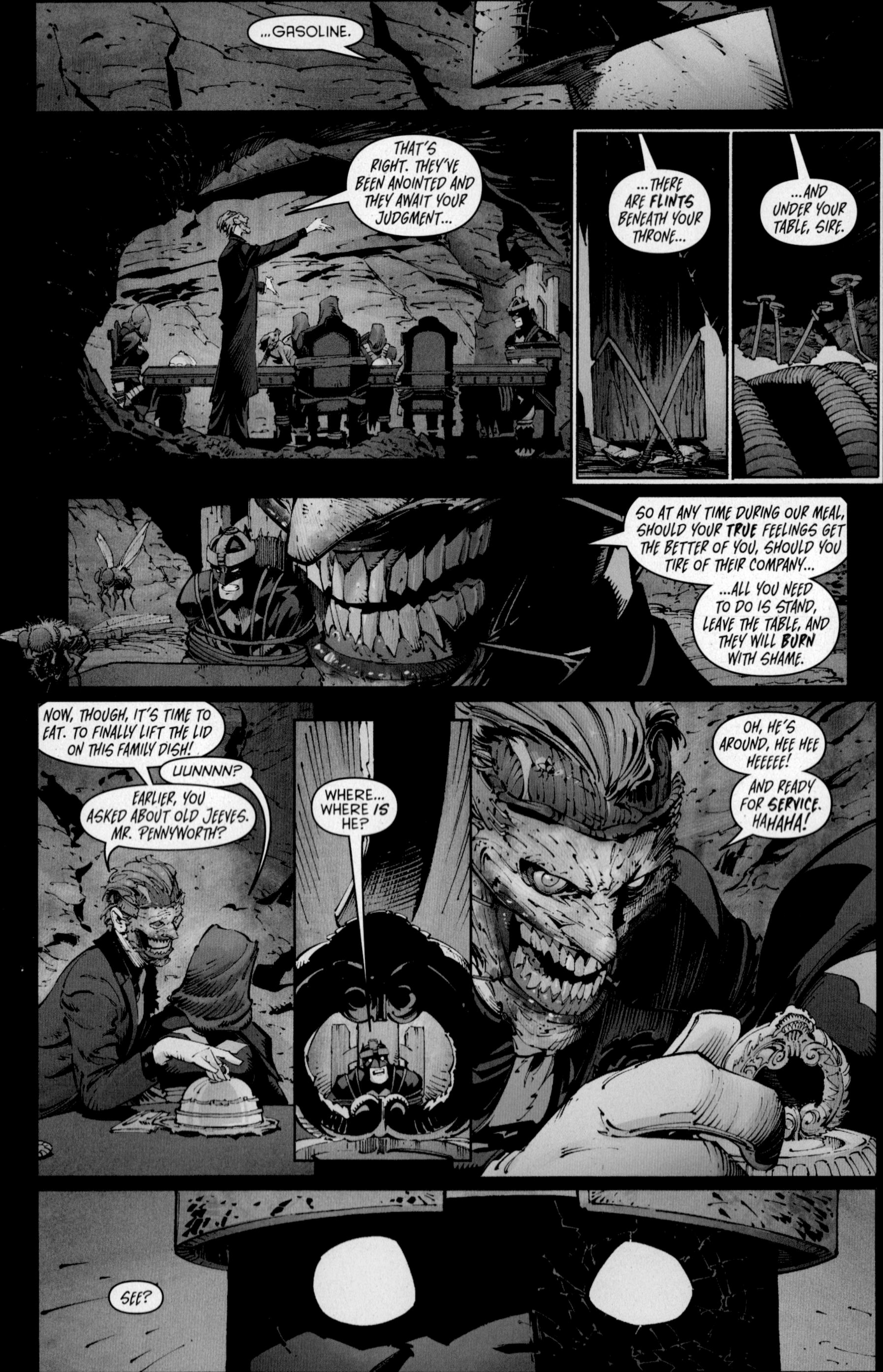
...GASOLINE.
THAT'S RIGHT. THEY'VE BEEN ANOINTED AND THEY AWAIT YOUR JUDGMENT...
...THERE ARE FLINTS BENEATH YOUR THRONE...
...AND UNDER YOUR TABLE, SIRE.
SO AT ANY TIME DURING OUR MEAL, SHOULD YOUR TRUE FEELINGS GET THE BETTER OF YOU, SHOULD YOU TIRE OF THEIR COMPANY...
...ALL YOU NEED TO DO IS STAND, LEAVE THE TABLE, AND THEY WILL BURN WITH SHAME.
NOW, THOUGH, IT'S TIME TO EAT. TO FINALLY LIFT THE LID ON THIS FAMILY DISH!
UUNNNN?
EARLIER, YOU ASKED ABOUT OLD JEEVES. MR. PENNYWORTH?
WHERE... WHERE IS HE?
OH, HE'S AROUND, HEE HEE HEEEEE!
AND READY FOR SERVICE. HAHAHA!
SEE?

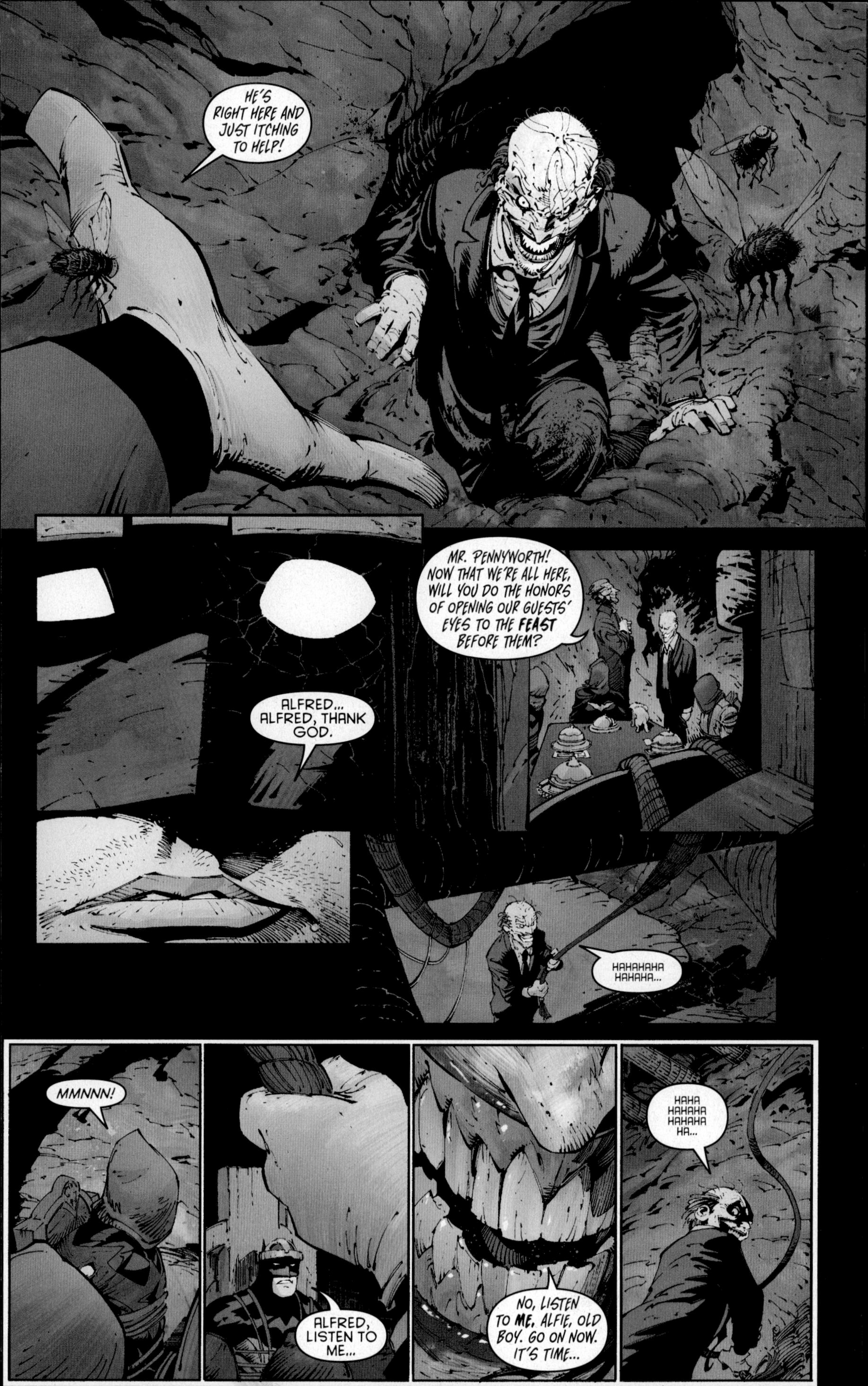
HE'S RIGHT HERE AND JUST ITCHING TO HELP!
MR. PENNYWORTH! NOW THAT WE'RE ALL HERE, WILL YOU DO THE HONORS OF OPENING OUR GUESTS' EYES TO THE FEAST BEFORE THEM?
ALFRED... ALFRED, THANK GOD.
HAHAHAHA HAHAHA...
MMNNN!
ALFRED, LISTEN TO ME...
NO, LISTEN TO ME, ALFIE, OLD BOY. GO ON NOW. IT'S TIME...
HAHA HAHAHA HAHAHA HA...

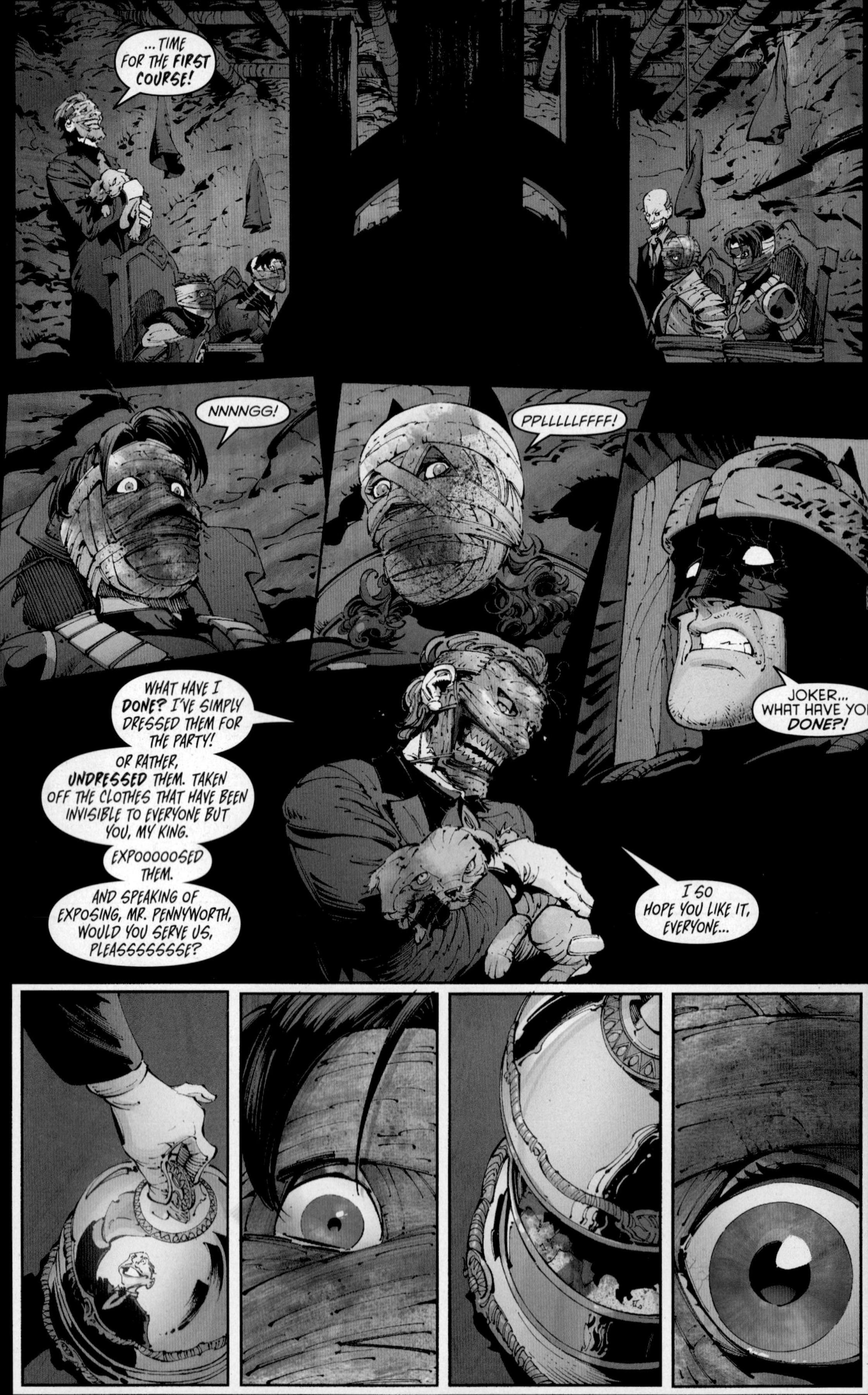
...TIME FOR THE FIRST COURSE!
NNNNGG!
PPLLLLLLFFFF!
JOKER... WHAT HAVE YO DONE?!
WHAT HAVE I DONE? I'VE SIMPLY DRESSED THEM FOR THE PARTY!
OR RATHER, UNDRESSED THEM. TAKEN OFF THE CLOTHES THAT HAVE BEEN INVISIBLE TO EVERYONE BUT YOU, MY KING.
EXPOOOOOSED THEM.
AND SPEAKING OF EXPOSING, MR. PENNYWORTH, WOULD YOU SERVE US, PLEASSSSSSSE?
I SO HOPE YOU LIKE IT, EVERYONE...

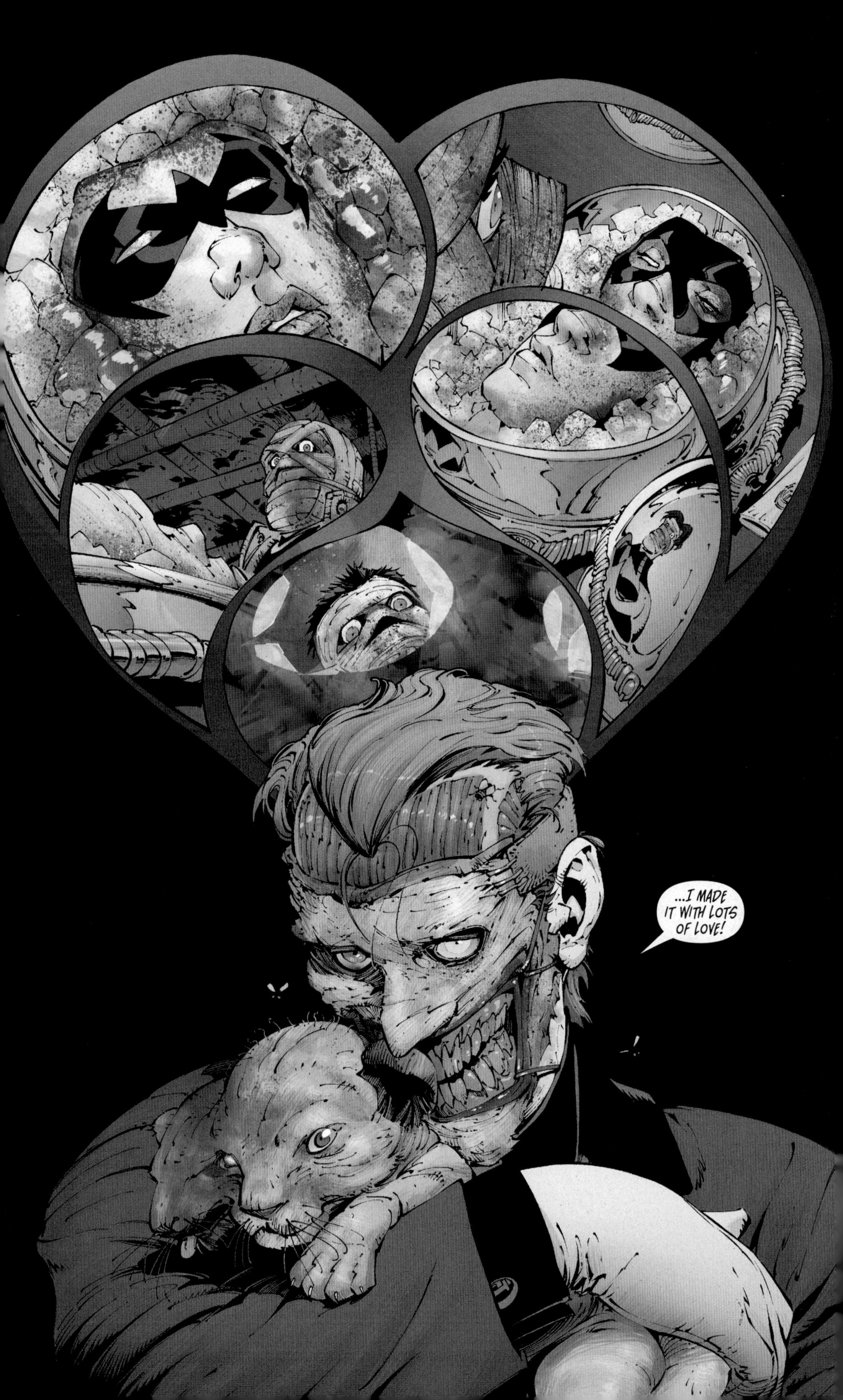
...I MADE IT WITH LOTS OF LOVE!

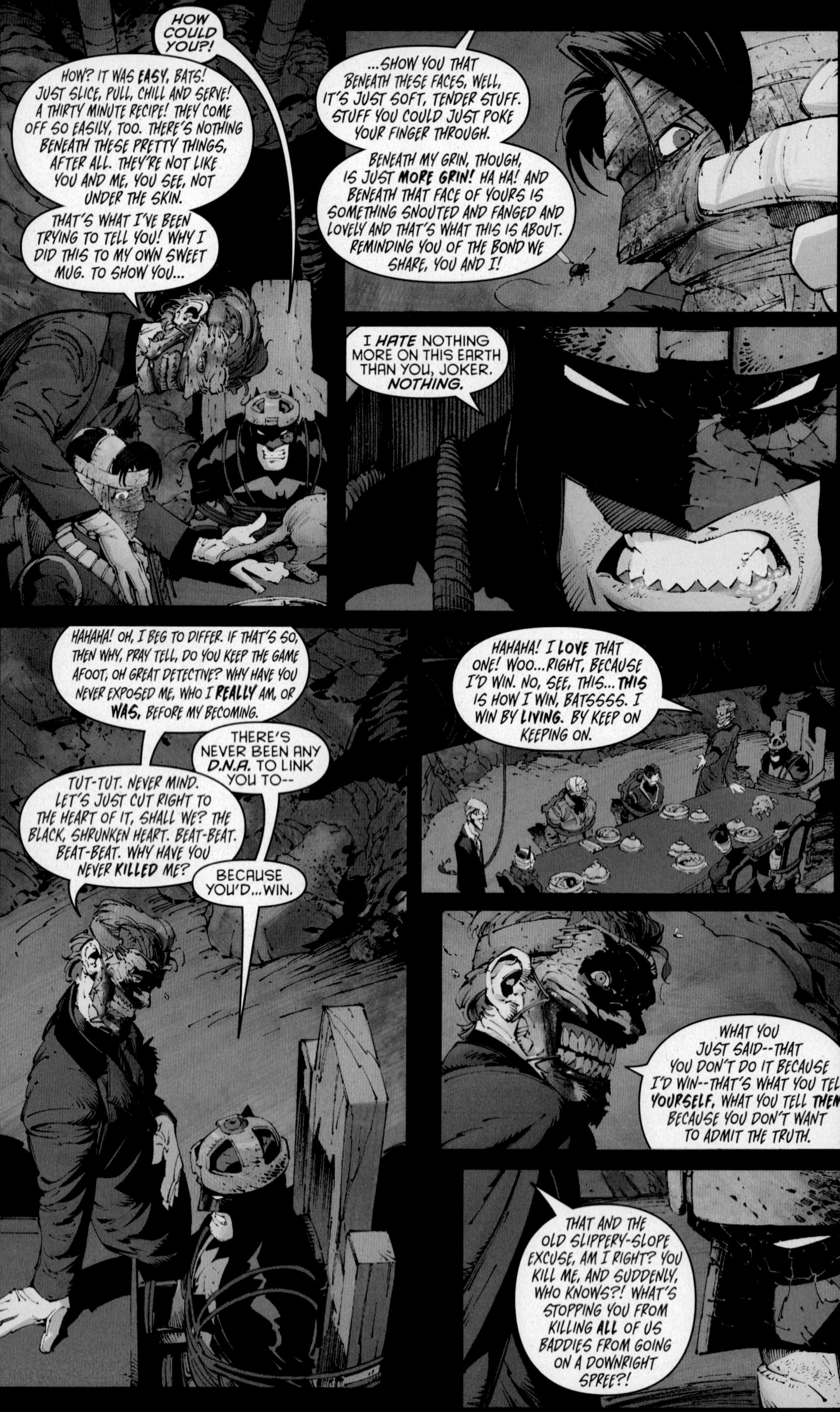
HOW COULD YOU?!
HOW? IT WAS EASY, BATS! JUST SLICE, PULL, CHILL AND SERVE! A THIRTY MINUTE RECIPE! THEY COME OFF SO EASILY, TOO. THERE'S NOTHING BENEATH THESE PRETTY THINGS, AFTER ALL. THEY'RE NOT LIKE YOU AND ME, YOU SEE, NOT UNDER THE SKIN.
THAT'S WHAT I'VE BEEN TRYING TO TELL YOU! WHY I DID THIS TO MY OWN SWEET MUG. TO SHOW YOU...
...SHOW YOU THAT BENEATH THESE FACES, WELL, IT'S JUST SOFT, TENDER STUFF. STUFF YOU COULD JUST POKE YOUR FINGER THROUGH.
BENEATH MY GRIN, THOUGH, IS JUST MORE GRIN! HA HA! AND BENEATH THAT FACE OF YOURS IS SOMETHING SNOUTED AND FANGED AND LOVELY AND THAT'S WHAT THIS IS ABOUT. REMINDING YOU OF THE BOND WE SHARE, YOU AND I!
I HATE NOTHING MORE ON THIS EARTH THAN YOU, JOKER. NOTHING.
HAHAHA! OH, I BEG TO DIFFER. IF THAT'S SO, THEN WHY, PRAY TELL, DO YOU KEEP THE GAME AFOOT, OH GREAT DETECTIVE? WHY HAVE YOU NEVER EXPOSED ME, WHO I REALLY AM, OR WAS, BEFORE MY BECOMING.
THERE'S NEVER BEEN ANY D.N.A. TO LINK YOU TO--
TUT-TUT. NEVER MIND. LET'S JUST CUT RIGHT TO THE HEART OF IT, SHALL WE? THE BLACK, SHRUNKEN HEART. BEAT-BEAT. BEAT-BEAT. WHY HAVE YOU NEVER KILLED ME?
BECAUSE YOU'D...WIN.
HAHAHA! I LOVE THAT ONE! WOO...RIGHT, BECAUSE I'D WIN. NO, SEE, THIS... THIS IS HOW I WIN, BATSSSS. I WIN BY LIVING. BY KEEP ON KEEPING ON.
WHAT YOU JUST SAID--THAT YOU DON'T DO IT BECAUSE I'D WIN--THAT'S WHAT YOU TELL YOURSELF, WHAT YOU TELL THEM BECAUSE YOU DON'T WANT TO ADMIT THE TRUTH.
THAT AND THE OLD SLIPPERY-SLOPE EXCUSE, AM I RIGHT? YOU KILL ME, AND SUDDENLY, WHO KNOWS?! WHAT'S STOPPING YOU FROM KILLING ALL OF US BADDIES FROM GOING ON A DOWNRIGHT SPREE?!

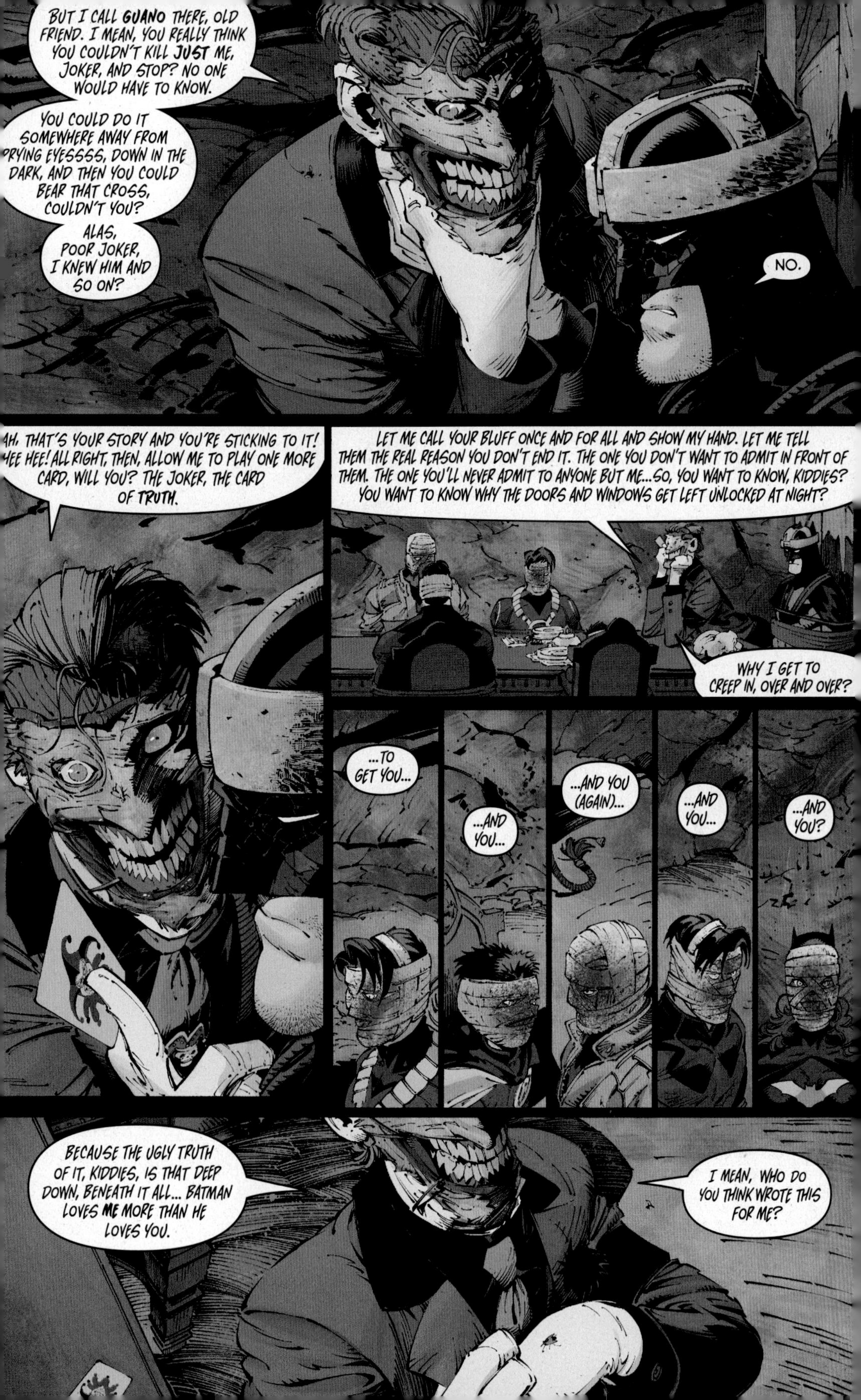
BUT I CALL GUANO THERE, OLD FRIEND. I MEAN, YOU REALLY THINK YOU COULDN'T KILL JUST ME, JOKER, AND STOP? NO ONE WOULD HAVE TO KNOW.
YOU COULD DO IT SOMEWHERE AWAY FROM PRYING EYESSSS, DOWN IN THE DARK, AND THEN YOU COULD BEAR THAT CROSS, COULDN'T YOU?
ALAS, POOR JOKER, I KNEW HIM AND SO ON?
NO.
AH, THAT'S YOUR STORY AND YOU'RE STICKING TO IT! HEE HEE! ALL RIGHT, THEN, ALLOW ME TO PLAY ONE MORE CARD, WILL YOU? THE JOKER, THE CARD OF TRUTH.
LET ME CALL YOUR BLUFF ONCE AND FOR ALL AND SHOW MY HAND. LET ME TELL THEM THE REAL REASON YOU DON'T END IT. THE ONE YOU DON'T WANT TO ADMIT IN FRONT OF THEM. THE ONE YOU'LL NEVER ADMIT TO ANYONE BUT ME...SO, YOU WANT TO KNOW, KIDDIES? YOU WANT TO KNOW WHY THE DOORS AND WINDOWS GET LEFT UNLOCKED AT NIGHT?
WHY I GET TO CREEP IN, OVER AND OVER?
...TO GET YOU...
...AND YOU...
...AND YOU (AGAIN)...
...AND YOU...
...AND YOU?
BECAUSE THE UGLY TRUTH OF IT, KIDDIES, IS THAT DEEP DOWN, BENEATH IT ALL... BATMAN LOVES ME MORE THAN HE LOVES YOU.
I MEAN, WHO DO YOU THINK WROTE THIS FOR ME?

...IT WAS **YOU**, BATS.

YOU WROTE THIS LITTLE LOVE LETTER, THIS BACKWARDS MAP, THIS HIT LIST...AND YOU WRITE IT AGAIN AND AGAIN, EVERY TIME YOU KEEP ONE OF **US** ALIVE, BUT LET ONE OF **THEM** FALL. AND THEY WILL FALL, MAYBE ONE BY ONE, MAYBE TOGETHER...BUT LOOK TO THE FUTURE, REALLY LOOK, AND YOU KNOW IT'S COMING...

...THAT DAY WHEN THEY'RE ALL DEAD AND BURIED, IN THEIR COLD BAT-GRAVES (HEE-HEE). BUT LOOK! THERE'S ME AND MY FRIENDS, AND...WHY, WE'RE STILL ALIVE AND KICKING! AND THERE YOU ARE, BATSSS...CHASING US, FOREVER CHASING!

AND WHY? BECAUSE IT'S WHAT YOU WANT TO HAPPEN. IT'S WHAT YOU **NEEEEED**. BECAUSE YOU SEE, WITH **US** YOU'RE MORE! WITH **US**, YOU TRANSSSCEND! WITH **US**, YOU'RE ALWAYS.

BUT **THEM**, THEY MAKE YOU EVERYTHING YOU WANT TO FORGET THAT YOU ARE, EVERYTHING YOU'RE AFRAID OF. AND YOU WERE AFRAID, WHEN YOU TOOK **THEM** IN. I KNOW. IT'S OKAY, OLD FRIEND. IT WAS A MOMENT OF WEAK-NESSSSS...THE DIRT WAS PULLING.

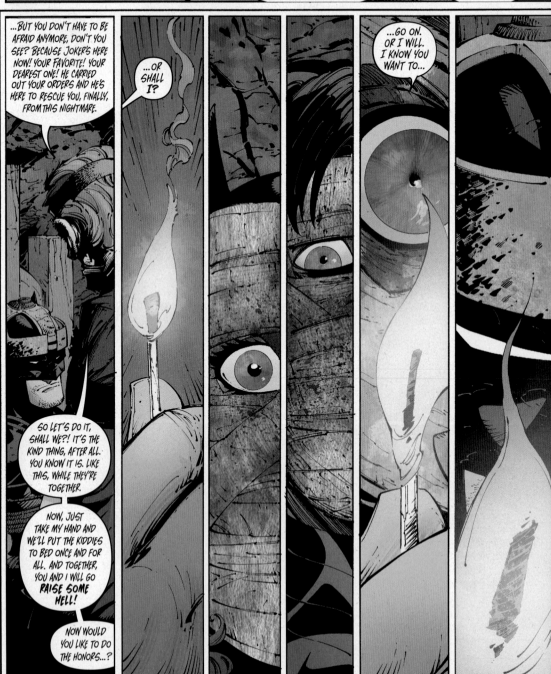

...BUT YOU DON'T HAVE TO BE AFRAID ANYMORE, DON'T YOU SEE? BECAUSE JOKER'S HERE NOW! YOUR FAVORITE! YOUR DEAREST ONE! HE CARRIED OUT YOUR ORDERS AND HE'S HERE TO RESCUE YOU, FINALLY, FROM THIS NIGHTMARE.

...OR SHALL I?

...GO ON. OR I WILL. I KNOW YOU WANT TO...

SO LET'S DO IT, SHALL WE?! IT'S THE KIND THING, AFTER ALL. YOU KNOW IT IS. LIKE THIS, WHILE THEY'RE TOGETHER.

NOW, JUST TAKE MY HAND AND WE'LL PUT THE KIDDIES TO BED ONCE AND FOR ALL. AND TOGETHER, YOU AND I WILL GO **RAISE SOME HELL!**

NOW WOULD YOU LIKE TO DO THE HONORS...?

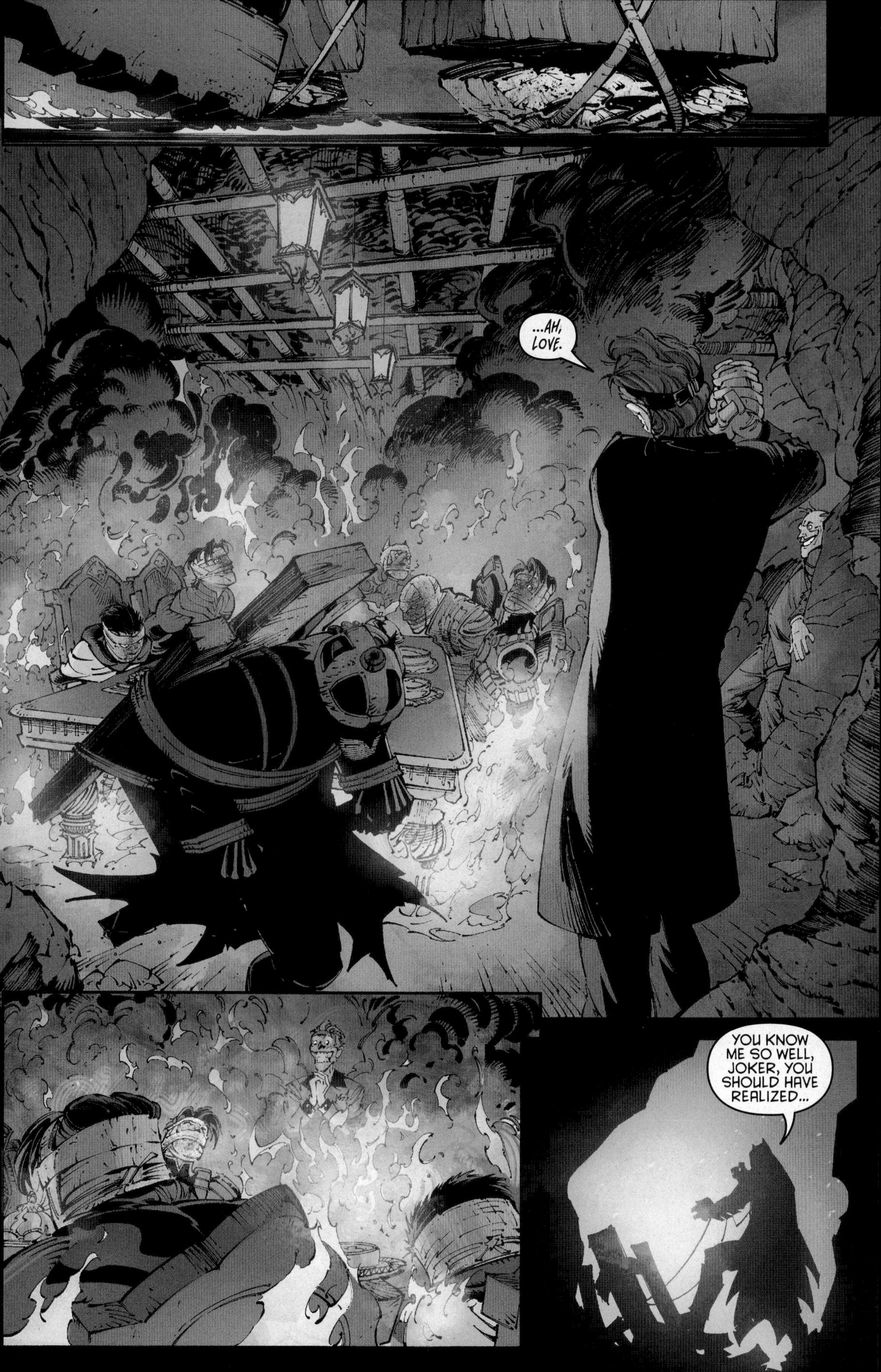
...AH, LOVE.
YOU KNOW ME SO WELL, JOKER, YOU SHOULD HAVE REALIZED...

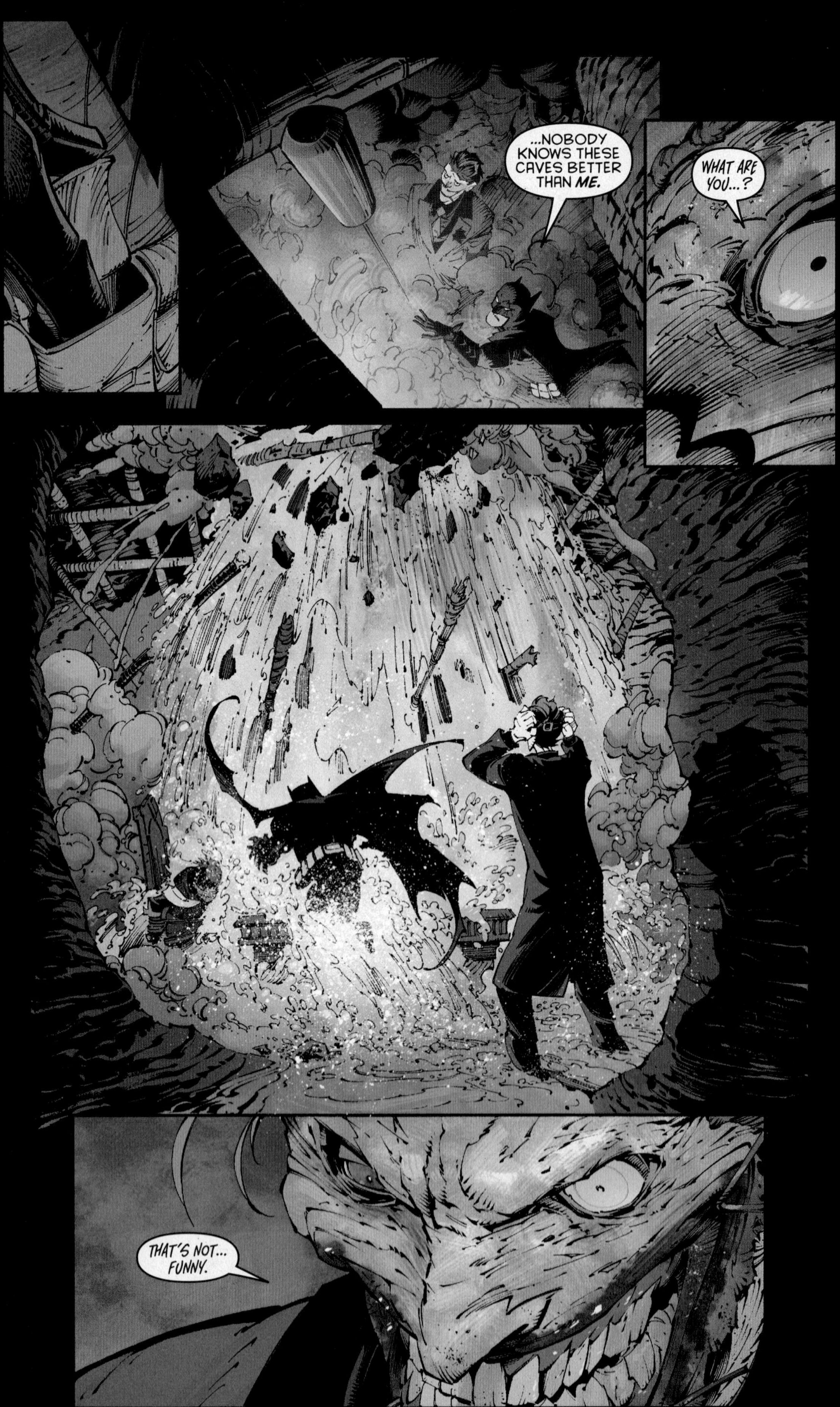
...NOBODY KNOWS THESE CAVES BETTER THAN *ME.*
WHAT ARE YOU...?
THAT'S NOT... FUNNY.

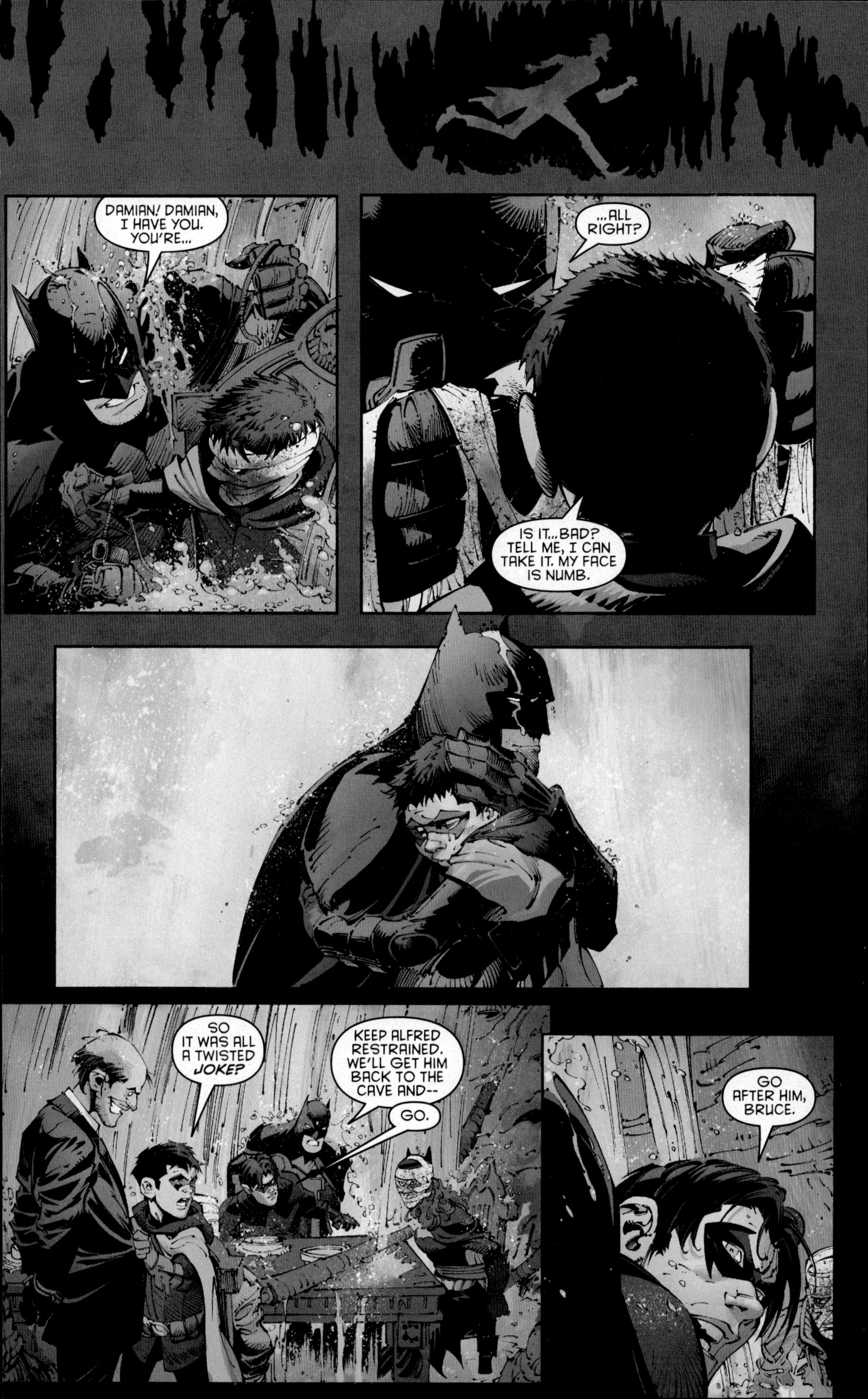
DAMIAN! DAMIAN, I HAVE YOU. YOU'RE...
...ALL RIGHT?
IS IT...BAD? TELL ME, I CAN TAKE IT. MY FACE IS NUMB.
SO IT WAS ALL A TWISTED JOKE?
KEEP ALFRED RESTRAINED. WE'LL GET HIM BACK TO THE CAVE AND--
GO.
GO AFTER HIM, BRUCE.

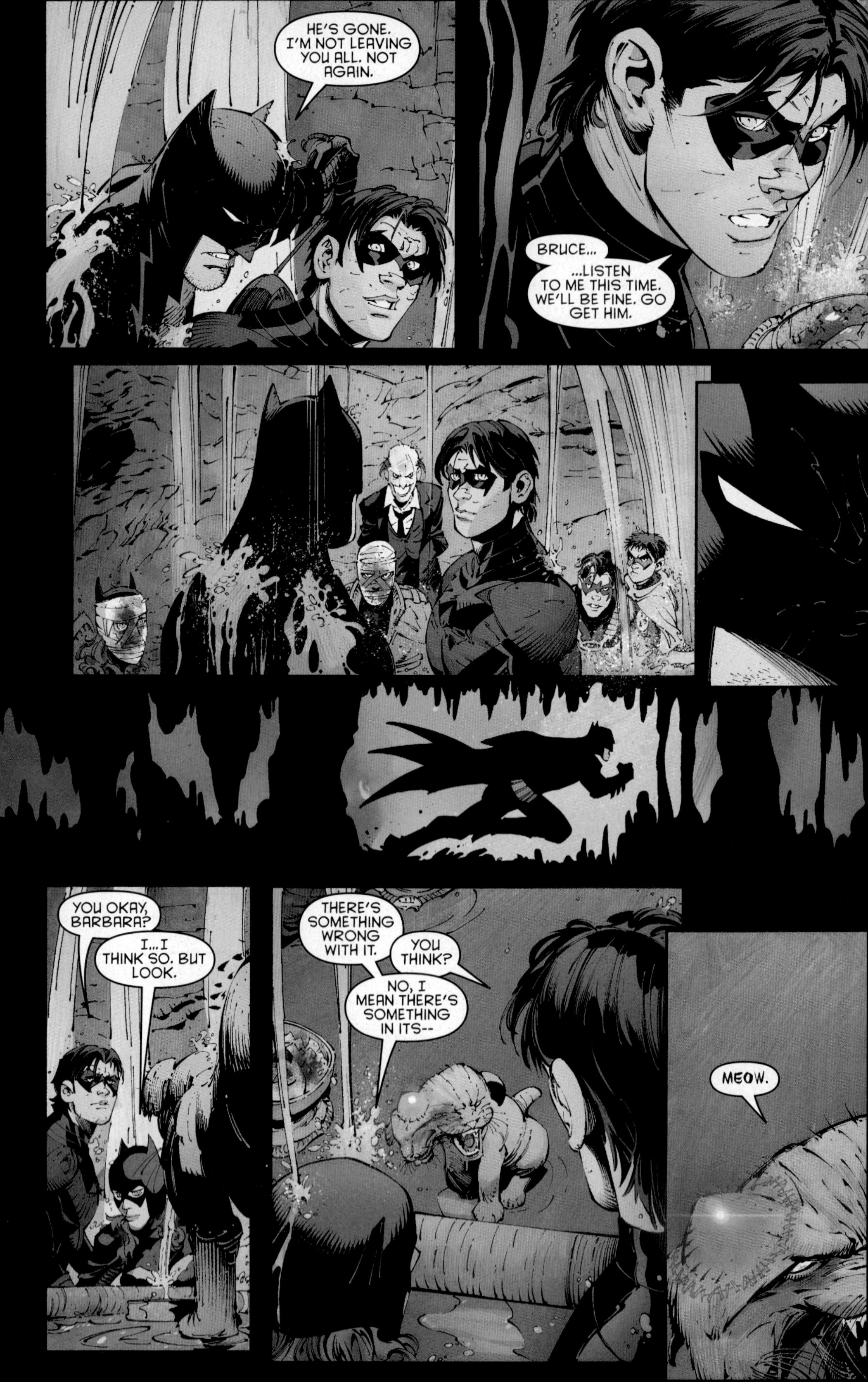
HE'S GONE. I'M NOT LEAVING YOU ALL. NOT AGAIN.
BRUCE...
...LISTEN TO ME THIS TIME. WE'LL BE FINE. GO GET HIM.
YOU OKAY, BARBARA?
I...I THINK SO. BUT LOOK.
THERE'S SOMETHING WRONG WITH IT.
YOU THINK?
NO, I MEAN THERE'S SOMETHING IN ITS--
MEOW.

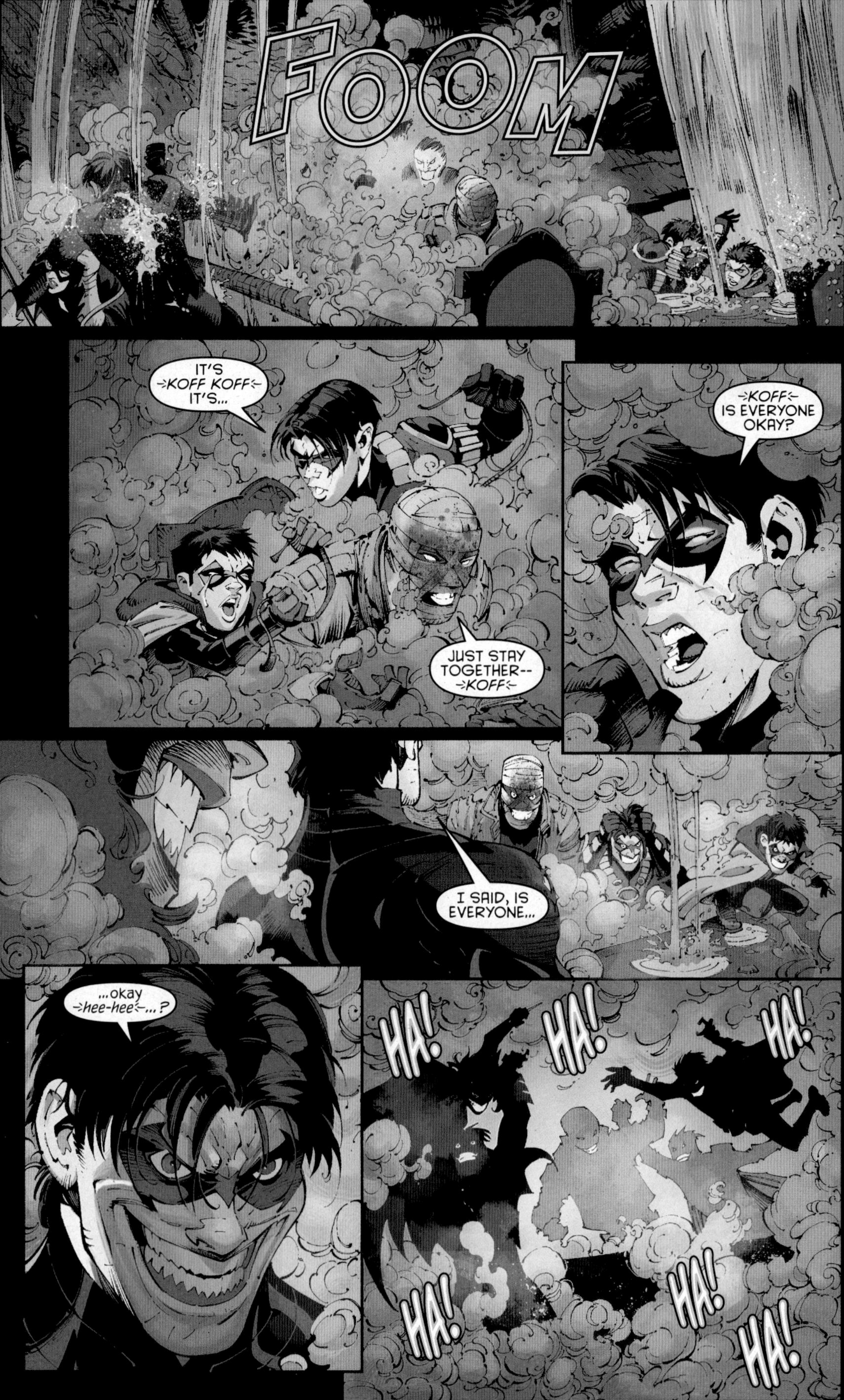
FOOM
IT'S -KOFF KOFF- IT'S...
JUST STAY TOGETHER-- -KOFF-
-KOFF- IS EVERYONE OKAY?
I SAID, IS EVERYONE...
...okay -hee-hee-...?
HA! HA! HA!
HA! HA! HA!

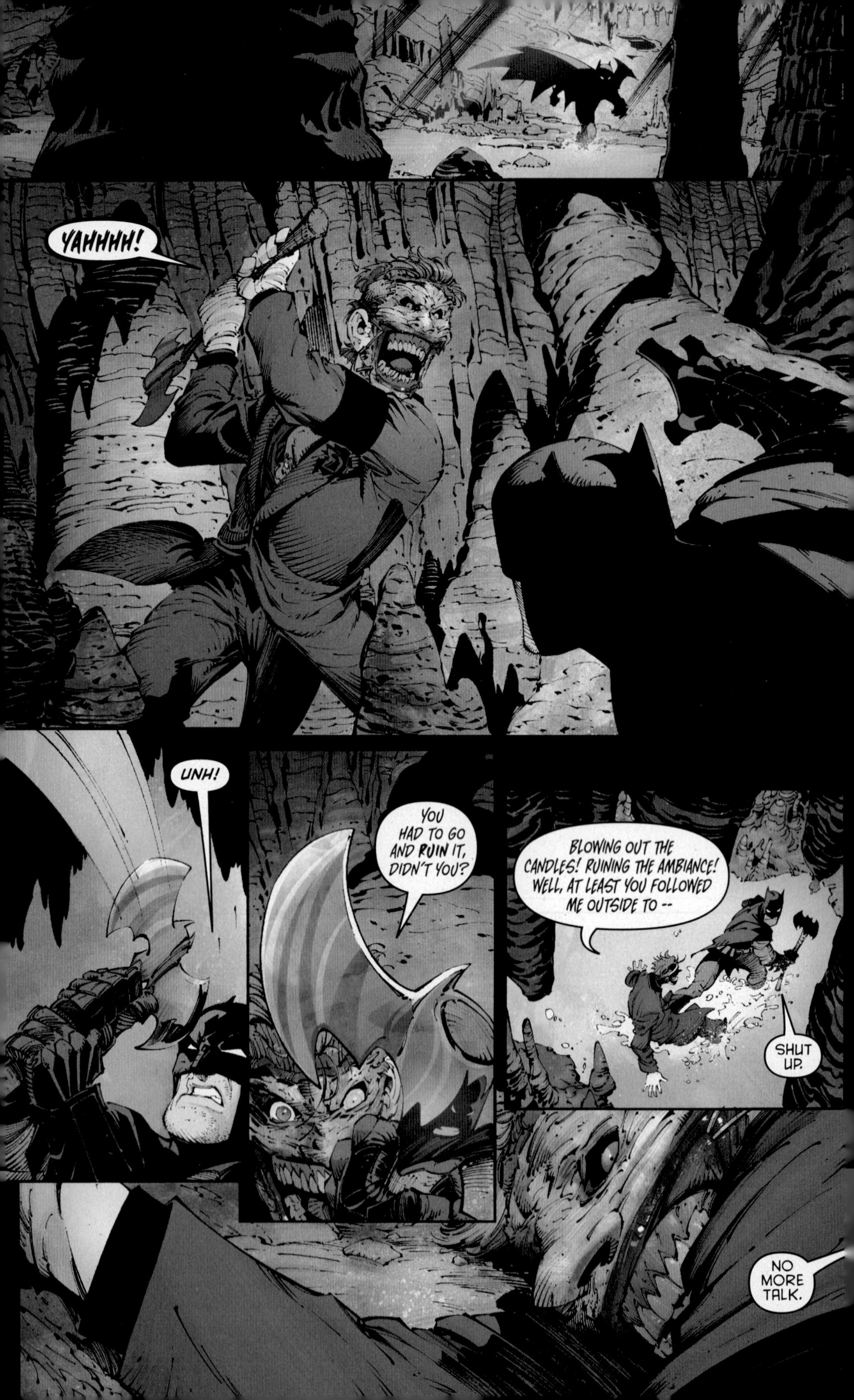
YAHHHH!
UNH!
YOU HAD TO GO AND RUIN IT, DIDN'T YOU?
BLOWING OUT THE CANDLES! RUINING THE AMBIANCE! WELL, AT LEAST YOU FOLLOWED ME OUTSIDE TO --
SHUT UP.
NO MORE TALK.

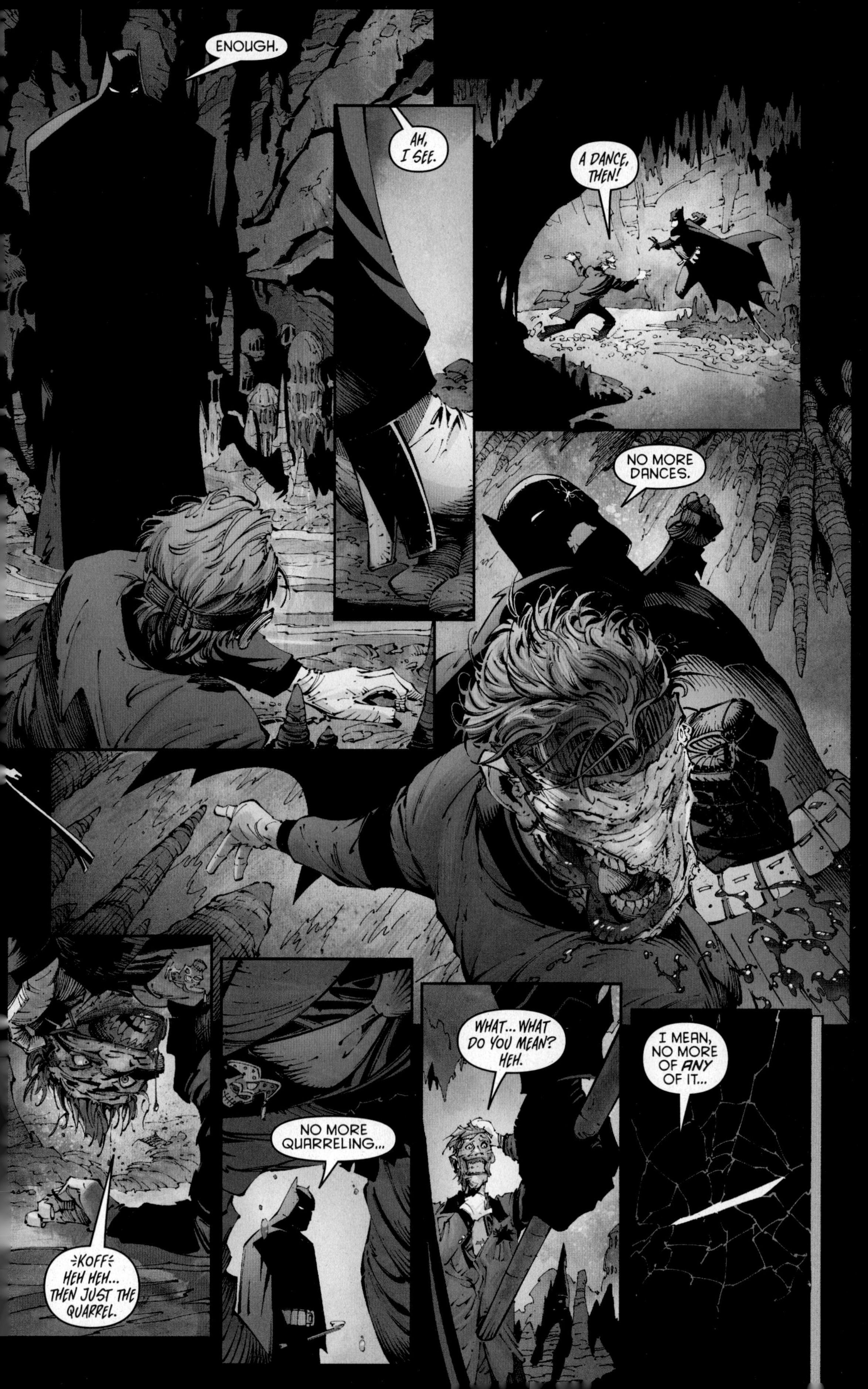
ENOUGH.
AH, I SEE.
A DANCE, THEN!
NO MORE DANCES.
KOFF HEH HEH... THEN JUST THE QUARREL.
NO MORE QUARRELING...
WHAT... WHAT DO YOU MEAN? HEH.
I MEAN, NO MORE OF ANY OF IT...

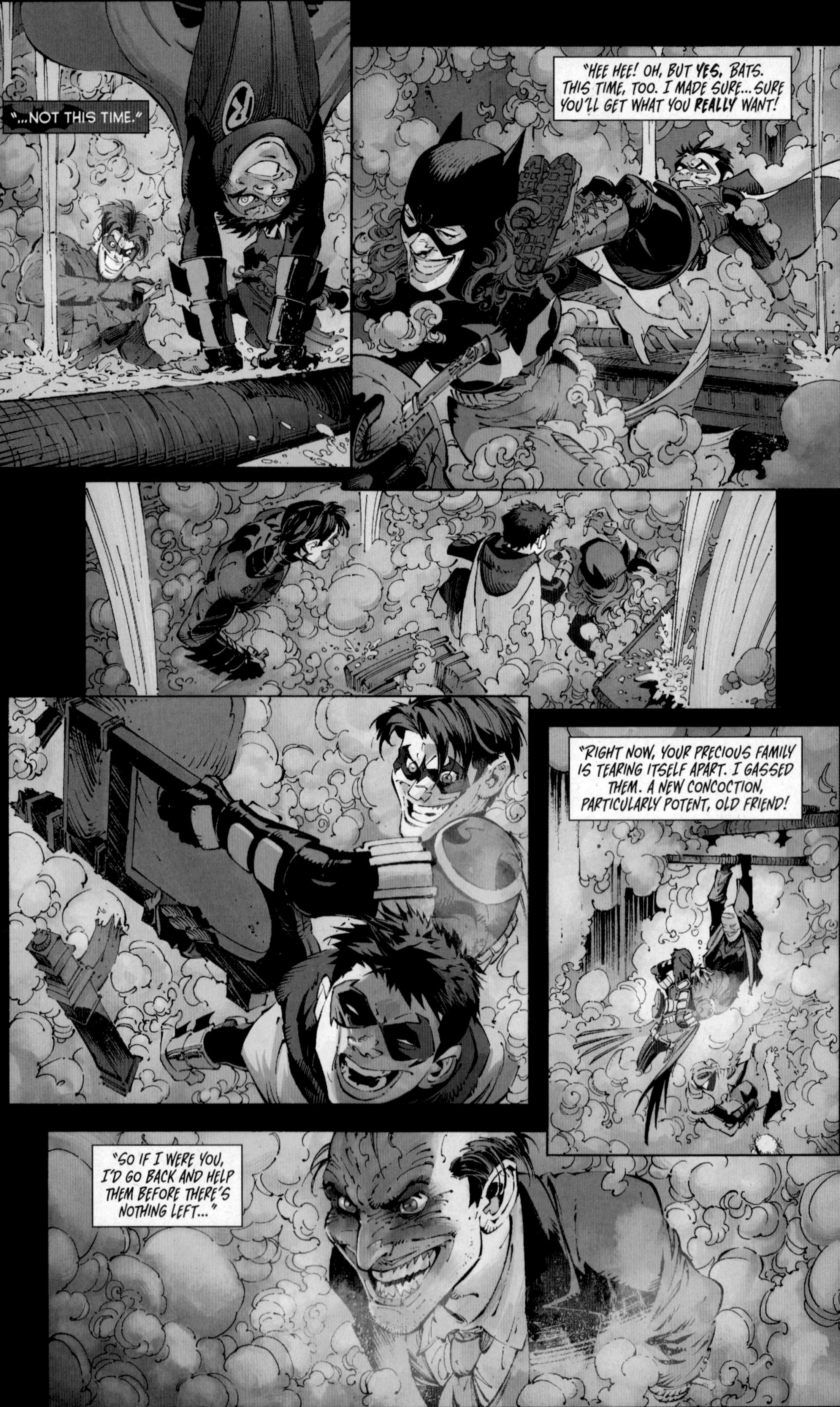
"...NOT THIS TIME."
"HEE HEE! OH, BUT YES, BATS. THIS TIME, TOO. I MADE SURE... SURE YOU'LL GET WHAT YOU REALLY WANT!
"RIGHT NOW, YOUR PRECIOUS FAMILY IS TEARING ITSELF APART. I GASSED THEM. A NEW CONCOCTION, PARTICULARLY POTENT, OLD FRIEND!
"SO IF I WERE YOU, I'D GO BACK AND HELP THEM BEFORE THERE'S NOTHING LEFT..."

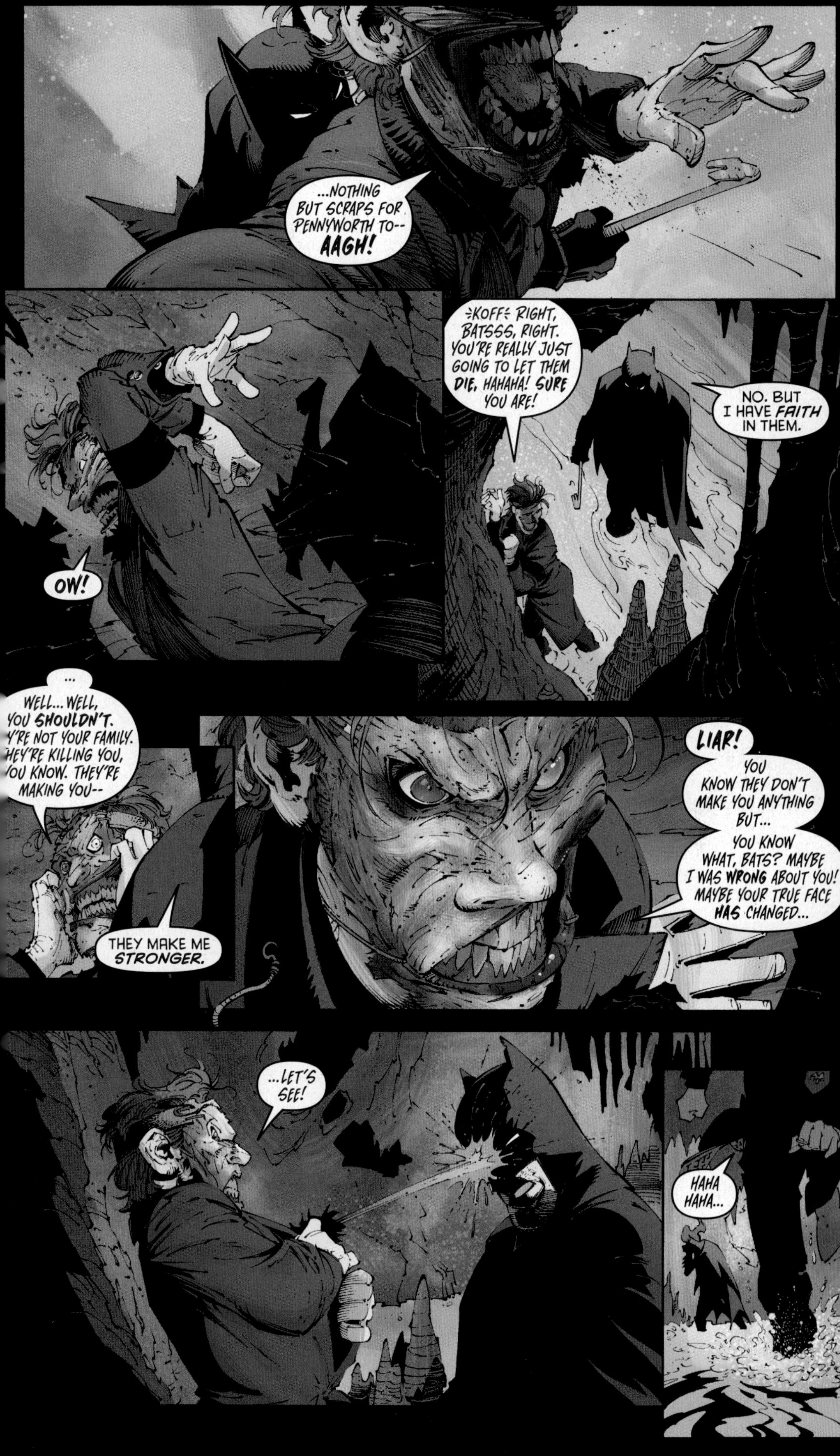
...NOTHING BUT SCRAPS FOR PENNYWORTH TO-- AAGH!
OW!
≑KOFF≑ RIGHT, BATSSS, RIGHT. YOU'RE REALLY JUST GOING TO LET THEM DIE, HAHAHA! SURE YOU ARE!
NO. BUT I HAVE FAITH IN THEM.
... WELL... WELL, YOU SHOULDN'T. Y'RE NOT YOUR FAMILY. HEY'RE KILLING YOU, YOU KNOW. THEY'RE MAKING YOU--
THEY MAKE ME STRONGER.
LIAR! YOU KNOW THEY DON'T MAKE YOU ANYTHING BUT... YOU KNOW WHAT, BATS? MAYBE I WAS WRONG ABOUT YOU! MAYBE YOUR TRUE FACE HAS CHANGED...
...LET'S SEE!
HAHA HAHA...

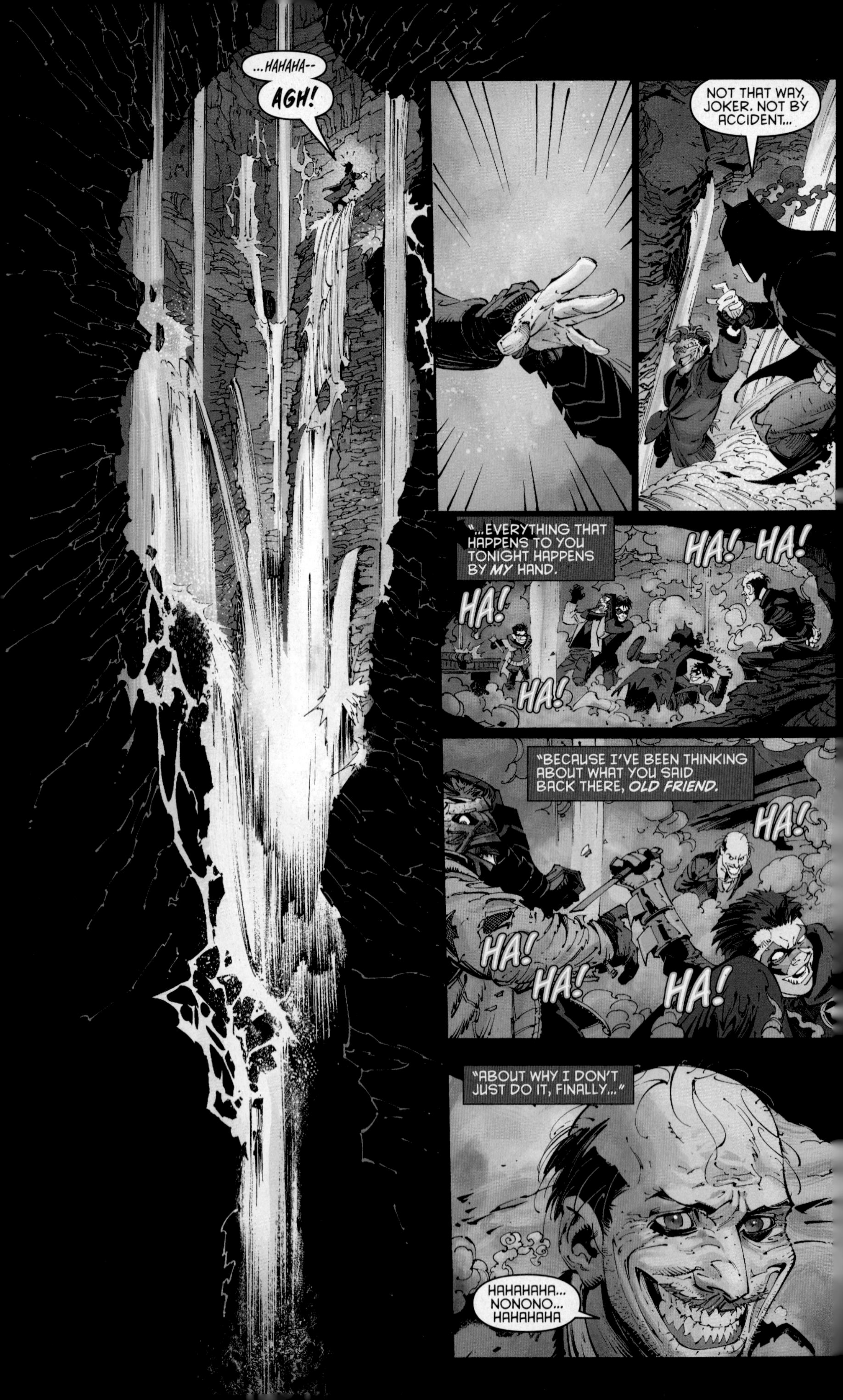

...HAHAHA--
AGH!
NOT THAT WAY, JOKER. NOT BY ACCIDENT...
"...EVERYTHING THAT HAPPENS TO YOU TONIGHT HAPPENS BY MY HAND.
HA! HA!
HA!
HA!
"BECAUSE I'VE BEEN THINKING ABOUT WHAT YOU SAID BACK THERE, OLD FRIEND.
HA!
HA!
HA!
HA!
"ABOUT WHY I DON'T JUST DO IT, FINALLY..."
HAHAHAHA... NONONO... HAHAHAHA

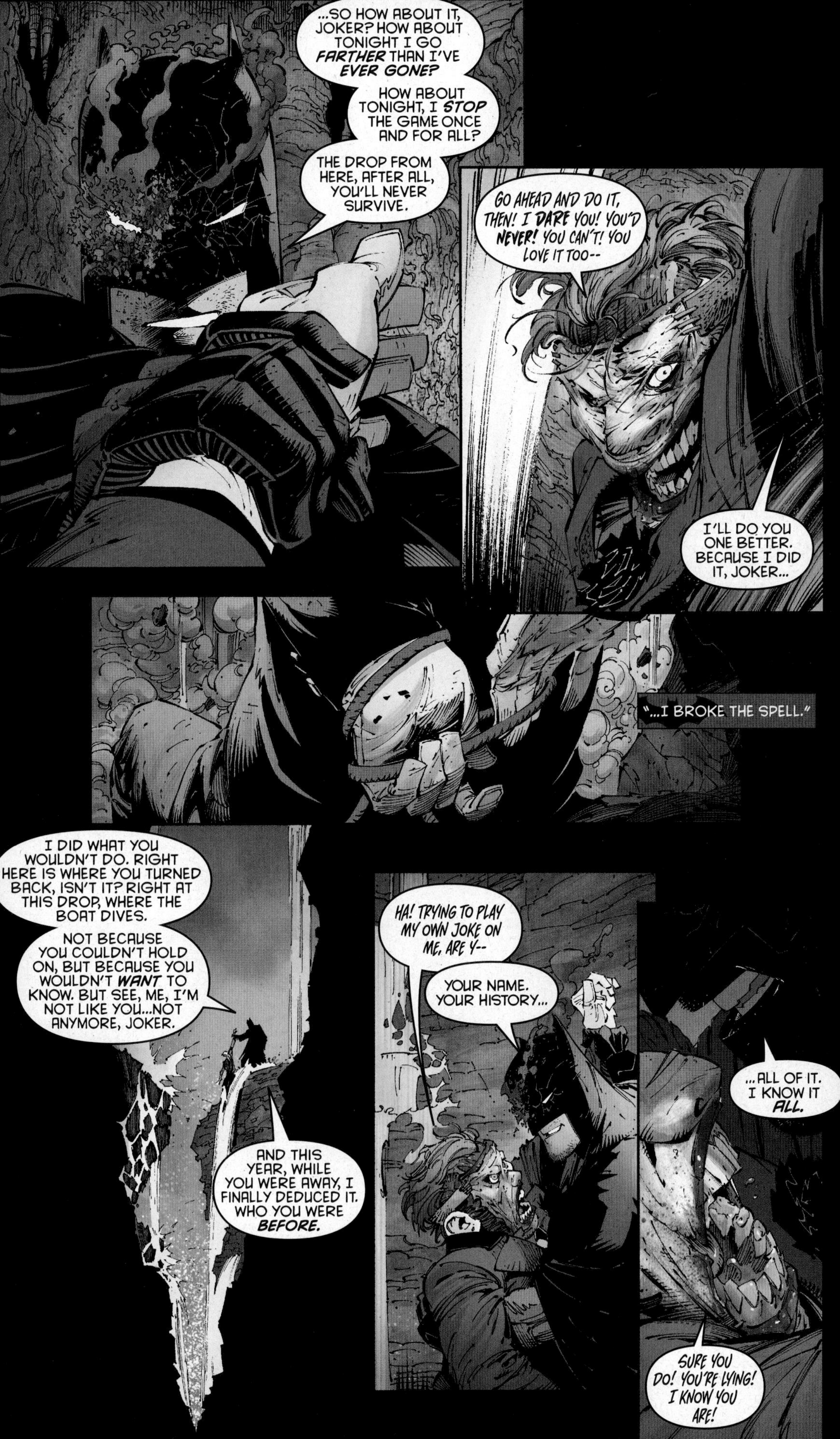
...SO HOW ABOUT IT, JOKER? HOW ABOUT TONIGHT I GO FARTHER THAN I'VE EVER GONE?
HOW ABOUT TONIGHT, I STOP THE GAME ONCE AND FOR ALL?
THE DROP FROM HERE, AFTER ALL, YOU'LL NEVER SURVIVE.
GO AHEAD AND DO IT, THEN! I DARE YOU! YOU'D NEVER! YOU CAN'T! YOU LOVE IT TOO--
I'LL DO YOU ONE BETTER. BECAUSE I DID IT, JOKER...
"...I BROKE THE SPELL."
I DID WHAT YOU WOULDN'T DO. RIGHT HERE IS WHERE YOU TURNED BACK, ISN'T IT? RIGHT AT THIS DROP, WHERE THE BOAT DIVES.
NOT BECAUSE YOU COULDN'T HOLD ON, BUT BECAUSE YOU WOULDN'T WANT TO KNOW. BUT SEE, ME, I'M NOT LIKE YOU...NOT ANYMORE, JOKER.
AND THIS YEAR, WHILE YOU WERE AWAY, I FINALLY DEDUCED IT. WHO YOU WERE BEFORE.
HA! TRYING TO PLAY MY OWN JOKE ON ME, ARE Y--
YOUR NAME. YOUR HISTORY...
...ALL OF IT. I KNOW IT ALL.
SURE YOU DO! YOU'RE LYING! I KNOW YOU ARE!

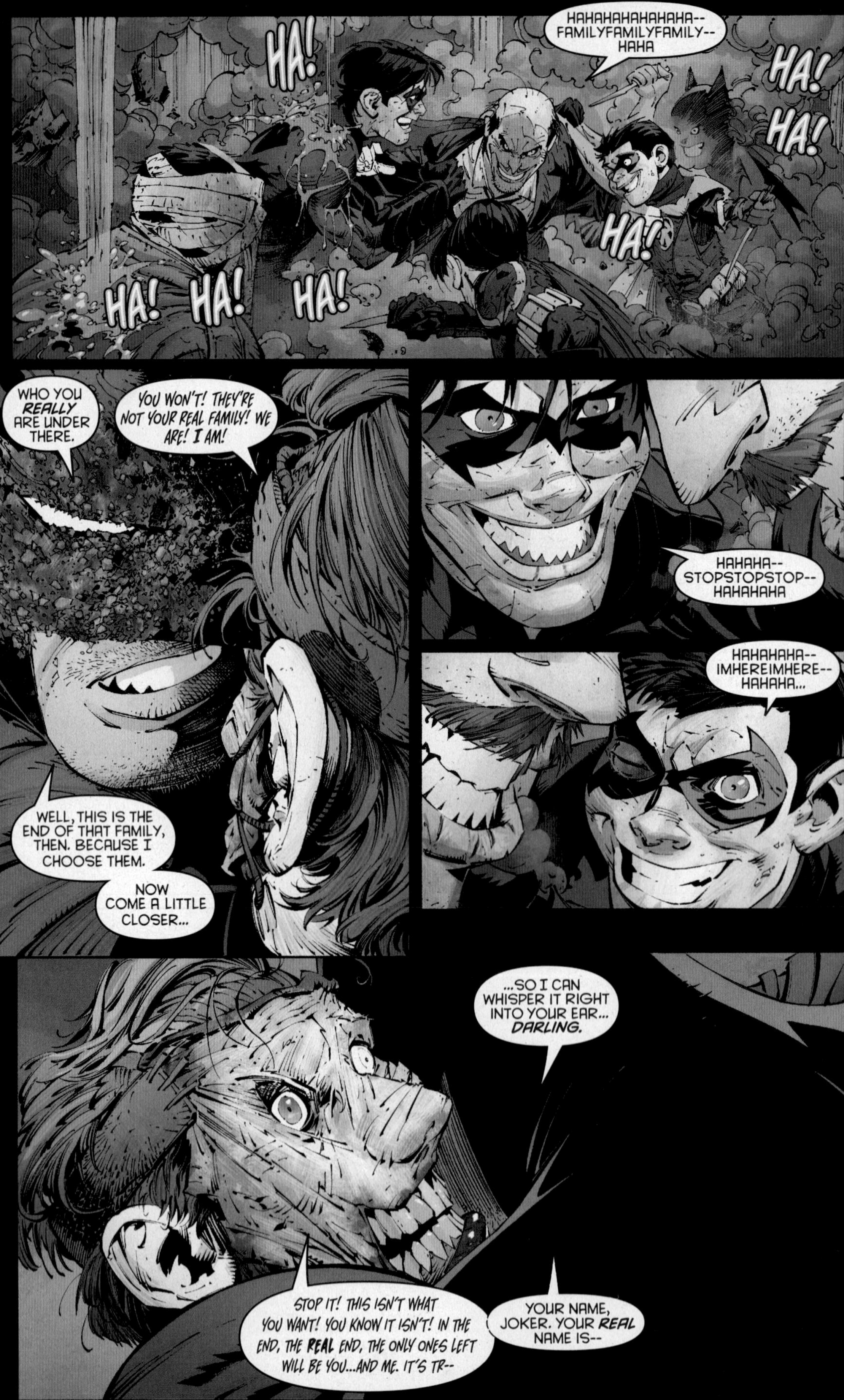
HA!
HAHAHAHAHAHAHA--
FAMILYFAMILYFAMILY--
HAHA
HA!
HA!
HA!
HA! HA! HA!
WHO YOU REALLY ARE UNDER THERE.
YOU WON'T! THEY'RE NOT YOUR REAL FAMILY! WE ARE! I AM!
WELL, THIS IS THE END OF THAT FAMILY, THEN. BECAUSE I CHOOSE THEM.
NOW COME A LITTLE CLOSER...
HAHAHA-- STOPSTOPSTOP-- HAHAHAHA
HAHAHAHA-- IMHEREIMHERE-- HAHAHA...
...SO I CAN WHISPER IT RIGHT INTO YOUR EAR... DARLING.
STOP IT! THIS ISN'T WHAT YOU WANT! YOU KNOW IT ISN'T! IN THE END, THE REAL END, THE ONLY ONES LEFT WILL BE YOU...AND ME. IT'S TR--
YOUR NAME, JOKER. YOUR REAL NAME IS--

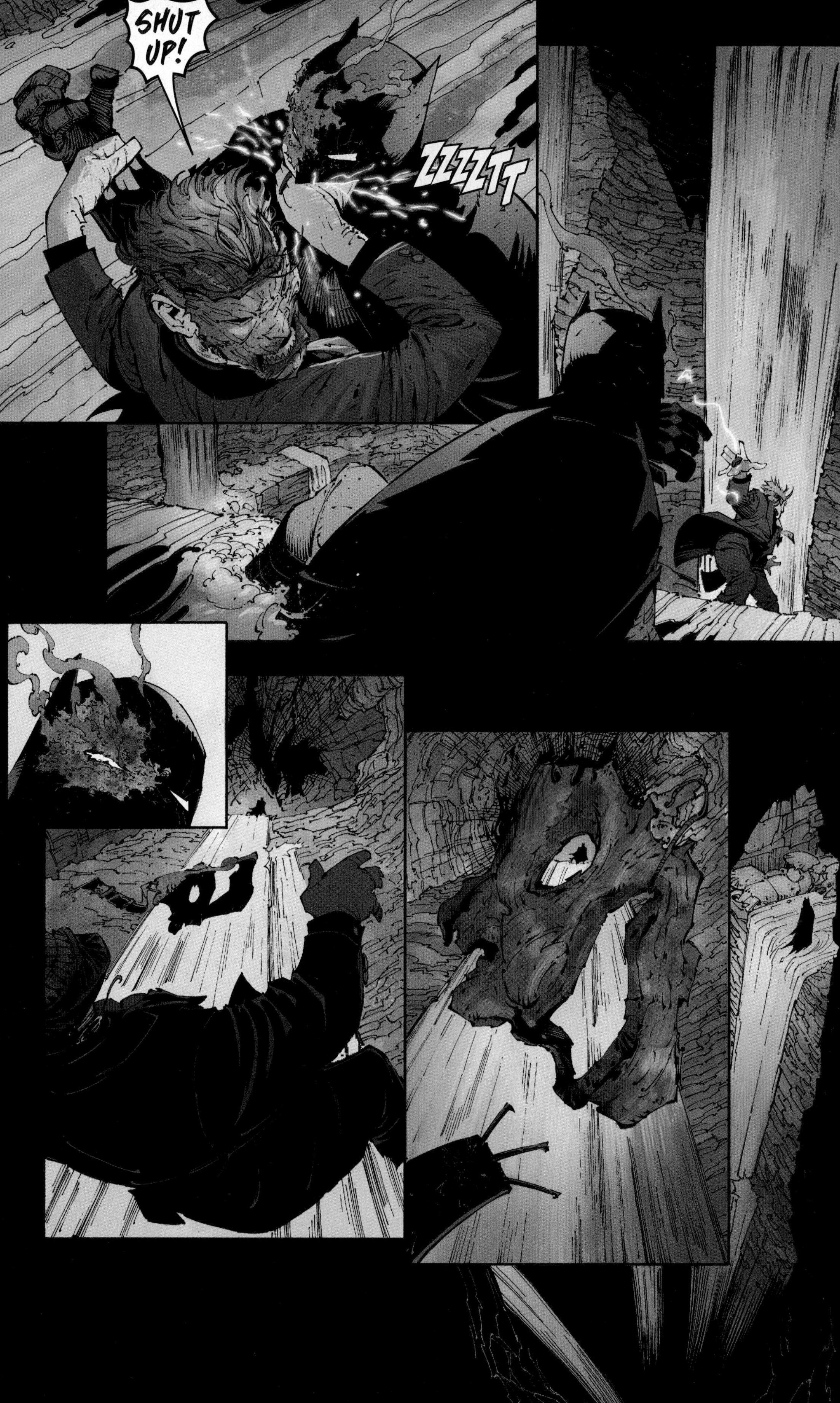
SHUT UP!
ZZZZTT

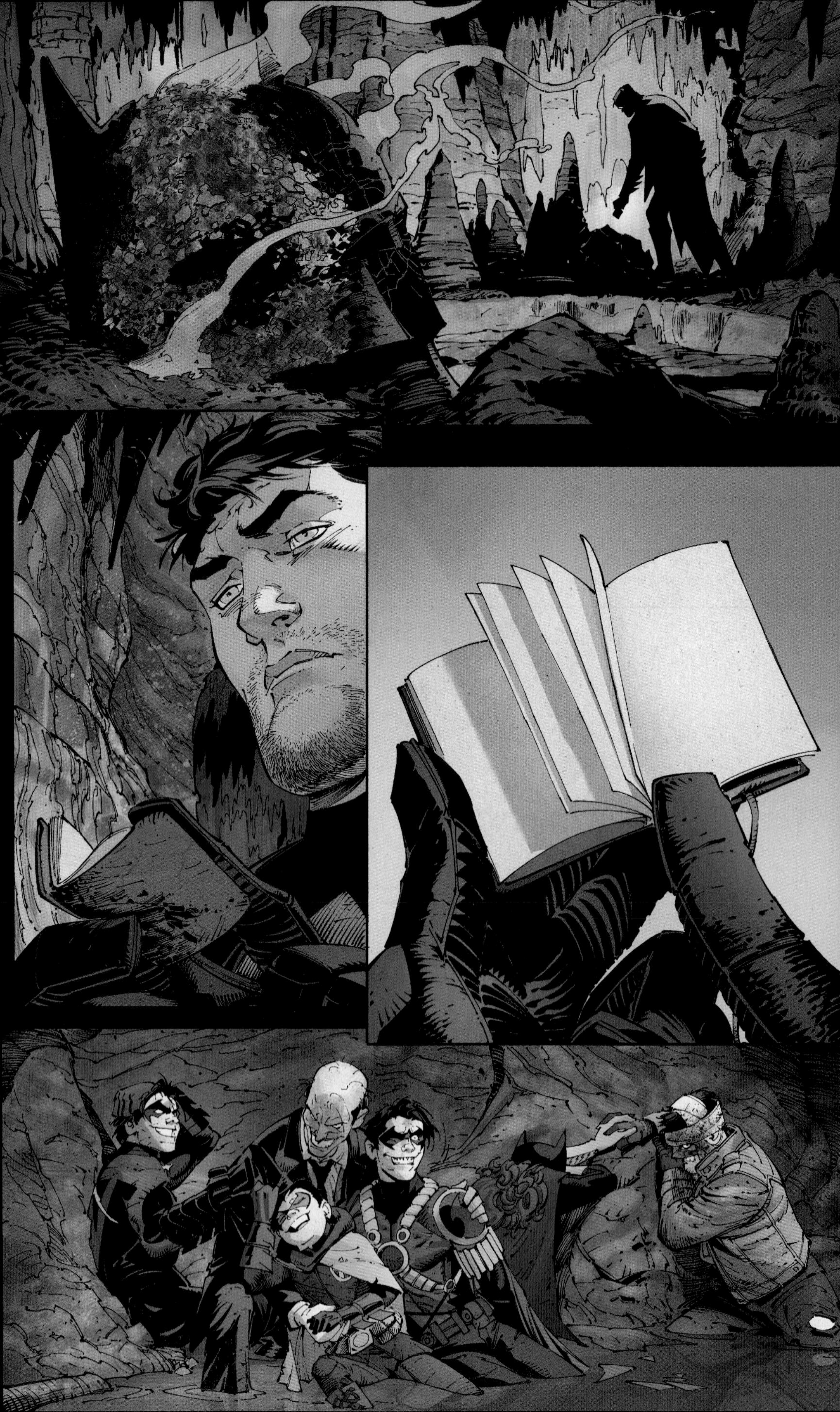

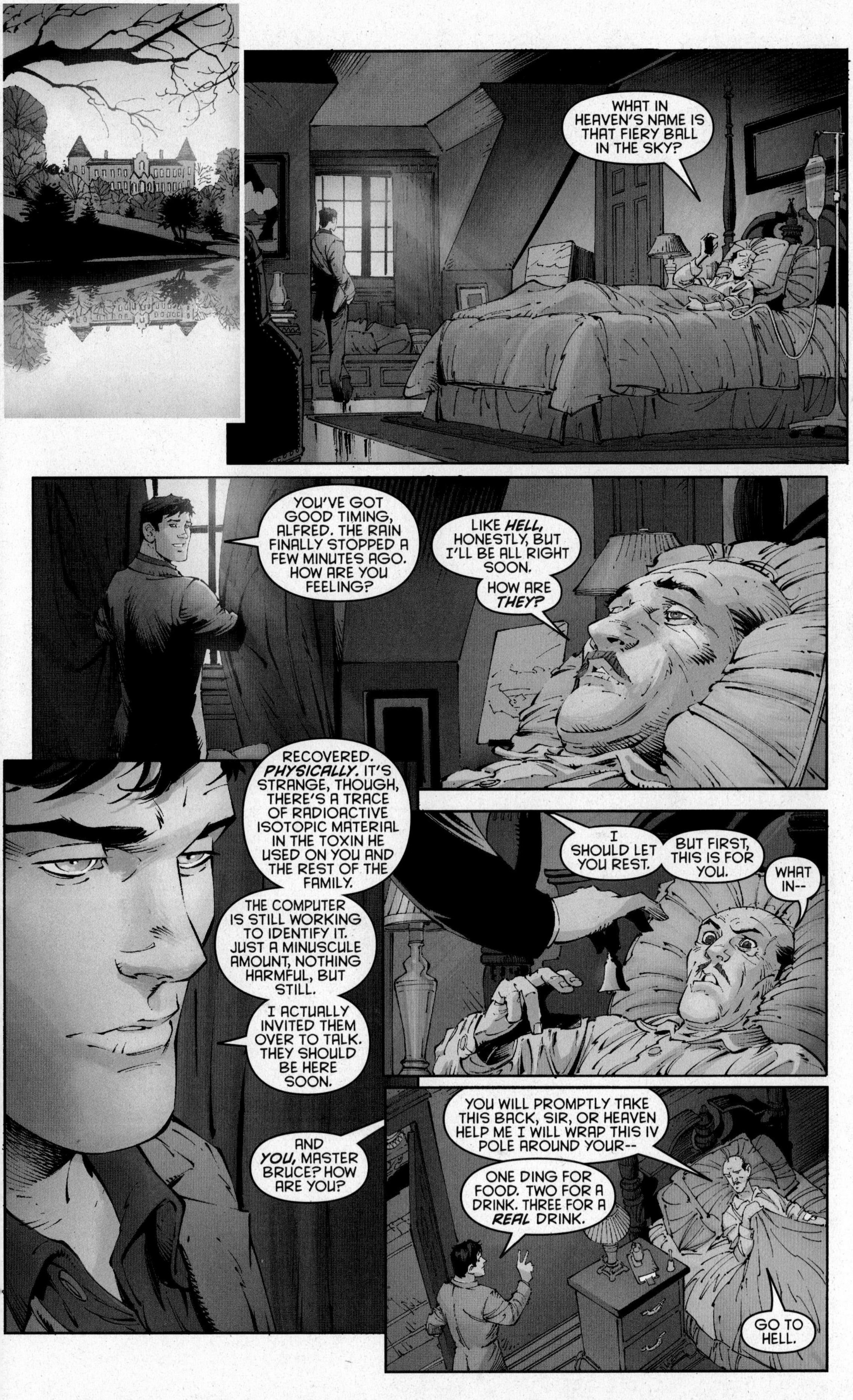
WHAT IN HEAVEN'S NAME IS THAT FIERY BALL IN THE SKY?
YOU'VE GOT GOOD TIMING, ALFRED. THE RAIN FINALLY STOPPED A FEW MINUTES AGO. HOW ARE YOU FEELING?
LIKE *HELL,* HONESTLY, BUT I'LL BE ALL RIGHT SOON.
HOW ARE *THEY?*
RECOVERED. ***PHYSICALLY.*** IT'S STRANGE, THOUGH, THERE'S A TRACE OF RADIOACTIVE ISOTOPIC MATERIAL IN THE TOXIN HE USED ON YOU AND THE REST OF THE FAMILY.
THE COMPUTER IS STILL WORKING TO IDENTIFY IT. JUST A MINUSCULE AMOUNT, NOTHING HARMFUL, BUT STILL.
I ACTUALLY INVITED THEM OVER TO TALK. THEY SHOULD BE HERE SOON.
AND *YOU,* MASTER BRUCE? HOW ARE YOU?
I SHOULD LET YOU REST.
BUT FIRST, THIS IS FOR YOU.
WHAT IN--
YOU WILL PROMPTLY TAKE THIS BACK, SIR, OR HEAVEN HELP ME I WILL WRAP THIS IV POLE AROUND YOUR--
ONE DING FOR FOOD. TWO FOR A DRINK. THREE FOR A *REAL* DRINK.
GO TO HELL.

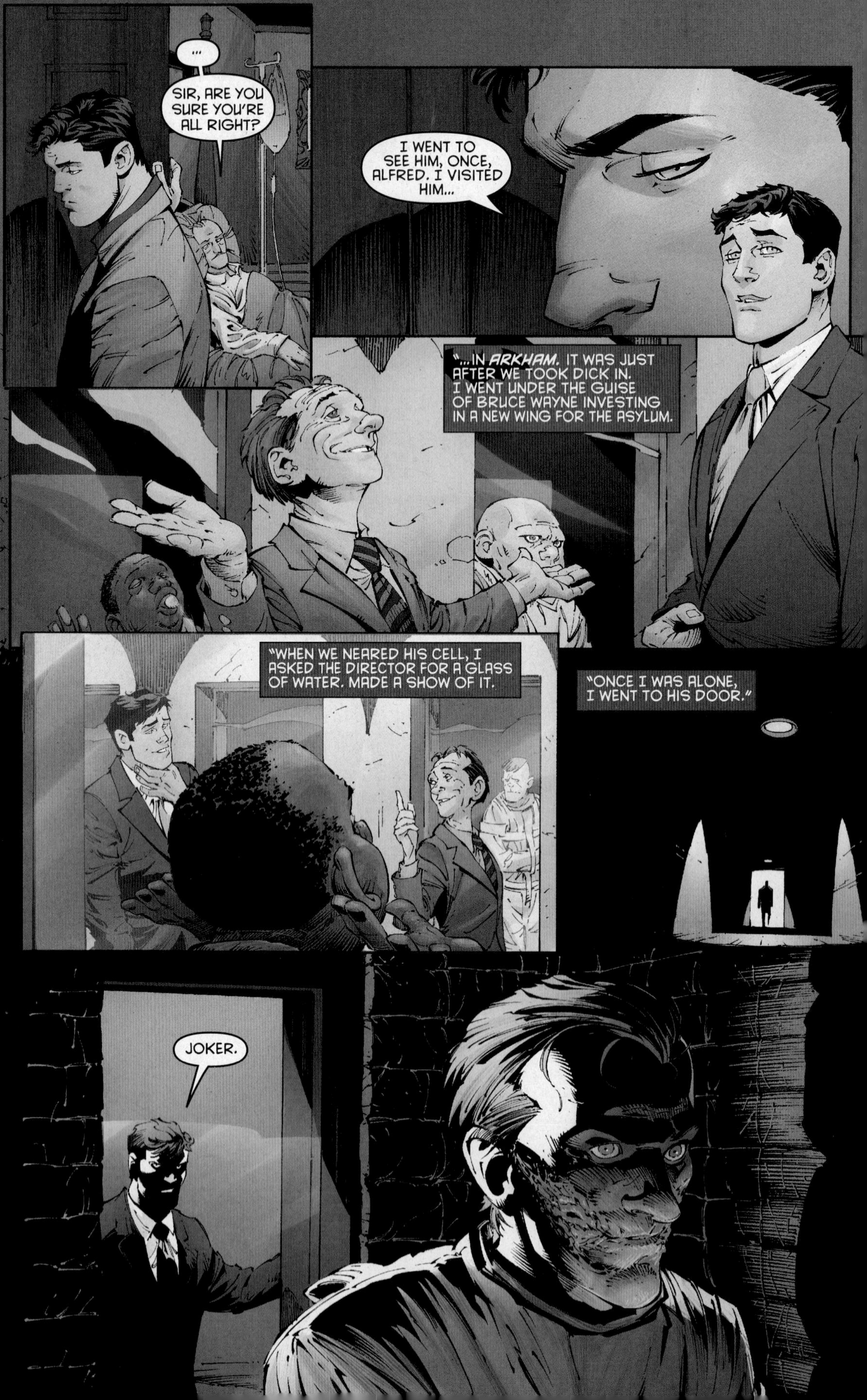
...
SIR, ARE YOU SURE YOU'RE ALL RIGHT?
I WENT TO SEE HIM, ONCE, ALFRED. I VISITED HIM...
"...IN ARKHAM. IT WAS JUST AFTER WE TOOK DICK IN. I WENT UNDER THE GUISE OF BRUCE WAYNE INVESTING IN A NEW WING FOR THE ASYLUM.
"WHEN WE NEARED HIS CELL, I ASKED THE DIRECTOR FOR A GLASS OF WATER. MADE A SHOW OF IT.
"ONCE I WAS ALONE, I WENT TO HIS DOOR."
JOKER.

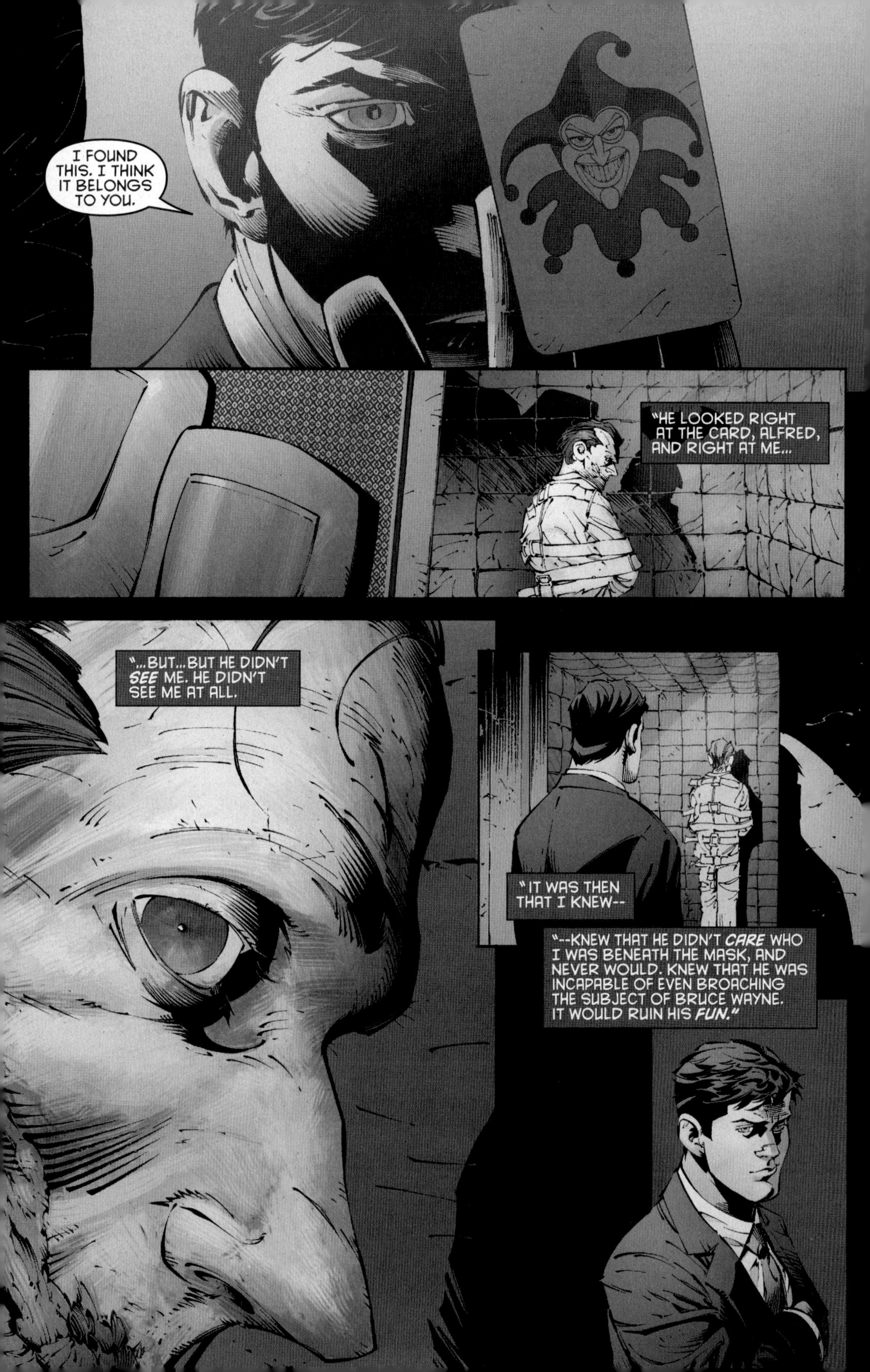
I FOUND THIS. I THINK IT BELONGS TO YOU.
"HE LOOKED RIGHT AT THE CARD, ALFRED, AND RIGHT AT ME...
"...BUT...BUT HE DIDN'T *SEE* ME. HE DIDN'T SEE ME AT ALL.
"IT WAS THEN THAT I KNEW--
"--KNEW THAT HE DIDN'T *CARE* WHO I WAS BENEATH THE MASK, AND NEVER WOULD. KNEW THAT HE WAS INCAPABLE OF EVEN BROACHING THE SUBJECT OF BRUCE WAYNE. IT WOULD RUIN HIS *FUN*."

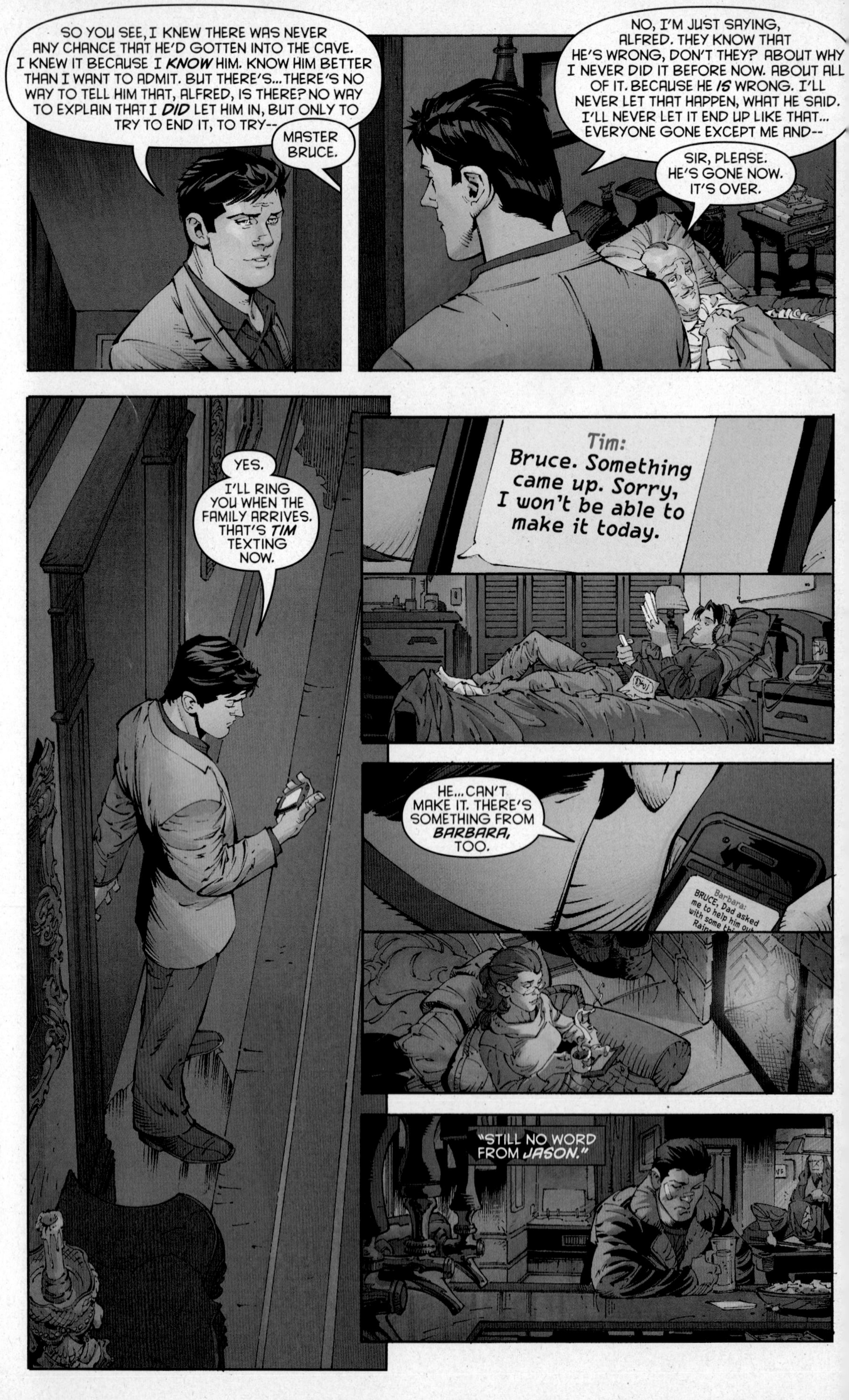
SO YOU SEE, I KNEW THERE WAS NEVER ANY CHANCE THAT HE'D GOTTEN INTO THE CAVE. I KNEW IT BECAUSE I *KNOW* HIM. KNOW HIM BETTER THAN I WANT TO ADMIT. BUT THERE'S...THERE'S NO WAY TO TELL HIM THAT, ALFRED, IS THERE? NO WAY TO EXPLAIN THAT I *DID* LET HIM IN, BUT ONLY TO TRY TO END IT, TO TRY--
MASTER BRUCE.
NO, I'M JUST SAYING, ALFRED. THEY KNOW THAT HE'S WRONG, DON'T THEY? ABOUT WHY I NEVER DID IT BEFORE NOW. ABOUT ALL OF IT. BECAUSE HE *IS* WRONG. I'LL NEVER LET THAT HAPPEN, WHAT HE SAID. I'LL NEVER LET IT END UP LIKE THAT... EVERYONE GONE EXCEPT ME AND--
SIR, PLEASE. HE'S GONE NOW. IT'S OVER.
YES.
I'LL RING YOU WHEN THE FAMILY ARRIVES. THAT'S *TIM* TEXTING NOW.
Tim:
Bruce. Something came up. Sorry, I won't be able to make it today.
HE...CAN'T MAKE IT. THERE'S SOMETHING FROM *BARBARA,* TOO.
Barbara:
BRUCE, Dad asked
me to help him out
"STILL NO WORD FROM *JASON.*"

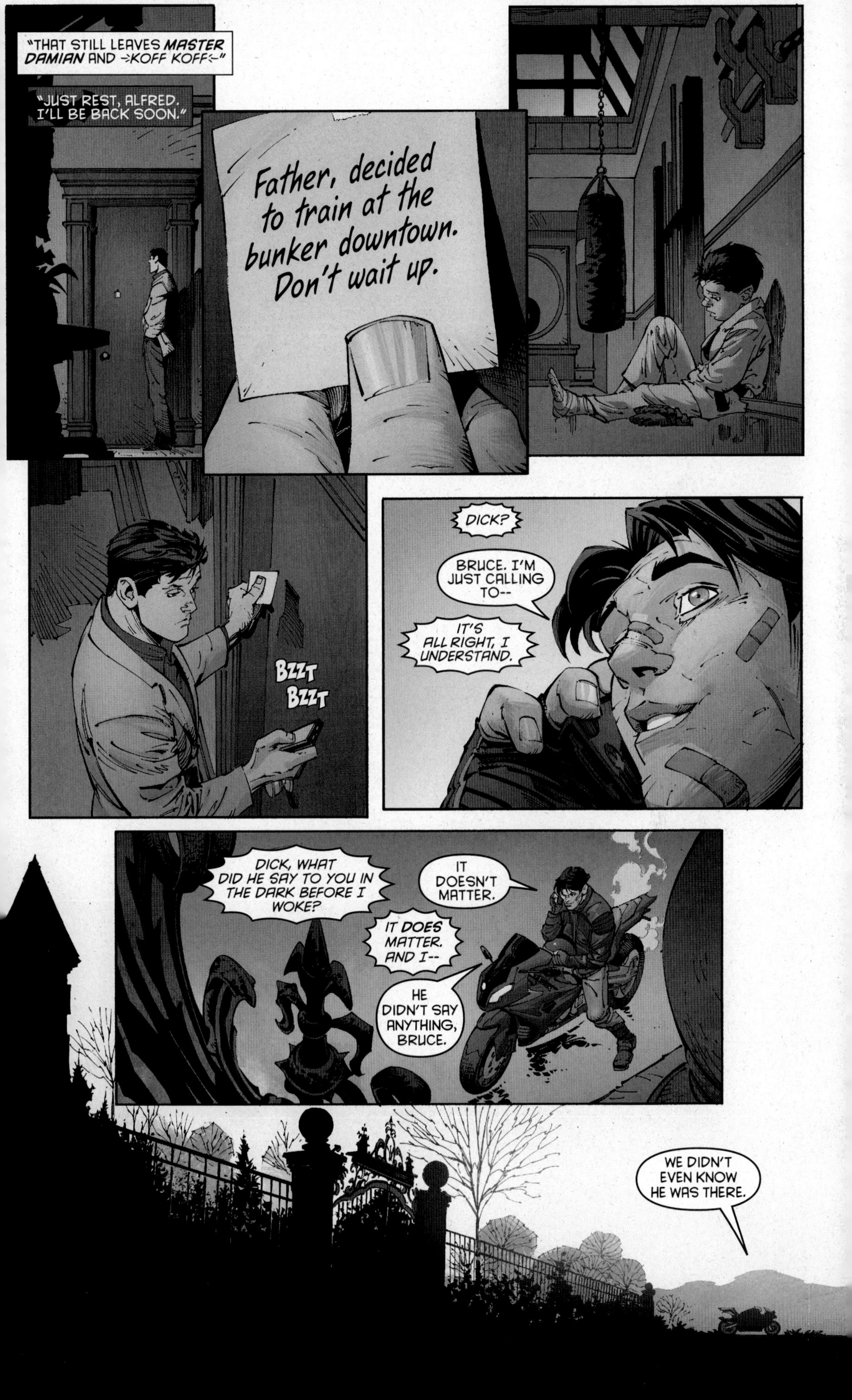
"THAT STILL LEAVES MASTER DAMIAN AND ⇢KOFF KOFF⇠"
"JUST REST, ALFRED. I'LL BE BACK SOON."
Father, decided to train at the bunker downtown. Don't wait up.
BZZZT BZZZT
DICK?
BRUCE. I'M JUST CALLING TO--
IT'S ALL RIGHT, I UNDERSTAND.
DICK, WHAT DID HE SAY TO YOU IN THE DARK BEFORE I WOKE?
IT DOESN'T MATTER.
IT DOES MATTER. AND I--
HE DIDN'T SAY ANYTHING, BRUCE.
WE DIDN'T EVEN KNOW HE WAS THERE.

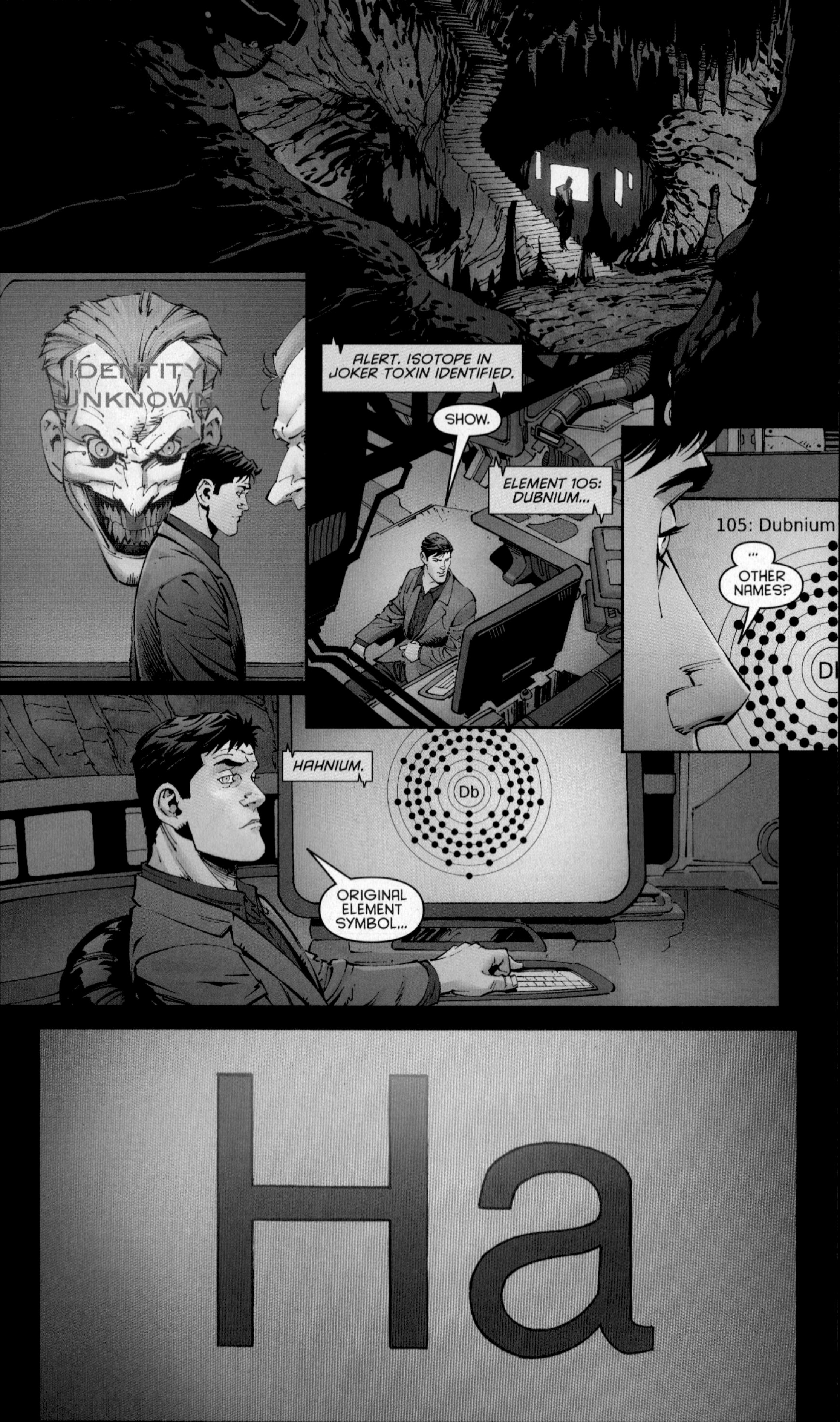
IDENTITY
UNKNOWN
ALERT. ISOTOPE IN JOKER TOXIN IDENTIFIED.
SHOW.
ELEMENT 105: DUBNIUM...
105: Dubnium
... OTHER NAMES?
HAHNIUM.
Db
ORIGINAL ELEMENT SYMBOL...
Ha

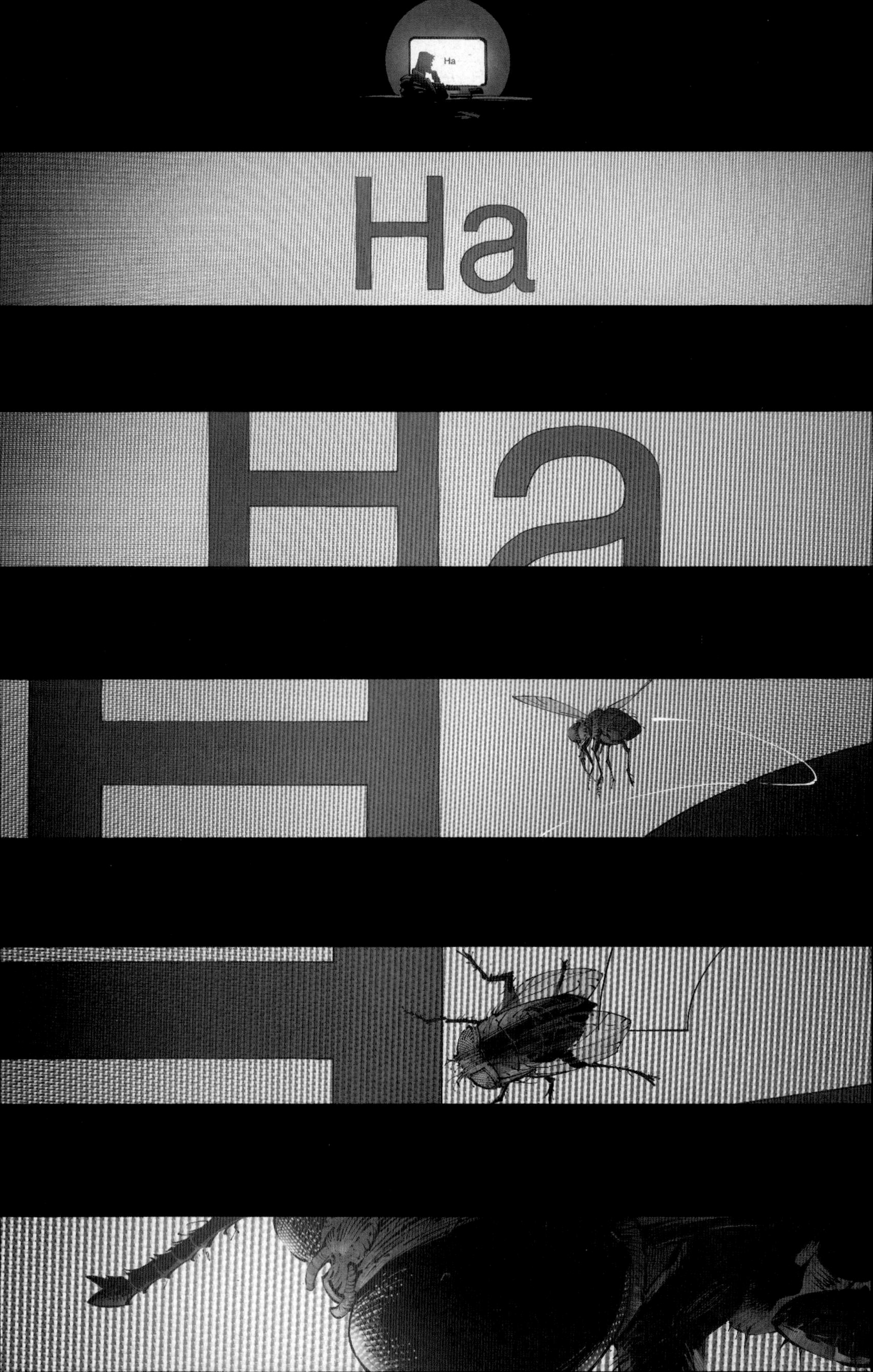
Ha
Ha

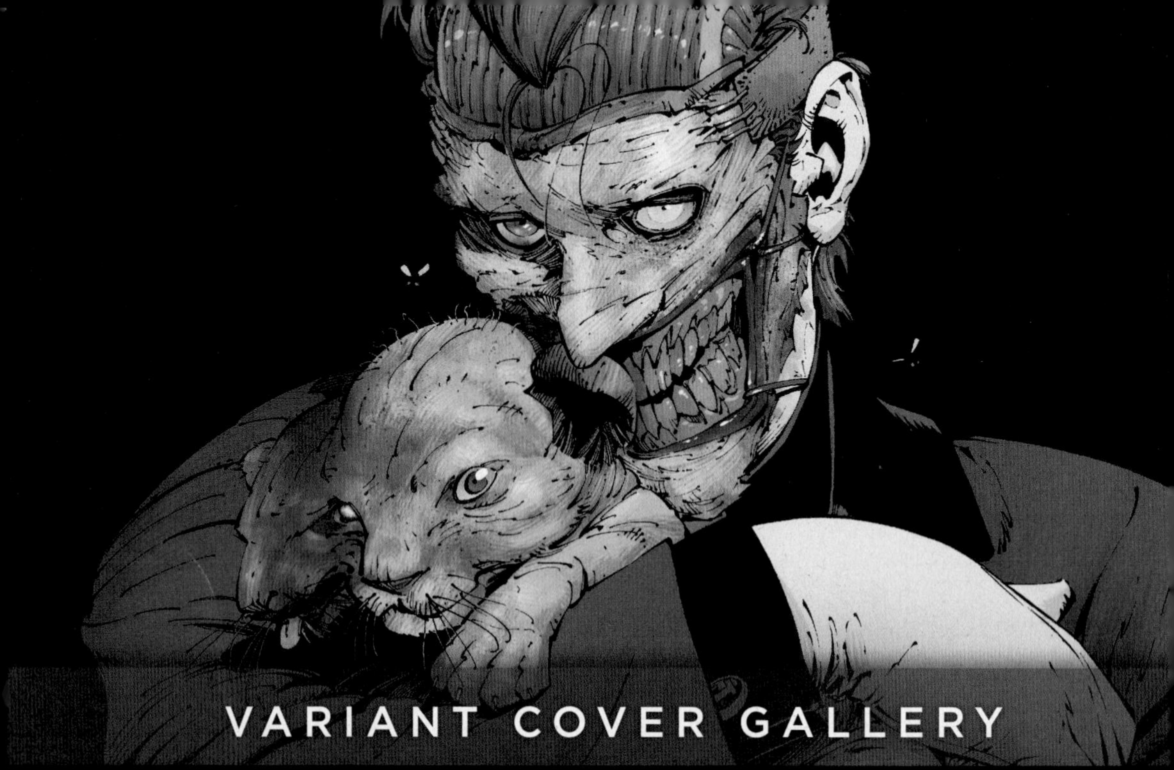

VARIANT COVER GALLERY

BATMAN 13
by Greg Capullo & FCO Plascencia

BATMAN 13 – New York Comic Con exclusive
by Greg Capullo & FCO Plascencia

BATMAN 13 – 2nd printing
by Aaron Kuder & Nathan Fairbairn

BATMAN 14
by Trevor McCarthy

BATMAN 15
by Greg Capullo & FCO Plascencia

BATMAN 16
by Alex Garner

BATMAN 17
by Tony Daniel, Matt Banning & Tomeu Morey

BATMAN 17 – Wonder Con exclusive
by Greg Capullo & FCO Plascencia

The Joker - overcover art
by Greg Capullo & FCO Plascencia

BATMAN: Death of the Family HC
by Greg Capullo & FCO Plascencia

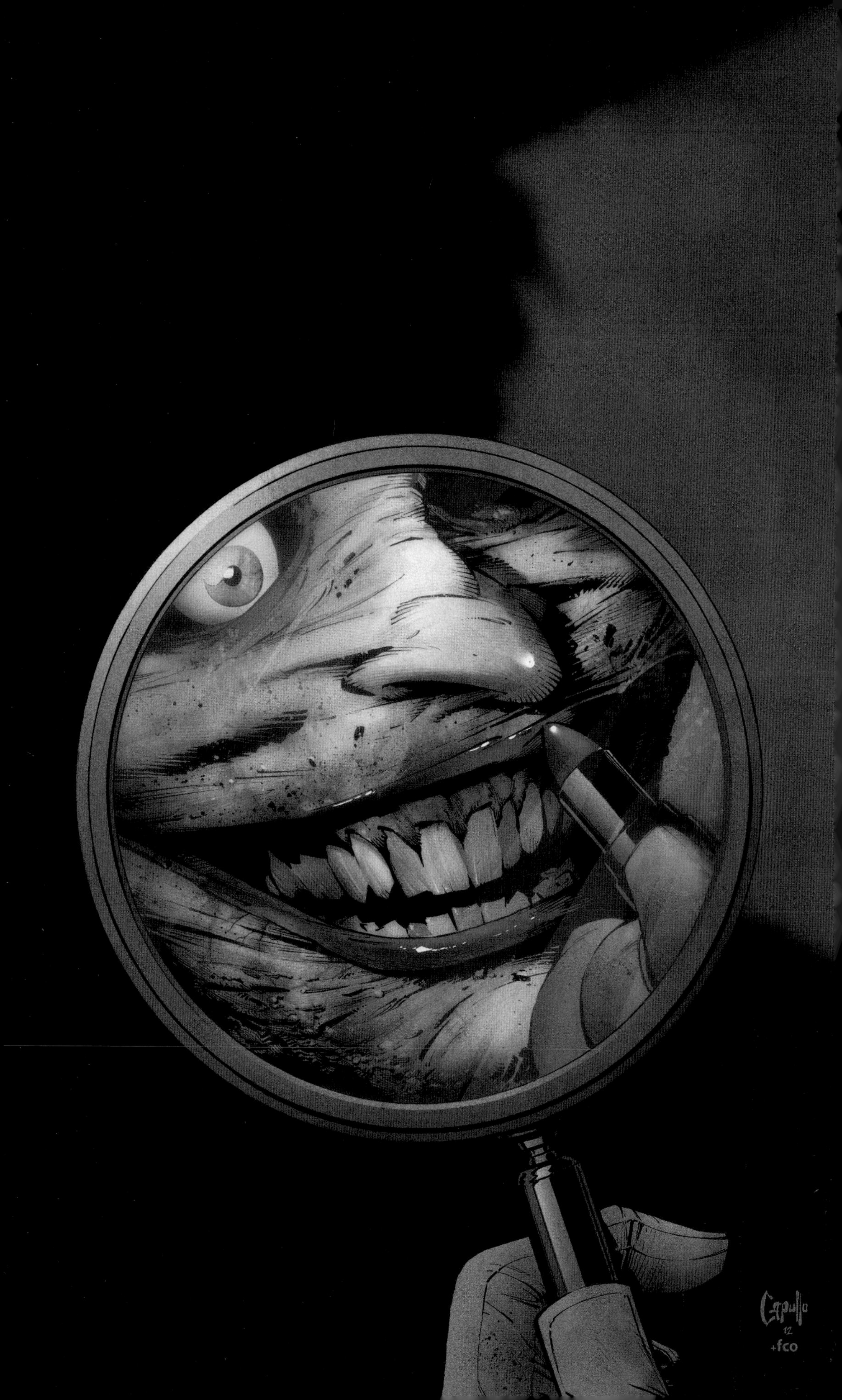
Capullo
12
+fco

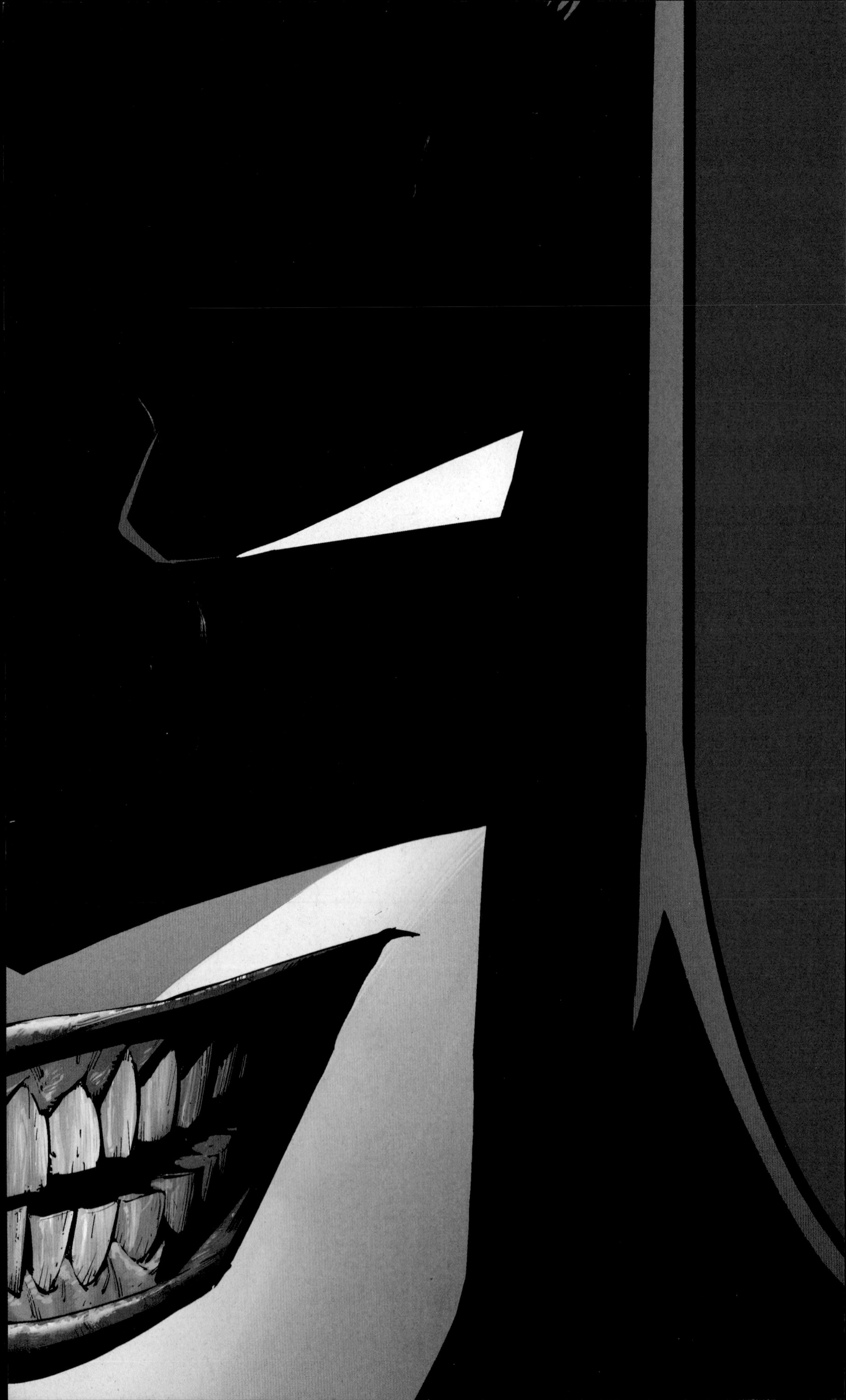

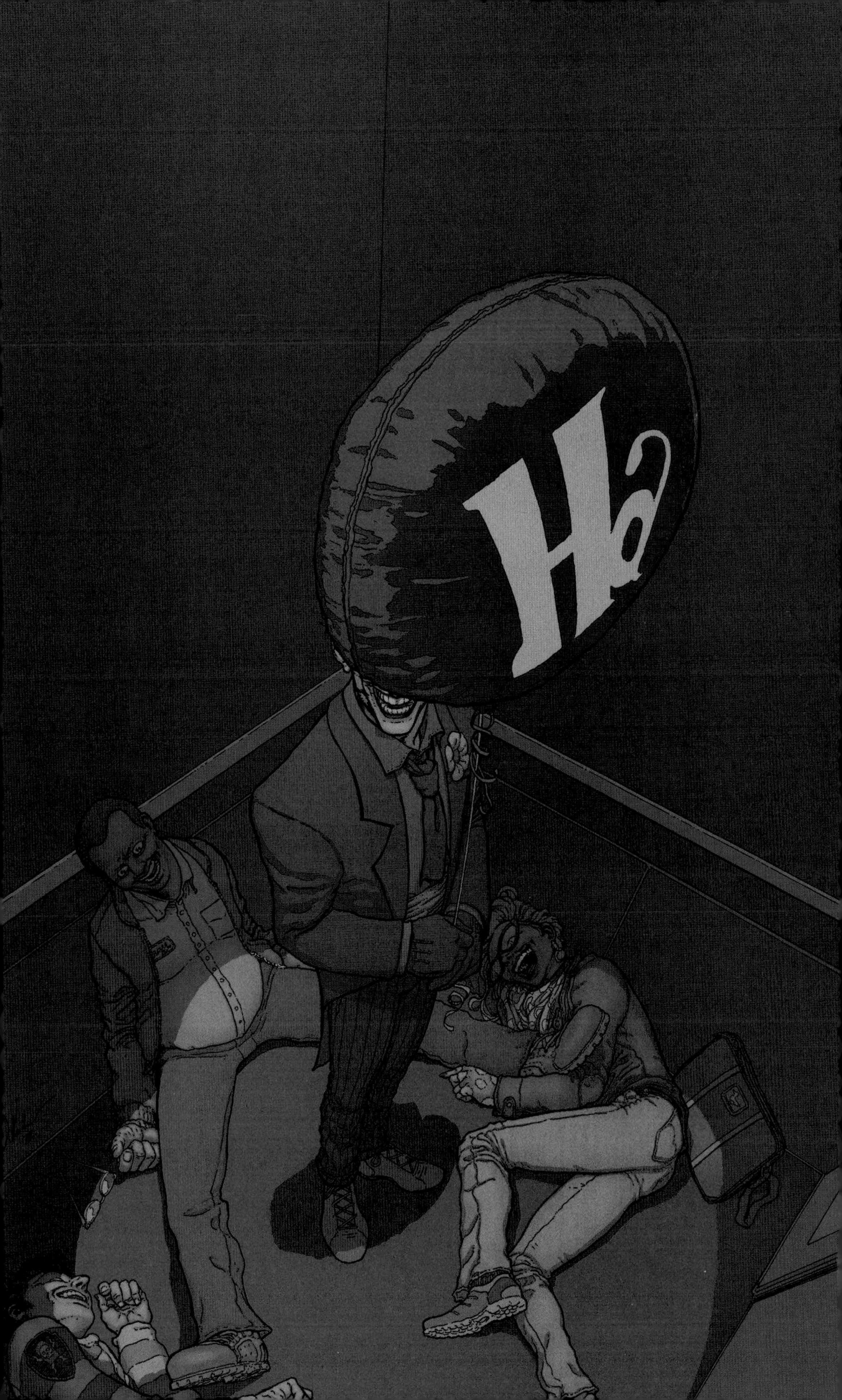
Ha

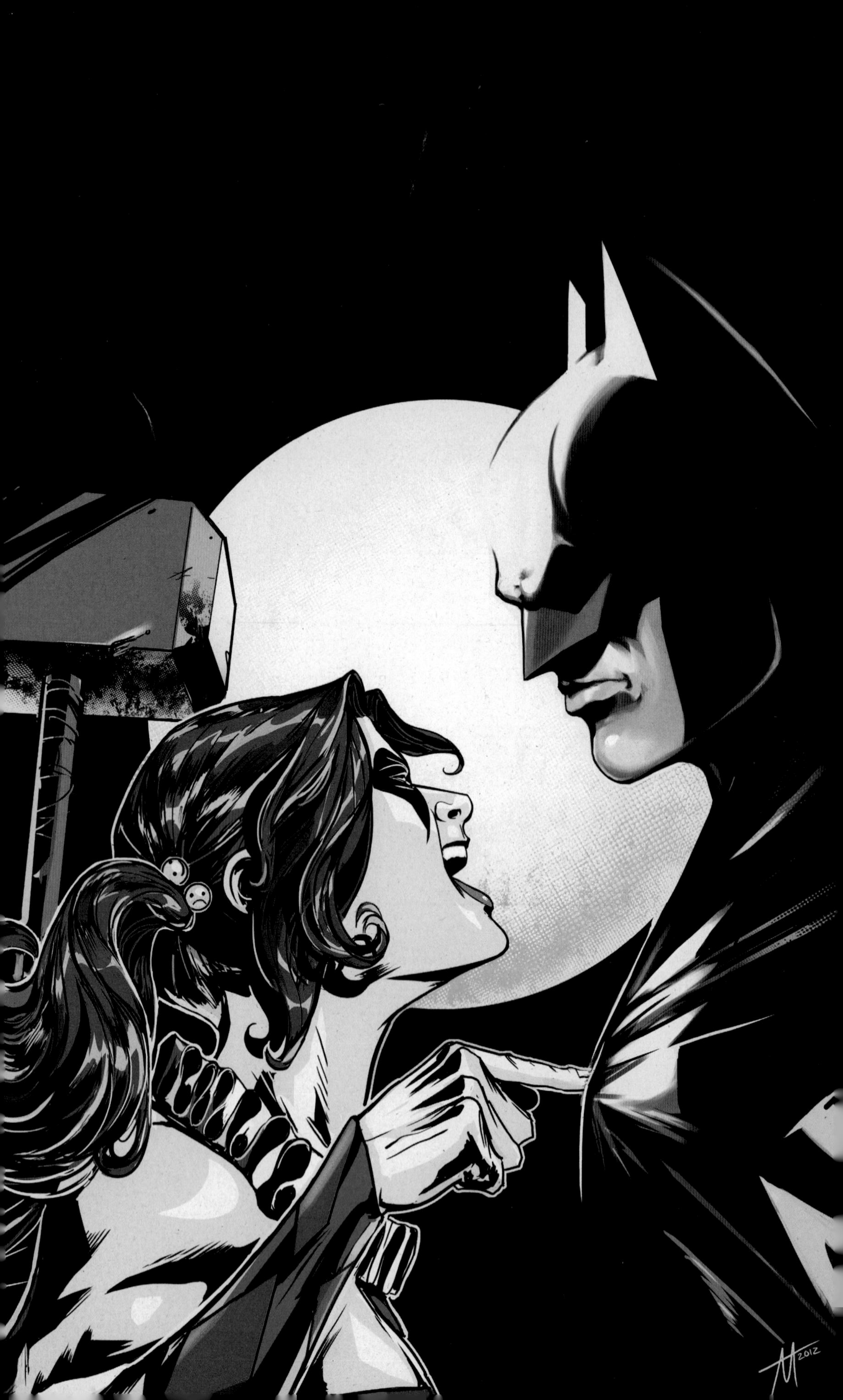

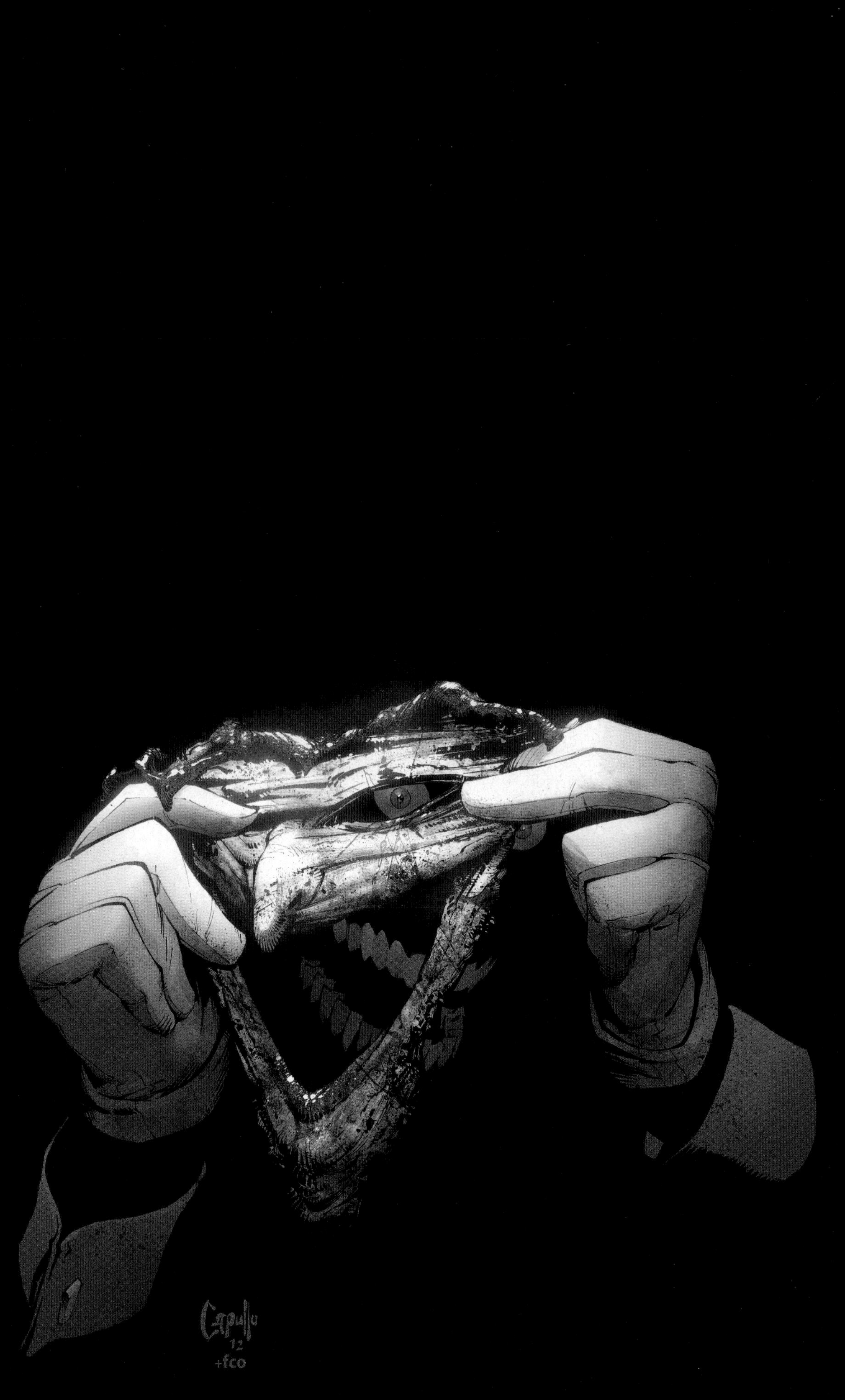
Capullo
12
+fco

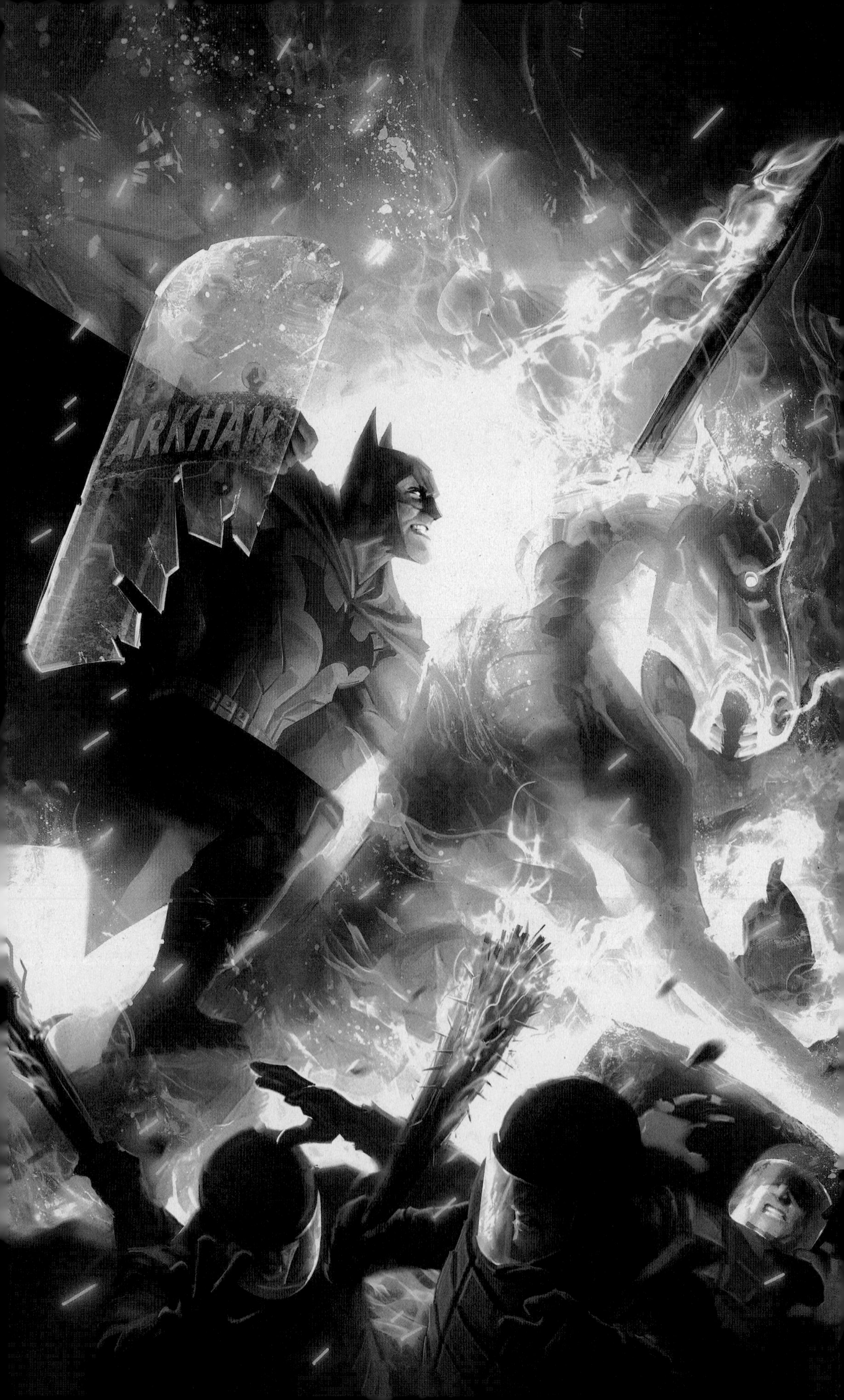
ARKHAM

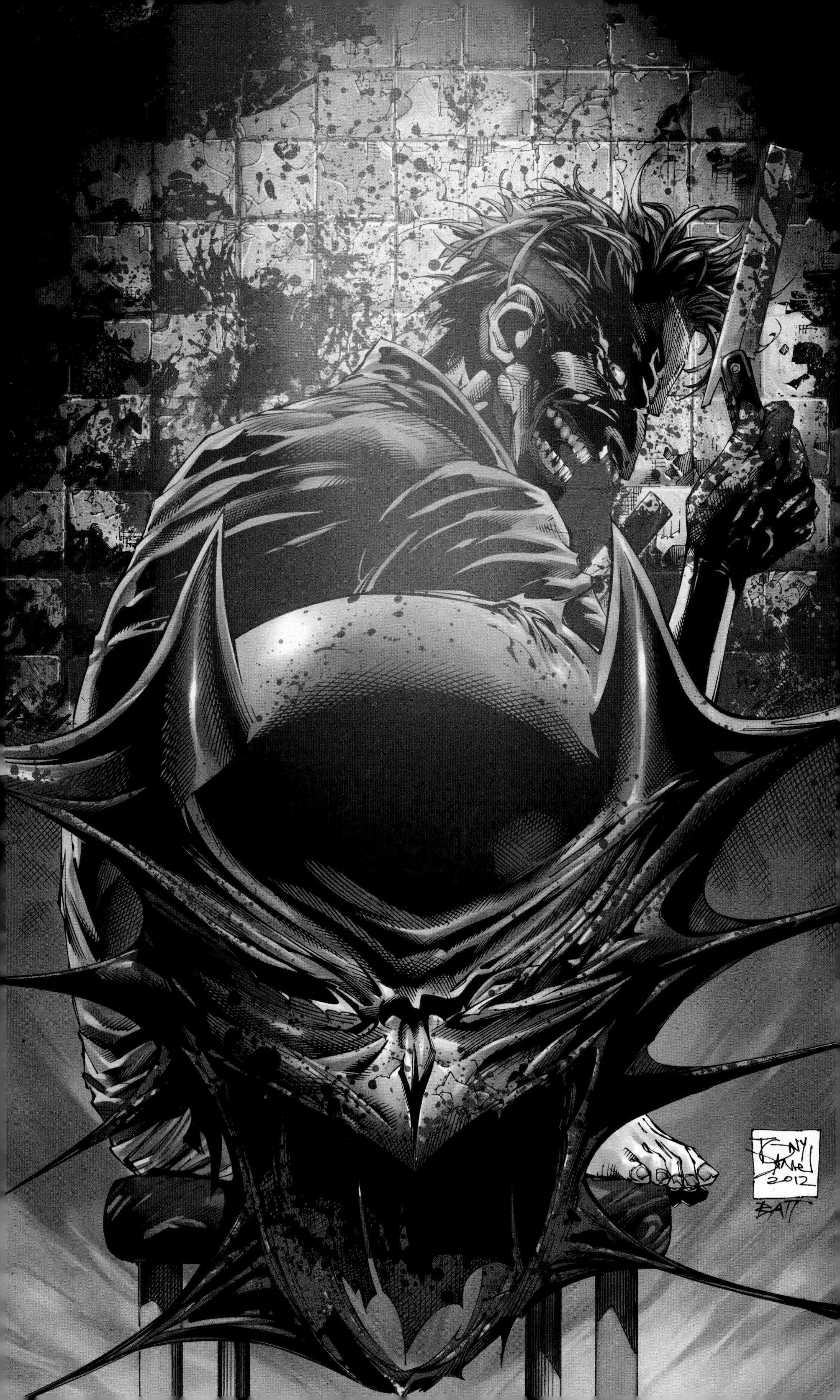

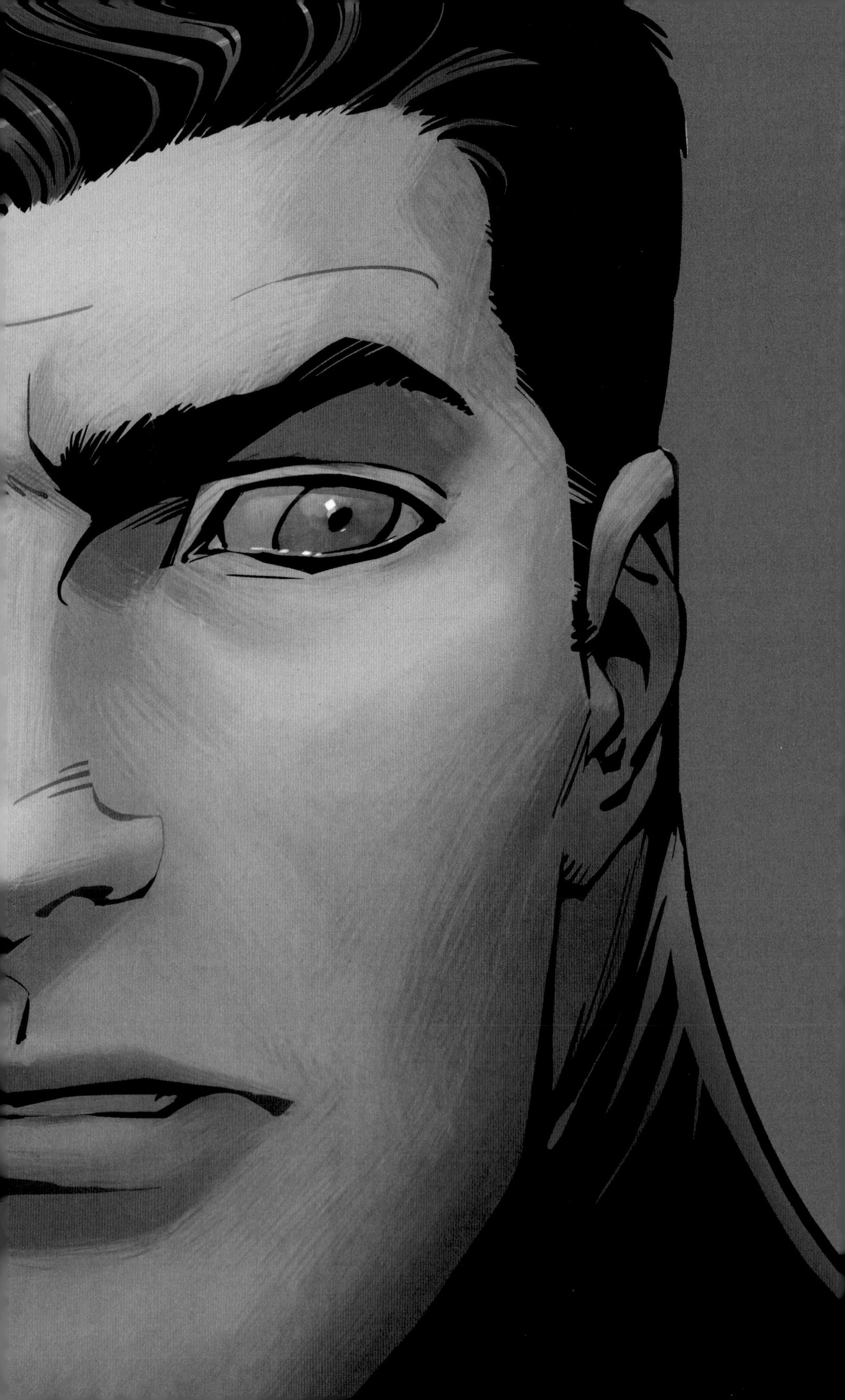

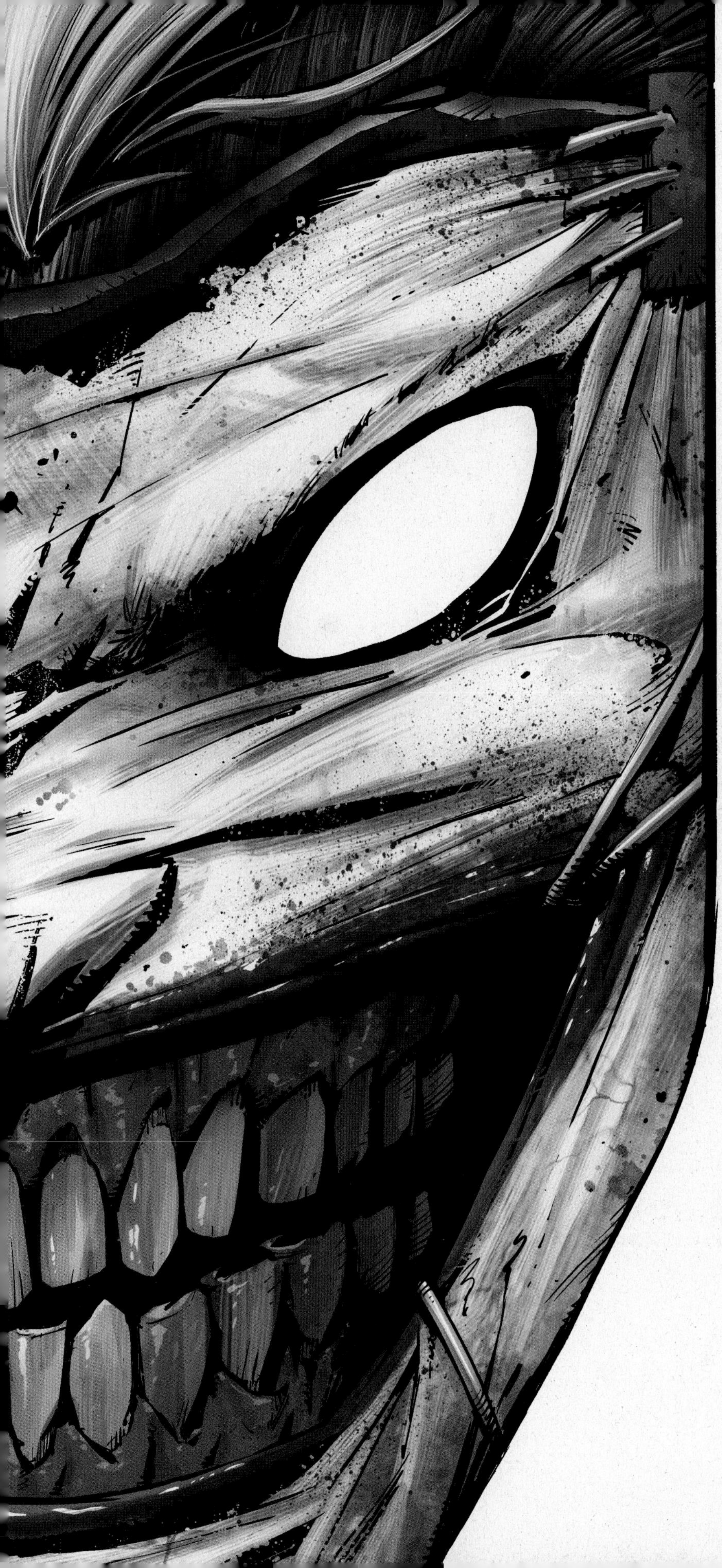

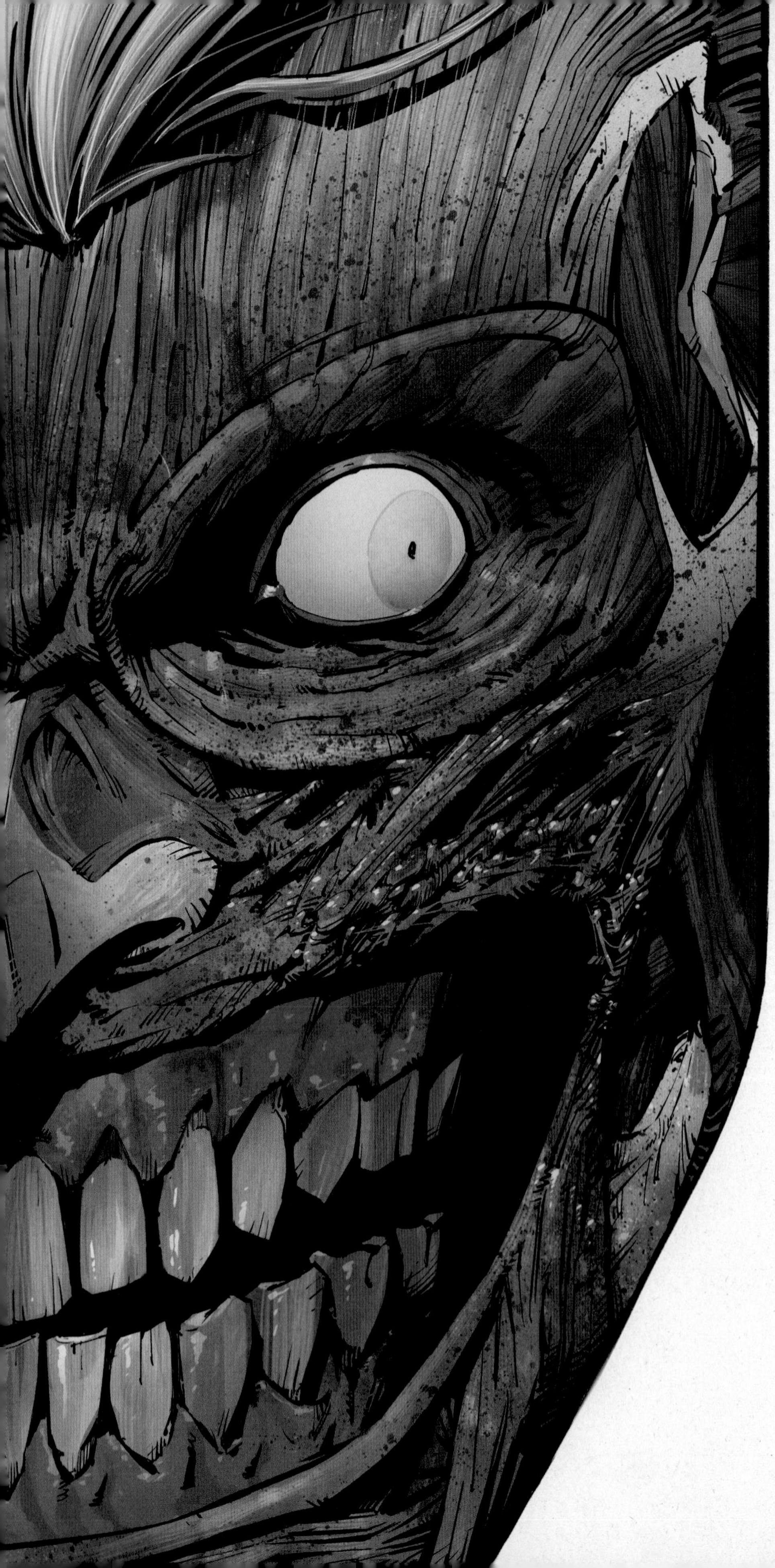

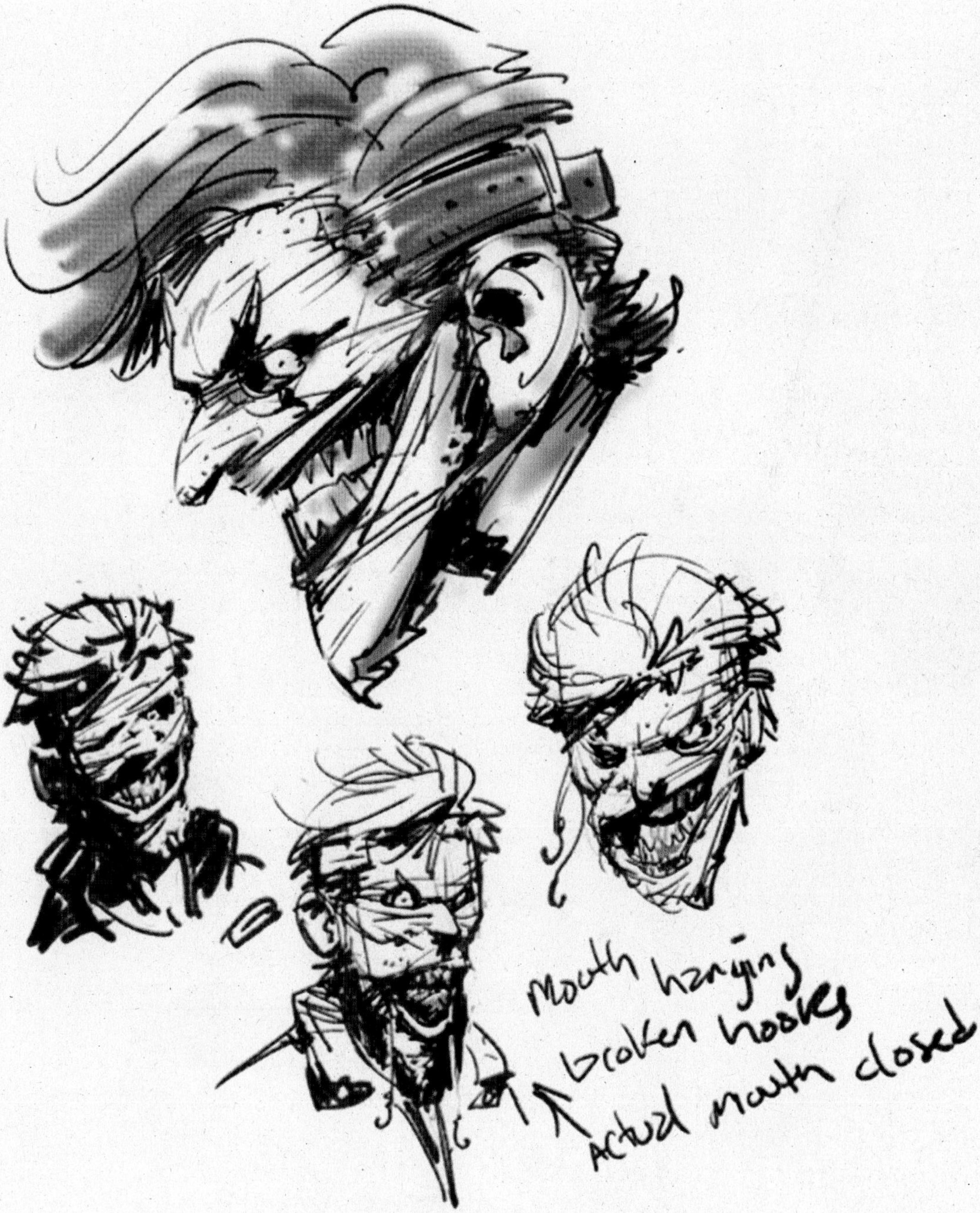
Mouth hanging
broken hooks
Actual mouth closed

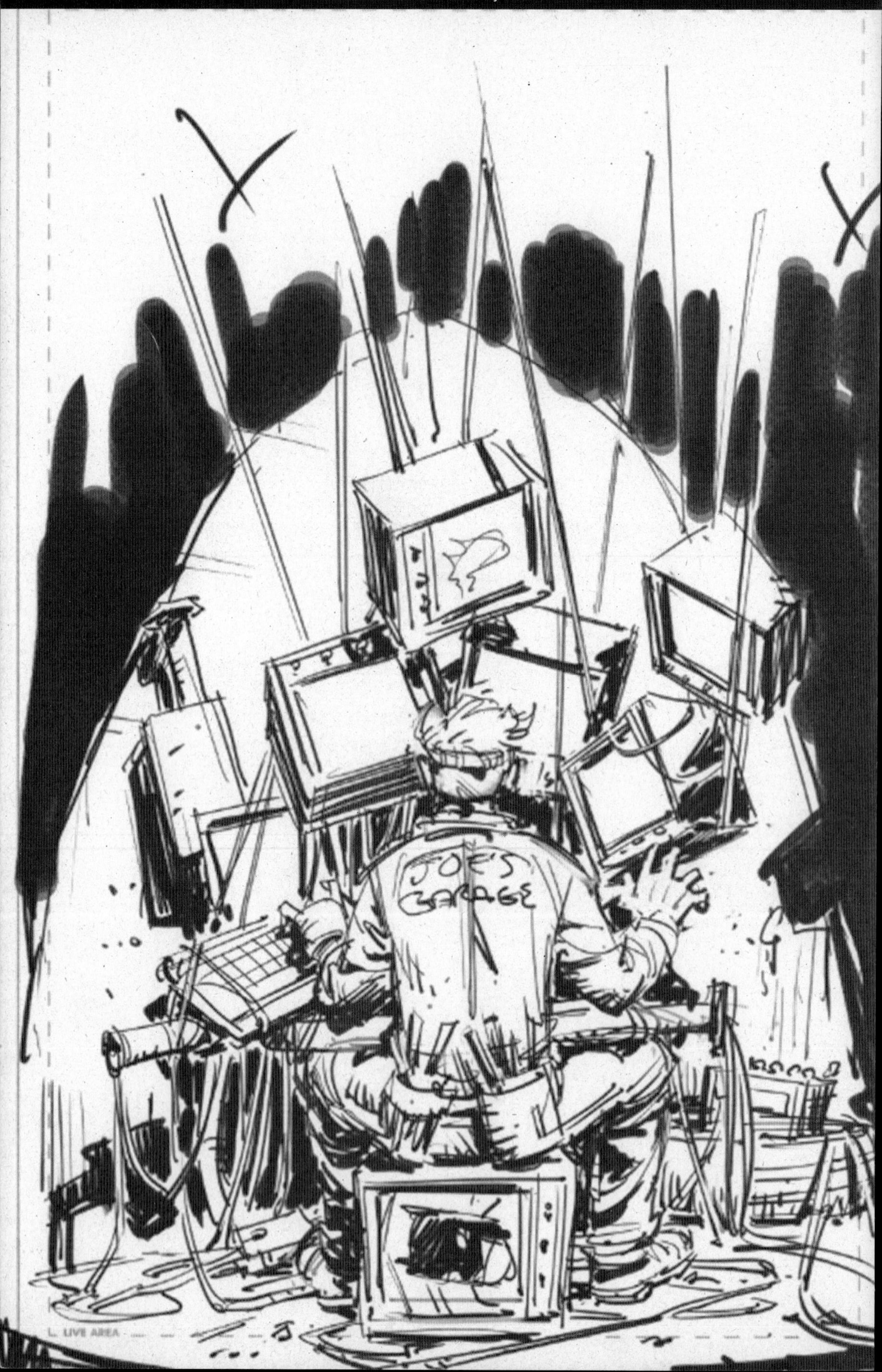
JOE'S
GARAGE
LIVE AREA

BATMAN #17 alternate color version by GREG CAPULLO with FCO PLASCENCIA

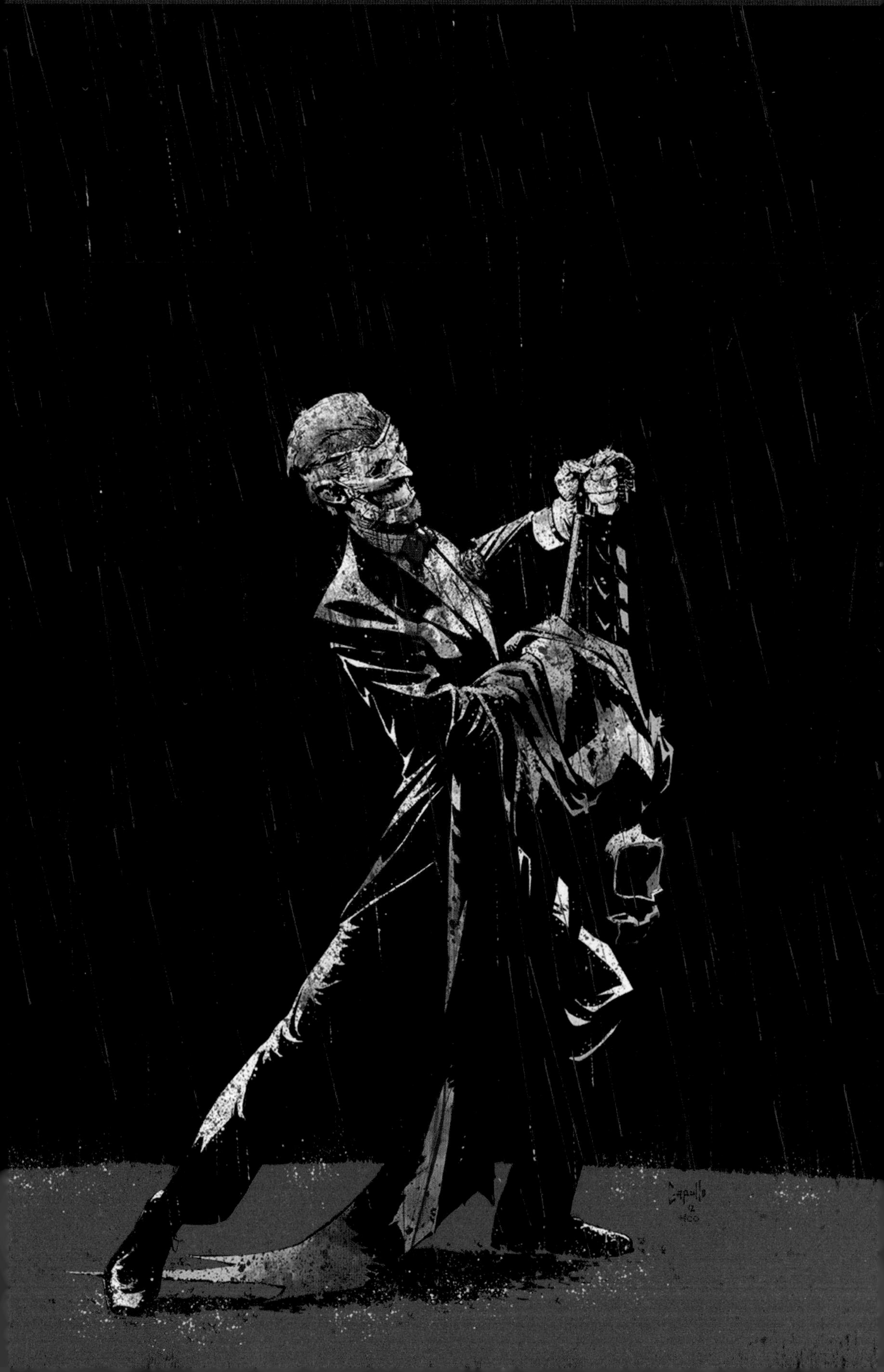

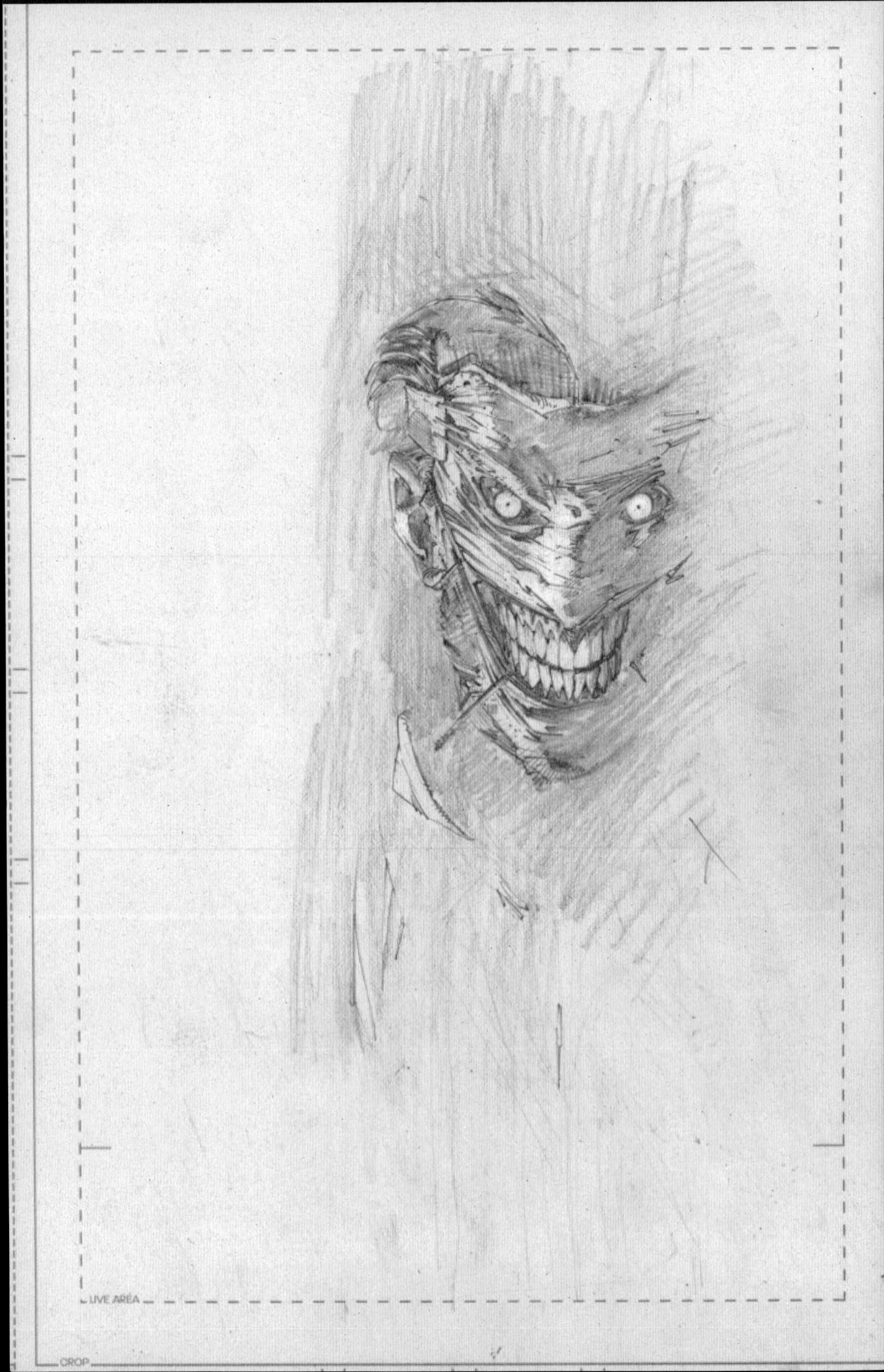
LIVE AREA
CROP

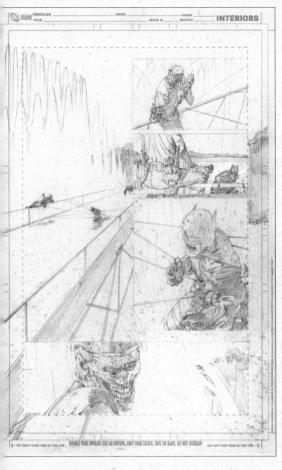

PENCILLER INKER PAGE#

TITLE ISSUE # MONTH

INTERIORS

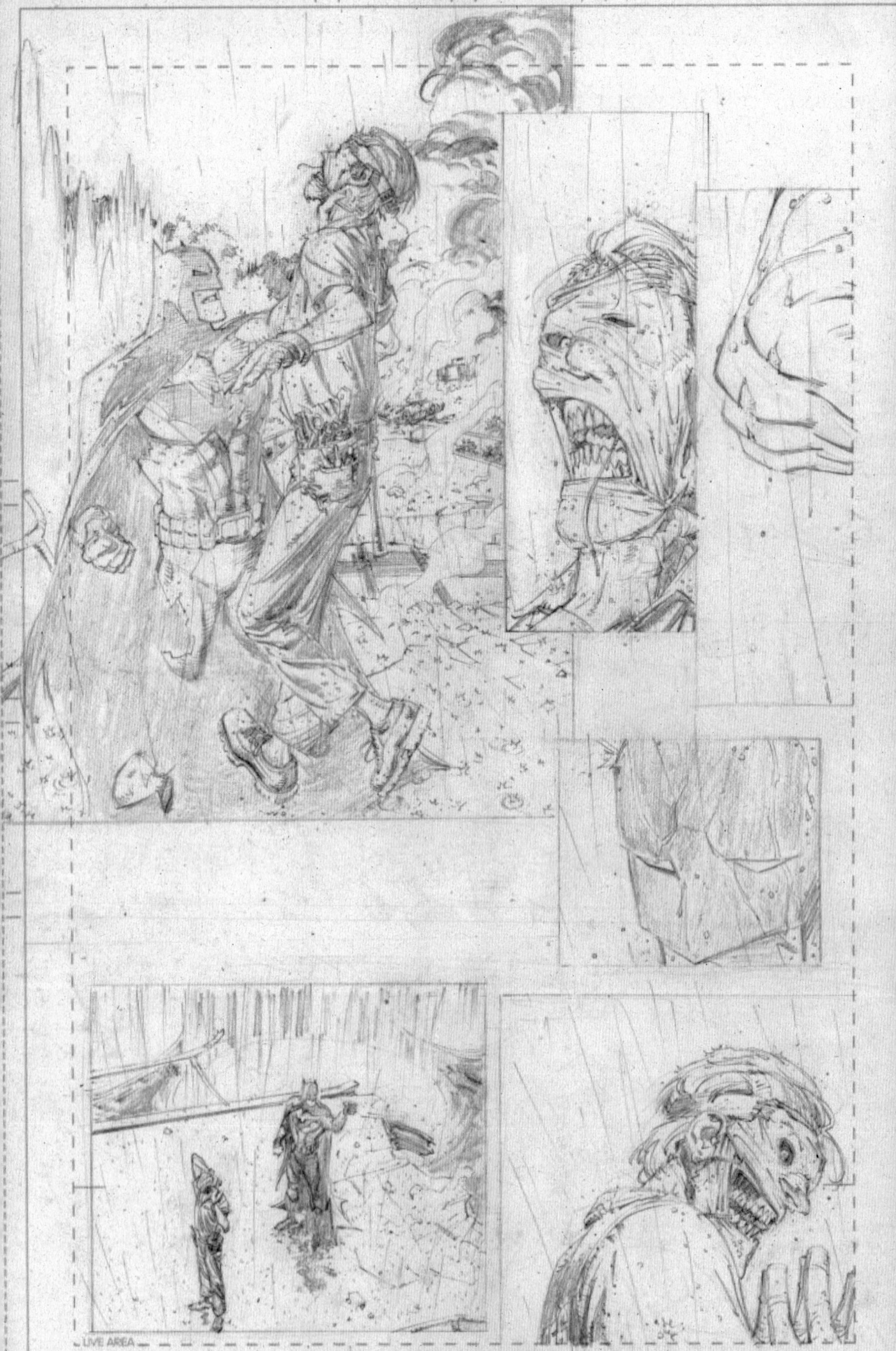

LIVE AREA

CROP

BLEED

DOUBLE PAGE SPREAD: CUT AS SHOWN, ABUT PAGE EDGES, TAPE ON BACK, DO NOT OVERLAP

← CUT RIGHT-HAND PAGE AT THIS LINE CUT LEFT HAND PAGE AT THIS LINE →